Medical Astrology
Healing for the 21st Century

MEDICAL ASTROLOGY

Healing for the 21st Century

MARCIA STARCK

EARTH MEDICINE BOOKS
SANTA FE, NEW MEXICO

Cover illustration is a detail of a painting by Rohmana d'Arezzo
Cover and book interior design by Janice St. Marie

Permission to print Anatomical Meanings of Zodiacal Degrees from the Aquarian Agent

Astrological charts courtesy of Solar Fire program, Astrolabe Inc., Brewster, MA

To contact the author write:

Earth Medicine Booksss
PO Box 5435
Santa Fe, NM 87502
(505) 983-8779
earthmed@aol.com
www. earthmedicineways.com

Starck, Marcia.
Medical astrology: Healing for the 21st century/by Marcia Starck; with foreword by Jeff Jawer.—1st ed.

p. cm.
ISBN 0-9644232-1-9

1. Medical astrology. 2. Naturopathy.
3. Alternative medicine. I Title.

BF1718.S73 2002 133.5'861
QB102-701452

Dedicated to all those healers and teachers
who have graciously shared their wisdom
and for my mother, Helen Kaplan Rittenberg Cantor,
who has recently departed to the spirit world

Other Books By Marcia Starck

Astrology, Key to Holistic Health

Healing with Astrology

Women's Medicine Ways: Cross Cultural rites of Passage

The Dark Goddess: Dancing with the Shadow

The Dark God: Exploring the Male Shadow

Handbook of Natural Therapies: The Spiral of Healing

Acknowledgments

With gratitude and many thanks to the following people who were instrumental in birthing this book:

All of my friends, clients, students, and colleagues who provided me with case histories

Janice St. Marie for her expertise and artistic ability in designing the lay out of the book

Joe Mowrey, for all of his work on the book's interior

Rohmana D'Arezzo, my dear friend, for her beautiful art work on the cover

Merrylin LeBlanc for her careful editing of the astrological material

Sally Eauclare for her editing of the supplement recommendations and her help in keeping me informed on the most recent nutritional supplements

Michael Guttman for helping to scan portions of the book and his work on advertising the book through my web site

Sandra Schank for her help with case histories as well as keeping my body in balance

Jeff Jawer, Jeannine Parvati Baker and Alan Oken, old friends and colleagues, for their words of wisdom

Steven Mc Fadden for his practical advice and suggestions

Contents

Foreword by Jeff Jawer 11

Introduction 15

CHAPTER 1 **History of Medical Astrology** 19

CHAPTER 2 **Analyzing the Horoscope: Elements and Quadruplicities** 23

CHAPTER 3 **Planets** 31

CHAPTER 4 **Signs and Houses** 39

CHAPTER 5 **Asteroids, Chiron, Moon's Nodes** 45

CHAPTER 6 **Declinations and Fixed Stars** 51

CHAPTER 7 **Midpoints** 56

CHAPTER 8 **Progressions, Transits, and Eclipses** 65

CHAPTER 9 **Diseases of the Immune System** 79

CHAPTER 10 ***Metabolic* Diseases** 102

CHAPTER 11 **Gastrointestinal Problems** 115

CHAPTER 12 **Cardiovascular Disease** 127

CHAPTER 13 **Gynecological Problems** 140

CHAPTER 14 **Eyes** 153

CHAPTER 15 **Arthritis** 164

CHAPTER 16 **Alcoholism and Drug Addiction** 176

CHAPTER 17 **Cancer** 189

CHAPTER 18 **AIDS and HIV Infections** 203

CHAPTER 19 **Neuromuscular Diseases: Multiple Sclerosis** 215

CHAPTER 20 **Neurodegenerative Diseases: Parkinson's and Altzheimer's** 227

CHAPTER 21 **Attention Deficit Disorder** 246

CHAPTER 22 **Bipolar Disorder** 257

CHAPTER 23 **Schizophrenia** 271

CHAPTER 24 **Electional Charts** 285

Appendices

Appendix A: ***Calculation of Midpoints*** *295*

Appendix B: ***Anatomical Meaning of Zodiacal Degrees*** *297*

Appendix C: ***Astrological Birth Control*** *305*

Appendix D: ***Decumbiture Charts*** *307*

Appendix E: ***Supplement Recommendations*** *309*

Appendix F: ***Herbal Recommendations*** *323*

Bibliography

General Astrology *327*

Medical Astrology *331*

Health and Healing *333*

Foreword

By Jeff Jawer

The last few decades have seen remarkable developments in medicine along two distinctly different paths. Allopathic medicine has used modern technology to produce new drugs, diagnostic tools and surgical techniques. Holistic medicine, on the other hand, has been recovering traditional methods of healing including herbs, acupuncture, astrology and many others. While the first seems to be taking us further and further away from our connection with the natural environment, the latter has reminded us of our place on this planet. As organic beings, it seems that the holistic path is the one with the greatest potential for redressing the imbalances that are the root causes of disease.

Modern astrology functions primarily as a tool for understanding ourselves through its descriptions of energetic patterns in psychological terms, as well as marking the ongoing cycles of our lives. This evolution of astrology from a more deterministic, event based system to one that functions as a therapeutic tool has done much to elevate the field. However, along the way we seem to have forgotten the body. It's almost as if astrology has become separated from the physical world in the way that modern technology separates us from our environment. Yet we know that psyche and soma are not two separate aspects of the human condition. They are, rather, two closely linked perspectives on who we are and how we function.

Self understanding frequently comes from seeing how apparently disparate pieces of our lives fit together. Behavior patterns are transformed from unconscious habits to acts of will when their origins are understood. Hearing the voice of father or mother coming out of our mouths is disconcerting, but is also a vital step in unraveling the mystery of our own conditioning. In the same way, health issues are not merely problems to be dispatched, but clues to the meaning of our very existence. Disease can be a teacher when it is framed within a context of meaning, rather than rejected as something foreign to us that must be destroyed. Healing, then, is not the exclusion of a part of us, or necessarily the elimination of something "bad." It is more frequently the integration of some aspect of ourselves that is out of balance.

The reality for most of us is that we live in a world that has been radically altered from that of our great grandparents. The nature of the air we breathe and the water we drink has been changed by the technology that dominates much of the environment. Even those living away from big cities drinking purified water and eating organic food are touched by changes in the earth's atmosphere and the ever-present power lines that permeate the landscape. We can interpret this as a sad loss or the next step in our evolutionary process. In either case, the tools of astrology can offer meaning and direction in these fast changing times.

This book is a powerful reminder that astrology is not only about what is above (in our minds), but what is below (in our bodies). It draws no distinction between the two, but builds a bridge between them. It also builds a bridge in time by drawing on the traditions of Medical Astrology and combining them with modern ideas about holistic health. The symbols of the birth chart describe both psyche and soma. Each provides clues about the other, connecting the varied strands of our existence. For the student of astrology, the symbols of the chart are not mere keywords or singular ideas. Each planet, sign, house and aspect contains many meanings that go beyond simple language. Different perspectives bring new awareness that enriches the student, advances the practitioner and opens the lay person to this universal language.

The ideas Marcia Starck has gathered for this book come from the astrological tradition and Marcia's decades of experience as a Medical Astrologer and student of holistic health. They are presented in a language and format which make it easy for one to move from concept to concept while building a solid foundation of knowledge. Like life, the subject may seem vast and complex on the surface. Careful digging, however, reveals an underlying structure and logic that makes sense to anyone who is open to learning.

Last, it is important to remember that healing is a process, not a singular act or the end product of a linear event. Healing is an ongoing awareness of how we are and how we fit into the world of family, friends, culture and climate. It is, of course, about the wholeness that underlies and connects this world with all the other worlds. Psyche, spirit, soma and soul flow as one beneath and above our ordinary perceptions. Combining the earthly arts of healing and the heavenly vision of astrology gives us an information rich framework that allows us to see them all working at once.

Introduction

M*edical Astrology: Healing For the Twenty-first Century* is not just another book on Medical Astrology. Its purpose is to define what Medical Astrology has become in the new century and how it can be used in the modern world with the current systems of healing.

In the western world, we have not had a specific system of medicine such as Ayurvedic medicine in India, which works along side Jyotish astrology, or Traditional Chinese Medicine which interfaces with Chinese astrology. Medicine in the middle ages was based around the four humors, which were related to the planets in determining an individual's temperament. The alchemists utilized planetary energies and cycles in making herbs and elixirs. However, western medicine departed from astrological knowledge and natural remedies. Through new technological advances into chemical medicines and pharmaceuticals, the attempt was to eliminate symptoms by masking them. Unfortunately, this usually leaves the body in a state of imbalance and often with other symptoms.

In the 1960's, with the outer planets Uranus and Pluto in Virgo, and Chiron in Pisces, there was a strong re-awakening to natural forms of healing, often termed alternative or complementary medicine. Vitamin and mineral supplements derived from natural organic sources, herbs, flower remedies, and homeopathic medicine became increasingly popular. So, too, did Traditional Chinese Medicine, Ayurvedic medicine, massage and body manipulation, chiropractic, and osteopathy, as well as colonic therapy and cleansing. Natural childbirth and home deliveries assisted by mid-wives became part of life again. Growing of organic vegetables and fruits, range fed beef and lamb, chickens and eggs without hormones, and whole grains without pesticides became so popular that they created a new venue, the Natural Foods Store or Health food industry.

Parallel to this movement was a resurgence and growth of metaphysical and spiritual studies. Astrology saw a revitalization and a trend away from the predictive astrology of the nineteenth and early twentieth centuries into a more psychological and person centered awarenes. Influenced by

Marc Edmond Jones and Dane Rudyhar, a humanistic astrology developed, emphasizing an individual's potential to transform and change. Cosmic patterns then became indicators to assist our understanding, and not the basis for determining our future.

Political and social movements such as feminism were reflected in astrology by the incorporation of four major asteroids, all with female names, adding some feminine psychology and balancing the predominantly male planet line-up. Astrology is now seen as an important tool with which to view human potential and can be linked up with the burgeoning fields of depth psychology and transformational psychology.

To utilize astrology now with the ancient art of medicine, the same process is necessary. Systems of healing which are based on the rhythms of the earth and her seasonal cycles have always been compatible with astrology; so, too, are medicines derived from natural and herbal sources which, in the ancient hermetic system, are ruled by the planets.

The new Medical Astrology calls for practitioners who are not only schooled in astrological techniques, but can integrate with this a knowledge of healing, nutrition, herbology, depth psychology, and spiritual practices. All of this is part of the ancient alchemical system that has to be updated and placed in our modern world, full of chemical substances and pollutants, food preservatives, and environmental toxins. We have more complex diseases than were ever dreamed of in the middle ages. Most of them are caused by ingested chemicals in our water and food, inhaled pollutants in our homes and environments, and of course, pharmaceutical drugs which create even more problems.

It is not enough to cast a chart for the onset of a "disease" or imbalance and see how long it might last; the Medical Astrologer needs to understand why these conditions might manifest as certain symptoms. Not only does she (or he) need to understand the psychological and spiritual state of the client, but she needs to have an understanding of the client's organs and teeth. Mercury amalgams on a certain tooth that corresponds to a particular meridian in the body may be the underlying cause of a health problem. Research from the Paracelsus clinic in Zurich, Switzerland reveals that all but two from thousands of cases of breast cancer studied had mercury amalgams on teeth whose meridians correspond to the breast.

The Medical Astrologer practicing in the twenty first century seeks to advise her clients what might be at the root of their problem; perhaps she will also recommend cleansing procedures, herbs, supplements, psychotherapeutic work, or spiritual practices that might be helpful. And certainly, the astrologer needs to be aware of practitioners in the healing arts that can assist her clients to balance their bodies and psyches.

This is not a simple job; perhaps that is why we have so few Medical Astrologers practicing in the west. Becoming a Medical Astrologer involves years of study and research, as well as being aware of new developments in the nutritional field and other healing modalities. For example, many of our children who are autistic or who are being diagnosed with various types of ADD (attention deficit disorder) are suffering from lead toxicity and other heavy metals. This is not something we would know simply by examining the astrological chart.

This book, then, is an attempt, to share some of the basics of Medical Astrology as I have learned them and practiced them in the past thirty years. It also seeks to explain the origins of various disease symptoms and suggest ways of healing, knowing that, just as our planetary configurations change each day, so too does the world of healing and disease.

CHAPTER 1

History of Medical Astrology

WHAT IS MEDICAL ASTROLOGY?

Medical Astrology utilizes the astrological horoscope as a tool to determine where there are physiological imbalances and how they are related to psychological and spiritual components of the native's life. The language of astrology is symbolic and works on many levels. The sign Libra rules the kidneys but also rules relationships. I had a client many years ago who had lost one kidney and was on dialysis machines so that she wouldn't lose the other. Looking at her horoscope, I noticed several planets in Libra. I asked her what was happening with her relationships, and she broke down sobbing. Her relationship with both her husband and son were extremely difficult. After realizing that the kidney problems were a manifestation of her relationships, she underwent some deep psychotherapy and was able to turn the physical problem around.

Medical Astrology has many uses—as a diagnostic tool, it can specify which organs or body systems are involved with the problems we are having. It also provides a way of keeping our bodies in balance through preventive measures. By combining astrology with the study of herbs and natural remedies, a Medical Astrologer can recommend various body therapies, dietary regimes, supplements, and homeopathic remedies, as well as crystal and gems.

Determining the best times for surgeries and treatments is another function of Medical Astrology. Transits to the natal chart, and daily aspects help to choose optimum times for surgeries or dental extractions, as well as times to take particular remedies. Timing of progressions and transits is also important for the planning of pregnancies.

HISTORY OF MEDICAL ASTROLOGY

Astrology has been used in healing and in medicine since ancient times. This tradition, however, of combining astrology and medicine in the west has been broken and piecemeal unlike Jyotish astrology in India which has always walked hand in hand with Ayurvedic medicine. In the western world, the full application of astrology to medicine came through a combination of Greek and Egyptian sources in Hellenistic Egypt after the time of Alexander the Great. Astrology arrived in Greece from its birthplace in Babylon at the end of the fifth century B.C.E. and was included in the medical writings of Hippocrates. However, it was in Egypt that the full development of astrological medicine took place. The earliest text was attributed to Hermes Trismegistos, or "thrice greatest Hermes", also known in Egypt as the god Thoth. This text was the *Iatromathematica of Hermes Trismegistos to Ammon the Egyptian* of the 2nd Century B.C.E.

Astrological medicine has as its roots Greek metaphysical thought stemming from Plato, Stoic philosophy which emphasized the relationship between human life and the stars, as well as the mystery religions and magical beliefs in Egypt. The most famous textbook of this classical period was Ptolemy's *Tetrabiblios*, the 'four books' on Astrology written in the 2nd century AD. Ptolemy sought to establish a scientific basis for astrology based on the moments of conception and birth. He was somewhat critical of the Egyptian astrologer-physicians who cast a horoscope for the time a patient first consulted them or became sick. This type of horoscope is called a *decumbiture* chart and is still in use today; it is related more to horary astrology and has a predictive component. (see Appendix D). Ptolemy was more interested in the individual's natal chart in order to assess health and fate.

In the middle ages Marsilio Ficino, a Christian priest, astrologer, and physician, translated the writings attributed to Hermes from Greek to Latin.

Ficino then went on to write *Three Books on Life* (1489), of which the third, *On Comparing Life with the Heavens*, dealt specifically with astrology and medicine. Ficino enumerated a practice of astrological medicine which recognized the free will of the human soul, identified a natural intermediary between the celestial and elementary world which he called the 'world spirit', and spoke of the purpose of healing the diseases of human beings. In this way, he was able to create a marriage of astrology with the Christian beliefs in practice then.

At the time of the publication of Ficino's work, a remarkable man was born in Switzerland, who came to be known as Paracelsus. Schooled in Hermetic philosophy and mystical teachings, Paracelsus contributed to the development of alchemical knowledge, which utilized astrology in understanding and curing disease. Paracelsus believed that we are connected to the universe by energy correspondences. Everything that lives—from the tiniest organism in a drop of water, to a small herb, to a huge animal—is a focal point of universal life energy. Paracelsus advised physicians to examine "the celestial constellations of the sky, the terrestrial constellations upon the earth, and the physiological constellations within man." For every star in the sky there is a flower in the meadow, and for each ray that comes out of space, there is an integration on every level of structure." Paracelsus pointed out the importance of astrology and astronomy in the healing realm; we need to understand the cosmic influences that are affecting all living matter before we can look specifically at each human being.

In enumerating five causes of disease, the first cause Paracelsus mentioned was "sidereal and astral influences acting upon the invisible etheric or vital body of man." These influences set in motion various vibrations which are diffused throughout the physical body and are possible causes of imbalance. Magnetic rays from a comet in the solar system, as it moves close to earth, operate on the earth's magnetic field and affect the health of humans. This phenomenon happened in July 1995 when the planet Jupiter was hit by a comet. Observing the changes on Jupiter's surface through telescopes and binoculars, we also witnessed strange weather patterns here on earth. These increased electrical energies led to more physical imbalances and illnesses.

By understanding cosmic influences, we can remain healthy and stabilize our own magnetic fields. For example, Paracelsus writes of the magnetic field surrounding the endocrine glands, which store and regulate the distribution of energy. If we deplete our resources too rapidly when no restorative energies are available, we may find ourselves fatigued or devitalized. Paracelsus believed that epidemics are not cured by medical skill, but may be caused and ended by mutations in the atmosphere, configurations of planets, and broad psychic disturbances that might result from war, panic, or fanaticism. According to him, humans possess the capability to store up psychic and spiritual energy so that they might retain their life force during "psychic mutations of nature." This idea is similar to the concept in shamanic cultures of learning to preserve personal power or "chi".

The alchemists of the middle ages in Europe worked with plants, metals, and gems in helping to transform energies and create balance. They attributed certain organs to specific planets and then listed appropriate herbs that came under the rulership of these planets. Utilizing the individual's horoscope, they created special herbal remedies to take internally and jewelry to wear externally.

In the 17th century Nicholas Culpeper, an English astrologer and herbalist, made an extensive list of herbs to correspond with the planets and planetary signatures which are still in use today. Culpeper is known as one of the originators of western holistic medicine; he worked with the four elements and the four basic qualities—hot, cold, moist, and dry, in determining the four temperaments of individuals. These "humors" were derived from the planets in terms of their elemental qualities and signs in which they resided.

As industrialization and technology advanced, departing from the seasonal rhythm of the earth and her elements, so, too, did the field of medicine become divorced from natural remedies and herbs, substituting newly discovered chemicals that altered the body and changed symptoms, often masking the real causes of disease. Western allopathic medicine has not been connected to the metaphysical realm, the spiritual realm, or even the psychological realm of mind/body relationship until the very end of the twentieth century.

In the early twentieth century, Alan Leo, a British astrologer who wrote many volumes on astrology, utilized some of Ptolemy's rules in determining health and working with the *hyleg* in the horoscope. The *hyleg* is the point upon which health and life depend; it may be the Sun or Moon or ascendant depending on the chart being studied.

Modern Medical Astrology tends to view the entire horoscope to assess an individual's health since psychological well being and spiritual balance are now considered prime components in what we refer to as our "health".

CHAPTER 2

Analyzing the Horoscope: Elements and Quadruplicities

SUN

The Sun represents the basic constitutional vitality—our inherent "prana" or "chi". Ruling the sign Leo, the Sun governs the heart and the circulatory system. Without the heart, we could not have life; if the heart is impaired or sluggish, our whole body will suffer. Aspects to the Sun from the Moon, ascendant, and other planets determine our type of metabolism and quality of our life force. Hard aspects include the conjunction, opposition, square, semi-square (45) sesquiquadrate (135) and quincunx or inconjunct which is 150 degrees. The inconjunct is the most important aspect medically. It is the most difficult to deal with as it involves constant adaptation. With a Yod (two planets inconjunct to a third and sextile with each other) there may be poor health at some time in the life; there may also be psychological repression.

Hard aspects from the Sun to the Moon can imply poor vitality and a blockage of energy; there is the need to eat wholesome organic foods as well as get plenty of exercise to keep the vital flow moving. There are no hard aspects from the Sun to Mercury except the conjunction, as Mercury can never be more than 28 degrees from the Sun. Venus can conjunct the Sun or be semi-square the Sun; this could indicate problems with the thyroid, or an acid-alkaline imbalance.

Hard aspects from Mars speed up the metabolism, indicating that one burns up energy quickly; eating small amounts of food regularly helps to replenish energy. Hard aspects from Jupiter may indicate heart problems or problems with blood sugar stemming from the liver and pancreas. Hard aspects from Saturn slow down the metabolism; these individuals can exist on fewer meals eaten over a longer time period; however, they do need frequent exercise to overcome lethargy and strengthen the body structure. Sun Uranus hard aspects give a very sensitive nervous system and may indicate spasms; there is also a tendency to have problems with the cardio-vascular system, since Uranus is the ruler of Aquarius. Sun Neptune hard aspects can deplete the vital forces through a leak of etheric energy; this is like trying to fill up a balloon when the balloon has a hole in it. These individuals may have frail health and prolonged time for healing. Hard aspects between the Sun and Pluto refer to the regenerative ability of the body; they can also act like Sun Mars aspects where the individual tends to over-do, and needs to slow down.

MOON

The Moon in the horoscope shows how the vital forces flow through the body. The Moon is our "amperage" whereas the Sun is our "voltage" (amperage is the flow of the current; voltage is the pressure behind the energy which causes the flow.) The Moon rules all the fluids in the body. Moon Mercury hard aspects could indicate digestive upsets since the Moon rules the digestive processes in the stomach which involve hydrochloric acid. Hard aspects between the Moon and Venus can indicate a tendency to indulge in sweets or low blood sugar. Moon Mars hard aspects can indicate anemia, high blood pressure, or excessive bleeding during child birth or surgeries. Moon Jupiter hard aspects may indicate liver ailments, digestive problems involving assimilation of fats, or blood sugar inconsistencies. Hard aspects between Saturn and the Moon may indicate skin problems, difficulties with the bones or teeth as well as problems with the menstrual cycle due to a lack of calcium. Moon Uranus hard aspects indicate a very sensitive nervous system that can be easily overstressed. Plenty of magnesium and B vitamins can help to balance these tendencies. With hard aspects between the Moon and Neptune, one tends to have low blood sugar and a sensitive immune system that needs constant bolstering from bioflavonoids and zinc. These individuals are super sensitive to drugs and even to certain herbs and supplements. They should be given smaller amounts and tend to do well with vibrational medicines such as homeopathy. Moon Pluto hard aspects can indicate problems with the reproductive system; for men, this can indicate impotency whereas women may have problems with miscarriages and still births.

ASCENDANT

The ascendant acts as the general conductor of energy throughout the body. It is primarily our outer covering or the physical image we present to the world at large. Fire signs on the ascendant followed by air signs are the best conductors of energy. Earth and water signs are weaker, though this may be modified by Sun, Mars, or Jupiter near the ascendant. Planetary aspects are also important in determining how the energy is conducted throughout the body.

ELEMENTS

In order to have a full picture of the individual from his horoscope, we need to understand the elements. It was the Greek philosopher Empedocles (490-430 BCE) who ascertained that each thing in nature was composed of four elements: Fire, Air, Water, and Earth. The primary qualities of these elements is hot, cold, moist, and dry. Fire was said to be hot and dry, air—hot and moist, water—cold and moist, and earth—cold and dry.

In establishing the western tradition of medicine and astrology, the four elements were associated with the four temperaments of humans or the four humors. Fire was associated with choler and the choleric temperament—the planets Sun and Mars; Air was associated with blood and the sanguine temperament—the planet Jupiter; Water with phlegm and the phlegmatic temperament—the planets Venus and Moon; Earth with melancholy and the melancholic temperament—the planets Saturn and Mercury. Since the ancients did not know of Uranus, Neptune, or Pluto, they had no associations.

From these temperaments and their combinations, the ancients determined the type of skin, pulse, hair, stature, digestion, and many other qualities. Early Medical Astrologers used the elements in determining the type of temperament of the individual and made health recommendations on that basis.

Climate certainly affects the element balance. In cold climates and in winter, phlegm (water and earth) accumulates in the body, particularly in the lungs. When the warm weather comes, it dissipates. Fire accumulates during the summer, and those whose fire element is aggravated, may experience skin rashes, fevers, and heat stroke. Air accumulates during spring and may have the effect of dehydration.

If we include the signs and houses along with the planets, we can obtain a fairly good idea of the element balance in the individual horoscope. Some planets such as Jupiter and Pluto are hard to characterize with one element—Jupiter is the ancient ruler of Pisces, and modern ruler of Sagittarius; the ancients saw Jupiter as an air planet and many of the conditions associated with Jupiter are expansive such as obesity and tumors. However, Jupiter also has a fiery quality, but not as strong as the Sun or Mars. Pluto, on the other hand, is the ruler of Scorpio, and relates to conditions that develop in the unconscious or under the surface, such as transformation of cells in the diseases known today as cancer. Venus also can be described as water since personal love and creativity can be emotional; however, other qualities of Venus as social grace give Venus an affinity with air.

For modern Medical Astrology and the health problems we observe today, I would classify Mercury as an air planet along with Uranus; these planets are related to nervous conditions, respiratory conditions (breathing air), and electrical energy. Sun and Mars are definitely fire planets, and Jupiter is also partially fire; these planets are involved with our vitality and "chi" energy; fire also refers to digestion. Moon, Venus, and Neptune are watery; they relate to emotional states and circulation of fluids in the body. Pluto is also somewhat watery. Saturn is earthy; earth relates to our body structure and skeleton.

ELEMENT	**PLANET**	**SIGN**	**HOUSE**
FIRE	Sun, Mars, Jupiter, Pluto	Aries, Leo, Sagittarius	1, 5, 9
EARTH	Saturn	Taurus, Virgo, Capricorn	2, 6, 10
AIR	Mercury, Uranus	Gemini, Libra, Aquarius	3, 7,1 0
WATER	Moon, Venus, Neptune, (Pluto)	Cancer, Scorpio, Pisces	4, 8, 12

Although a horoscope may seem to lack a certain element by analyzing the planets in signs and houses, if a planet is angular or conjoined the Sun or Moon, that element may be emphasized. For example, Sun conjoined Mars would be very fiery as would Mars near the ascendant or mid-heaven.

Fire gives us warmth and feeling; it provides us with comprehension and insights as well as giving us an optimistic demeanor. Physically, fire relates to our skin color, digestion, and temperature. A lack of fire in the horoscope can indicate depleted vitality, lethargy, depression, poor circulation and problems with cold, poor digestion, pale skin, lack of self confidence, and lack of courage. These individuals need physical exercise as well as the practice of chi gung, tai chi, or yoga to keep the vital energy flowing in the body. A student with her Sun conjunct Neptune in Virgo, Aquarius Moon and Gemini rising comes to mind. She would wear heavy clothes even in summer months and used a blanket to cover herself in class. After starting a daily yoga practice and going to the gym a few times a week, her circulation got much better and she no longer needed the extra layer of clothes. She also became a much more optimistic person.

Preponderance of fire may indicate a person who burns herself out and does not conserve physical energy. It often brings on skin eruptions and rashes, boils, fevers, heart burn, inflammation, and aggressive behavior which can become angry, violent and reckless. A friend with four planets in Leo, Aries Moon, and Sagittarius rising did construction work. After work and on week-ends, he often helped his family with other outdoor jobs and ran around doing errands. Every few months he would totally collapse and be in bed for a few days with adrenal depletion. When he finally realized his pattern, he started to pace himself and also took a thermos to work of *fo ti*, a good herb for the adrenals and vital energy

The earth element refers to solidity and our sense of stability and security. It rules the bones, skin, teeth, nails, and cartilage, all that is solid in our bodies. Earth also relates to practicality and dependability. A lack of earth often suggests pale skin, little stamina, trouble repairing body tissue, impracticality, and difficulty manifesting ideas. For those who lack earth, buying groceries, cooking, and exercising may seem a waste of time. One woman with four planets in Gemini including her Sun, Libra rising, and Cancer Moon, remarked, "Wouldn't it be simpler to swallow a pill each time we need to eat?"

An abundance of the earth element may indicate sluggishness, adhesions, excessive materialism, and resistance to change. These people do enjoy exercising, cooking, gardening, but can get too obsessed with their bodies. A Taurus client with Virgo rising changed his diet to macrobiotic, then to raw foods, and then back to a more moderate diet. In the course of these changes, he first gave away his coffee pot, then his other pots when he began the raw foods diet. Of course he later asked for all his pots back.

Air relates to movement and breathing. Without air, our movements and perceptions would be slow, and we would lack a sense of relationship with others that results from movement. Air thus pertains to communication and ideas. If our air element is balanced, we have a strong sense of aesthetics and social graces. We also have a good sense of objectivity in our communications. Lack of air indicates slowness of movement, dizziness, shortness of breath, a weak nervous system, and difficulty expressing ideas. A client with no air in his horoscope developed a nervous stutter until he began counseling others, and became confident of his ability to express himself.

Preponderance of planets in air can make one prone to restlessness, insomnia, nervousness, palpitations, and rapid breathing. These people may have overly dry skin, brittle bones and nails, and sometimes premature signs of aging. A neighbor who is a triple air sign and extremely anxious developed symptoms of arthritis; after working with some yoga exercises and breathing as well as mineral supplements, the symptoms stopped.

Water gives the body softness and fluidity. Water is associated with the fluids in our body including saliva, the sense of taste. Our personal subjective feelings are a function of the water element; objective ideas are a function of air. A balanced water element can make one gentle and compassionate. An individual having few planets in water may be insensitive, lack fluids in her body, and tend to accumulate toxins. Drinking more liquids and juice fasts are helpful in eliminating toxins. These people need to learn how to project their feelings so that their reasons for action carry weight.

With an excess of the water element, emotionally caused conditions are prominent. These people are more prone to chills and cold, tend to put on excess weight, and accumulate phlegm and mucous easily. Water retention in the body is often symbolic of carrying around too much emotional baggage. Learning to detach from feelings and become more objective is a strong lesson. A client who has eight planets in water signs had been suffering from cancer; as she did some deep therapeutic work and learned to detach from other people's problems, her cancer went into remission.

CARDINAL, FIXED, AND MUTABLE SIGNS

Along with the elements, the distribution of planets in cardinal, fixed, and mutable signs as well as angular, succedent, and cadent houses is most important in analyzing the horoscope for health problems. First, see how many planets occupy each of the signs by element, and tally them to see where the majority are. Planets in the houses have a subtle vibration of the energy relating to the element so consider the planets in the three types of houses as well. For example, planets in the third house would have an air quality regardless of the sign they are in.

The planets may be involved in a T-square; this indicates two planets opposite each other and square a third; the empty sign may be an area where the problem is manifest. For example, I have seen several clients with a Taurus Sun square a planet in Aquarius, opposite a planet in Scorpio, and no planets in Leo, that have manifested heart problems. Sometimes the ascendant or mid-heaven will form one arm of the T-square. There may also be a grand cross, which means that four planets are all square each other. This can indicate blockages or held back energy that may be associated with health problems.

The cardinal signs consist of Aries and Libra, Cancer and Capricorn. With this emphasis, individuals usually take initiative for treating their ailments, follow through, and are open to alternative and natural ways of treatment. Problems often involve the body structure, spine and bones, or teeth, all ruled by Saturn. Gastrointestinal problems involve the stomach, ruled by the Moon, and the gall bladder, ruled by Saturn. Many problems that involve pains in the arm or heartburn may be caused by gall stones or some restrictions of bile flow. Kidney problems of course are governed by Libra and can create acid/alkaline imbalance which affects digestion; if the kidneys are plugged up, renal retention and spasm can occur. Problems of "burn-out" or adrenal depletion are also evident here as the adrenals are governed by Mars.

Taurus and Scorpio, Leo and Aquarius, comprise the fixed signs. Individuals with this predominance tend to more chronic conditions and are often very fixed in their habit patterns, resist change, and are more reticent of trying new remedies and treatments. Scorpio rules the colon and this is the root of so many health problems; the colon can become clogged up from poor diet, little exercise, and lack of regular cleansing. When the colon is clogged, fecal matter builds up in the intestinal walls, and toxins accumulate in the body. This can lead to heart problems (Leo), as well as problems of the throat and sinuses (Taurus) and poor circulation (Aquarius). Cataracts and glaucoma can also form in the eyes with a clogged up colon and poor circulation. Other problems with these signs involve the thyroid (Taurus); hyperthyroidism can result in nervous problems and heart palpitations while hypothyroidism causes fatigue, lethargy, and mental slowness.

The mutable signs include Gemini and Sagittarius, Virgo and Pisces. These individuals have many acute problems and are the most prone to colds and flus. They are open to change and will try new treatments but unfortunately, rarely follow through for a period of time on either the supplements, herbs, or dietary recommendations. Virgo rules the digestive system which is the root of many problems here; since Virgo governs the small intestine where so much of the digestive process takes place, there are often problems with indigestion as well as hypoglycemia and diabetes due to the failure of the pancreas to secrete the proper amount of insulin which takes place in the small intestine. Pisces rules the lymphatic system and when these glands become clogged through poor diet and toxic substances, many symptoms will arise as well as frequent colds and flus. Gemini and Sagittarius govern the lungs and breathing; respiratory allergies may be prevalent as well as diseases such as pneumonia. Since Jupiter rules the liver, toxic and sluggish liver conditions can affect digestion and cause allergic reactions.

CHAPTER 3

Planets

IN MEDICAL ASTROLOGY, THE PLANETS indicate how a specific organ or bodily function will be affected. The sign in which a planet is placed at birth plus the aspects it makes with other planets, provide information physiologically. For example, Mars rules inflammations, flaring up of a condition, excess heat. If Mars is placed in Cancer, there may be excess heat in the stomach, which translates to excess hydrochloric acid. People with Mars in Cancer have problems with fruits and acidic foods; they usually complain about drinking orange juice on an empty stomach.

The vitamins and minerals have an affinity with the planets. In some cases, there is an obvious rulership such as calcium and Saturn; in other cases, there is simply an affinity such as chromium, which is related to the blood sugar, and Jupiter.

SUN

The Sun is our inherent vitality, the "prana" or "chi" flowing through us. The sign that the Sun is in and the aspects that it makes with other planets will show us how strong our vital force is, and what we can do to increase it. The Sun rules the sign Leo and thus is related to the cardiovascular system and the circulatory system.

The Sun is related to the heart chakra and according to Dr. William Davidson, it rules the etheric body, the fine filament that encases the physical body and keeps it functioning. If the etheric body is damaged by x-rays or radiation, this container develops a hole and an etheric leak appears. Dr. Davidson recommends sunshine and certain substances such as anhydrous lanolin applied to the chest and back to seal this leak. He mentions those with hard aspects between their Sun and Neptune as having etheric leaks and needing to regenerate their energy through the Sun.

The Sun rules vitamins D, A, and F. During the winter months, we may need to take vitamin D along with extra calcium and magnesium which help vitamin D to assimilate. Vitamin A helps the heart and eyes and is often taken along with vitamin D in the winter. Vitamin F consists of the essential fatty acids that make it easy for oxygen to be transported to the cells and work with vitamin D in making calcium available.

Since the Sun governs the cardiovascular system, it also has dominion over the mineral magnesium. The electrical conductivity of the heart is ruled by the planet Uranus and magnesium helps to keep the electrical energy in balance. Chlorophyll is the magnesium ion; it is found in green plants and leafy green vegetables. Drinking liquid chlorophyll is important if we are not getting enough greens in our diet. Without the Sun, there would be no chlorophyll.

MOON

The Moon shows how the vital force is being directed, and may show how healthy a person is. With several hard aspects to the Moon, the individual may tend to have health problems even though her vitality may be strong.

The Moon rules the sign Cancer and has dominion over our emotions and all the fluids in the body such as water, blood, and serum. It also rules the eyes, the stomach, and the breasts.

An individual with a prominent Moon or several planets in Cancer may tend to put on weight due to accumulation of fluids in the body. If one holds back or suppresses emotions, other symptoms may appear in addition to weight gain. (weight gain is often excess fluids that pad or protect the body when one is feeling overly sensitive.)

Potassium is ruled by the Moon as it helps to control the balance of fluids in the body as well as the acid-alkaline balance. Often, women lack potassium before their menstrual cycle; it is helpful to take additional potassium and magnesium five days before menstruation and during menstruation.

MERCURY

Mercury rules the nervous system and the respiratory system. Difficult aspects between Mercury and other planets can indicate conditions of stress and worry that affect physiological processes.

Since Mercury rules Gemini, it governs the lungs and the tubes in the body, the channels through which blood and oxygen flow as well as hormones. Allergies that affect the respiratory system are often found in individuals where Mercury is angular, several planets are in Gemini, and Mercury has hard aspects from Mars, Saturn, Uranus, Neptune, or Pluto.

Mercury also rules Virgo and is thus involved with the pancreas' breakdown of sugar into glucose, which occurs in the small intestine, ruled by Virgo. With Mercury in Virgo or having hard aspects from Mars or Saturn in Virgo, there can be problems with indigestion, flatulence, or diarrhea.

Since Mercury is the messenger, it is also connected with speech; often speech impediments or stutters are related to hard aspects between Mercury and Saturn.

Mercury rules the B complex vitamins in general, which help to balance the nervous system. Specific B complex vitamins are ruled by other planets as well.

VENUS

Venus, as ruler of Taurus, governs the thyroid gland and conditions of hypo and hyper thyroid. When Venus receives hard aspects from Saturn, there may be hypothyroidism; with hard aspects from Uranus, the thyroid is erratic and this may lead to either condition.

Venus rules sugars and sweets and with hard aspects to Jupiter, Neptune and sometimes the Moon, there may be a tendency to hypogly-cemia or diabetes. These individuals often crave sweets, eat excessive sweets especially when they are feeling unloved, and need dark green leafy vegetables and proteins to maintain their blood sugar.

As ruler of Libra, Venus governs the kidneys, and the acid-alkaline balance in the body. With several planets in Libra, or hard aspects from Saturn to Venus, there may be kidney problems and also skin problems which develop when the kidneys are very toxic.

Venus also has dominion over the venous circulatory system, a series of small blood vessels that branch out. Difficult aspects to Venus can bring weak artery or vein walls and poor circulation.

Two minerals, iodine and copper, are ruled by Venus. Iodine, found primarily in seaweeds and fish, helps thyroid conditions. Copper is necessary to assimilation of iron, which is ruled by Mars. Copper is also important when one is taking zinc supplements.

MARS

Ruler of Aries, Mars governs the blood and adrenal glands. Mars' placement in the horoscope indicates our activity level and how the gas pump stimulates our vital engine. Mars in fire signs may indicate one who has a high level of physical activity and may also be very aggressive as well as burn out. Mars in air signs has incredible mental energy for technical and intellectual projects but can also experience mental exhaustion. Mars in water signs may not have a lot of physical endurance unless Mars is angular or in strong positive aspect to the Sun, but they have lots of drive toward spiritual and healing endeavors. Mars in earth signs can manifest strong and solid energy; they can keep on going for many hours and maintain their energy.

Mars can be involved in blood disorders such as anemia; this occurs often when Mars is in a water sign with hard aspects to the Sun, Saturn, or Neptune. The individual will need extra iron as well as vitamin B-12 and folic acid.

Mars can indicate inflammation, fevers, redness and itchiness, and swelling. Mars in Virgo for example could be inflammation in the intestinal linings while Mars in Scorpio could indicate colitis. With a strong Mars in her chart, an individual will burn off illness quickly, often with a fever, and recuperation will be quick. With Mars in the water and earth signs, recuperation is often slower.

Mars transits and progressions can also indicate accidents, especially if Uranus is involved.

Mars rules the mineral iron, which is difficult to assimilate without proper amounts of vitamin B-12 and folic acid, another B vitamin, both of which help in preventing anemia and in synthesizing DNA. Mars also has an affinity with vitamin K, which helps to form prothrombin, a chemical involved in blood clotting.

JUPITER

Jupiter, the largest planet, rules the liver, the largest organ, and the pancreas; it is involved in conditions of hypoglycemia and diabetes. Jupiterian people may suffer from conditions of excess such as overweight and over-indulgence in food and drink. Another manifestation of Jupiter's excesses is growths and tumors.

Those with Jupiter conjoined the Sun, Moon, or an angle of the chart, along with those who have a strong Sagittarian element, often tend to have problems with the liver. The liver may have difficulty breaking down fats and dispensing with them; it therefore becomes clogged. Lecithin is often called for since it helps to break down the fats.

Since Jupiter rules fats in the body, it is also connected to the cholesterol levels. Hard aspects between Jupiter and Neptune as well as Jupiter and Venus relate to the blood sugar and indicate problems with carbohydrate metabolism; a diet low in carbohydrates and chromium supplements are helpful.

Jupiter rules the B-vitamins biotin, choline, and inositol . Biotin assists in the oxidation of fatty acids and carbohydrates. Choline and inositol form lecithin, which breaks down fats. Pangamic acid or vitamin B-15 is also ruled by Jupiter; pangamic acid helps regulate fat and carbohydrate metabolism and also helps to control the levels of cholesterol. The minerals chromium and manganese are also related to Jupiter. A manganese deficiency can affect glucose tolerance, resulting in the inability to remove excess sugar from the blood. It activates enzymes that are necessary to regulate fatty acids and cholesterol. Chromium produces an enzyme like substance called the GTF, glucose tolerance factor, which helps to utilize insulin, thus balancing the blood sugar.

SATURN

Saturn is the structural principle and thus rules the bones, joints, and teeth. Saturn also rules the gall bladder where the bile is stored. Whatever sign Saturn inhabits in the natal chart usually indicates a malfunctioning of that area of the body. For example, Saturn in Gemini indicates problems with the respiratory system and lungs.

Since Saturn rules the principle of crystallization, gall stones are one of its manifestations. Arthritis is another condition of crystallization that may occur in individuals with a strong Saturn or dominant Capricorn theme.

Saturn is a cold planet and those governed by Saturn usually like warm climates and warm temperatures. Rheumatism is also a Saturnian condition. Saturn also rules the skin, in the sense that the skin is a barrier that protects us; Venus rules the outer covering of the skin.

Often problems with the teeth and gums as well as the bones and joints occur under transits of Saturn. That is when our dental bills are highest.

The minerals calcium, phosphorus, sulfur, and fluorine are ruled by Saturn. Calcium is required for our bones and teeth; phosphorus speeds up the healing process with bone fractures and is necessary for proper skeletal growth and tooth development. Sulfur is important for the hair and fingernails as well as the skin. Fluorine strengthens the bones and helps reduce the formation of acids in the mouth. vitamin C and bioflavonoids (vitamin P) are also Saturn ruled as is PABA. Vitamin C helps form collagen; bioflavonoids are necessary in producing vitamin C in the body and work with circulation in keeping the capillaries elastic. PABA, one of the B vitamins, is important for healthy skin.

URANUS

Uranus governs the higher nervous system and electrical impulses. It is related to spasms, cramps, shocks, and paralysis. Menstrual cramps indicate a lack of calcium and magnesium. Epilepsy is also a Uranian condition and can be helped by high doses of magnesium, manganese, and the B complex vitamins.

Stress is often apparent under transits of Uranus. Since Uranus rules the electrical conductivity system of the heart, heart attacks and strokes occur under its transits. Uranus stays in a sign for seven years, so its house placement and aspects are more important.

Uranus has rulership over the mineral magnesium, manganese along with Jupiter, and the B complex vitamins, along with Mercury. Magnesium works with the electrical conductivity of the heart and helps to prevent cramps and spasms. Manganese nourishes the brain and nervous system and treats schizophrenia and Parkinson's disease.

NEPTUNE

Neptune often causes inaccurate diagnoses and strange symptoms. If Neptune is very prominent, the individual may be addicted to alcohol or some type of drugs, including prescription drugs. The individual could also be super-sensitive and have allergic reactions to medications. Usually, subtle remedies such as homeopathy and flower remedies work well with strong Neptunian or Piscean individuals.

Neptune rules the lymphatic system which can become clogged due to excess mucous and toxins in the body. It also rules the pineal gland, which gives us intuitive information, as well as the thymus gland and the spleen.

People with a strong Neptune usually have sensitive immune systems and are prone to flus and colds. This is often due to a weak spleen, which can be fortified with Chinese herbs and supplements. Neptune also governs poisonings and over-doses, especially from mysterious substances. Neptune stays in a sign for fourteen years, so again, its house placement and aspects are more important.

Neptune rules pantothenic acid, which helps the adrenal cortex in producing adrenalin when one is wiped out and under stress. The mineral zinc is also related to Neptune, which is very important for a strong immune system and helps the spleen.

PLUTO

Pluto governs the reproductive system and the excretory system. Since Pluto has the ability to transform our emotions and desires, it also transforms our cells, which some times results in life or death. As ruler of the reproductive system, Pluto aspects and transits are linked with still births and miscarriages. Pluto also governs the large intestine or colon and thus is associated with diseases of the colon and bowel such as colitis and hemorrhoids.

Pluto's action is underground and we are often not aware of the transmutation of our cells. We may have changes happening in the body that are diagnosed under a Pluto transit—the diseases known as cancer are associated with Pluto. Pluto stays in a sign for many years; since its orbit is erratic, its duration in each sign varies; therefore it is more important to check its house position and aspects.

Pluto rules vitamin E, B-6, and also B-17 or laetrile. Vitamin E is an antioxidant important to the reproductive organs and endocrine system. It helps to balance the hormones. B-6 or pyridoxine is related to hormonal balance in women; prior to menstruation women need additional B-6 which aids nervousness and irritability. B-17 or laetrile is a fairly new vitamin produced from apricot kernels that is being used in treating cancer. Pluto also rules the mineral selenium, which works closely with vitamin E in the production of normal growth and fertility. Selenium is an antioxidant and is helpful to women during menopause and other hormonal changes.

VITAMIN AFFINITIES

A	Sun
B complex	Mercury, Uranus
B-6	Pluto
Biotin	Jupiter
Choline	Jupiter
Inositol	Jupiter
Pantothenic acid	Neptune
PABA	Saturn
Folic Acid	Mars
B-12, Cobalamin	Mars
B-15, Pangamic acid	Jupiter
B-17, Laetrile	Pluto
C	Saturn
D	Sun
E	Pluto
F	Sun
K	Mars
P, Bioflavonoids	Saturn

MINERAL AFFINITIES

Calcium	Saturn
Magnesium	Uranus, Sun
Phosphorus	Saturn
Potassium	Moon
Iron	Mars
Copper	Venus
Iodine	Venus
Zinc	Neptune
Chromium	Jupiter
Manganese	Uranus, Jupiter
Sulfur	Saturn
Fluorine	Saturn
Selenium	Pluto

CHAPTER 4

Signs and Houses

THE SIGNS HELP TO DETERMINE which parts of the body are affected physiologically and what psychological issues may be behind the malfunctioning of particular organs or body processes. I use the signs in polarity as they represent similar energies but show different aspects of that energy, the yin and the yang.

ARIES-LIBRA

Aries is the personal, the "I am" indicating individual energy and initiative. Aries rules the head in general, the motor sections of the brain, and the circulation of the blood through the skull area. When one is too mental or too much "in the head", headaches may be common.

Libra is the "we are" referring to relationships and contracts. Libra governs the kidneys which eliminate the liquid wastes of the body. Libra also rules the acid alkaline metabolism, balancing the body through maintaining enough acid and enough alkaline. Diets high in meat or too many fruits and fruit juices can cause the body to become too acidic. Whole grains, dark green vegetables, potato peel broth, and parsley tea can help to alkalinize the body.

Aries rules the adrenal glands which respond to stress; strong Aries individuals often "burn out." Headaches may occur as a result of sluggish kidneys, digestive upsets (Cancer), or gall bladder problems (Capricorn). Skin problems may also manifest as a result of toxicity in the kidney area.

The kidneys can become blocked through deposits of cholesterol and other waste products; this may result in nephritis or inflammation, low back pain, and weight gain. If one is having problems with relationships, it usually manifests through the kidneys.

TAURUS-SCORPIO

Taurus and Scorpio, fixed signs of will and desire, nurture the body as well as cleanse and purify it by ridding it of waste material. Taurus rules the mouth and throat while Scorpio governs the prostate gland, reproductive system, colon, and excretory system. If we ingest any spoiled food or poisons, our body immediately cleanses itself through one or both of these doorways. Likewise, if we become too emotional or take in too many negative experiences, our body may seek to cleanse itself in a similar fashion.

Taurus rules the thyroid gland as well as the larynx and tonsils. Malfunctioning of the gland may be due to emotional stress as well as poor diet, or to a toxic colon (Scorpio), blockages of the arteries and circulation problems (Leo and Aquarius). Those who have a hyperthyroid condition can be very nervous, experience heart palpitations, sweating, and lose weight. Hypothyroidism, on the other hand, can lead to obesity, dry skin, low blood pressure, extreme sensitivity to cold, and constipation.

Problems from a congested or toxic colon may interfere with all bodily processes. A diet of natural organic foods with enough roughage as well as high enemas and colonics will keep the colon healthy. Otherwise, toxins can go back into the bloodstream, tissues, and bones.

GEMINI-SAGITTARIUS

Gemini and Sagittarius, the body's communication network, control the nervous system for distributing messages. Gemini rules the arms, hands, shoulders, lungs and respiratory system, nerves and nervous system. Sagittarius rules the thighs and hips, the liver (our largest organ), the pancreas, and the sciatic nerve (our largest nerve). If we are under pressure, nervous or tense, our breathing may become too shallow and we can develop problems in the area of the lungs; states of tension and anxiety may also lead to problems with the sciatic nerve.

Gemini also governs the tubes of the body—the trachea, bronchial tubes of the lungs, eustachian tubes of the ears, ureter tubes from the kidneys to the bladder, the urethra from the bladder to its outside opening, and the fallopian tubes near the uterus.

Gemini, the twins, and Sagittarius, the archer and bow, are mutable signs relating to inhalation and exhalation. Food allergies and digestive problems (Virgo) as well as lymphatic congestion (Pisces) can affect the lungs and produce problems with breathing as well as congestion and excess mucous in the lung area.

CANCER-CAPRICORN

Cancer and Capricorn, the security oriented signs, home and profession, provide us with the foundation and structure for our bodies. Capricorn rules the skeletal frame, the bones, teeth, joints, cartilage, skin, knees, and gall bladder, while Cancer rules the stomach and digestive process in the stomach, the coverings over the eyeballs, brain, sinus cavities, lung and heart membranes, and bone marrow. When something goes awry in our emotional life or professional work, it is often our body's structure that gives way with a broken bone or slipped disc; we may also develop a stomach ulcer or gastritis.

Since the stomach is the place for protein digestion, not enough hydrochloric acid or too much can cause problems with digestion; these problems can lead to headaches (Aries) and acid-alkaline imbalance (Libra). If the food is not broken down in the stomach through peristalsis, then when it enters the duodenum and intestinal tract, the minerals and vitamins will not be absorbed.

Capricorn governs the gall bladder which secretes a liquid called bile into the duodenum. Bile digests the fats, breaking them down so they are assimilated into the digestive tract. If there is a blockage in the gall bladder, there can be pains around the chest or heart area. Holding back feelings or ideas can lead to a blockage and to constipation.

LEO-AQUARIUS

Leo and Aquarius, creativity and the expression of it to humanity, govern circulation and oxygenation. Leo rules the heart, the center of the circulatory system, which in Aquarius sends out the energy to all the cells of the body. Aquarius also rules the calves and ankles; swollen ankles may result from circulatory dysfunction. If we do not open our hearts, or block our emotions in any way, we tend to have poor circulation and feel cold.

Those with a strong Aquarian element need to conserve their oxygen so that it will go to all the cells of the body. Eating heavy foods robs the body of oxygen; deep breathing exercises will help to eliminate carbon dioxide and take in more oxygen.

Aquarius and Leo also rule the spinal cord. Problems here may produce back aches and also nerve related diseases such as multiple sclerosis.

VIRGO-PISCES

Virgo and Pisces are signs of health and healing, elimination and digestion. Virgo rules the small intestine and the entire digestive process. Pisces governs the feet and the duodenum, where food receives bile from the gall bladder and juices from the pancreas. Pisces also rules the lymphatic system whose cells attack and neutralize invading bacteria. Thus Virgo discriminates and purifies while Pisces immunizes. When we take on too many projects, especially of a mental nature, as Virgo is ruled by Mercury, we may have difficulty assimilating our experiences and develop digestive problems.

Virgo rules the pancreas along with Jupiter; the function of the pancreas is to release pancreatic juices into the small intestine where digestion takes place. From the pancreas come the hormones, insulin and glycogen, which are key players in carbohydrate metabolism.

Pisces is a very sensitive sign; Pisces governs the immune system as well as lymphatic system. Individuals with strong Pisces placements tend to be very sensitive to drugs and certain foods. This is also true of those with strong Virgo placements.

HOUSES

In Medical Astrology, the houses can be helpful in futhur describing physiological symptoms. A preponderance of planets in one house accentuates that house and may also bear a similar vibration to the sign naturally associated with that house. For example, one client had four Pisces planets including his Sun in the third house; he suffered from respiratory and lung problems. The third house corresponds to the sign Gemini.

First House

Those with several first house planets may be aggressive and strong individuals. They keep going, rarely take time to rest, and often "burn out." Since they are strong individualists, they may develop health problems when these tendencies are repressed.

Second House

People with many planets in the second house are sometimes obsessed with piling up material investments, properties, or even higher degrees, to prove their self worth. They may often indulge in heavy food and experience problems from excess carbohydrates and fats. They can also manifest this energy in growing gardens with organic vegetables and living a healthy life style.

Third House

A preponderance of third house planets may place stress on the nervous system. These people are always involved in communicating, whether it is at work or to help their families or neighbors. They need to have some time to themselves and learn to be alone and quiet.

Fourth House

The fourth house represents attitudes and conditioning from the parents. There may be a lot of emotional factors to deal with for those who have several planets here as well as the possibility of repressed anger and resentment. One may need to get in touch with healthier ways of living than what was shared by the parents.

Fifth House

Those with strong fifth houses have a need for attention and love. Often they can receive attention from creative self-expression, though sometimes it is through a series of disappointing love affairs. If they have children or work with children, their fifth house energies may be satisfied. Planets in this house tend to manifest their energies in the cardiovascular system.

Sixth House

Being one of the health houses in the horoscope, the sixth house can describe the areas where there might be physiological problems, depending on the signs on the cusps of the sixth and twelfth houses. Those with several planets in the sixth feel the need to serve others and may experience guilt when they are not doing this. Guilt feelings often translate into intestinal problems and other symptoms. When one learns how to balance serving others with taking care of one's own body, positive health can be experienced.

Seventh House

Those with many planets in this house may not feel complete on their own. They may have a strong need to be in partnerships, and give over some of their lives to their partners. Often they suffer from kidney problems. However, one with a strong seventh house may feel secure within herself and not manifest any health problems.

Eighth House

A conglomeration of planets in this house could show deep psychological issues that have become internalized. This can indicate serious health problems, especially with the colon, until the issues are examined and brought out into the open.

Ninth House

Often people with several planets in this house have a strong faith and belief in higher ideals. They may encounter health problems in their travels as a result of eating food that is not prepared properly or water that is not clean. This depends upon how well they take care of their bodies, especially the liver, which is associated with Sagittarius and thus this house as well. Since this house is opposite the third, problems with the respiratory system can also be indicated here.

Tenth House

Those with strong tenth houses may tend to spend a lot of time working in the outside world and not enough time cooking meals or exercising. They may have chronic health problems, especially with shoulders, back, and neck until they take time to care for their bodies.

Eleventh House

Many planets here can affect the nervous system. Since this is the natural house of Aquarius, there can also be some circulatory difficulties.

Twelfth House

Along with the sixth house, this is one of the health houses. The twelfth house indicates hospitalizations as well as confinements in sanatoriums and rest homes. It can also show psychological problems as well as subconscious fears. These issues need to be brought out in the open so that they will not cause problems with the immune system or other areas of the body.

CHAPTER 5

Asteroids, Chiron, Moon's Nodes

ASTEROIDS

In delineating a horoscope for health purposes, it is helpful, though not necessary, to place the four major asteroids, Hygeia, and Chiron in the horoscope.

Ceres

Ceres and Vesta represent aspects of Virgo. Ceres, the goddess of grain and harvest, appears to be the indicator of child bearing and fertility along with the Moon. The sign and house where Ceres is placed usually shows where and how one's nurturing capacities may manifest. Ceres also is connected with food problems, not getting enough to eat as well as over-eating. Since the goddess Demeter or Ceres stopped food production when her daughter was taken to the underground, difficult aspects to Ceres could indicate one who was punished as a child by a parent holding back meals as well as other nurturing. Food disorders such as anorexia (starvation) and bulemia (binging and purging) are related to Ceres.

A client with Ceres conjoined her natal Neptune in the eleventh house has no children of her own but through her spiritual and healing work, constantly mothers friends and acquaintances. Another client, with Ceres conjunct her seventh house cusp, has played a mothering role with each of her partners. An old friend has Ceres conjoined his Mars in Pisces near the ascendant. He practices various forms of healing such as acupuncture and Jin Shinn Do, thus nurturing people by working with their bodies and transmitting energy to them.

A woman with Ceres conjoined her Moon and Saturn in Taurus has been suffering from bulemia for many years.

Progressions and transits also are important. For a client who was having difficulty conceiving a child, the year she finally adopted one, Ceres came by solar arc to her Sun. Another client had an abortion when Ceres conjoined her Mars by solar arc. She had conceived the child with Pluto conjoined her natal Ceres.

Vesta

Vesta, the virginal goddess of the hearth, is a devoted worker and serves many. A strong Vesta in the natal chart indicates one who works hard, is dedicated to service, and may undergo many sacrifices. Vesta brings trials through which people learn and grow. She also brings purification, often through pain. Vesta's symbol , the perpetual flame on the hearth, shows the cleansing nature of fire. The house and sign where Vesta is placed indicates where one sacrifices mundane goals and personal desires for greater service.

A woman who has no Virgo planets in her chart nor any sixth house emphasis, has Vesta in a funnel formation at her nadir. (A funnel formation indicates a single planet in a hemisphere which acts to funnel the rest of the energy.) She does shiatsu and other healing work as well as maintaining a bookkeeping business; she is extremely careful about her health habits, eats a macrobiotic diet, and very dedicated to her healing work. Another friend had Vesta conjoined her Neptune in the third house. She did therapy and spiritual counseling when she was alive and has written several books. However, she was blind for a period of years after which her vision was restored through glaucoma surgery. During that time she sacrificed her outer vision for developing inner vision. Another man who has his Sun conjoined Neptune and Vesta had two accidents as a child which made him blind for the rest of his life.

One client conceived a child when her ascendant by solar arc squared Vesta; one month later she lost the child. Another client had glaucoma diagnosed when Saturn by solar arc conjoined natal Vesta. At the time, she was overworking and under a great deal of tension.

Vesta is often prominent in the horoscopes of women who are infertile and cannot bear children as well as men who are impotent.

Pallas Athena

Pallas and Juno symbolize aspects of Libra. Pallas Athena was the protector of cities and dealt with artistry and skill. She was the warrior goddess, born from the head of Jupiter, and was active in social and political causes. Pallas was one of the goddesses of healing and has always been associated with the snake that she wears on her breast plate. The snake is a symbol of re-generation. Those with Pallas prominent in their horoscopes often work with psychological therapies and with other types of healing such as past life regression and hypnotherapy. Difficult aspects to Pallas may point to problems with learning, poor hand eye coordination, and visual problems, particularly dyslexia.

A student with Pallas conjoined Pluto in the ninth house maintains a counseling practice using astrology and past life regressions. (Pluto represents the deep subconscious and that which lies beneath the surface.)

Three clients with dyslexia have Pallas prominent: one has Pallas, Neptune and Vesta conjoined in the sixth house, the other has Pallas on the descendant, and the third has Pallas on the ascendant opposite Mars.

Some individuals who suffer from manic depression have stressful aspects to Pallas. One has Pallas conjoined her Sun, another has Pallas opposite his Sun, and a third has Pallas exactly square Uranus and opposite Neptune.

Juno

Juno governs committed relationships, marriages, engagements, and ceremonies involving relationships. Juno can also indicate deception and betrayal; Juno (Hera) was always being betrayed by her husband Jupiter (Zeus). A client with her Sun conjoined Juno spends most of her time focused on her relationship and has a difficult time doing things by herself.

Juno also relates to childbirth. A friend had Juno transiting her ascendant when her son was born; a student had Juno conjoined her Sun when she gave birth, and a client had it transiting her Venus at the birth of her daughter.

Hygeia

Hygeia was the Greek goddess of healing and daughter of Asclepius. Since we now have the asteroid Hygeia in our horoscopes through the Solar Fire computer program, we can see how Hygeia is placed in the charts of those with serious health problems.

The sign and house where Hygeia is may give us some indications as to those areas of our life where we need healing. When Hygeia is conjoined another planet or closely aspecting another planet, it emphasizes the energy of that planet.

In many horoscopes with serious health problems, I have seen Hygeia conjunct the Moon. A young man who has had ADD as well as learning disabilities, has Hygeia in the same degree as his Sagittarian Moon which is also conjoined Neptune and Pallas. His mother claims that he was emotionally abused while he was growing up by his father, so his emotional body needs the healing. A woman with MS has her Moon conjoined Hygeia and Juno in Pisces squared by Saturn and opposing Jupiter. She was not allowed to express her sensitivity when she was younger. A young man who is epileptic has his Moon in Aquarius opposite Hygeia in Leo. A woman with severe allergies from foods has Hygeia conjunct her Aries Moon; she is prone to headaches.

Several people with serious respiratory allergies have Hygeia conjoined Mercury. One of them had such weak lungs that she died during an asthma attack. Her Hygeia was conjoined Mercury in Gemini, but she also had a grand square with her Sun, Mars, and Venus in Gemini opposite Jupiter in Sagittarius and square Saturn in Pisces and Neptune in Virgo.

In the horoscopes of those with the diseases referred to as cancer, I have found Hygeia near the ascendant. One woman who has had two surgeries for uterine cancer and is doing well, has Hygeia in Sagittarius conjoined Chiron, Ceres, and ascendant while squaring Saturn in Virgo. A man who has since passed away from cancer of the liver, had Hygeia on his ascendant in Aquarius square Venus in Taurus and inconjunct Saturn in Cancer. His Pisces Sun was opposite Jupiter in Virgo.

CHIRON

Chiron, the planetoid or comet that orbits between Saturn and Uranus has indeed been called a maverick, due to its eccentric orbit. Chiron's discovery on Nov. 1, 1977 was symbolic of the burgeoning holistic health movement with its emphasis on body work, herbology, nutritional supplements,

Oriental systems of healing, and vibrational therapies, as well as studies on death and dying.

Chiron was the wounded healer in Greek mythology who did not achieve immortality, but instead had to go to the underworld and undergo a period of darkness first. In our horoscopes, Chiron symbolizes where we have been wounded and how (through sign and house) we can connect with and transform our wounding. Chiron combines the Saturnian respect for the past with the Uranian creative vision.

Those individuals who contract serious health problems as well as those who undergo a major healing crisis have Chiron angular or conjoined the Sun, Moon, or ascendant. Chiron is also prominent in the charts of healers and doctors, often conjoined the midheaven or ascendant.

Chiron is usually found to be active by transit or progression when physical symptoms manifest. It is often involved in conceptions, births, abortions, and mis-carriages. One woman had a child born when transiting Chiron was opposing her Moon; several years later she lost a child due to a uterine infection when Chiron was opposing Neptune. A client who had difficulty becoming pregnant conceived when transiting Chiron trined her Chiron; her son was born with Chiron on her Moon. Another client had an abortion with transiting Chiron square her Sun. Five years later, she adopted a child with transiting Chiron square Pluto.

MOON'S NODES

The nodes of the Moon are extremely important in the interpretation of the horoscope. Like the Moon, the nodes are associated with emotional vulnerability and sensitivity. The signs where the nodes are found and the aspects to them are very important in determining health problems.

The signs indicate areas of the body where there might be some problems; for example, the nodes in Aries/Libra could suggest possible difficulty in the head or sinus area, the adrenals, or kidneys. If there are hard aspects from Mars, Saturn, Pluto, and even from Uranus or Neptune, this makes the case stronger.

Particularly in the sixth and twelfth houses, the nodes may describe physiological and psychological problems. A client has her south node in Aries conjoined Saturn in the sixth house; her problems are with her sinuses and occasional sinus headaches. Since she does healing work, she has learned to balance her body and in fact, her health is quite good.

Another client with south node in Sagittarius conjoined the midheaven and Venus and north node in Gemini conjoined the fourth house cusp, has problems with multiple sclerosis involving back pain and severe shakiness. Being a triple Aquarius with Sun, Moon, and Mercury in the twelfth house, she has a very sensitive nervous system.

CHAPTER 6

Declinations and Fixed Stars

DECLINATIONS

Planetary positions in our horoscopes are based on the longitude of the planets which is the vertical co-ordinate; we also need the horizontal co-ordinate for a full delineation

Declination is the horizontal co-ordinate of the planets; it is the degrees north or south of the Celestial Equator. The change in declination is caused by the tilt of the earth as it revolves around the Sun. The Sun's declination varies from 23.5 degrees north to 23.5 degrees south. At summer solstice, the Sun is at its highest point, 23.5 north declination; at winter solstice it is at its opposite point, 23.5 south. At spring and fall equinox, the Sun is between these two points or at 0 degrees declination.

Two planets which are in the same degree (within an orb of one and a half degrees) and on the same side of the equinox line are said to be parallel. A parallel acts much like a conjunction in the chart, uniting the energies of the two planets. Two planets which are on opposite sides of the equinox line (one north and one south) are said to be contra-parallel. This might be thought of as comparable to an opposition.

For most of the time, the planets stay in the range of the higher numbers, between 22 and 25 degrees; therefore one would have more parallels and contra-parallels natally at these degrees. Parallels and contra-parallels are also important in progressions and transits.

In the case of a client with severe eczema, her Sun is parallel Mars, which can indicate redness and itching. Her Moon is contra-parallel Mercury, suggesting possible respiratory allergies or problems from inhalants. Neptune is contra-parallel Saturn, which may make her immune system very sensitive. Uranus is parallel Pluto and contra-parallel the MC; this shows the ability for strong healing and transformation. Longitudinally, her Sun is conjoined Mars in Taurus, her Moon is conjoined Neptune in Libra, and she has Pisces rising. She also has a Venus Uranus conjunction in Cancer. The longitudinal positions point out her sensitive immune system and tendency to have problems with redness and itchiness. By looking at the declinations, we find the Moon Mercury contact which actually describes the causes of her eczema—extreme sensitivity to inhalants.

A woman with diabetes most of her life has Virgo rising with Neptune in the twelfth house near the ascendant. Neptune is opposite Saturn in Pisces and square Jupiter in Sagittarius. Her Moon is in Leo square Venus in Scorpio. By declination, her Moon is parallel Uranus, so it is difficult for her to stick to her diet, and contra parallel Venus, indicating that she craves sweets. Pluto is parallel her MC and contra-parallel Jupiter, so she does have the will to discipline herself with diet and supplements thereby controlling the diabetes.

A group who calls themselves the Magi Society have done a lot of research with declinations and work with a declination chart. They have published several books and gone deeply into explaining the value of declinations. Studying some of their work can be very helpful. I have used the declinations by transit in my own chart for many years and find that they are important in understanding the cycles I am experiencing. They help to illuminate certain issues, adding to the information that I receive from the transits.

FIXED STARS

The fixed stars of the zodiac may be considered in working with certain disease conditions such as eye problems. As Bernadette Brady points out in her excellent book, *Brady's Book of Fixed Stars*, it is important to determine whether the star is rising, setting, or culminating and also whether another star or planet is rising at the same time, known as a paran relationship. It is also necessary to work only with the stars rising at the place of birth.

IMPORTANT STARS IN MEDICAL ASTROLOGY

Aculeus and Acumen

Both are in the constellation of Scorpius, 25 and 28 degrees of Sagittarius. (These are given in their 1950 longitude). Since they are a nebula, they have traditionally been linked to blindness or inner vision. As a pair of stars, they are related to attacks—not just physical but mental, verbal, and spiritual. Aculeus represents the light side, attacks that strengthen, and Acumen the dark side, attacks that weaken. A woman who had glaucoma and was blind for seven years has her Moon conjoined Acumen. She developed her inner sight and began doing channeling and counseling work while she was blind. The second case history in the chapter on Gynecological Problems has her Sun conjoined Aculeus and her Mercury conjoined Acumen. She has had a long history of fibroids but also has written about and taught Feng Shui for many years.

Algol

Algol is the severed head in the constellation of Perseus. It is at 25 degrees of Taurus. Algol is a binary star system where a smaller star orbits a larger star, eclipsing it every few days. Earlier writers considered it the most evil star in the sky. It seems to signify a strong consuming passion and anger. The second case history in the Gastrointestinal Problems chapter has her Sun at this degree. Though she is only 25 years old, she has had many serious health problems including Krohn's disease and an ulcer. The second case history in the Cancer chapter has Uranus on this degree opposite her Mercury. Although she had a hysterectomy in her 30's, she has been in good health and is still teaching at the age of 61.

Antares

Antares is the most imporant star in the constellation of Scorpius. Its longitude is 9 degrees Sagittarius. Antares is one of the brightest stars in the sky; it appears red as we view it. Considered a royal star, Antares has the nature of both Mars and Jupiter and can take things to extremes. The first eye case history in this book has his north node on Antares;

he had two accidents at an early age which made him blind. He also died of colon cancer at the age of 42. However, he was a very intelligent and talented person, and accomplished a lot in his short life. The first case history in the chapter on MS has her south node conjoined Antares. She has had MS for many years and is in a lot of pain. However, she did have a successful career as a nurse and still hopes to recover and write a book.

Aselli

The North and South Asellus are in the constellation of Cancer; their longitudes are 7 and 8 degrees of Leo. They are part of a stellar cluster known as the Manger and are known as the northern and southern donkeys. They have an affinity with the Sun and Mars, and may indicate a very strong person. The woman with glaucoma who was blind for many years, had her natal Jupiter conjoined the south Asellus; she wrote several books and did counseling while she was blind. The second case history in Diseases of the Immune System has her nodes on the south Asellus. She has had many severe allergic reactions that involve a lot of redness and itchiness (Mars). Her life and work are very versatile; she does accounting, electrical work, has written an astrology book, and is involved with publishing.

Castor and Pollux

Castor and Pollux are the brightest stars in the constellation of Gemini; their longitude is 19 degrees of Cancer. Since they are twin stars, they involve working with polarity. These stars are often found in the charts of writers. The woman who had glaucoma and was blind for seven years has her north node on this degree; she wrote four books and many articles. The second case history in the Altzheimer's chapter has Neptune conjoined these stars; in her youth, she also wrote poetry and many articles.

The Hyades

The Hyades are a cluster of five to seven stars on the forehead of the bull in Taurus. Their longitude is 4-6 degrees of Gemini. Since the Hyades refer to water or rain drops, they have the influence of Mars and Neptune. The first case history in the chapter on AIDS had his north node conjoined the Hyades; he was the leader of a gay marching band and a very skilled musician.

The Pleiades

The Pleiades or seven sisters, are a group of seven stars in the constellation of Taurus; their longitude is 29 degrees Taurus. There are many legends connected to the Pleiades; they are a nebula which has been connected to blindness as well as inner vision. The first case history in the chapter on Neurodegenerative Diseases has the Pleiades rising exactly opposite her Mercury. She has had Parkinson's disease for many years, but has continued to function and did raise a child by herself. Her Jupiter is also conjoined Antares. The first case history in the Bipolar chapter has his Mars square the Pleiades; he tends to "burn out" and become depressed much of the time. He also has his ascendant conjoined Antares. The second case history in the same chapter has his Uranus square the Pleiades. He is usually in a very "hyper" state.

CHAPTER 7

Midpoints

MIDPOINTS ARE A RELATIVELY MODERN TECHNIQUE in the history of astrology; they were known in Medieval and Renaissance astrology but became popular through the use of the 90 degree dial in both the Uranian (also known as the Hamburg school) of Alfred Witte and the school of Cosmobiology. However, it is not necessary to utilize the dial or the other techniques of these systems in order to work with midpoints.

Midpoints are actually a very important tool because one can derive so much information from midpoints without even using signs and houses. When a planet is connected through its midpoints to other planets in the chart, it furthur defines that planet's functioning. Midpoints are also responsive to progressions and transits.

Finding a midpoint is relatively easy, especially since computer programs print out lists of midpoints. Midpoints can also be seen on a 90 degree dial. To calculate a midpoint, one calculates the distance between two planets and divides by two. This will yield a nearer midpoint and a farther midpoint, which will of course be opposite each other. There are also two midpoints square to those and all four of these are called direct midpoints. (see Appendix A for calculation of midpoints). The other four midpoints are those points 45 degrees away from the midpoints, known as indirect midpoints. If a planet equals a midpoint, we have a combination that is similar to a T square. For example, if Mars equals the Sun/Venus midpoint, it is comparable to a T square between Sun, Venus, and Mars. Orbs on midpoints are small, one and a half degrees. Only hard aspects are used, including the semi-square and sesquiquadrate, which are multiples of 45.

With these combinations, one can see more clearly certain psychological patterns and predispositions to physiological manifestations. Dividing the circle by four, or aspects based on the fourth harmonic, lead to manifestations on the physical plane; these may be events or could be health problems. One would pay more attention to a certain midpoint if there are several located at the same degree (or opposite or square it). This degree or degrees then are especially sensitive and would be particularly responsive to transits and progressions.

I use six midpoints when working on a health analysis for a client. Though I have found these six to be the most important, I might also look at other midpoints when particular symptoms are manifested, or if a specific disease has been diagnosed.

When I first started to study midpoints, I kept track of my own and was amazed at what I found. The Saturn/Neptune midpoint is known as the health axis; Pluto transited my Saturn/Neptune midpoint in 1975 and 1976, which marked my strongest health crisis, and corresponded to my first fast, subsequent dietary changes, and my introduction to colonics. When my Sun/Moon midpoint was transited by Neptune, I had allergic reactions to foods that I had never previously experienced. I also had the flu at the beginning of this transit, which persisted for a few months; I have not actually had a major flu bug since that time. Transiting Neptune over the Mars/Uranus midpoint in a client's chart set off the worst bout of eczema she had ever suffered. (Neptune rules allergies and Mars/Uranus the nervous system.)

IMPORTANT HEALTH MIDPOINTS

Sun/Moon

This is the most important midpoint in the horoscope. The soli-lunar angle reflects the phase of the moon under which a person was born. A planet or chart angle falling on the Sun/Moon midpoint is involved in the soli-lunar angle and thus receives much emphasis. Sun/Moon equals the basic vitality and balance of body fluids.

For example, if Uranus = Sun/Moon midpoint, the person may have an extremely nervous temperament. With Saturn = Sun/Moon, there would be difficulty in expressing the emotions, lack of vital energy, and the body would be prone to the type of crystallizing effect found in arthritis or rheumatism.

Saturn/Neptune

This is the health axis or cardinal point of disease. When a planet equals the Saturn/Neptune midpoint, it may signify difficulty with the organ or organs ruled by that planet. For example, if Jupiter = Saturn/Neptune, there is often trouble with the liver or pancreas. This may manifest in several ways—the individual may be diabetic or hypoglycemic at some point in life, could contract hepatitis or some other liver disease, or may simply have a sluggish liver or pancreas and need to be careful about what she eats and drinks. How this manifests depends upon the rest of the horoscope and whether the individual takes care of herself in regard to diet, exercise, sleep patterns, and emotional stress. A friend had hepatitis during Neptune's transit of her Moon. When calculating her midpoints, I found her Saturn/Neptune midpoint equaled Jupiter, indicating the tendency for problems in the area of the liver and pancreas. The transit itself could have manifested physiologically in many ways, such as allergies or the flu. A client, injured in an accident at age fourteen and crippled as a result, has his Saturn/Neptune midpoint = Pluto, indicating conditions of a more serious or chronic nature.

Mars/Saturn

Mars and Saturn in combination refer to the body structure as well as the inhibition or restriction of some bodily function. When Mars/Saturn =Venus, there may be thyroid problems or restricted glandular functioning. In the horoscopes of some of the women who have had difficulty conceiving, the Mars/Saturn midpoint = Venus.

Mars/Uranus

This midpoint corresponds to the nervous system, injuries, accidents, or operations. People with sensitive nervous systems or diseases of nervous origin often have their Sun, Moon or ascendant equal this midpoint. This is true of those who are accident-prone and suffer many injuries.

Mars/Neptune

This midpoint is the point of toxicity, susceptibility to infections and epidemics, as well as toxic conditions from poisons and drugs. When the Sun, Moon, or ascendant equals Mars/Neptune, it often indicates a person who contracts infections easily. In a medical astrology class, a student told us about her son, who was sent home from school in his early years whenever anyone else became ill, because he would invariably get the same illness. On calculating his midpoints, she found that his Sun = Mars/Neptune, and realized his extreme sensitivity to infections and toxins. Another client whose Mars/Neptune midpoint = Moon, had a serious staph infection in her uterus, which was caused by an intrauterine device (the Moon rules female organs).

Mars/Pluto

This midpoint refers to heavy accidents, destruction of cells, and destruction of life in some form. I have noted this midpoint active in horoscopes of women who have had miscarriages or abortions. In most cases the Mars/Pluto midpoint = Sun, Moon, or ascendant; in one or two cases, Venus or Neptune.

MIDPOINT EQUIVALENCIES

Listed here are a few suggestions for the meaning of midpoints when they equal natal planets or when they are activated by progression or transit. It is important to remember that these are only potential meanings; by keeping one's body in balance the negative implications do not have to manifest. Also, as always, it is essential to examine the rest of the horoscope.

Sun = Saturn/Neptune

Health problems throughout the life; the person may be involved with healing

Sun = Mars/Saturn

Weak vitality; need for work on body structure; strong power of endurance

Sun = Mars/Uranus

Sensitive nervous system; a strong body capable of making sudden efforts; possible accidents or surgeries when aspected by progression or transit

Sun = Mars/Neptune

Susceptibility to infections and toxins; allergic tendencies; capable of working with higher vibrations of energy

Sun = Mars/Pluto

Serious or chronic conditions; strong will and regenerative power

Moon = Saturn/Neptune

Disorder of female organs; emotional depression; ability to channel emotions into higher states

Moon = Mars/Saturn

Inhibition of feelings or emotions; for women, possible difficulty in conceiving; good control and focus of emotions

Moon = Mars/Uranus

Highly sensitive nervous system; possible surgeries involving female organs; intuitive and inspirational abilities

Moon = Mars/Neptune

Tendency to infections especially of female organs; sensitivity to allergies and toxins; possible hypoglycemic tendency; strong psychic and intuitive powers

Moon = Mars/Pluto

Problems with female reproductive cycle; emotional upheavals; powerful and deep emotional encounters

Mercury = Saturn/Neptune

Diseases of nervous system, respiratory ailments, allergies; intuitive and structured thought processes

Mercury = Mars/Saturn

Problems with hearing; possible blockage in respiratory system; organized and powerful mind

Mercury = Mars/Uranus

Possible injuries and accidents to neurological system; highly sensitive nervous system; respiratory allergies; quick and inspirational mind; independence in ideas

Mercury = Mars/Neptune

Nervous conditions resulting from use of drugs or alcohol; highly intuitive thinking and psychic faculties

Mercury = Mars/Pluto

Tendency to overstimulation of nervous system; hyper-activity; deep and probing mind

Venus = Saturn/Neptune

Glandular disorders; kidney problems; a more compassionate love nature

Venus = Mars/Saturn

Inhibited function of endocrine glands particularly the thyroid; possible problems in conception for women; ability to structure creative energy

Venus = Mars/Uranus

Hormonal imbalance; erratic functioning of thyroid gland; possible surgery involving reproductive organs; creative inspiration

Venus = Mars/Neptune

Infections in reproductive system; venereal diseases; kidney and bladder infections; compassionate and sympathetic nature

Venus = Mars/Pluto

Problems involving reproductive system; hemorrhoids and problems with excretory system; ability to transform sexual energy

Mars = Saturn/Neptune

Lack of energy; low vitality; depletion of adrenal energy; problems with spine and body structure; arthritis; rheumatism; hard worker with strong motivations

Jupiter = Saturn/Neptune

Possible dysfunction of liver or pancreas; weight loss; focus on inner and spiritual growth

Jupiter = Mars/Saturn

Metabolic problems; restricted functioning of liver and pancreas; protection in cases of broken bones and other problems with body structure

Jupiter = Mars/Uranus

Erratic functioning of liver and pancreas; protection in accidents or surgeries

Jupiter = Mars/Neptune

Difficulty metabolizing carbohydrates; tendency to hypoglycemia; personal expansion through study of metaphysical and spiritual disciplines

Jupiter = Mars/Pluto

Strong regenerative and recuperative ability; chronic problems with liver and pancreas

Saturn = Mars/Uranus

Blockage of energy in neurological system; serious accidents; long term surgeries; ability to use new and unusual ideas

Saturn = Mars/Neptune

Low vitality; body structure out of alignment; arthritis; rheumatism; ability to utilize higher metaphysical concepts

Saturn = Mars/Pluto

Severe and chronic conditions; chronic problems with reproductive system; hard worker with strong motivations

Uranus = Saturn/Neptune

Sudden or unexpected illnesses; problems with nervous system; independence and inventiveness

Uranus = Mars/Saturn

Possible blockage in neurological system; body structure out of alignment; manifests new ideas

Uranus = Mars/Neptune

Diseases of neurological origin; paralysis; changes in energy level; involvement with metaphysical and psychic studies

Uranus = Mars/Pluto

Long-term surgeries and disabling conditions; ability to transform nervous energy

Neptune = Mars/Saturn

Lowering of vitality through toxic conditions, use of drugs and alcohol; ability to ground physical energy while working in states of higher consciousness

Neptune = Mars/Uranus

Possible infections resulting from surgery or injuries; channeling of energy into metaphysical and psychic studies

Neptune = Mars/Pluto

Poor ability to recuperate or regenerate body; transforming patterns related to alcoholism or drugs

Pluto = Saturn/Neptune

Serious illness; chronic disability; changing health patterns through diet and other healing techniques

Pluto = Mars/Saturn

Serious defects in body structure, such as missing organs or limbs; transformation of body structure through exercise and other physical therapies

Pluto = Mars/Uranus

Possible long-term surgery and disabling conditions; transformation of nervous energy to manifest in a creative way

Pluto = Mars/Neptune

Infections and toxic conditions leading to long-term illnesses and disabilities; transforming allergic tendencies

MIDPOINT COMBINATIONS

The following meanings apply when the three planets are found in a T square or involved in a midpoint equivalency. These eight combinations are commonly found.

Mars/Jupiter/Neptune

Difficulty metabolizing carbohydrates (one of the hypoglycemic signatures), adrenal depletion, toxic conditions resulting from the liver and pancreas, (often found in horoscopes of alcoholics). These people generally need frequent small meals of whole grains and vegetables, easily digested proteins like fish, yogurt and other soured milk products, a small amount of fruit and fruit juice, no sugar or honey (stevia may be substituted), no salt, no alcohol, and small amounts of carbohydrates.

Venus/Jupiter/Neptune

Difficulty metabolizing carbohydrates, craving for sweets, prone to excesses in diet, (often found in horoscopes of alcoholics). Diet same as above.

Mars/Saturn/Neptune

Prone to certain conditions arising from body structure such as arthritis, rheumatism, and dental problems. These individuals need high amounts of calcium, magnesium, and B-complex vitamins. Their diet should consist of whole grains such as brown rice, buckwheat and millet; fish and organic poultry; dark green leafy vegetables such as collard greens, kale, mustard greens, chard, and arugula which are high in calcium and magnesium; herbs such as comfrey (high in calcium), borage and red raspberry leaf (high in magnesium), and wintergreen and sarsaparilla root.

Mars/Venus/Neptune

Faulty glandular functioning; need for extra iodine. Fish, dulse, kelp, and other sea vegetables are particularly good. The herb, nettles, is rich in iron and iodine.

Saturn/Neptune/Venus

May indicate a tendency to diabetes, or a restriction of the thyroid gland. Diet should include whole grains and leafy green vegetables, fish and organic poultry, dulse, kelp, and other sea vegetables. No sugar or honey.

Mars/Mercury/Uranus

Nervous and respiratory conditions. Need for good B complex supplement and magnesium. Diet should include whole grains, which are high in the B vitamins, dark green leafy vegetables, which are high in magnesium, and herbs such as borage and red raspberry leaf for magnesium content.

Mars/Pluto/ Moon

Lack of iron with possible anemic tendencies; occasional irregularities of the menstrual function and miscarriages. Need for iron-rich foods such as organic calves' liver, wheatgrass juice, and beets. Also helpful are B-complex vitamins, vitamin E and selenium.

Sun/Moon /Neptune

Lack of tone and vitality which may manifest as a pranic leak or 'leaky aura'; hard to maintain the vitality at a steady level. An adequate amount of sleep and rest is needed; also exercises like yoga and tai chi which involve deep breathing are beneficial. A balanced diet with sufficient protein and dark green leafy vegetables is important.

CHAPTER 8

Progressions, Transits, And Eclipses

PROGRESSIONS

Progressions, transits, and eclipses play a role in the timing of illness and may also focus on particular organs where there are problems. Secondary progressions should be calculated. Aspects from the progressed Sun and ascendant would be the most important in relating to the health. Monthly aspects of the progressed Moon are also relevant in determining energy levels and in timing; they may set off other progressions and transits.

For example, the progressed Sun conjunct Mercury or square Mercury might indicate a time to nurture the nervous system, take extra B vitamins and magnesium, and be aware of any respiratory allergies. This is especially true if these tendencies are present in the natal chart. If the progressed Sun makes a hard aspect to natal Mars, there could be less vitality, even possibly a tendency to anemia; additional exercise to build vitality and a diet rich in iron and copper could be helpful.

The sign and house of the progressed Moon are interesting to observe. One client developed a kidney problem when her progressed Moon was in Libra. Another client had cancer diagnosed the month the progressed

Moon opposed her natal Pluto. For someone who had a history of heart problems, the progressed Moon going through his fifth house exacerbated this condition.

A progressed planet making a hard aspect to one of the health midpoints is also important. A woman had progressed Mars on her Mars/Pluto midpoint the year she had a miscarriage. In another case when progressed Venus squared a client's Saturn/Neptune midpoint, a thyroid problem was diagnosed.

Solar arc directions also provide information, although the astrologer does not always have the time to use all of these systems. Solar arc directions are determined by advancing each position in the natal chart by the arc of the progressed Sun. The true solar arc would take the difference in longitude between the natal Sun and the secondary progressed Sun, using the day for a year method. The mean solar arc takes the average daily movement of the Sun, used uniformly each year. For one client, allergy problems started when solar arc Mercury conjoined his natal Neptune; he had to eliminate certain foods that had not been a problem previously. Another woman had symptoms of hypoglycemia when solar arc Neptune hit her natal Jupiter; she had to adjust her diet and take some additional supplements.

TRANSITS

Transits of the outer planets can affect us physically as well as emotionally and spiritually. Often we have more than one major transit and these also have to be combined with the secondary progressions, and of course, the tendencies in our natal horoscopes. We can learn how to handle our transits in a positive way which will affect our growth and enable us to expand our abilities under these transits. Often, it is necessary to balance our bodies physiologically, so that we can take advantage of a transit and not feel overburdened with health problems. If we are in tune with our bodies, we know when we are lacking a certain mineral or vitamin; if we are in tune with our transits, we can be aware of those deficiencies before they manifest in physical symptoms. For example, many people become depressed during Saturn transits; however, if the calcium and magnesium are balanced, one can simply utilize the transit to work on projects and establish new structures. Or one might have sleepless nights during transits of Uranus and feel "burnt out." Increasing physical exercise and supplementing the diet with more magnesium, manganese, and B complex vitamins can make the transits of Uranus exciting.

The physiological effects of the various transits follows (only the hard aspects are included):

TRANSITS OF SATURN

Saturn transits teach us lessons. If we have been ignoring our physical bodies the transits of Saturn may seem restrictive and limiting in terms of health. Since Saturn rules calcium, calcium deficiencies are often prominent at this time, bringing on problems with teeth, bones or various parts of the skeletal frame. For calcium depletion, calcium-magnesium capsules or liquid calcium-magnesium, as well as the herbs comfrey root, comfrey leaf, and oatstraw have proved helpful. Magnesium and vitamin D are important in assisting the calcium to assimilate. Foods high in calcium include sesame seeds, sea vegetables, and dark green leafy vegetables.

Aspects from **Saturn** to the **Sun** usually indicate low vitality; there is a need to build up the system with nourishing food and physical exercise to overcome the inertia of Saturn. The cardiovascular system can be affected, with poor circulation and heart problems as a result.

Saturn transiting the **Moon** affects the emotions and may manifest physiologically as a period of lowered resistance to colds and flus as well as crystallizations in the body resulting in arthritic and rheumatoid conditions. One time when Saturn conjoined my Moon in Gemini I had frequent colds; another time I had a periodontal chip placed under one tooth to help heal the gums. One client had acute bursitis in her shoulder when Saturn hit her Cancer Moon. Many of these conditions have been helped by calcium and magnesium supplements, which also alleviate the depression brought on by this transit.

Transits from **Saturn** to **Mercury** relate to the nervous system, speech and hearing. One of my clients developed a nervous stutter under a square from Saturn to Mercury. Foods rich in B-vitamins, such as whole grains, plus a B-complex supplement, were effective in controlling his symptoms once he understood the emotional reasons for the stutter. Others have had allergies and hives under this transit, especially when Saturn is in a mutable sign and transits Mercury.

Venus and **Saturn** combinations often manifest as skin conditions, kidney problems, and thyroid deficiencies. A student of mine had Saturn conjoined her Venus over a long period. During this time her face broke out in a rash which continued to bother her throughout the transit. She also experienced a good deal of depression and limitations in her social life. Another client developed hypothyroidism when Saturn squared Venus.

Saturn-Mars combinations can bring frustrations of various kinds. They are somewhat like driving a car with the brakes on. The lesson from these transits is one of patience, but it may take an accident, some broken bones or high blood pressure to get the point across. Arthritis, rheumatism, and hardening of the arteries may manifest during this time. The iron in the body may be lowered during this transit and it is necessary to supplement with foods rich in iron (beets, cherries, prunes and dark red foods), herbs like nettle leaves, wheatgrass juice, and liquid dulse.

With **Saturn** making aspects to itself, hard testing and inner struggle are often experienced. Weak knees and knee problems may develop during this transit. When Saturn squared my natal Saturn in the sixth house, I experienced discomfort in my knees, especially while driving. Although I was taking a calcium supplement at the time, I still had a deficiency and needed a stronger supplement. A friend snapped her kneecap while bowling under a square from Saturn to natal Saturn.

Saturn transits to **Uranus** exacerbate mental tensions and frustrations. It is extremely important at this time to examine any aspects of the personality which have become crystallized and rigid. Breaking through these old habit patterns may release much of the tension. Foods rich in B vitamins and some of the nervine herbs (herbs that help relax the nervous system) like spearmint, camomile, catnip, scullcap and wood betony have helped cool down Uranian vibrations.

Saturn in combination with **Neptune** brings symptoms which are difficult to diagnose. One is more susceptible to toxins and has a lowered resistance under this transit; adequate rest, regular meals, and exercise are especially important. If an individual is ill and a drug is administered, it should be done with caution because of increased sensitivity at this time. Many people have developed allergies to drugs as a result. Respiratory and food allergies and hypoglycemic reactions have also started with Saturn transiting Neptune. One of my clients reported a very strong reaction to drinking wine during this period with Saturn conjunct her natal Neptune in Virgo.

Under **Saturn-Pluto** aspects one may take on more than one can handle; overwork and extra burdens drain the physical vitality. Transformations in diet and lifestyle are frequent at this time, often as a result of some illness or operation. When Saturn conjoined my natal Pluto in Leo I had a problem with the colon (ruled by Pluto) and with assimilating food. I was able to heal myself through fasting and subsequent change to a lighter diet.

TRANSITS OF URANUS

The most common physical manifestations of Uranus are nervous conditions and accidents. The energy of Uranus needs to be grounded through exercise and meditative practices so that it can be used in a positive way—in new ideas, projects, and inventions. For all transits of Uranus, it is advisable to nourish the nervous system by eliminating coffee and regular tea (orange pekoe and black teas contain caffeine) and substituting with the nervine herb teas: spearmint, camomile, catnip, scullcap, wood betony, vervain, and hops. The mineral magnesium is usually depleted during Uranus transits and therefore conditions involving pain and spasm result. Foods high in magnesium are dark green leafy vegetables, kelp and sea vegetables, almonds, and cashews. Supplemental means of obtaining magnesium include liquid chlorophyll, magnesium capsules, as well as the herbs borage and red raspberry leaf. A B-vitamin supplement may also be recommended during this transit; be sure to obtain one without a yeast base.

Aspects from **Uranus** to the **Sun** often lead to heart disease and hypertension (the Sun ruling the heart and Uranus the electrical system). This is true especially when Uranian energies are suppressed and tension builds up within. One client with Sun conjunct Mars in Libra had a heart attack when Uranus transited this conjunction. He was in his early 40's at the time and experiencing tension and frustrations with his job. His heart problems lasted several years until he made the big breakthrough and completely changed his vocation. A student with her natal Sun in the eighth house had an automobile accident in which her car was totally demolished when Uranus exactly opposed her Sun. Fortunately, she experienced no serious bodily injuries except for a whiplash and some nerve damage in one hand.

Uranus-Moon combinations have produced many unwanted pregnancies as well as a few desired ones. One client who conceived with Uranus opposite her Moon later miscarried. Another client, who had been trying to conceive for several years, finally was successful through the use of artificial insemination when Uranus was opposite her Moon. Emotional upsets from this transit have thrown many into states of nervousness and confusion.

Uranus-Mercury combinations may produce extreme nervous problems and spasms. Epileptic seizures have often started under this influence. A former student of mine ran a home for disturbed children, several of whom were epileptic. She noticed that many of them had seizures under Uranus Mercury transits.

Transits from **Uranus** to **Venus** often manifest in skin conditions, kidney and bladder problems, and malfunctioning of the thyroid gland. Dulse, kelp, and seaweeds high in iodine, iron, and other minerals have been helpful to many who experience erratic functioning of the thyroid.

Uranus-Mars combinations arouse restless physical energy which sometimes lead to mishandling of machinery or carelessness in driving. One can also experience a good deal of sexual restlessness. One friend, who had Uranus conjoined her Mars in Scorpio, went swimming every day to release her physical and sexual energy. She also became pregnant twice during this transit. Another client with Uranus conjunct Mars developed a skin rash with itching and blisters as a result of repressing sexual energy. Surgery can also occur during this transit. Several female clients had hysterectomies when Uranus conjoined their natal Mars in Scorpio.

Uranus-Jupiter transits often relate to erratic functioning of the liver and pancreas. One client with Uranus transiting her Jupiter had severe pains in her stomach. Doctors diagnosed it as indigestion resulting from nervous tension and prescribed tranquilizers. Finally a Chinese doctor discovered that not enough bile was being produced (bile is made by the liver); he gave her some herbal teas and put her on a diet of grains and vegetables The condition soon cleared up.

With **Uranus** transiting **Saturn**, the opportunity for breaking up old patterns is present. In the course of these changes, bones often get broken, back problems may often occur (re-structuring of the body), and occasionally conditions like arthritis and rheumatism develop when there is great resistance to these changes.

Uranus transiting **Uranus** can cause nervous conditions that may manifest in all parts of the body as one goes through the cycle of changes. With Uranus' transit of Libra (1968-75), bladder and kidney problems were frequent. In Scorpio (1975-81), Uranus stirred up problems in the reproductive system and colon. (Scorpio rules the colon and excretory system.) There was also an increase in venereal disease. Many women receiving the opposition of Uranus in Scorpio to their natal Uranus in Taurus experienced pre-menopausal symptoms and irregular menstrual cycles. Herbs for toning the female system, blessed thistle and raspberry leaf, and herbs that contain estrogens such as sarsaparilla root are helpful for this cycle. Supplements of magnesium, vitamin B-6, evening primrose oil or some other source of GLA, and vitamin E would also be advised. Uranus' transit of Sagittarius (1981-88) brought out more problems with the respiratory system and allergies. With Uranus moving through Capricorn (1989-96), there were more manifestations of arthritis and rheumatism. Uranus in Aquarius (1996-2003) has caused problems with the electrical conductivity system of the heart, spasms, and colitis.

Uranus-Neptune combinations catalyze changes in consciousness. Often under these transits consciousness-expanding drugs have been used and occasionally unpleasant side effects have resulted. In older people there may be a tendency to withdraw from the world with the mind lapsing into a kind of dormant state, often termed senility. Proper nourishment of the nervous system is important in aiding one to stay grounded and not be carried away with too many unrealistic plans.

Uranus aspecting natal **Pluto** brings about transformation on many levels. Change of diet and lifestyle may occur, along with alterations in one's physical appearance. Often there is a weight loss as one gets involved in more exercise and a lighter diet. Sometimes skin tone, hair texture, and other physical features are changed. One client practiced yoga during this transit and reported that a body area which had been rigid all her life became supple as a result.

TRANSITS OF NEPTUNE

With transits of Neptune there is a greater tendency to disease and infection. Since Neptune rules the auto-immune system, susceptibility to toxins becomes stronger. One is also more predisposed to develop symptoms that are difficult to diagnose. It is important to meditate during this transit in order to gain more clarity.

Malfunctions in the metabolism often develop during Neptune's transits. One client had her first severe symptoms of hypoglycemia when Neptune transited her Sagittarian ascendant. The symptoms continued while Neptune conjoined her other Sagittarian planets.

Sensitivity to the outside world makes one feel more reclusive during Neptune transits and often one builds up anxieties and fears. The wearing of crystals and other gems may prove helpful in neutralizing any negative energy. One should be careful to take additional protective measures in doing any kind of healing work or spiritual readings.

Caution should also be exercised regarding the use of drugs, chemical or recreational, as well as alcohol. Habit patterns that are started during Neptune transits may be difficult to break. Treating ailments with natural substances is best.

Transits of **Neptune** to the **Sun** may bring about allergic reactions, multiple chemical sensitivities, and a weakened immune system. One of my students developed an allergy to fish when Neptune conjoined her Sagittarian Sun. Still another developed nasal allergies.

With **Neptune-Moon** combinations, eye problems such as cataracts have become prevalent, since the Moon deals with fluids in the body and Neptune vision. A friend had an eye operation with Neptune conjunct her natal Moon. It might be important to have your eyes examined during this transit. Also the kidneys, which are a reflex of the eyes, and balance the fluids, should be checked. With the Moon ruling Cancer (the stomach), Neptune transiting the Moon has also brought about some digestive disturbances and food allergies.

Neptune-Mercury combinations can produce extremely anxious states, often associated with confusion. It is helpful to be able to relax as much as possible under this transit—to go away for a few weeks, to spend time on the earth, and in the water. Films, music, and poetry can be a source of inspiration at this time. Foods and supplements rich in B vitamins as well as the nervine herbs are important. In extreme conditions, this combination can produce considerable strain, resulting in a nervous breakdown. Two clients were hospitalized when Neptune conjoined natal Mercury in Sagittarius.

Neptune transiting **Venus** may cause problems with the thyroid; the metabolism can also be thrown off with subsequent sugar imbalance. Curb any tendency to overindulge in sweets and alcohol at this time. It is important to eat alkaline foods such as whole grains, vegetables, some fish or organic poultry if desired, and eliminate most fruits and acidic foods. This transit can make the body very acidic and prone to candida and herpes infections.

Neptune-Mars combinations can, on occasion, cause anemic conditions. Foods rich in iron such as organic beef and veal liver, wheatgrass, beets, dulse and sea vegetables should be increased, as well as nettle leaf tea. Infections that have been difficult to diagnose and cure can begin under this transit.

Neptune aspects to **Jupiter** often catalyze metabolic disturbances like hypoglycemia and diabetes as well as other conditions involving liver toxicity. Excesses in diet, alcohol, and recreational drugs are common. One student developed hepatitis when Neptune squared his natal Jupiter; he had to make changes in his diet and exercise pattern in order to maintain his health.

The influence of **Neptune** on natal **Saturn** may manifest in several ways. Often conditions of crystallization such as arthritis have developed because people were unwilling to release old habit patterns. Many children with natal Saturn in Gemini had their teeth coming in crooked with the opposition of Neptune in Sagittarius. Feelings of lethargy and the tendency to "space out" have been experienced with the transit of Neptune over natal Saturn. One student with Neptune square his natal Saturn in Virgo started jogging because of his lethargic feeling; he ended up injuring his foot (Neptune) and then decided to surrender himself to the lethargy.

Neptune-Uranus combinations stimulate the nervous system. Often individuals experiencing these transits are bewildered by the events occurring in their lives. Confusion and disorientation in thinking have resulted, and on occasion, some people have resorted to drugs or alcohol as an escape mechanism. Allergies have often manifested during this transit, especially in those with natal Uranus in mutable signs.

The first square of **Neptune** to its own place occurs in the early 40's when one has already completed the Uranus opposition and is ready for spiritual catalyzation. This can be an upsetting emotional period or a very productive, creative, and spiritual time. Several clients experienced a recurrence of childhood allergies. One person was working out an emotional relationship and kept repeating old patterns. He came down with the worst case of hay fever in twenty years. Another friend developed an allergy to a dog that he bought for his children and had to resolve some of his own childhood fears regarding dogs.

Transits of **Neptune** to **Pluto** indicate a time of intense inner and spiritual growth. Often old habit patterns are left behind and new ways of eating and taking care of the body are adopted. Many with natal Pluto in Gemini experienced surgery (removal of one of their organs) with the opposition of Neptune in Sagittarius. Some of those with natal Pluto in Cancer underwent major dietary changes when Neptune in Capricorn opposed Pluto. A few of those with Pluto in Leo had heart problems when Neptune opposed in Aquarius; one client had cataract surgery.

TRANSITS OF PLUTO

Transits of Pluto can often lead to a transformation of health patterns and diet. Through some illness or physical breakdown, one is forced to go through a period of purification and purging, a rebirth on a physiological level. Surgery, involving the removal of one part of the body with another organ taking over that particular process, often occurs. Many women have undergone hysterectomies, especially with Pluto squaring its natal position.

Hidden transformations in the body that have not manifested physiologically prior to this time often come to the surface. One young client had cancer diagnosed when Pluto hit his ascendant, though the process inevitably started prior to the actual conjunction. The reproductive system is often involved under Pluto transits, with infection and diseases prevalent. Problems with the excretory system may also manifest at this time.

Transits of **Pluto** to the **Sun** affect changes in the entire body, especially the circulatory system since the Sun rules the heart. Squares and oppositions of Pluto to the Sun often bring on poor circulation. More aerobic exercise and herbs such as red clover blossoms can be helpful.

Pluto-Moon combinations may indicate digestive disturbances (Moon governs the stomach) and require a change of diet. Transits of Pluto to the Moon can also aggravate allergies since the Moon rules fluids and mucous. One client with Moon conjunct Neptune in Libra in her natal chart developed an extreme case of eczema when Pluto transited this conjunction. The exacerbation of her condition forced her to seek out the help of a homeopathic physician, which resulted in an alleviation of the symptoms. Under **Pluto-Moon** transits, miscarriages and stillbirths have occurred. As Pluto rules birth and death, many situations are possible which force the individual to undergo some kind of transformative process. Someone asked a doctor, who assisted in home deliveries, how he felt about his responsibility in delivering children that were stillborn. He replied that he had seen both the mother and father undergo as much of a personal transformation through the delivery of a dead child as through a live one.

Pluto transiting natal **Mercury** can lead to nervous exhaustion and, in extreme cases, breakdowns. Under a Pluto transit one tends to go so deeply into the study of a subject that one may experience acute strain. Relaxation, meditation and physical exercise will help to balance out the intense mental energy.

Pluto contacting the **Venusian** energy may stir up sexual energies. This can result in skin rashes, particularly herpes infections. Venus rules the blood sugar so candida may also be prevalent. It is important to eat an alkaline diet with few fruits and sweets. Venereal diseases, such as gonorrhea and syphilis, may also occur under this transit.

Mars-Pluto contacts can bring out the expression of violent explosive energies. Accidents are common under this transit. The individual can become physically exhausted from overdoing. Repressed sexual energy often manifests in the excretory system with symptoms of hemorrhoids.

Transits of **Pluto** to **Jupiter** mark a time of strong transformation and growth. This may be a period to clean up any excesses in the life style. Problems with the pancreas and liver may surface during this transit, particularly if there is a need to cleanse the body and purify the diet.

Pluto-Saturn combinations often mark dramatic periods of change in the life when old structures are released and transformed. This may necessitate new dietary habits, exercise routine, and other daily regimes. Cancer has often been diagnosed during Pluto-Saturn transits. When Pluto uncovers fixations that have been dormant, it is an opportunity to release old patterns, emotional and otherwise, and evolve new ones.

Pluto transiting natal **Uranus** is certain to bring some new events into one's life. With Pluto in Libra, kidney problems and eye problems surfaced. One client, with Pluto opposing her natal Uranus in Aries, developed swelling under her eyes, and also discovered she had kidney problems. Another student had her fallopian tubes tied when Pluto squared her natal Uranus in Cancer. With Pluto in Scorpio opposite natal Uranus in Taurus, many women had problems with the reproductive system. One client had fibroid tumors diagnosed with this opposition. Another began menopause with hot flashes. So far, Pluto in Sagittarius opposite natal Uranus in Gemini and square natal Uranus in Virgo, has brought on more allergic conditions.

The energy of **Pluto** transiting **Neptune** is responsible for many inner or spiritual transformations. Certain inherent sensitivities which, on the physical level, often lead to allergies or chemical sensitivities, may be brought out by this transit. The increased sensitivity toward the environment may bring about conditions that are common to many individuals. One client with natal Neptune in Virgo in her eleventh house began her studies of astrology under Pluto's transit. She also developed allergies to shell fish and cranberries, and broke out in hives after eating both of these foods.

Pluto aspecting natal **Pluto** often leads to a change of appearance; old habit patterns leave and are replaced with new ones. If surgery is performed, it may involve a new medical technique or replacing a diseased organ with an organ from another person. Many women underwent hysterectomies when Pluto in LIbra squared their natal Pluto in Cancer, bringing about changes in their hormone levels and menstrual cycles. Unfortunately, in many cases, surgery only compounded the difficulties and they still had to deal with their emotional and physical changes through diet, exercise, and other therapies. Pluto in Scorpio square natal Pluto in Leo brought some strong healing experiences to many. Several clients experienced psychic surgery by Phillipine healers and in Brazil, which helped to alleviate conditions of chronic fatigue and environmental illness.

LUNATIONS AND ECLIPSES

Lunations refer to the 13 new Moons and 13 full Moons each year. It is important to observe where these fall in the horoscope, especially if they are making a close hard aspect to a planet. Often on new Moons we begin new dietary and exercise programs; on full Moons physical symptoms may manifest, as full Moons bring the energy out into the open.

Twice a year we usually have an eclipse series which consists of one solar eclipse (new Moon) and one lunar eclipse (full Moon) separated by two weeks. Eclipses amplify the effect of lunations and may have an effect for six months afterward and a few months beforehand. Some eclipses are partial and some are total; solar eclipses have different eclipse paths which pass through particular geographic areas where they can be seen. Lunar eclipses can be seen anywhere if the sky is clear.

Some eclipses are conjunct the north node and some the south node. A south node eclipse may function as a release point; releasing old psychological patterns could manifest in physical symptoms. When an eclipse makes a hard aspect to a natal planet, an angle, or a health midpoint, physical manifestations may be present. (the orb is about 3 degrees).

Eclipses come in series called Saros cycles; each Saros cycle has a particular quality depending on the first eclipse in the series. Each series produces a solar eclipse every 18 years plus 9-11 days, depending on leap years. Each series starts as a tiny partial eclipse near the north or south pole; it takes about 650 years to produce an eclipse conjunct the nodal axis. Meanwhile, each eclipse will be one half to one degree closer to the nodal axis; when it reaches the nodal axis, each eclipse will move one half to one degree furthur away from the axis until it produces a tiny partial eclipse 18 degrees behind the axis.

The pre-natal eclipse point refers to the solar eclipse before birth. The degree of the pre-natal eclipse should be included in the horoscope since significant time periods in one's life occur when a progression, major transit, or eclipse, makes a hard aspect to this point. Note whether the eclipse point conjoins the north or south node; individuals with the south node conjunction seem to experience more serious health problems. Children who manifested cancer at an early age had the south node conjunction.

An example of eclipse action is a client who had very severe eczema. Her symptoms started at her eleventh birthday when the solar eclipse opposed her sixth house Pluto. At the age of fifteen, when her hand became very swollen and infected, the solar eclipse conjoined her Mars. When she began working with a homeopathic doctor, which led to a healing crisis, the solar eclipse conjoined her Moon Neptune conjunction in the eighth house.

A woman who was blind for four and a half years had the solar eclipse sesquiquadrate her Neptune and the lunar eclipse square Neptune when she began to lose her sight. (Neptune refers to sight as well as inner vision.) The year she underwent her surgery for glaucoma, the solar eclipse made a sesquiquadrate to her Jupiter (good fortune) and the lunar eclipse conjoined it. After the surgery, she got her new prescription for glasses when the solar eclipse opposed Neptune.

CHAPTER 9

Diseases of the Immune System

THERE IS BARELY A PERSON in our modern world that has not suffered from some impairment of the body's immune system. For many who have various types of allergies (food, respiratory, skin) as well as multiple chemical sensitivities (MCS), their immune systems are not working up to par; for others who have auto-immune diseases such as rheumatoid arthritis and lupus, their immune systems are over-active and are eating up their own bodies.

A substance capable of triggering an immune response is called an *antigen*. An antigen can be a virus, a bacterium, a fungus, a parasite, tissues or cells from another individual, or a foreign substance such as ragweed pollen or cat's hair. When these apparently harmless substances set off a reaction, it is known as an allergy and the antigens become allergens.

The organs of the immune system are located throughout the body and are referred to as lymphoid organs since they are in charge of the growth, development, and deployment of lymphocytes, the white blood cells that are the key players in the immune system.

There are two major classes of lymphocytes—B cells and T cells. B cells complete their maturation in the bone marrow; T cells migrate to the thymus, which lies behind the breastbone. In these places, they multiply and mature into cells capable of producing an immune response. Some lymphocytes leave the bone marrow and the thymus to cluster in immune organs and lymph nodes. Others use the blood circulation as a network of lymphatic vessels to transport lymph, a fluid that bathes the body's tissues, carrying foreign antigens to the lymph nodes where they can be filtered out and presented to the immune cells.

B cells secrete antibodies into the body's fluids; antibodies match up with antigens and can block viruses from entering cells or coat bacteria to disable them. Antibodies belong to a large family of molecules known as immunoglobulins. There are nine different types of immunoglobulins, each of which plays a different role in the immune defense strategy.

To maintain a healthy immune system, one needs to eat good clean foods, take additional nutritional supplements when needed, get enough exercise, some relaxation and meditation daily, and a sufficient amount of sleep. One also needs to be aware of stress factors and how they impact the physical body. Avoiding chemicals and preservatives in foods, which means eating organic foods or cleaning the foods with a solution of food grade hydrogen peroxide, is probably the most important step one can take. In addition, making sure that one's home is free from chemical detergents, chemical cleaning fluids, leakage of carbon monoxide, and toxic substances in paints and rugs is also crucial.

Foods are both sprayed with pesticides and irradiated to preserve freshness; many of our foods are also genetically engineered now. Eating any of these foods can lead to the creation of fungus, mold, or even parasites in the system, which our immune cells will try to eliminate, causing a weakened immune defense system.

Stress affects not just the white blood cells in the immune system but the kidneys, which regulate the composition of the blood and tissues through eliminating certain chemicals from the body and adjusting blood pressure. It also affects the thyroid, which releases hormones that stimulate the metabolism of every other tissue. The liver is involved as well, since it regulates the concentration of sugar, protein, and other important tissue foods in the blood. It plays an important role in detoxifying poisonous substances and environmental pollutants that arise in the body.

Allergies create a hypersensitive state in which the body overreacts to foreign substances; this reaction may stimulate histamine production.

Wheezing and difficulty breathing in asthma, red itchy skin in eczema or from insect bites, diarrhea from certain foods, are all symptoms of an allergic reaction. Allopathic medicine often recommends an anti-histamine pill or salve to stop the reaction; this damages the immune system even more.

Allergic disorders range from those which affect the respiratory passages (asthma, hay fever, allergic rhinitis) to skin allergies (eczema, hives), gastrointestinal allergies (which may cause diarrhea or constipation), as well as allergies affecting the neurological system (resulting in migraines, fatigue, and other symptoms).

Important ways of maintaining health and preventing both allergic reactions and chemical sensitivities include the following: **Colonic irrigations** or high enemas which get rid of old waste material, help to cleanse the liver, and purify the blood. A **liver flush** done every morning for a week before a colonic will help to detoxify the liver. The liver produces an enzyme called histiminase which serves as a natural anti-histamine. If the liver is congested with fats or accumulated toxins, it cannot produce histiminase. Maintaining a good **acid alkaline balance** is also important. Many people eat too many acidic foods such as coffee, fruits, and sugar; they also eat food high in sodium such as salt, tamari (soy sauce), and miso (soybean paste). Alkaline foods such as whole grains and vegetables balance the body; *candida albicans*, which is a yeast that lives in the intestine producing herpes and other symptoms, cannot grow in an alkaline environment. Bioflavonoids or vitamin P nurture the kidneys and help to maintain the acid alkaline balance. **Nourishing the adrenal glands** is also important: the adrenal cortex releases a natural cortisone which inhibits inflammation as well as the hormone aldosterone, that fights stress and prevents fatigue. B complex vitamins and magnesium, which is found in liquid chlorophyll (the magnesium ion) and dark green vegetables, aid in producing these hormones. **Maintaining the health of the mucous membranes** is also crucial. Since allergic reactions often result in inflammation of the mucous membranes, it is important to maintain these in a healthy state. Mucous protects all the organ linings from invasion by bacteria. When this is not being produced, membranes are vulnerable to irritation by germs, which may result in an uncontrolled increase in the production of mucous. Oils rich in the essential fatty acids such as flax seed oil, borage oil, black currant seed oil, and evening primrose oil are important for this. Also certain herbs are healing to the mucous membranes; mullein and comfrey are particularly good for the bronchial mucosa while slippery elm is soothing to stomach and intestinal linings.

PSYCHOLOGICAL FACTORS

Allergic and chemically sensitive individuals are hypersensitive people (Neptune, Moon, and water sign emphasis) who react strongly to emotional conditions as well as to external substances. Often they lack self confidence and tend to suppress their feelings so that the allergic reaction to a substance provides an outlet for pent up emotions. Many types of events serve to trigger these reactions—moving away from a known environment, change of job, entering into a new relationship such as marriage or separating from an old one, death of a family member, health problems, financial problems, and other worries.

Anger and hostility may be held back; often these individuals develop symptoms of redness, itchiness, and swelling. These symptoms are ruled by Mars, the god of war. Those with skin allergies who manifest these symptoms are dealing with a toxic liver; when the liver cannot detoxify properly, the skin may break out. In Traditional Chinese Medicine, the liver is related to anger, another connection to Mars.

Asthma is certainly one of the most complex and scary of the allergic manifestations. Breath is the first requisite of life and respiration is a strong step in biological independence. Difficulty breathing may be a subtle protest in being separated from the mother. Dependency on the mother seems to be a prime characteristic of asthmatics. Asthmatic children often have problems adapting to new surroundings and events. They may tend to be compulsive in their habit patterns. As teenagers, they frequently experience conflicts around sex, which may reappear later in life. An asthma attack may provide an outlet for emotional release and sometimes is a substitute for crying.

ASTROLOGICAL PATTERNS

Neptune and Pisces are often seen where allergies and chemical sensitivities are present. Neptune may be angular, conjunct the Sun or Moon or another planet. Pisces may be rising or the Moon or Sun could be in Pisces; often there are several planets in Pisces or its opposite sign Virgo. There is usually a strong water sign emphasis. Jupiter or the sign Sagittarius may also be prominent as Jupiter and Sagittarius govern the liver, which is always involved in both allergic reactions and chemical sensitivity.

The Moon rules fluids and has much to do with mucous and swelling; the Moon may be angular in the horoscope and the sign Cancer strong, especially in cases of gastrointestinal allergies.

Mutable signs are often pre-dominant, particularly where respiratory allergies or multiple chemical sensitivities are prevalent. Mercury is also involved with respiratory allergies and asthma, as are the signs Gemini and Sagittarius, and the third and ninth houses. Virgo and Pisces, the other two mutable signs, are involved with food allergies and multiple chemical sensitivities since Virgo governs the digestive process. Four degrees of Virgo and Pisces and eighteen degrees Gemini and Sagittarius are sometimes seen with respiratory allergies.

Venus and Saturn are implicated in cases of skin allergies. Hard aspects from Venus to Saturn are found in eczema; to Pluto where there are skin growths, warts, or tumors; to Mars where there is swelling or blistering. Venus in Capricorn is common, with hard aspects to either Saturn or Pluto or both.

Allergies and MCS often begin with transits of Neptune to major planets or angles, or progressed planets hitting Neptune. Transits of Pluto also can bring on these cycles, particularly those that continue for long time periods. Uranus, Neptune, or Pluto making hard aspects by transit to Mercury may be the beginning of respiratory allergies. When these same planets transit the natal Moon, more reactions to food are found, necessitating diet changes.

MIDPOINTS

Some of the general health midpoints are important here:

Saturn/Neptune—the health axis indicates restriction
Saturn/Neptune often equals Jupiter, Mercury, or Venus

Mars/Neptune—shows sensitivity to toxic substances
Mars/Neptune often equals Jupiter or Mercury

In addition, check the following:

Moon/Neptune—indicates hyper-sensitivity and over accumulation of water in the tissues

Venus/Neptune—blood sugar

Allergies—Woman 1
Natal Chart
Jun 9, 1921, 11:45 PM PST +8:00
San Francisco
37N46 30 122W25 06

Geocentric
Tropical
Koch
True Node

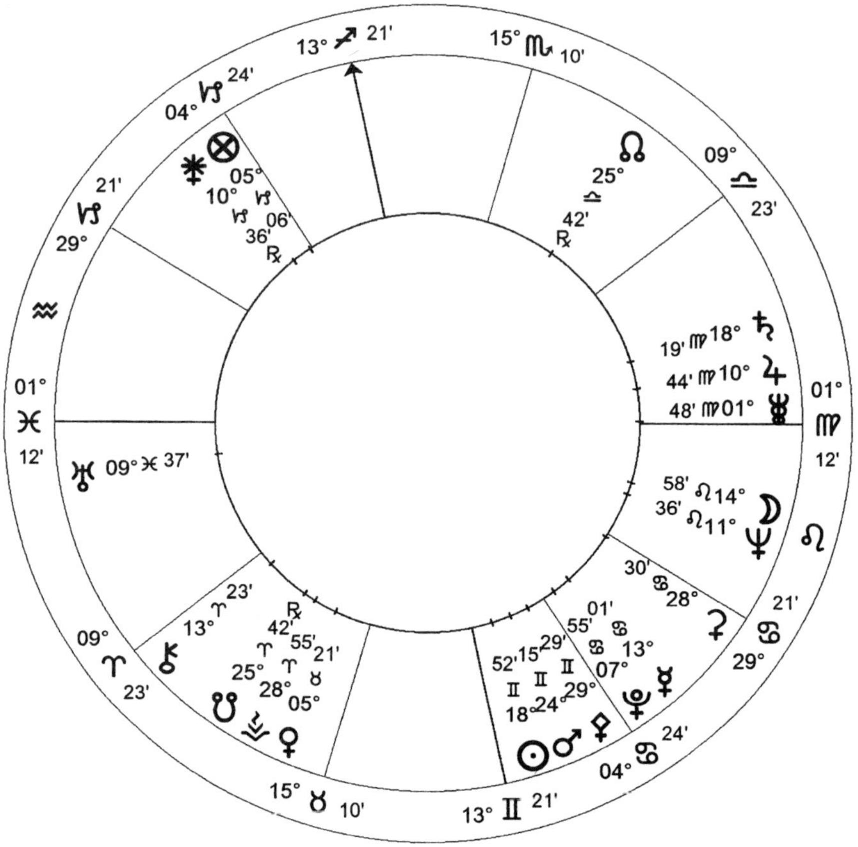

CASE HISTORIES

Case History #1

This woman has had respiratory and food allergies most of her life; they started at the age of 5. At the age of 15, in high school, they were pretty bothersome; she used anti-histamines and other medications to control the symptoms. When she was 20, she had some skin problems, hives and itching. At the age of 27, she became allergic to certain foods and changed

Midpoint Listing

Allergies • Woman 1 • Natal Chart
In Planetery Sequence • Modulus 360°00'

☽	14°♌58	*☿*	13°♋01	♂/♆	17°♋55	*♅*	09°♓37	⚷/⚸	22°♊35
☽/☉	16°♋55	☿/♀	09°♊11	♂/♇	01°♋05	♅/♆	25°♉37	⚷/☊	19°♑32
☽/☿	29°♋00	☿/♂	03°♋38	♂/⚷	18°♉49	♅/♇	08°♉46	⚷/⊗	24°♒14
☽/♀	25°♊09	☿/♃	11°♌52	♂/⚳	26°♉35	♅/⚷	26°♓30	*⚳*	28°♈55
☽/♂	19°♋36	☿/♄	15°♌40	♂/⚴	26°♊52	♅/⚳	04°♈16	⚳/⚴	29°♉12
☽/♃	27°♌51	☿/♅	11°♉19	♂/⚵	02°♈25	♅/⚴	04°♉33	⚳/⚵	04°♓46
☽/♄	01°♍38	☿/♆	27°♋18	♂/⚶	11°♋23	♅/⚵	10°♒07	⚳/⚶	13°♊43
☽/♅	27°♉18	☿/♇	10°♋28	♂/⚸	28°♋01	♅/⚶	19°♉04	⚳/⚸	00°♋21
☽/♆	13°♌17	☿/⚷	28°♉12	♂/☊	24°♌58	♅/⚸	05°♊43	⚳/☊	27°♋19
☽/♇	26°♋26	☿/⚳	05°♊58	♂/⊗	29°♓40	♅/☊	02°♑40	⚳/⊗	02°♓01
☽/⚷	14°♊10	☿/⚴	06°♋15	*♃*	10°♍44	♅/⊗	07°♒22	*⚴*	29°♊29
☽/⚳	21°♊56	☿/⚵	11°♎49	♃/♄	14°♍31	*♆*	11°♌36	⚴/⚵	05°♈03
☽/⚴	22°♋13	☿/⚶	20°♋46	♃/♅	10°♐10	♆/♇	24°♋45	⚴/⚶	14°♋00
☽/⚵	27°♎47	☿/⚸	07°♌24	♃/♆	26°♌10	♆/⚷	12°♊29	⚴/⚸	00°♌38
☽/⚶	06°♌44	☿/☊	04°♍22	♃/♇	09°♌19	♆/⚳	20°♊15	⚴/☊	27°♌36
☽/⚸	23°♌23	☿/⊗	09°♎04	♃/⚷	27°♊03	♆/⚴	20°♋32	⚴/⊗	02°♈18
☽/☊	20°♍20	*♀*	05°♉21	♃/⚳	04°♋49	♆/⚵	26°♎06	*⚵*	10°♑36
☽/⊗	25°♎02	♀/♂	29°♉48	♃/⚴	05°♌06	♆/⚶	05°♌03	⚵/⚶	19°♎33
☉	18°♊52	♀/♃	08°♋02	♃/⚵	10°♏40	♆/⚸	21°♌42	⚵/⚸	06°♏12
☉/☿	00°♋56	♀/♄	11°♋50	♃/⚶	19°♌37	♆/☊	18°♍39	⚵/☊	03°♐09
☉/♀	27°♉06	♀/♅	07°♈29	♃/⚸	06°♍16	♆/⊗	23°♎21	⚵/⊗	07°♑51
☉/♂	21°♊33	♀/♆	23°♊28	♃/☊	03°♎13	*♇*	07°♋55	*⚶*	28°♋30
☉/♃	29°♋48	♀/♇	06°♊38	♃/⊗	07°♏55	♇/⚷	25°♉39	⚶/⚸	15°♌09
☉/♄	03°♌35	♀/⚷	24°♈22	*♄*	18°♍19	♇/⚳	03°♊25	⚶/☊	12°♍06
☉/♅	29°♈15	♀/⚳	02°♉08	♄/♅	13°♐58	♇/⚴	03°♋42	⚶/⊗	16°♎48
☉/♆	15°♋14	♀/⚴	02°♊25	♄/♆	29°♌57	♇/⚵	09°♈15	*⚸*	01°♍48
☉/♇	28°♊23	♀/⚵	07°♓59	♄/♇	13°♌07	♇/⚶	18°♋12	⚸/☊	28°♍45
☉/⚷	16°♉07	♀/⚶	16°♊56	♄/⚷	00°♋51	♇/⚸	04°♌51	⚸/⊗	03°♏27
☉/⚳	23°♉53	♀/⚸	03°♋34	♄/⚳	08°♋37	♇/☊	01°♍48	*☊*	25°♎42
☉/⚴	24°♊10	♀/☊	00°♌32	♄/⚴	08°♌54	♇/⊗	06°♎30	☊/⊗	00°♐24
☉/⚵	29°♓44	♀/⊗	05°♓14	♄/⚵	14°♏28	*⚷*	13°♈23	*⊗*	05°♑06
☉/⚶	08°♋41	*♂*	24°♊15	♄/⚶	23°♌25	⚷/⚳	21°♈09		
☉/⚸	25°♋20	♂/♃	02°♌29	♄/⚸	10°♍03	⚷/⚴	21°♉26		
☉/☊	22°♌17	♂/♄	06°♌17	♄/☊	07°♎01	⚷/⚵	26°♒59		
☉/⊗	26°♓59	♂/♅	01°♉56	♄/⊗	11°♏43	⚷/⚶	05°♊57		

her diet slightly, but still used the anti-histamines and medication. She was also drinking quite a bit of alcohol in her 20's and 30's, which did not help her liver and made the allergies worse. She gave birth to a healthy child in October 1955. In 1967, when she was 46, she had some allergy tests; she tested out positive to many pollens and grasses as well as certain foods. In 1979, close to the time of her second Saturn return, cancer of the uterus was diagnosed; she had a total hysterectomy in March 1979.

Interpretation of Horoscope

With the Sun conjoined Mars in Gemini, there is the tendency to weak lungs and respiratory problems; Mars would also indicate redness, itchiness, and inflammation. This combination is square Saturn in Virgo, which shows that the allergies are connected to digestion, suggesting food allergies as well. With a Pisces ascendant, there is a sensitive emotional nature and a weak immune system. Uranus in Pisces close to the ascendant would indicate that the nervous system needs nurturing, plenty of magnesium and B complex vitamins. Uranus opposing Jupiter suggests erratic functioning of the liver and Jupiter conjunct Saturn in Virgo also shows that there is a problem metabolizing fats. Moon in Leo is conjoined Neptune in the sixth house; this indicates allergies and immune system problems; it also suggests there may be a problem with alcohol, drugs, or sensitivity to prescription medicines. Venus is in Taurus square Neptune, which leads to idealism as regards love relationships as well as problems metabolizing carbohydrates. Mercury in Cancer conjoined Pluto indicates problems with the respiratory system; fortunately this conjunction is trine Uranus and sextile Venus and Jupiter. The south node conjoined Vesta suggests strong service work; with the Pisces ascendant, there may be a tendency to be self sacrificing as well.

By declination, the Sun is parallel both Mercury and Mars, again emphasizing the respiratory and nervous systems. The Moon is parallel Venus, suggesting possible blood sugar problems, and Jupiter is contra-parallel Uranus which is similar to the opposition between the two, indicating erratic liver functioning..

Midpoints

Mars/Uranus = Sun and Saturn, indirect—problems with the nervous system and allergies

Mars/ Neptune = ascendant, indirect—sensitivity to toxic substances and an exceptionally vulnerable immune system

Saturn/ Neptune falls between Mercury and Pluto (15 degrees cardinal), direct, suggests that the health axis involves the lungs

Venus/ Neptune = Mars, direct—again showing problems with blood sugar

Transits and Progressions

In 1926, her allergies began—transiting Pluto was conjoined Mercury.

In 1936, allergies were bad in high school. Transiting Neptune was opposing Uranus.

In 1941, there was redness and itching of the skin. Transiting Pluto was square natal Venus.

In 1948, her allergies intensified and her diet changed. Secondary progressed Mars was conjoined natal Mercury, progressed Moon was conjoined natal Neptune and Moon, transiting Neptune was at 13 Libra squaring Mercury.

In 1955, when she gave birth, Neptune at 28 Libra was opposed Vesta and square Ceres (aspects to Ceres often occur with birth or pregnancy). Pluto at 28 degrees Leo was almost conjoined her 7th house cusp, and Saturn at 18 degrees Scorpio was sextile natal Saturn and inconjunct her Sun.

In 1967, she underwent allergy tests. Pluto was conjoined her natal Saturn in Virgo.

In March 1979, she had a total hysterectomy. Progressed Sun conjoined natal Moon, transiting Saturn opposed natal Uranus, transiting Pluto trined natal Sun, and transiting Jupiter conjoined Ceres. The solar eclipse a few weeks before was at 8 Pisces conjunct natal Uranus.

Case History #2

Many types of allergic reactions have plagued this woman. As a child, she had severe reactions to poison ivy beginning at age 11 when there was a fire in which poison ivy was burning. This attack lasted about 3 1/2 weeks as she was also very allergic to the calamine lotion that was used. In October 1991, at the age of 29, she was exposed to a campfire on which someone had thrown poison ivy, thinking it was wood. She was given cortisone in an emergency room, to which she was allergic. Another time, in December 1996, she drove through a field where they were burning weeds but was able to use stinging nettles to stop the reaction from the poison ivy.

Asthma attacks began in high school at the age of 16. She coughed herself to sleep every night but her parents thought it was bronchitis. In medical school at the age of 22, she had trouble breathing in a cadaver lab; she was allergic to the formalin. At first it was diagnosed as TB because she was coughing up blood. Later, another doctor diagnosed it as adult onset bronchial asthma. She started taking theophylline, inhaled steroids, to which she had a bad reaction, and then inhaled albuterol, which contains

Allergies—Woman 2
Natal Chart
Aug 16, 1962, 518 PM CST +6:00
Biloxi
30N23 45 088W53 07

Geocentric
Tropical
Koch
True Node

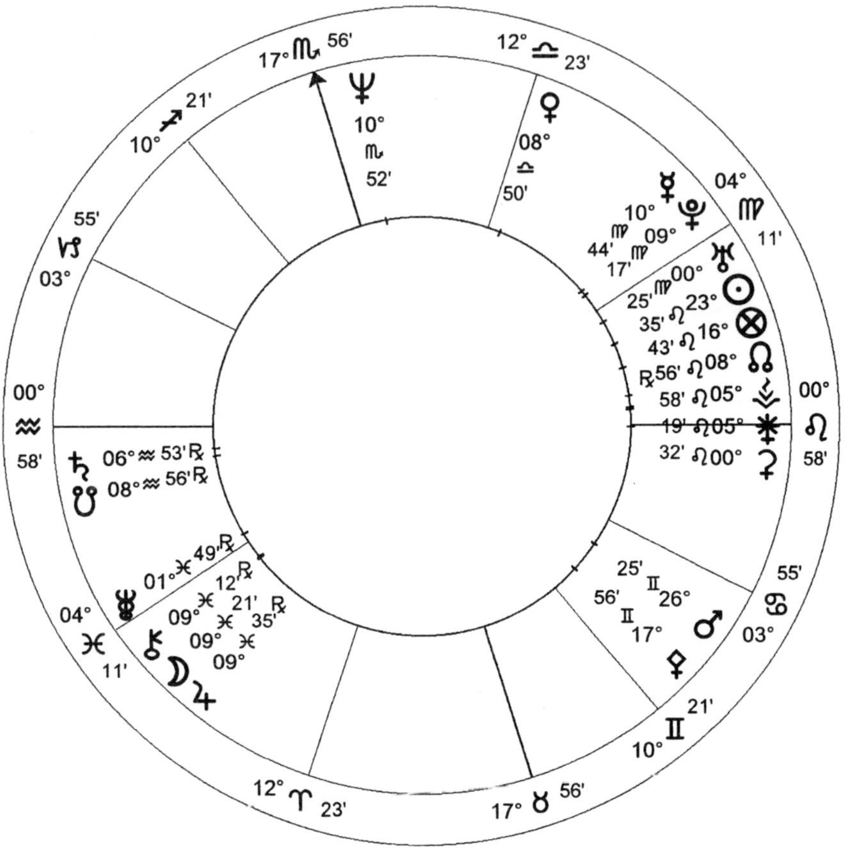

a "non-active" ingredient to which she is allergic. She is also sensitive to theophylline so only takes the minimum. The asthma flared up again in the spring of 1986, when she was 24 years old and undergoing a divorce. After five years of taking very high doses of theophylline, she was able to reduce the dose.

There are also several food allergies she deals with; she has had severe reactions to mushrooms (which are a fungus) and Nutra-sweet (which is of

Midpoint Listing

Allergies • Woman 2 • Natal Chart
In Planetery Sequence • Modulus 360°00'

☽*	09°♓21	*☿*	10°♍44	♂/♆	03°♍39	*♅*	00°♍25	⚷/⚶	05°♓30
☽/☉	01°♊28	☿/♀	24°♍47	♂/♇	02°♌51	♅/♆	05°♎39	⚷/☊	24°♉04
☽/☿	10°♐02	☿/♂	03°♌35	♂/⚷	02°♉48	♅/♇	04°♍51	⚷/⊗	27°♉58
☽/♀	24°♐05	☿/♃	10°♐10	♂/⚸	16°♋11	♅/⚷	04°♊49	*⚸*	05°♌58
☽/♂	02°♉53	☿/♄	23°♏49	♂/⚴	22°♊10	♅/⚸	18°♌11	⚸/⚴	11°♋57
☽/♃	09°♓28	☿/♅	05°♍35	♂/⚵	15°♋52	♅/⚴	24°♋10	⚸/⚵	05°♌38
☽/♄	23°♒07	☿/♆	10°♎48	♂/⚳	13°♋28	♅/⚵	17°♌52	⚸/⚳	03°♌15
☽/♅	04°♊53	☿/♇	10°♍01	♂/⚶	29°♈07	♅/⚳	15°♌29	⚸/⚶	18°♉53
☽/♆	10°♑06	☿/⚷	09°♐58	♂/☊	17°♋41	♅/⚶	01°♊07	⚸/☊	07°♌27
☽/♇	09°♊19	☿/⚸	23°♌21	♂/⊗	21°♋34	♅/☊	19°♌41	⚸/⊗	11°♌21
☽/⚷	09°♓16	☿/⚴	29°♋20	*♃*	09°♓35	♅/⊗	23°♌34	*⚴*	17°♊56
☽/⚸	22°♉39	☿/⚵	23°♌02	♃/♄	23°♒14	*♆*	10°♏52	⚴/⚵	11°♋37
☽/⚴	28°♈38	☿/⚳	20°♌38	♃/♅	05°♊00	♆/♇	10°♎04	⚴/⚳	09°♋14
☽/⚵	22°♉20	☿/⚶	06°♐16	♃/♆	10°♑14	♆/⚷	10°♑02	⚴/⚶	24°♈52
☽/⚳	19°♉56	☿/☊	24°♌50	♃/♇	09°♊26	♆/⚸	23°♍25	⚴/☊	13°♋26
☽/⚶	05°♓35	☿/⊗	28°♌44	♃/⚷	09°♓24	♆/⚴	29°♌24	⚴/⊗	17°♋20
☽/☊	24°♉08	*♀*	08°♎50	♃/⚸	22°♉47	♆/⚵	23°♍06	*⚵*	05°♌19
☽/⊗	28°♉02	♀/♂	17°♌38	♃/⚴	28°♈45	♆/⚳	20°♍42	⚵/⚳	02°♌56
☉*	23°♌35	♀/♃	24°♐13	♃/⚵	22°♉27	♆/⚶	06°♑20	⚵/⚶	18°♉34
☉/☿	02°♍10	♀/♄	07°♐52	♃/⚳	20°♉04	♆/☊	24°♍54	⚵/☊	07°♌08
☉/♀	16°♍13	♀/♅	19°♍38	♃/⚶	05°♓42	♆/⊗	28°♍48	⚵/⊗	11°♌01
☉/♂	25°♋00	♀/♆	24°♎51	♃/☊	24°♉16	*♇*	09°♍17	*⚳*	00°♌32
☉/♃	01°♊35	♀/♇	24°♍04	♃/⊗	28°♉09	♇/⚷	09°♐14	⚳/⚶	16°♉10
☉/♄	15°♏14	♀/⚷	24°♐01	*♄*	06°♒53	♇/⚸	22°♌37	⚳/☊	04°♌44
☉/♅	27°♌00	♀/⚸	07°♍24	♄/♅	18°♏39	♇/⚴	28°♋36	⚳/⊗	08°♌38
☉/♆	02°♎14	♀/⚴	13°♌23	♄/♆	23°♐53	♇/⚵	22°♌18	*⚶*	01°♓49
☉/♇	01°♍26	♀/⚵	07°♍05	♄/♇	23°♏05	♇/⚳	19°♌54	⚶/☊	20°♉22
☉/⚷	01°♊23	♀/⚳	04°♍41	♄/⚷	23°♒02	♇/⚶	05°♐33	⚶/⊗	24°♉16
☉/⚸	14°♌46	♀/⚶	20°♐19	♄/⚸	06°♉25	♇/☊	24°♌06	*☊*	08°♌56
☉/⚴	20°♋45	♀/☊	08°♍53	♄/⚴	12°♈24	♇/⊗	28°♌00	☊/⊗	12°♌50
☉/⚵	14°♌27	♀/⊗	12°♍47	♄/⚵	06°♉06	*⚷*	09°♓12	*⊗*	16°♌43
☉/⚳	12°♌03	*♂*	26°♊25	♄/⚳	03°♉42	⚷/⚸	22°♉35		
☉/⚶	27°♉42	♂/♃	03°♉00	♄/⚶	19°♒21	⚷/⚴	28°♈34		
☉/☊	16°♌15	♂/♄	16°♈39	♄/☊	07°♏55	⚷/⚵	22°♉16		
☉/⊗	20°♌09	♂/♅	28°♋25	♄/⊗	11°♏48	⚷/⚳	19°♉52		

course a chemical) as well as coffee. She also avoids common food allergies such as peanuts, sugar, dairy products, soy, and wheat which create allergens. Other known allergies are to calamine lotion and all phenol drugs.

Interpretation of Horoscope

Her horoscope shows Sun broadly conjunct Uranus, indicating a sensitive nervous system, while the Moon, Jupiter, and Chiron are all conjoined in

Pisces opposite Mercury and Pluto in Virgo. Pisces Moon indicates a weak immune system, made worse by Jupiter, which rules the liver. Mercury conjoined Pluto points to a weak respiratory system and in Virgo, suggests that digestion and foods are at the basis of her problems. Neptune is elevated in the chart and is square her nodes and Saturn. Neptune squaring the nodes points to a weak and highly sensitive immune system. Saturn is inconjunct Mercury and Pluto, suggesting blockages in the lungs. Mars is in Gemini, sesquiquadrate Neptune and the south node. Mars in Gemini indicates problems with the respiratory system; it is often an indicator of asthma. Venus in Libra is trine Saturn and the south node, but inconjunct Chiron, Moon, and Jupiter in Pisces pointing up problems with blood sugar. Saturn conjoined the south node in Aquarius, as well as Aquarius rising, suggests poor circulation.

By declination, Saturn is contra parallel Pluto while the Moon is contra parallel Uranus. Saturn contra parallel Pluto can indicate blockages in the colon, which is on the same meridian as the lungs. Moon with Uranus again points to a sensitive nervous system.

Midpoints

Sun/Moon = Uranus, direct—independent nature and rebellious, highly sensitive nervous system

Mars/Saturn = Uranus, indirect—poor circulation, sudden attacks that inhibit vitality

Saturn/Neptune = Mars, direct—Mars in Gemini falling on the health axis indicates problems with respiratory system and lungs

Transitions and Progressions

In August 1973, she had her first serious poison ivy reaction. Secondary progressed Moon was exactly square Neptune, transiting Jupiter was conjoined Saturn, Neptune was hitting the Mars/Neptune direct midpoint (3 mutable) while Uranus was hitting the indirect midpoint (18 cardinal).

In November 1978 was the beginning of asthma. Secondary progressed Sun was conjoined natal Pluto while progressed Mars was inconjunct natal Saturn. Transiting Jupiter was inconjunct her Chiron, Moon, Jupiter combination. Saturn was conjunct Mercury, Uranus was conjunct MC, and Pluto was hitting the Mars/Neptune indirect midpoint. The solar eclipse on Oct. 2 had hit her Venus.

In the fall of 1984, in medical school, she had trouble breathing and lost her short term memory. Progressed Moon was opposite Mars in Gemini in September; transiting Mars was also opposing Mars that month. Saturn was conjoined the MC while Uranus was square her Chiron, Moon, and Jupiter. The lunar eclipse in November of that year conjoined her fourth house cusp.

In the spring of 1986, there was her divorce and flare ups. Transiting Pluto was square Saturn, and Uranus was 45 degrees from the Saturn south node conjunction. Saturn was square Chiron, Moon, and Jupiter, and it was her Jupiter return.

In October 1991, she had a bad poison ivy attack followed by an allergic reaction to cortisone. Transiting Jupiter was conjoined Pluto, Pluto was conjunct MC, and Saturn was conjunct ascendant, moving into her first Saturn return.

In December 1996, she had a poison ivy attack but used stinging nettles to control it. Progressed Venus was exactly conjunct progressed Neptune. Transiting Uranus was approaching Saturn, Neptune was inconjunct Mars and 135 degrees from Mercury, Pluto was hitting the Mars /Neptune direct midpoint.

Case History #3

Here is the case of someone with multiple chemical sensitivities who is living a fairly normal life by controlling her symptoms in natural ways. In her late teens, she was prone to bladder infections and digestive problems. Digestive problems plagued her throughout her life. In 1993, she noticed that perfumes and incense bothered her. In late 1995-1996, she had some very strong symptoms including migraines, muscle cramping, chronic tiredness, food allergies, and foggy thinking. She went to an allergist who did some food testing and gave her some de-sensitization shots; there was a negative reaction to the first series of shots. She also had blood tests and a digestive stool analysis which revealed some non beneficial bacteria.

Her treatment included intra-venous vitamins A, E, and C along with supplements of magnesium citrate, zinc, and molybdenum. She was also given a nutritional colon cleanse. At some point in 1996, she quit working, stayed home and starting examining what she had done to co-create the situation. She spent her time in emotional and spiritual cleansing, looking at all of her old patterns, and also began meditation for longer periods.

MCS—Woman
Natal Chart
Aug 29, 1954, 12:04 PM EST +5:00
Laurinburg
34N46 26 079W27 47

Geocentric
Tropical
Koch
True Node

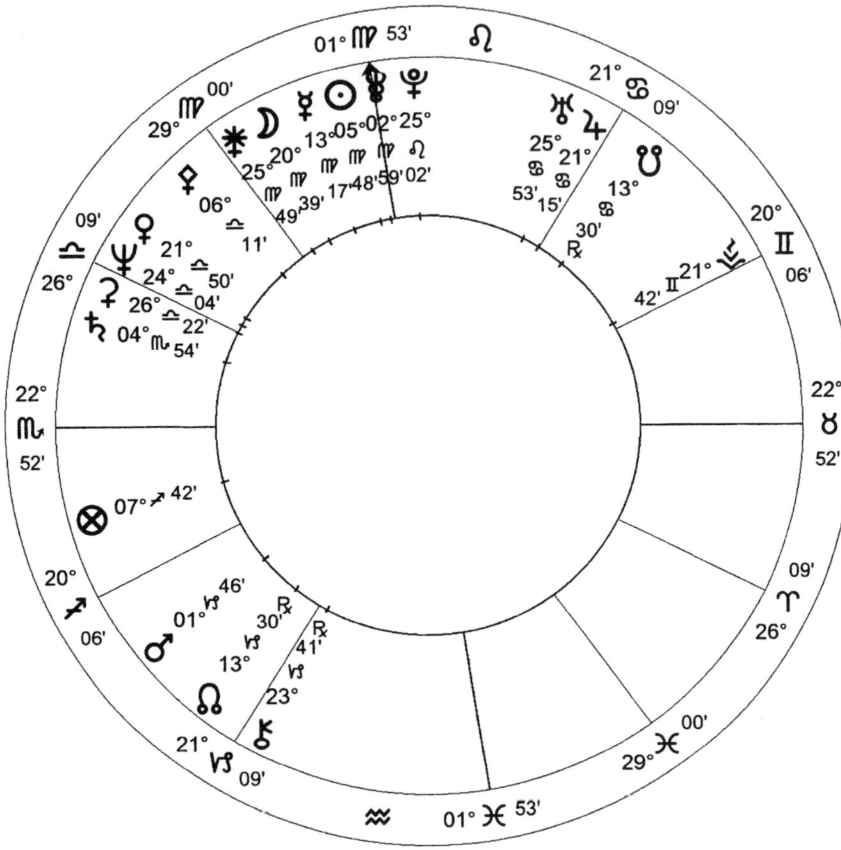

By 1997, she felt much more stable and had her symptoms under control. At this time she met her husband.

Currently she takes an anti-oxidant containing vitamins A, C, and E; she does some exercise, particularly walking, though at times she is too tired. She still experiences chronic fatigue and needs an afternoon nap. If she is in contact with things that irritate her such as strong perfumes or incense, her lungs can get congested. She does travel but has to alert the places she stays

Midpoint Listing

MCS • Woman • Natal Chart
In Planetery Sequence • Modulus 360°00'

☽	20°♍39	*☿*	13°♍17	♂/♆	27°♏55	*♅*	25°♋53	⚷/⚶	13°♏20
☽/☉	13°♍14	☿/♀	02°♎34	♂/♇	28°♎24	♅/♆	09°♍59	⚷/☊	18°♑35
☽/☿	16°♍58	☿/♂	07°♏32	♂/⚷	12°♑44	♅/♇	10°♌28	⚷/⊗	00°♑42
☽/♀	06°♎14	☿/♃	17°♌16	♂/⚸	26°♓44	♅/⚷	24°♎47	*⚸*	21°♊42
☽/♂	11°♏13	☿/♄	09°♎06	♂/⚴	18°♏59	♅/⚸	08°♋48	⚸/⚴	13°♌57
☽/♃	20°♌57	☿/♅	19°♌35	♂/⚵	13°♏48	♅/⚴	01°♍02	⚸/⚵	08°♌45
☽/♄	12°♎47	☿/♆	03°♎41	♂/⚳	29°♏04	♅/⚵	25°♌51	⚸/⚳	24°♌02
☽/♅	23°♌16	☿/♇	04°♍10	♂/⚶	02°♏23	♅/⚳	11°♍08	⚸/⚶	27°♋21
☽/♆	07°♎21	☿/⚷	18°♏29	♂/☊	07°♑38	♅/⚶	14°♌26	⚸/☊	02°♈36
☽/♇	07°♍51	☿/⚸	02°♌30	♂/⊗	19°♐44	♅/☊	19°♎42	⚸/⊗	14°♍42
☽/⚷	22°♏10	☿/⚴	24°♍44	*♃*	21°♋15	♅/⊗	01°♎48	*⚴*	06°♎11
☽/⚸	06°♌10	☿/⚵	19°♍33	♃/♄	13°♍05	*♆*	24°♎04	⚴/⚵	01°♎00
☽/⚴	28°♍25	☿/⚳	04°♎50	♃/♅	23°♋34	♆/♇	24°♍33	⚴/⚳	16°♎17
☽/⚵	23°♍14	☿/⚶	08°♍08	♃/♆	07°♍39	♆/⚷	08°♐53	⚴/⚶	19°♍35
☽/⚳	08°♎31	☿/☊	13°♏24	♃/♇	08°♌09	♆/⚸	22°♌53	⚴/☊	24°♏51
☽/⚶	11°♍49	☿/⊗	25°♎30	♃/⚷	22°♈28	♆/⚴	15°♎08	⚴/⊗	06°♏57
☽/☊	17°♏04	*♀*	21°♎50	♃/⚸	06°♋28	♆/⚵	09°♎57	*⚵*	25°♍49
☽/⊗	29°♎11	♀/♂	26°♏48	♃/⚴	28°♌43	♆/⚳	25°♎13	⚵/⚳	11°♎06
☉	05°♍48	♀/♃	06°♍32	♃/⚵	23°♌32	♆/⚶	28°♍32	⚵/⚶	14°♍24
☉/☿	09°♍33	♀/♄	28°♎22	♃/⚳	08°♍48	♆/☊	03°♐47	⚵/☊	19°♏39
☉/♀	28°♍49	♀/♅	08°♍52	♃/⚶	12°♌07	♆/⊗	15°♏53	⚵/⊗	01°♏46
☉/♂	03°♏47	♀/♆	22°♎57	♃/☊	17°♎22	*♇*	25°♌02	*⚳*	26°♎22
☉/♃	13°♌31	♀/♇	23°♍26	♃/⊗	29°♍28	♇/⚷	09°♏22	⚳/⚶	29°♍41
☉/♄	05°♎21	♀/⚷	07°♐46	*♄*	04°♏54	♇/⚸	23°♋22	⚳/☊	04°♐56
☉/♅	15°♌51	♀/⚸	21°♌46	♄/♅	15°♍24	♇/⚴	15°♍37	⚳/⊗	17°♏02
☉/♆	29°♍56	♀/⚴	14°♎01	♄/♆	29°♎29	♇/⚵	10°♍26	*⚶*	02°♍59
☉/♇	00°♍25	♀/⚵	08°♎49	♄/♇	29°♍58	♇/⚳	25°♍42	⚶/☊	08°♏15
☉/⚷	14°♏45	♀/⚳	24°♎06	♄/⚷	14°♐18	♇/⚶	29°♌01	⚶/⊗	20°♎21
☉/⚸	28°♋45	♀/⚶	27°♍25	♄/⚸	28°♌18	♇/☊	04°♏16	*☊*	13°♑30
☉/⚴	21°♍00	♀/☊	02°♐40	♄/⚴	20°♎33	♇/⊗	16°♎22	☊/⊗	25°♐36
☉/⚵	15°♍49	♀/⊗	14°♏46	♄/⚵	15°♎22	*⚷*	23°♑41	*⊗*	07°♐42
☉/⚳	01°♎05	*♂*	01°♑46	♄/⚳	00°♏38	⚷/⚸	07°♈41		
☉/⚶	04°♍24	♂/♃	11°♎30	♄/⚶	03°♎57	⚷/⚴	29°♏56		
☉/☊	09°♏39	♂/♄	03°♐20	♄/☊	09°♐12	⚷/⚵	24°♏45		
☉/⊗	21°♎45	♂/♅	13°♎50	♄/⊗	21°♏18	⚷/⚳	10°♐02		

ahead of time to be careful with laundry detergent on the linens and other scents that might be bothersome. She continues to see a physician who recommends supplements, and a chiropractor when necessary. A few years ago she had some acupuncture treatments but is not currently pursuing this. Basically, she works in the mornings when her energy is up and rests in the afternoons. She attributes her healing of the strong symptoms to some of the deep inner work she has done, in addition to the physical treatments.

Interpretation of Horoscope

This horoscope shows a dominant Virgo theme with the Sun, Moon, and Mercury in Virgo in addition to the asteroids Hygeia and Juno. The Sun is conjoined Hygeia, which often indicates that the person has done a lot of healing work on herself and on others. Here Hygeia and the Sun are close to the MC. Mercury is strong as it is on the Sun/Moon midpoint in addition to being the ruler of the Sun and Moon. The Virgo theme indicates a sensitive digestive system. Venus conjoined Neptune shows a very creative individual with possible bladder problems and low blood sugar. This conjunction squares the Jupiter Uranus conjunction (strong intuition) so we know that the liver is heavily involved, with the tendency to build up toxins (square to Neptune) and possibly cravings for sugar (square to Venus). Saturn is in Scorpio in the twelfth house indicating blockages in the colon; Scorpio ascendant is also square Pluto, again ruling the colon. However, the Scorpio ascendant is trine the Jupiter Uranus conjunction and sextile the Moon, so this individual has the potential to keep her system balanced through colon cleansing and detoxifying the liver. Mars is well placed in Capricorn and trine the Sun Hygeia conjunction, providing her with good vitality and the will to follow through on cleansing and dietary recommendations. The Sun in the tenth house is also well placed for vital energy. The north node is in Capricorn and exactly trine Mercury, adding to her capacity for discipline and follow through. Chiron in Capricorn is in a T square with Jupiter Uranus in Cancer and Venus Neptune in Libra. This shows that her ability to heal herself will come through organized study and understanding, as Chiron is in the third house and Mercury is on her Sun/Moon midpoint. Working out in the world with Chiron in Capricorn and her full tenth house is something that is important for her. This horoscope lacks fire, though the Sun is angular and Mars is well placed in Capricorn, so the physical body is particularly sensitive and maintaining vitality is a challenge.

In terms of declination, her Sun is contra parallel both Venus and Saturn. This could indicate that she is more sensitive to cold and has poor circulation. Jupiter is parallel both Uranus and Pluto, suggesting the possibility of re-generating and cleansing the liver.

Midpoints

Sun/Moon = Mercury, direct—vulnerable respiratory system, strong mental abilities and communication skills

Mars/Saturn = Jupiter, indirect—tendency for the liver to become toxic and congested

Mars/Neptune = nodes, indirect—highly sensitive immune system, psychic and intuitive abilities

Transits and Progressions

In 1993, incense and perfumes began to bother her. Secondary progressed Mercury was exactly conjunct progressed Saturn at 8+ degrees Scorpio. In April of 1993, the progressed Moon at 8 Aquarius was also square this conjunction. Transit-wise, Pluto was crossing her ascendant, indicating the need for cleansing of the physical body, and letting go of old patterns. Both Uranus and Neptune were at 21 Capricorn, squaring Venus and Jupiter in her natal chart. This shows that the body was becoming more sensitive, with more toxins in the liver, and low blood sugar. Uranus square Venus also indicates possible thyroid and hormonal irregularities. Saturn in Aquarius was square the ascendant at this time, and in June 1993, the lunar eclipse was at 14 Sagittarius, exactly square her Mercury, which rules the lungs and respiratory system.

In 1996, she had strong symptoms including migraines, muscle cramping, food allergies, fogginess, chronic tiredness. Secondary progressed Mars was conjoined natal Chiron; Mars rules the muscles, and Mars conjoined Chiron certainly indicates the need for major healing. In April of 1996, she also had the full Moon phase of the progressed lunation cycle with progressed Moon in Pisces opposite her Moon in Virgo. Pisces governs the immune system, and often a progressed Moon in this sign will indicate a time period where there are more problems with the immune system. Transiting Neptune was square both natal Neptune and opposite natal Uranus. Neptune square Neptune has often been a time when people develop more allergies and sensitivities, change their diets, can no longer tolerate certain foods and substances. Transiting Uranus in early Aquarius was also square natal Saturn in Scorpio; breaking up old blockages in the colon was indicated. On April 4, 1996 the lunar eclipse squared her nodes in Capricorn and Cancer; on April 17, the solar eclipse was in her sixth house of health, squaring natal Uranus.

Case Hisory #4

This case history is of a woman who was the project director of a pharmaceutical company for many years and worked very hard in the

Chronic Fatigue—Woman
Natal Chart
April 18, 1945, 10:28 PM PWT +7:00
San Francisco
37N46 30 122W25 06

Geocentric
Tropical
Koch
True Node

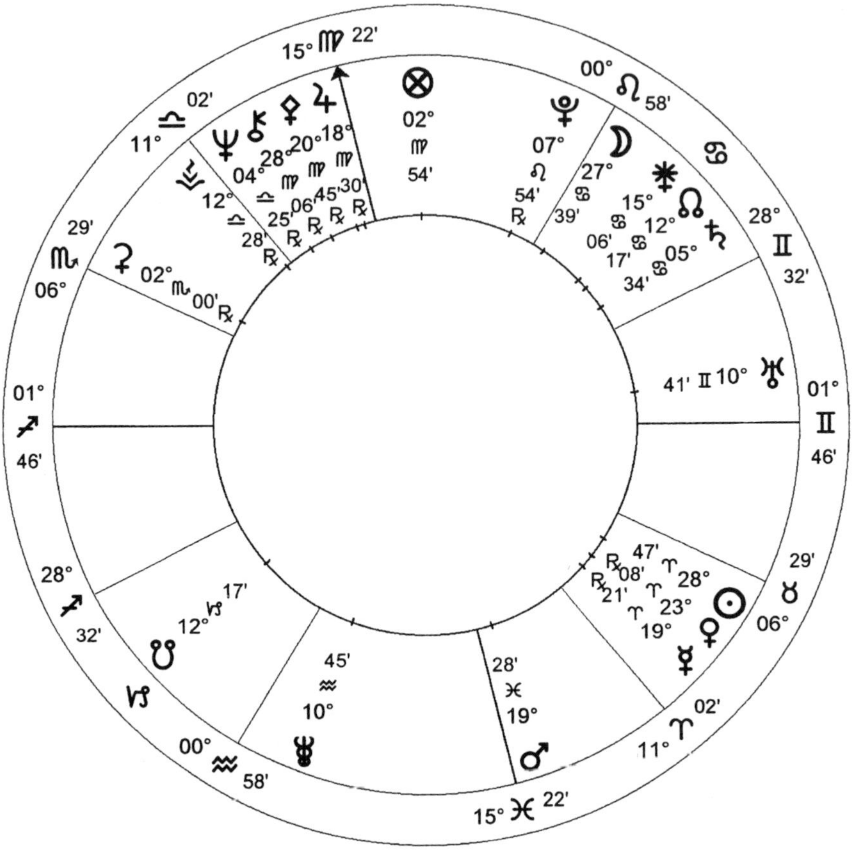

corporate world. She had lots of energy and suddenly was unable to work or think clearly; later she was diagnosed with Chronic Fatigue Syndrome. In March of 1993, when she started to experience symptoms of extreme tiredness and memory loss, she would go into work late and it would take her hours to do a simple chore. She had a blood test in May, which showed her to be hypoglycemic, so she began an exercise program and started on a few supplements. At this time, she had total adrenal exhaustion and her

Midpoint Listing

Chronic Fatigue • Woman • Natal Chart
In Planetery Sequence • Modulus 360°00'

☽	27°♋39	*☿*	19°♈21	♂/♆	26°♐57	*♅*	10°♊41	⚷/⯔	04°♐26
☽/☉	13°♊13	☿/♀	21°♈15	♂/♇	28°♉41	♅/♆	07°♌33	⚷/☊	20°♌12
☽/☿	08°♊30	☿/♂	04°♈25	♂/⚷	23°♐47	♅/♇	09°♋18	⚷/⊗	15°♍30
☽/♀	10°♊24	☿/♃	03°♋55	♂/⚳	00°♑58	♅/⚷	04°♌24	*⚳*	12°♎28
☽/♂	23°♉34	☿/♄	27°♉28	♂/⚴	20°♐07	♅/⚳	11°♌35	⚳/⚴	01°♎37
☽/♃	23°♌05	☿/♅	15°♉01	♂/⚵	17°♉17	♅/⚴	00°♌43	⚳/⚵	28°♌47
☽/♄	16°♋37	☿/♆	11°♋53	♂/⚶	10°♑44	♅/⚵	27°♊54	⚳/⚶	22°♎14
☽/♅	04°♋10	☿/♇	13°♊37	♂/⯔	00°♓07	♅/⚶	21°♌21	⚳/⯔	11°♐37
☽/♆	01°♍02	☿/⚷	08°♋43	♂/☊	15°♉53	♅/⯔	10°♈43	⚳/☊	27°♌23
☽/♇	02°♌47	☿/⚳	15°♋55	♂/⊗	11°♊11	♅/☊	26°♊29	⚳/⊗	22°♍41
☽/⚷	27°♌53	☿/⚴	05°♋03	*♃*	18°♍30	♅/⊗	21°♋48	*⚴*	20°♍45
☽/⚳	05°♍04	☿/⚵	02°♊13	♃/♄	12°♌02	*♆*	04°♎25	⚴/⚵	17°♌56
☽/⚴	24°♌12	☿/⚶	25°♑40	♃/♅	29°♋36	♆/♇	06°♍10	⚴/⚶	11°♎23
☽/⚵	21°♋23	☿/⯔	15°♓03	♃/♆	26°♍27	♆/⚷	01°♎15	⚴/⯔	00°♐45
☽/⚶	14°♍50	☿/☊	00°♊49	♃/♇	28°♌12	♆/⚳	08°♎27	⚴/☊	16°♌31
☽/⯔	04°♉12	☿/⊗	26°♊07	♃/⚷	23°♍18	♆/⚴	27°♍35	⚴/⊗	11°♍50
☽/☊	19°♋58	*♀*	23°♈08	♃/⚳	00°♎29	♆/⚵	24°♌45	*⚵*	15°♋06
☽/⊗	15°♌17	♀/♂	06°♈18	♃/⚴	19°♍38	♆/⚶	18°♎12	⚵/⚶	08°♍33
☉	28°♈47	♀/♃	05°♋49	♃/⚵	16°♌48	♆/⯔	07°♐35	⚵/⯔	27°♈56
☉/☿	24°♈04	♀/♄	29°♉21	♃/⚶	10°♎15	♆/☊	23°♌21	⚵/☊	13°♋42
☉/♀	25°♈58	♀/♅	16°♉55	♃/⯔	29°♏38	♆/⊗	18°♍40	⚵/⊗	09°♌00
☉/♂	09°♈08	♀/♆	13°♋47	♃/☊	15°♌24	*♇*	07°♌54	*⚶*	02°♏00
☉/♃	08°♋38	♀/♇	15°♊31	♃/⊗	10°♍42	♇/⚷	03°♍00	⚶/⯔	21°♐22
☉/♄	02°♊11	♀/⚷	10°♋37	*♄*	05°♋34	♇/⚳	10°♍11	⚶/☊	07°♍09
☉/♅	19°♉44	♀/⚳	17°♋48	♄/♅	23°♊08	♇/⚴	29°♌20	⚶/⊗	02°♎27
☉/♆	16°♋36	♀/⚴	06°♋57	♄/♆	20°♌00	♇/⚵	26°♋30	*⯔*	10°♒45
☉/♇	18°♊21	♀/⚵	04°♊07	♄/♇	21°♋44	♇/⚶	19°♍57	⯔/☊	26°♈31
☉/⚷	13°♋26	♀/⚶	27°♑34	♄/⚷	16°♌50	♇/⯔	09°♉20	⯔/⊗	21°♏50
☉/⚳	20°♋38	♀/⯔	16°♓57	♄/⚳	24°♌01	♇/☊	25°♋06	*☊*	12°♋17
☉/⚴	09°♋46	♀/☊	02°♊43	♄/⚴	13°♌10	♇/⊗	20°♌24	☊/⊗	07°♌36
☉/⚵	06°♊57	♀/⊗	28°♊01	♄/⚵	10°♋20	*⚷*	28°♍06	*⊗*	02°♍54
☉/⚶	00°♒23	*♂*	19°♓28	♄/⚶	03°♍47	⚷/⚳	05°♎17		
☉/⯔	19°♓46	♂/♃	18°♊59	♄/⯔	23°♈10	⚷/⚴	24°♍26		
☉/☊	05°♊32	♂/♄	12°♉31	♄/☊	08°♋56	⚷/⚵	21°♌36		
☉/⊗	00°♋51	♂/♅	00°♉05	♄/⊗	04°♌14	⚷/⚶	15°♎03		

organs shut down. A few months later, with regular massage treatments, some hypnotherapy and re-birthing, she began to improve.

In August of 1994, she had a relapse and was in bed for 3 months. She left her job and career. She changed her diet to one that eliminated sweets, dairy products, and wheat; began colonics; read about and started using herbs, homeopathy, and acupuncture. In addition, she started studying astrology and working with shamanism. In 1995, she began practicing tai chi.

By 1995, she was able to travel and went to both Mexico and Egypt. In 1996 she went to Peru. By 1996, she had moved from Atlanta to Santa Fe and was in acupuncture school. She has since graduated, and has been involved in studying Ayurvedic medicine. She has also been to China twice to study Traditional Chinese Medicine. She is careful of her diet and uses herbs and supplements, along with keeping up massage, acupuncture, and colonics.

Interpretation of Horoscope

Her natal horoscope exhibits a strong fire sign emphasis with 3 planets in Aries and Sagittarius rising. Mars is also angular opposite Jupiter. Often people with angular Mars experience adrenal exhaustion, as they tend to over work and literally "burn out." Mars in Pisces opposite Jupiter in Virgo shows both sensitive immune and digestive systems. Cancer Moon is exactly square her Aries Sun, Venus, and Mercury, which tends to deplete her energy; the Moon squaring Venus can also indicate low blood sugar. Mercury is inconjunct Jupiter so she is prone to mental "burn out." In addition to the Sun and Moon being exactly square, Saturn in Cancer is exactly square Neptune in Libra, which shows a weak immune system. The ruler of her chart, Jupiter, is opposite Mars and squared by Uranus, so liver toxicity can be an issue.

Her moon is parallel Saturn, Uranus, and the node, indicating a very sensitive neurological system as well.

Midpoints

Sun/Pluto = Mars and Jupiter, direct—the need to constantly regenerate her vital organs

Transits and Progressions

In March 1993, her symptoms began. Progressed Moon was conjoined natal Mercury; transiting Uranus Neptune conjunction was square her Venus showing blood sugar and immune system problems while Saturn was semi-square her Capricorn south node. All through the year, the Uranus Neptune conjunction squared both her Mercury and Venus, so her mental energy was low and her mind felt foggy. In May of 1993, the solar eclipse was exactly opposite her ascendant; in June, the lunar eclipse was square both her Mars and Jupiter.

In August 1994, she had a relapse and was in bed for 3 months. Progressed Mars was squaring her natal Moon. Transiting Uranus and Neptune were still square Venus; Pluto was trine her natal Moon, enabling her to change her life style and begin studies in astrology and shamanism. In the end of May, the lunar eclipse was conjoined her ascendant.

In 1995, she began tai chi and traveled to Mexico and Egypt. Pluto was transiting her natal ascendant.

In 1996, she moved to Santa Fe, traveled to Peru, continued studies of astrology and shamanism. Progressed Mars was conjunct her natal Sun. Transiting Neptune was square her Sun and opposite her Moon. In April the solar eclipse was conjoined her Sun.

SUPPLEMENT RECOMMENDATIONS FOR IMMUNE SYSTEM DEFICIENCIES

There are many types of supplements that are important to consider for strengthening the immune system. Each person is different and will require various combinations of these nutritional supplements and different amounts.

Quercetin, among the Bioflavonoids, is one of the most important supplements in dealing with these conditions. It stabilizes certain cells and inhibits release of histamine and other inflammatory chemicals.

Vitamin C activates white blood cells and increases production of lymphocytes, the white cells important in antibody response. It can also decrease the production of histamine and thus can reduce allergic reactions. It also increases interferon production, and so can activate the immune response to viruses.

Vitamin E is used for its antioxidant properties.

Vitamin A or Beta carotene is also a strong antioxidant that is crucial not only for the eyes and the skin, but it moisturizes the mucous linings helping to fight off infectious agents and environmental toxins.

Pantothenic Acid or Vitamin B-5 is the anti-stress vitamin since it supports the adrenal glands in the production of cortisone and other adrenal hormones to help counteract stress.

Vitamin B-12 or Cobalamin is often lacking in those who are allergic or who have MCS.

GLA oil (Gamma linolenic acid) is very important for allergies and asthma, skin disorders such as eczema and dermatitis, MCS, and rheumatoid arthritis.

EPA and DHA (Eicosapentaenoic acid and Decosahexaenoic acid) are helpful in rheumatoid arthritis, asthma, migraine, and MCS.

Zinc is the most important mineral for the immune system. It improves antibody response and helps regulate the function of the white blood cells. A high amount of zinc in the diet can increase the production of T lymphocytes.

Selenium is an antioxidant which is low in some soils and may be required as a supplement. It helps prevent cell degeneration from free radicals and protects from the toxic effects of heavy metals and other substances.

Probiotics produce immunity in the body, help with food allergies, and in herpes infections.

Digestive Enzymes are sometimes called for when there are food allergies and digestive problems. Usually it is pancreatic enzymes that are most helpful which include lipases, amylases, and proteases.

Coenzyme Q-10 or Ubiquinone is an antioxidant and immune stimulant.

Glutathione and L-cysteine—Glutathione is an antioxidant that helps to protect against environmental toxins, heavy metals, cigarette smoke, and radiation exposure by detoxifying these chemicals into less toxic forms. It is especially good for skin conditions. Glutathione is often obtained from N-acetyl cysteine.

Adrenal glandulars are often helpful for fatigue, stress, allergies, environmental sensitivities, and low blood sugar.

L-carnitine is necessary to transform fatty acids into energy for muscular activity. It is being used for those who have MCS and experience tiredness with difficulty exercising.

MSM or Methylsulfonyl Methane is a sulfur compound that may have some anti-inflammatory and antioxidant properties. It is currently being used in treating inhalant allergies and arthritis.

HERBAL RECOMMENDATIONS

There are several herbs that are important in supporting the immune system and also in detoxifying the liver.

Garlic is a natural antibiotic with some immune stimulating properties. It treats bacterial and fungal conditions, including candida/yeast problems.

Goldenseal root—Goldenseal powder from the root has many uses including antibacterial and antiparasitic; it is good for yeast, worms, and other types of germs. It is also a detoxifier as it is a bitter herb and so works well for certain liver and gastro-intestinal problems.

Goldenseal leaf is excellent to detoxify and tone the liver.

Echinacea root is a powerful herb to purify the blood and the lymph. It is excellent for treating skin problems such as acne, boils, poison ivy, and oak.

Alfalfa is helpful for those with allergies and those with MCS, as it is such a strong source of nutrients.

Herbs that support the respiratory system are good for sensitivity to inhalants and asthma. These include coltsfoot, which is a good expectorant as well as containing zinc in its leaves, and mullein, which is also a good expectorant and tones the mucous membranes of the respiratory system

CHAPTER 10

Metabolic Diseases

METABOLIC DISEASES OCCUR when there is malfunctioning of one or more glands which disrupt the body's chemistry. With diabetes and hypoglycemia, there is an inability to metabolize carbohydrates and fats due to malfunctioning of the pancreas and adrenals.

In the pancreas there is a set of glands known as the Islets of Langerhans, which secrete insulin directly into the bloodstream. Insulin is essential for transporting glucose (sugar) into the cells. When there is not enough insulin, blood sugar rises. As blood sugar levels increase, the kidneys eliminate sugar into the urine; this high level of sugar makes one particularly susceptible to infection.

In hypoglycemia, excess insulin is produced; blood glucose levels drop and the individual feels weak and irritable. When the blood sugar gets very low, the adrenals secrete excess amounts of adrenalin and cortin. Excess amounts of these two hormones can make one extremely nervous and oversensitive. Other symptoms of hypoglycemia include hunger, fatigue, weakness, anxiety, and sometimes lack of coordination and mental confusion.

Allergies can cause hypoglycemia. When exposed to allergens, people experience a significant drop in blood sugar levels. Allergens cause a stress on the system, straining the adrenal glands and causing adrenal exhaustion, which contributes to low blood sugar. Alcohol also contributes heavily to low blood sugar; the symptoms referred to as "hang over" after a night of drinking are extreme hypoglycemic symptoms. Smoking destroys vitamin C; vitamin C deficiency is linked to disorders in the sugar control mechanism. Excessive salt intake also contributes to hypoglycemia; it causes a loss of blood potassium, which leads to low blood sugar. Coffee raises the blood sugar in diabetics and lowers it in hypoglycemics. Coffee and other caffeine drinks affect the adrenal glands, which are related to sugar metabolism.

PSYCHOLOGICAL FACTORS

Symptoms of both hypoglycemia and diabetes often occur during a period of stress in a person's life. People have manifested these symptoms after a traumatic shock regarding work or a relationship breaking up or a family member's death or illness. Under these conditions of stress, there is an increased release of adrenaline and cortin. Adrenaline raises the blood sugar and cortin causes the liver to make more glycogen, which is converted into glucose, thus raising the blood sugar.

Diabetics are often very bitter people. Life's circumstances have made them adopt these attitudes; the body compensates by producing an increased amount of sugar.

ASTROLOGICAL PATTERNS

Diabetes and Hypoglycemia are ruled by the planet Jupiter and the sign Sagittarius, since Jupiter governs the liver and pancreas. As a storage container for glycogen (the chief carbohydrate storage material) the liver is co-ruled by the Moon, which governs storage containers. When Jupiter is angular, conjoined the Sun or Moon or another planet, there may be a tendency to a weak or toxic liver or poorly functioning pancreas. This is also true with Sagittarian Sun, Moon, or ascendant. A strongly placed Jupiter may also indicate a condition of overweight, which contributes to diabetes.

Saturn in hard aspect to Jupiter inhibits the functioning of these organs. Uranus in hard aspect to Jupiter may create an erratic functioning of the liver and pancreas. Neptune in hard aspect to Jupiter indicates conditions of toxicity, as well as blood sugar problems, and possible use of alcohol and drugs. Pluto in hard aspect to Jupiter may indicate a chronic problem with the liver or pancreas.

Neptune rules the pituitary gland so a weakened Neptune or prominent Pisces theme may predispose the individual to imbalances in the metabolic system. Venus rules sugar and also the kidneys, which are involved in eliminating excess sugar, and also in helping to maintain the acid alkaline balance. Saturn rules the gall bladder, which stores the bile that the liver produces; hard aspects from Saturn to Jupiter are often found.

It is difficult to discern astrologically whether the manifestation will be toward hypoglycemia or diabetes. After seeing many case histories, I have found no difference in the astrological patterns; therefore some sort of testing is necessary.

MIDPOINTS

In addition to Saturn/Neptune, Mars/Neptune, Mars/Saturn, and Mars/Uranus, other relevant midpoints to check are:

Jupiter/Saturn—gall bladder, pancreas, and liver

Jupiter/Neptune—inability to deal with toxins

Venus/Jupiter—assimilation of carbohydrates

Venus/Neptune—weakened glandular functions, blood sugar problems

Combinations of planets that may point to a tendency toward metabolic imbalance when found in a T-square or midpoint configuration include:

Saturn, Neptune, and Jupiter
Mars, Neptune, and Jupiter
Venus, Neptune, and Jupiter
Saturn, Neptune, and Venus
Mars, Neptune, and Venus
Jupiter, Saturn, and Venus
Mars, Saturn, and Jupiter

CASE HISTORIES

Case History #1

The first case history is of a woman diagnosed with diabetes at her second Saturn return. She thinks she probably had it for a while before she was diagnosed. Her father was diabetic, though he never took insulin but did take pills. She was doing astrological counseling, teaching astrology, and also going daily to visit her mother-in law who was in the hospital, so it was a stressful period. She noticed that her energy was very low, despite the fact of taking good vitamin supplements. In December 1982, she went to the Joslin Clinic in Boston where she was diagnosed with diabetes and hemochromatosis (a disorder of iron metabolism with excess deposits of iron in the tissues and cirrhosis of the liver). She was given some pills, told to cut out sugar, and had to bring in a pint of blood twice a week for a year for testing. She remained on the pills for six years and four months.

Prior to the diagnosis of diabetes, she had a bout with arthritis in the summer of 1981. She was treated with ultrasonic ray therapy in July and within six months was much better. Her mother also had arthritis.

In April of 1989, she and her husband moved to Florida from the northeast. She found an Internist who specialized in diabetes; he put her in the hospital for a week to observe her and then prescribed insulin. Three years ago, she did chelation therapy, 40 treatments, and now she renews this treatment every six months. She does three or four boosters a week. Currently, she is taking insulin, and using many supplements, particularly chromium piccolinate and a pancreas tonic, as well as watching her food intake.

Interpretation of Horoscope

In this natal horoscope, Jupiter is in the twelfth house in Scorpio and conjoined the Moon. It is broadly square Neptune, which may indicate a toxic liver and low blood sugar. It is also inconjunct Venus (blood sugar) and Mercury in Gemini. Jupiter is part of a grand trine with Sun, Pluto, and Mars in Cancer and the south node, Hygeia, and Uranus in Pisces, which shows that this condition can be controlled. Neptune is close to the MC which indicates a high degree of sensitivity, indicated by the angular Moon as well. Neptune angular also points out a sensitive immune system. Neptune square the Moon often indicates blood sugar problems and a tendency to an acid body, which is part of the arthritis pattern. Neptune is also inconjunct Uranus in Pisces. The north node is in the tenth house in Virgo conjunct Vesta, a strong service theme which also shows the necessity of working on healing. With the nodes in Virgo and Pisces, the whole digestive tract is implicated. Chiron is in the sixth house in Aries, square Mars and inconjunct Vesta.

Diabetes—Woman
Natal Chart
Jun 24, 1923, 4:20 PM EDT +4:00
Summerville
42N23 15 071W 06

Geocentric
Tropical
Koch
True Node

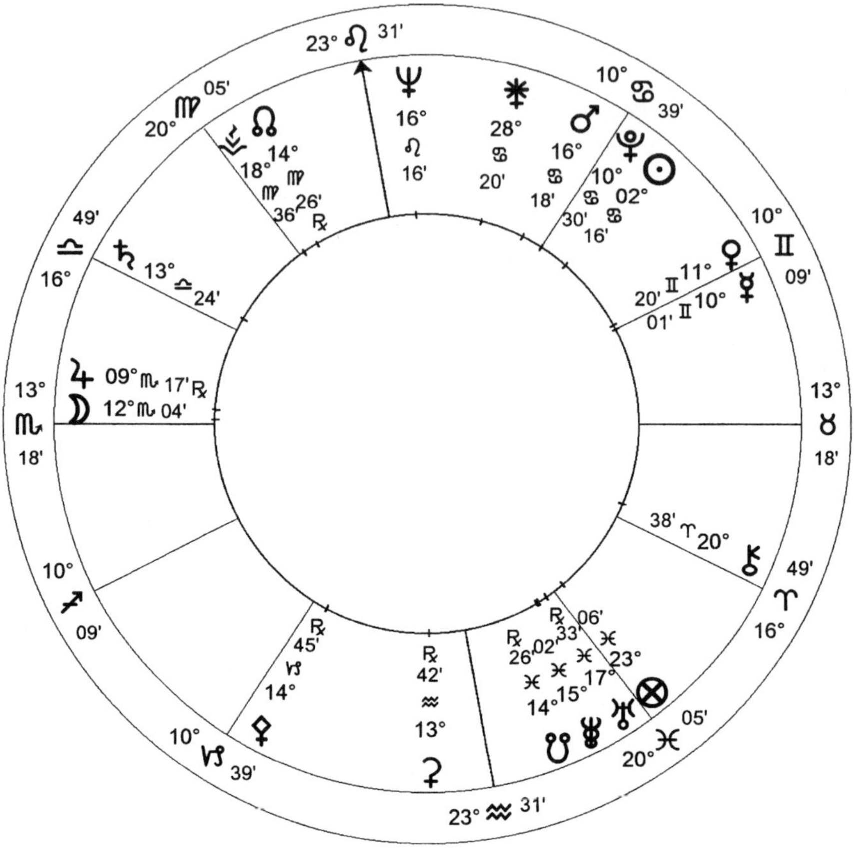

By declination, Venus is parallel Pluto, the need to heal blood sugar problems as well as relationships. Sun is parallel Mars which provides her with good energy.

Midpoints

Saturn/Neptune = nodes, Hygeia and Uranus, direct—sensitive nervous system, digestive problems

Midpoint Listing

Diabetes • Woman • Natal Chart

In Planetery Sequence • Modulus 360°00'

☽	12°♏04	*☿*	10°♊01	♂/♆	01°♌17	*♅*	17°♓33	⚷/⚶	02°♈50
☽/☉	07°♍10	☿/♀	10°♊40	♂/♇	13°♋24	♅/♆	01°♊54	⚷/☊	02°♋32
☽/☿	26°♌03	☿/♂	28°♊10	♂/⚷	03°♊28	♅/♇	14°♉01	⚷/⊗	06°♈52
☽/♀	26°♌42	☿/♃	24°♌39	♂/⚳	17°♌27	♅/⚷	04°♈06	*⚳*	18°♍36
☽/♂	14°♍11	☿/♄	11°♌43	♂/⚴	15°♎31	♅/⚳	18°♐04	⚳/⚴	16°♏40
☽/♃	10°♏41	☿/♅	28°♈47	♂/⚵	22°♋19	♅/⚴	16°♒09	⚳/⚵	23°♌28
☽/♄	27°♎44	☿/♆	13°♋09	♂/⯚	00°♉00	♅/⚵	22°♉56	⚳/⯚	01°♐09
☽/♅	14°♑49	☿/♇	25°♊15	♂/⚶	15°♉40	♅/⯚	00°♓37	⚳/⚶	16°♐49
☽/♆	29°♍10	☿/⚷	15°♉20	♂/☊	15°♌22	♅/⚶	16°♓18	⚳/☊	16°♍31
☽/♇	11°♍17	☿/⚳	29°♋19	♂/⊗	19°♉42	♅/☊	15°♊59	⚳/⊗	20°♊51
☽/⚷	01°♒21	☿/⚴	27°♓23	*♃*	09°♏17	♅/⊗	20°♓20	*⚴*	14°♑45
☽/⚳	15°♎20	☿/⚵	04°♋10	♃/♄	26°♎21	*♆*	16°♌16	⚴/⚵	21°♎32
☽/⚴	13°♐25	☿/⯚	11°♈52	♃/♅	13°♑25	♆/♇	28°♋23	⚴/⯚	29°♑13
☽/⚵	20°♍12	☿/⚶	27°♈32	♃/♆	27°♍47	♆/⚷	18°♊27	⚴/⚶	14°♒54
☽/⯚	27°♐53	☿/☊	27°♋14	♃/♇	09°♍53	♆/⚳	02°♍26	⚴/☊	14°♏35
☽/⚶	13°♑33	☿/⊗	01°♉34	♃/⚷	29°♑58	♆/⚴	00°♏30	⚴/⊗	18°♒55
☽/☊	13°♎15	*♀*	11°♊20	♃/⚳	13°♎56	♆/⚵	07°♌18	*⚵*	28°♋20
☽/⊗	17°♑35	♀/♂	28°♊49	♃/⚴	12°♐01	♆/⯚	14°♏59	⚵/⯚	06°♉01
☉	02°♋16	♀/♃	25°♌18	♃/⚵	18°♍48	♆/⚶	00°♊39	⚵/⚶	21°♉41
☉/☿	21°♊09	♀/♄	12°♌22	♃/⯚	26°♐30	♆/☊	00°♍21	⚵/☊	21°♌23
☉/♀	21°♊48	♀/♅	29°♈26	♃/⚶	12°♑10	♆/⊗	04°♊41	⚵/⊗	25°♉43
☉/♂	09°♋17	♀/♆	13°♋48	♃/☊	11°♎52	*♇*	10°♋30	*⯚*	13°♒42
☉/♃	05°♍47	♀/♇	25°♊55	♃/⊗	16°♑12	♇/⚷	00°♊34	⯚/⚶	29°♒22
☉/♄	22°♌50	♀/⚷	15°♉59	*♄*	13°♎24	♇/⚳	14°♌33	⯚/☊	29°♏04
☉/♅	09°♉54	♀/⚳	29°♋58	♄/♅	00°♑28	♇/⚴	12°♈37	⯚/⊗	03°♓24
☉/♆	24°♋16	♀/⚴	28°♓02	♄/♆	14°♍50	♇/⚵	19°♋25	*⚶*	15°♓02
☉/♇	06°♋23	♀/⚵	04°♋50	♄/♇	26°♌57	♇/⯚	27°♈06	⚶/☊	14°♊44
☉/⚷	26°♉27	♀/⯚	12°♈31	♄/⚷	17°♋01	♇/⚶	12°♉46	⚶/⊗	19°♓04
☉/⚳	10°♌26	♀/⚶	28°♈11	♄/⚳	01°♎00	♇/☊	12°♌28	*☊*	14°♍26
☉/⚴	08°♈30	♀/☊	27°♋53	♄/⚴	29°♏04	♇/⊗	16°♉48	☊/⊗	18°♊46
☉/⚵	15°♋18	♀/⊗	02°♉13	♄/⚵	05°♍52	*⚷*	20°♈38	*⊗*	23°♓06
☉/⯚	22°♈59	*♂*	16°♋18	♄/⯚	13°♐33	⚷/⚳	04°♋37		
☉/⚶	08°♉39	♂/♃	12°♍48	♄/⚶	29°♐13	⚷/⚴	02°♓42		
☉/☊	08°♌21	♂/♄	29°♌51	♄/☊	28°♍55	⚷/⚵	09°♊29		
☉/⊗	12°♉41	♂/♅	16°♉55	♄/⊗	03°♑15	⚷/⯚	17°♓10		

Mars/Neptune = nodes, Hygeia and Uranus, indirect—immune sensitivity

Jupiter/Neptune = ascendant and Moon, indirect—sensitive immune system, possibility of liver toxicity

Venus/Neptune = Saturn, direct—problems with blood sugar, possible thyroid problems

Venus/Jupiter = Pluto, indirect—need to work with the blood sugar and carbohydrate metabolism

Transits and Progressions

In July 1981, arthritis was diagnosed and she had ultrasonic ray therapy. The progressed Moon was in the first degree of Capricorn, which is ruled by Saturn and related to arthritic problems; progressed Mars, ruler of the 6th house, is conjoined the MC. Transiting Pluto is opposite Chiron in the 6th house; Neptune is semi-square Jupiter, the liver; the Jupiter Saturn conjunction at 3 degrees Libra is semi-square Neptune. On July 30, the solar eclipse was at 8 degrees Leo square Jupiter.

In December 1982, diabetes was diagnosed and treated. Progressed Venus was exactly conjunct progressed Mars just past the natal MC; progressed Sun was at 29 degrees Leo, about to enter Virgo, which is associated with digestion. Transiting Neptune was semi-square the Moon, transiting Saturn sesquiquadrate Uranus, and transiting Jupiter square the progressed Sun. On December 15, the solar eclipse was at 23 degrees Sagittarius semi-square Jupiter, and on December 30, the lunar eclipse was at 8 degrees Cancer conjoined Pluto.

In April of 1989, she moved to Florida and had her diabetes re-evaluated. Progressed Jupiter conjoined her ascendant. Transiting Pluto was conjunct her ascendant (transformation of physical body). Neptune and Saturn at 12 and 13 degrees Capricorn were square Saturn (re-evaluating her physical habits and regime) and opposite Pluto. Transiting Jupiter was inconjunct Jupiter. In March of 1989, the solar eclipse was conjoined natal Uranus; in February 1989, the lunar eclipse was semi-square Mars.

Case History #2

This is a woman who grew up in Holland and moved to the United States when she was 31 years old in November 1974. As a child, she remembers being very cranky and aggressive when she was hungry, or her meals were late. During her last six years of living in Holland, she was on a Macrobiotic diet which made her feel much better; she had stopped eating sugar altogether. When she came to the United States, she began to eat sugar again, though her diet was still basically good, comprised mostly of organic vegetables, grains and some fish. She thinks the sugar was very detrimental to her health. In the spring of 1975, she became pregnant; in September and October 1975 she had a vacation in Hawaii, where she contracted hepatitis. She became very ill; her skin actually turned yellow for a while. In December of 1975, her baby was still born. She remembers not being able to go into shopping centers for a long time; the lights and smells would bother her and she would become very 'spaced out'. Obviously, her liver was compromised at this time and she was having symptoms common to MCS (multiple chemical sensitivities). She made certain that her meals were regular, always carried snacks, used certain supplements like chromium, and by 1990, she feels she had recovered. At this time, her energy is quite good if she eats meals on time. She had a bout with arthritis in the year 2000 and it still affects her hands when she uses them too much. She gave up her career as a massage therapist and reflexologist and has begun more creative pursuits like painting and music.

Interpretation of Horoscope

This horoscope shows a Virgo Sun conjoined Venus in the twelfth house with Libra rising. The Sun Venus conjunction is in a T square with both Mars and Uranus in Gemini and Moon in Sagittarius. A tendency to blood sugar problems would be seen with the Sun conjoined Venus, particularly in Virgo, which governs digestion. Moon in Sagittarius does indicate weakness with the liver, especially with the opposition to Mars and Uranus, which shows a hyperactive nervous system. Neptune is close to the ascendant in the twelfth house, indicating a sensitive immune system. It is also conjoined Mercury, so the respiratory system bears watching. Pluto widely conjunct the Jupiter north node conjunction in Leo and sextile Mars Uranus in Gemini helps the vital energy. Pluto is also sextile Mercury in Libra and the Jupiter north node conjunction is trine the Moon. Saturn in Gemini is square Neptune, which affects the immune system and makes the lungs very sensitive.

By declination, the Sun is contra parallel Mercury, emphasizing weak lungs. Mars, Saturn, and Uranus are also parallel, relating to her sensitive nervous system, with Saturn parallel Pluto as well.

Midpoints

Saturn/Neptune = Jupiter, direct—weakness and restriction of liver and pancreas

Jupiter/Neptune = Mars and Uranus, direct—tendency to low blood sugar, difficulty metabolizing carbohydrates, immune problems manifest through nervous system

Hypoglycemia—Woman
Natal Chart
Sept 7, 1943, 9:18 AM -2:00
Amsterdam
52N22 004E54

Geocentric
Tropical
Koch
True Node

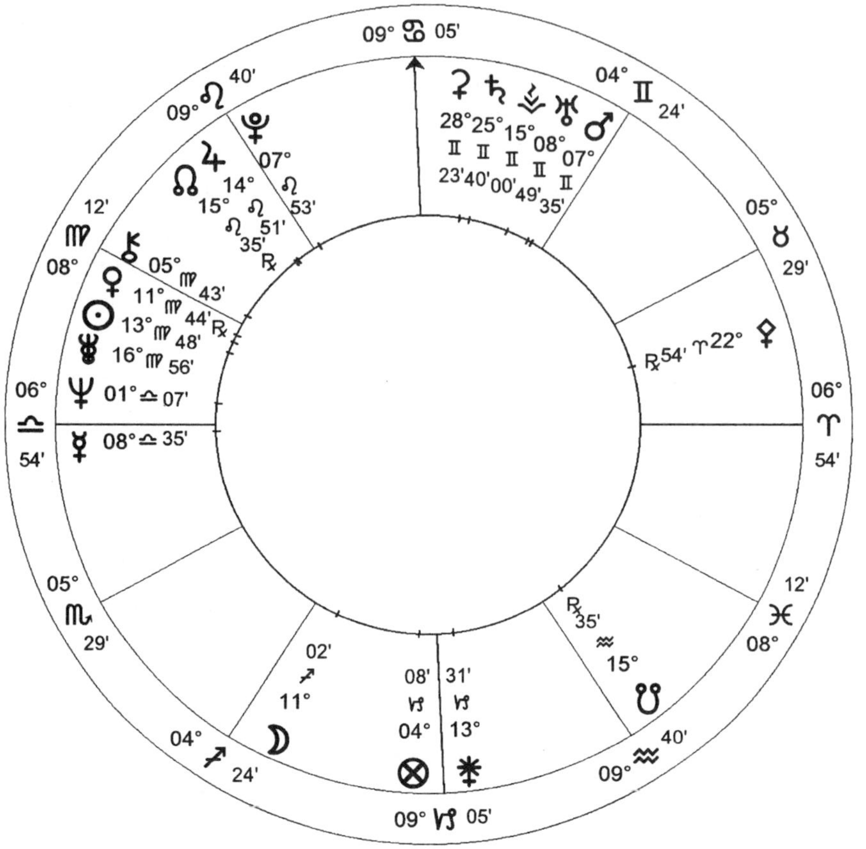

Venus/Neptune = Pluto, indirect—chronic blood sugar problems

Transits and Progressions

In April 1975, when she was 31 years old, her pregnancy began. Transiting Neptune was 8 degrees Sagittarius, opposite Mars and Uranus and conjoined the Jupiter/Neptune midpoint. Pluto was transiting the ascendant and Mercury. On May 11, 1975, the solar eclipse was 135 degrees

Midpoint Listing

Hypoglycemia • Woman • Natal Chart
In Planetery Sequence • Modulus 360°00'

☽	11°♐02	*☿*	08°♎35	♂/♆	04°♌21	*♅*	08°♊49	⚷/⚸	11°♍19
☽/☉	27°♎25	☿/♀	25°♍09	♂/♇	07°♋44	♅/♆	04°♌58	⚷/☊	25°♌39
☽/☿	09°♏48	☿/♂	08°♌05	♂/⚷	21°♋39	♅/♇	08°♋21	⚷/⊗	04°♏55
☽/♀	26°♎23	☿/♃	11°♍43	♂/⚳	11°♊18	♅/⚷	22°♋16	*⚳*	15°♊00
☽/♂	09°♓18	☿/♄	17°♌08	♂/⚴	15°♉15	♅/⚳	11°♊55	⚳/⚴	18°♉57
☽/♃	12°♎57	☿/♅	08°♌42	♂/⚵	25°♓33	♅/⚴	15°♉51	⚳/⚵	29°♓16
☽/♄	18°♍21	☿/♆	04°♎51	♂/⚶	17°♊59	♅/⚵	26°♓10	⚳/⚶	21°♊42
☽/♅	09°♓55	☿/♇	08°♍14	♂/⚸	27°♋15	♅/⚶	18°♊36	⚳/⚸	00°♌58
☽/♆	06°♏04	☿/⚷	22°♍09	♂/☊	11°♋35	♅/⚸	27°♋52	⚳/☊	15°♋18
☽/♇	09°♎27	☿/⚳	11°♌48	♂/⊗	20°♓52	♅/☊	12°♋12	⚳/⊗	24°♓34
☽/⚷	23°♎22	☿/⚴	15°♋44	*♃*	14°♌51	♅/⊗	21°♓28	*⚴*	22°♈54
☽/⚳	13°♍01	☿/⚵	26°♏03	♃/♄	20°♋16	*♆*	01°♎07	⚴/⚵	03°♓12
☽/⚴	16°♒58	☿/⚶	18°♌29	♃/♅	11°♋50	♆/♇	04°♍30	⚴/⚶	25°♉38
☽/⚵	27°♐16	☿/⚸	27°♍45	♃/♆	07°♍59	♆/⚷	18°♍25	⚴/⚸	04°♋55
☽/⚶	19°♍42	☿/☊	12°♍05	♃/♇	11°♌22	♆/⚳	08°♌04	⚴/☊	19°♊14
☽/⚸	28°♎59	☿/⊗	21°♏21	♃/⚷	25°♌17	♆/⚴	12°♋00	⚴/⊗	28°♒31
☽/☊	13°♎18	*♀*	11°♍44	♃/⚳	14°♋56	♆/⚵	22°♏19	*⚵*	13°♑31
☽/⊗	22°♐35	♀/♂	24°♋39	♃/⚴	18°♊53	♆/⚶	14°♌45	⚵/⚶	05°♈57
☉	13°♍48	♀/♃	28°♌18	♃/⚵	29°♎11	♆/⚸	24°♍01	⚵/⚸	15°♏13
☉/☿	26°♍11	♀/♄	03°♌42	♃/⚶	21°♋37	♆/☊	08°♍21	⚵/☊	29°♎33
☉/♀	12°♍46	♀/♅	25°♋16	♃/⚸	00°♍54	♆/⊗	17°♏37	⚵/⊗	08°♑49
☉/♂	25°♋41	♀/♆	21°♍25	♃/☊	15°♌13	*♇*	07°♌53	*⚶*	28°♊23
☉/♃	29°♌20	♀/♇	24°♌48	♃/⊗	24°♎30	♇/⚷	21°♌48	⚶/⚸	07°♌39
☉/♄	04°♌44	♀/⚷	08°♍43	*♄*	25°♊40	♇/⚳	11°♋27	⚶/☊	21°♋59
☉/♅	26°♋18	♀/⚳	28°♋22	♄/♅	17°♊15	♇/⚴	15°♊24	⚶/⊗	01°♈15
☉/♆	22°♍27	♀/⚴	02°♋19	♄/♆	13°♌24	♇/⚵	25°♎42	*⚸*	16°♍56
☉/♇	25°♌50	♀/⚵	12°♏37	♄/♇	16°♋47	♇/⚶	18°♋08	⚸/☊	01°♍15
☉/⚷	09°♍45	♀/⚶	05°♌03	♄/⚷	00°♌41	♇/⚸	27°♌24	⚸/⊗	10°♏32
☉/⚳	29°♋24	♀/⚸	14°♍20	♄/⚳	20°♊20	♇/☊	11°♌44	*☊*	15°♌35
☉/⚴	03°♋21	♀/☊	28°♌39	♄/⚴	24°♉17	♇/⊗	21°♎01	☊/⊗	24°♎51
☉/⚵	13°♏39	♀/⊗	07°♏56	♄/⚵	04°♈36	*⚷*	05°♍43	*⊗*	04°♑08
☉/⚶	06°♌05	*♂*	07°♊35	♄/⚶	27°♊02	⚷/⚳	25°♋22		
☉/⚸	15°♍22	♂/♃	11°♋13	♄/⚸	06°♌18	⚷/⚴	29°♊18		
☉/☊	29°♌41	♂/♄	16°♊38	♄/☊	20°♋38	⚷/⚵	09°♏37		
☉/⊗	08°♏58	♂/♅	08°♊12	♄/⊗	29°♓54	⚷/⚶	02°♌03		

from the ascendant; the lunar eclipse on May 25 was opposite Mars and square Chiron.

In September 1975, she contracted hepatitis in Hawaii. Transiting Neptune was almost on her Moon, still opposing Uranus. Transiting Pluto was on Mercury.

In December 1975, she had a child still born. Transiting Neptune was conjoined her Moon. Uranus was transiting her Venus/Neptune midpoint (indirect) and squaring natal Pluto. Mars was transiting Saturn, and Saturn was semi-square the asteroid Hygeia. The solar eclipse on November 3, 1975 was 135 degrees from Saturn; the lunar eclipse on November 18 was 133 degrees from Mercury.

In January 2000, her arthritis began. Secondary progressed Moon was in Capricorn, which is often the case when symptoms of arthritis start; it was also inconjunct natal Mars. Pluto was transiting her Moon; Neptune was starting to oppose Pluto, and Uranus was opposing Jupiter. The lunar eclipse on January 21 was semi-square her Sun while the February solar eclipse was opposite Jupiter.

NUTRITIONAL RECCOMENDATIONS FOR HYPOGLYCEMIA AND DIABETES

Chemical additives, processed foods, genetically altered foods, heavy sugar intake, lack of nutrients—all these contribute to these diseases. Some guidelines to help balance blood sugar follow:

1. No alcohol—Alcohol interferes with liver functions more than any other food substance. If alcohol is used for an occasion, sake or rice wine is the best choice, as fruit sugar is not involved.
2. No sugar and little honey, molasses or maple syrup. The best sweetener is stevia, which can be obtained in herbal stores.
3. No salt of any kind. Most vegetables have plenty of sodium; sea vegetables also have adequate amounts of sodium, which is balanced. Extra salt creates an acid alkaline imbalance. Tamari (soy sauce) is not that good either. Low salt substitutes as Veg it or Seasun, may be used instead.
4. Small amounts of fruit if it is tolerated; citrus, soured apples, rhubarb, pomegranates, should be not be taken as they are extremely acidic. No fruit juice.
5. Red meat should be eliminated as it is hard to digest. Organic poultry and fresh fish, preferably from wild ocean fish, and not farm raised, should be used.
6. Few heavy carbohydrates such as pasta, tortillas, and beans should be included. Whole grains should be the principal carbohydrate, with little wheat, which is the cause of allergies. Brown rice, buckwheat, millet, quinoa, barley, oats, rye, and amaranth, are all good choices.
7. Dairy products from cows should be eliminated. Substitute goats milk products as well as rice milk or almond milk

8. Soy products such as tofu, soy milk, soy cheese, are the cause of many allergies. They are difficult to digest since much of the soy is also genetically modified.
9. It is important to include fiber foods in the diet because they help elimination and good intestinal health. Aloe vera leaves and juice as well as psyllium seed husks are good; algar and alginate which are found in seaweeds are also strong fiber foods

SUPPLEMENT RECOMMENDATIONS FOR METABOLIC DISEASES

Pancreas glandular helps by providing pancreatic enzymes and, when taken after every meal, there is not the craving for sugar.

L-glutamine is an important amino acid in helping to relieve the craving for sugar.

Chromium is part of the glucose tolerance factor; it helps to regulate carbohydrate metabolism and prepares insulin function for proper use of glucose in the body.

Zinc is closely tied to the body's use of insulin. It is found in the healthy pancreas where insulin is manufactured.

Magnesium—Excess sugar or alcohol in the system interferes with magnesium, so it is important to supplement with extra magnesium. It also helps the nervous system and aids in sleep, which is crucial to maintaining blood sugar levels.

Manganese is an important mineral for its role in glucose metabolism.

Pantothenic acid or adrenal glandulars—Adrenal hormones, along with pancreatic enzymes, are crucial in keeping up blood sugar levels. Pantothenic acid works with the adrenal cortex and may be sufficient as a supplement unless the adrenals are very depleted, in which case, an organic adrenal glandular will help.

Bioflavonoids help the immune system and circulation and also protect vitamin C from oxidation.

Vitamin E is important for its antioxidant properties, helping to prevent the breakdown of nutrients by oxidation.

Vitamin A is also important as an antioxidant and for moisturizing mucous linings.

Vitamin B-6 helps in amino acid metabolism and also in regulating hormones for women.

Lipoic acid is essential for diabetics. It helps optimize the function of the insulin receptors on the cells. It is also important for hypoglycemic conditions since it helps the body in its utilization of sugar.

HERBAL RECOMMENDATIONS

Goldenseal leaf is used to detoxify and tone the liver.

Alfalfa leaves are high in chlorophyll, provide magnesium, and also contain the essential amino acids.

Stringbean pod tea is a source of insulin and good for diabetics.

Dandelion Root is helpful in maintaining blood sugar levels.

CHAPTER 11

Gastrointestinal Problems

THE DIGESTIVE TRACT IS AN AREA where we play out many of our emotions and stresses. Whenever we eat, we take in not just the physical quality of our food, but we also ingest whatever emotions we are experiencing at the time— our anxieties, fears, and anger at others.

At some time in our lives we all experience problems with the gastrointestinal system; it may be diarrhea after eating some food that is bad, or chronic constipation, or an acid stomach. However, it could also be more serious issues such as gastritis (inflammation of the stomach wall), colitis (inflammation of the colon or large intestine), ulcers (both duodenal and gastric), or peritonitis (inflammation of the peritoneum, the membrane lining the walls of the abdominal and pelvic cavities.)

Since the digestive process starts with the teeth, problems with the teeth and gums may also contribute to problems within the gastrointestinal tract.

In cases of severe nervousness, there can be a spasm of the muscles where the esophagus joins the diaphragm and the diaphragm joins the stomach. This is known as a hiatal hernia.

Many problems can occur while the food is in the stomach. The inner lining of the stomach is a mucous membrane in which are tiny glands that secrete a fluid called gastric juice. This juice contains hydrochloric acid and aids in breaking down proteins into smaller substances. It also contains various enzymes.

Sometimes the hyperacidity of the stomach causes gas to accumulate, which leads to a great deal of pain. When the stomach is chronically hyperacid and the individual under a great deal of tension and anxiety, a portion of the stomach wall may be irritated to form an ulcer.

The addition of the gastric juice reduces the food to a fluid called chyme, which then passes into the small intestine. Digestion completes itself in the small intestine with absorption taking place in the bottom part. The duodenum is in the first part of the small intestine; its role is to neutralize the acid chyme from the stomach through antacid secretions that pour into the duodenum from the pancreas and liver. When the lining of the duodenum becomes too acid, a duodenal ulcer may result.

In the small intestine, the pancreas secretes pancreatic juice, and the liver secretes bile, which is stored in the gall bladder between meals. These combine with the chyme, neutralizing it, and pass into the main portion of the small intestine. Here the enzymes from the intestinal juice help to break down carbohydrates and fats. If certain enzymes are missing, then there could be problems at this stage of the digestive process.

Food takes three hours to pass through the small intestine to the colon or large intestine where absorption takes place, especially absorption of water. As water is absorbed, the contents of the large intestine become more solid. These solid contents, containing the indigestible residues of food, make up the feces. When an individual is extremely tense, the peristaltic action of the colon may be slower than usual, which results in constipation. Nervous conditions or infections may also cause the food to be pushed through too quickly, which results in diarrhea and a severe loss of water.

PSYCHOLOGICAL FACTORS

Emotional upsets, tension, nervousness, anxieties, and deep fears are often played out in the digestive tract. Emotional upsets may lead to indigestion, stomach pains or cramping; often there is diarrhea or constipation as well. Deep seated tensions and anxieties contribute to the formation of ulcers, gastritis, and colitis.

Often, those who get ulcers tend to bottle up their fears in the region of the solar plexus. Sometimes they have not had much nurturing as children.

As they mature, they struggle between their unsatisfied dependency needs and social aspirations. They tend to work very hard and assume responsibility for others. When emotional conflicts arise, they vacillate between nurturing others and needing to be nurtured themselves. At these times, the stomach tends to produce more acid and the condition of hyperacidity that we refer to as ulcers develops.

Another common occurrence causing gastrointestinal problems is the inhibition of bile production. Bile is produced in the liver and stored in the gall bladder. In cases of emotional repression, especially anger, the liver may not produce enough bile or the gall bladder may not release it, which leads to constipation and other complaints.

ASTROLOGICAL PATTERNS

The entire digestive system is ruled by Virgo. In terms of individual organs, the stomach is governed by Cancer, the small intestine by Virgo, the duodenum (leading from the stomach to the small intestine) by Pisces, and the colon, by Scorpio.

Problems in the abdominal area may be seen with Mars or Saturn in Cancer, especially if there are hard aspects to the Sun, Moon, or ascendant. Certainly these individuals are working through particular emotional patterns. Mars in Cancer indicates too much hydrochloric acid in the body; these people need to be careful with their intake of coffee, fruits, and other acid foods. Saturn in Cancer may indicate a lack of hydrochloric acid, which may need to be added in the form of betaine hydrochoride, or lemon juice.

Mars in Virgo or Pisces with hard aspects to the Sun, Moon, Saturn, Uranus, or Neptune is often present as a signature in cases of duodenal ulcer. Sometimes it is Saturn in Virgo or Pisces with the same hard aspects. Stomach ulcers are often found with Mars or Saturn in Cancer. Gastritis (inflammation of the stomach lining caused by ulcers, digestive disorders, or other toxins) is characterized by Sun conjunct Mars in Cancer or Moon conjunct Mars in Cancer.

Mars also rules the muscles of the body; with Mars in Virgo or Pisces, the intestinal muscles may be affected. This can lead to constipation (one of the physical causes of constipation is improper nerve muscle coordination) or other abdominal conditions involving muscle spasm.

Problems in the area of the colon or large intestine may occur with strong Scorpio or Pluto influence. Sun, Moon, ascendant, Mars, or Saturn in Scorpio with hard aspects from Mars or Pluto are often signatures for colitis, or problems with the bowel or hemorrhoids.

With peritonitis, the inflammation of the membrane lining the abdominal cavity, often there is Sun, Moon, or Mars in Virgo with hard aspects from Saturn, Uranus, Neptune, or Pluto.

MIDPOINTS

The general health midpoints, Saturn/Neptune, Mars/Neptune, Mars/Uranus, and Mars/Saturn are used for gastrointestinal disorders. In addition, the following midpoints are used:

Jupiter/Saturn—liver, pancreas, and gall bladder functions

Jupiter/Uranus—peristalsis of the intestines, spastic colon

CASE HISTORIES

Case History #1

The first case history is that of a woman who has had some serious gastrointestinal problems. She also has arthritis and she has had chronic anemia. Her first symptoms of arthritis started in 1990 and 1991 when her fingers became swollen. In November of 1992, she started having bleeding, nausea, and diarrhea. Then she passed out and was taken to the hospital emergency room. At first they thought she was having a heart attack; then they realized it was a bleeding ulcer. She lost one half of her red blood cells, and needed both transfusions and oxygen. She was given an endoscopy, through which they determined that it was a stomach ulcer not a duodenal ulcer. They pumped her stomach to get rid of the remainder of the blood. Her treatment consisted of dietary changes and the use of the medication, Tagamat, which she only took for 2 weeks as it made her nauseous. She stopped drinking coffee for three months and drank 16-20 ounces of cabbage juice a day, with some carrot and celery juice added. She also used aloe vera juice, alkala—a powder to alkalinize her body, homeopathic remedies, and supplements. She did not have any reoccurrence of the ulcer.

In March of 2000, she began to have diarrhea, bleeding, and then cramping in her colon. A colonoscopy diagnosed ulcerative colitis and an inflamed colon. She used cortisone foam for two weeks, in addition to having acupuncture, changing her diet, and supplements. She was given a stool test which uncovered *klebsiella*, a type of organism that causes pneumonia in the respiratory tract; it is referred to as pneumonia of the gut and was treated with antibiotics. In December of 2000, she had another bleeding incident. In the spring of 2001, she did some chelation therapy, which helped the arthritis. In April, she had both an endoscopy and a colon-oscopy, which showed no signs of ulceration or gastritis. She continues using natural therapies and supplements, eats organic foods, but still does drink some coffee and wine.

Interpretation of Horoscope

Her natal horoscope shows Sun conjoined Chiron in Taurus in the eighth house square Mars in Leo; this can be a signature for anemia and low energy. The Sun trines Saturn in Capricorn and sextiles the Jupiter Pluto conjunction in Cancer, which helps the vital energy. Venus is conjoined the north node and Uranus in the seventh, square Jupiter Pluto in the tenth, and also broadly square Vesta, Saturn, and Moon in the fourth. The south node in Libra completes a grand square. Saturn Moon conjunct in Capricorn is a strong signature for arthritis. It suggests a difficult relationship with her mother, with the tendency to hold back emotions. Jupiter conjoined Pluto in Cancer, opposite Saturn Moon in Capricorn, may indicate problems in the stomach area. With Virgo rising, the whole intestinal area is implicated. Venus conjoined Uranus indicates possible thyroid irregularities, which she has had, and taken thyroid medications. With Venus, ruler of Taurus, square Jupiter, there is also a potential problem with blood sugar; she likes sweet things and gourmet dishes. Jupiter square Uranus and opposite Saturn shows that liver functions can be restricted and limited, building up toxic materials in the body. Moon is broadly square Uranus, which indicates a sensitive nervous system and tendency to anxiety and worry. Neptune is in Virgo in the twelfth, trine Mercury in Taurus, semi-square Pluto, and sesquiquadrate Uranus. This also shows a sensitive nervous system, which is related to her immune system, ruled by Neptune.

In terms of parallels of declination, she has Jupiter parallel Pluto, and contra parallel Saturn. This is the problem with digestion and the liver. She also has Venus parallel her north node, which can indicate blood sugar problems and a strong desire for sweets.

Midpoints

Saturn/Neptune = Mars, direct—shows the tendency to anemia and low energy

Gastrointestinal—Woman
Natal Chart
May 7, 1931, 3:45 PM EDT +4:00
New York, NY
40N43 074W00

Geocentric
Tropical
Koch
True Node

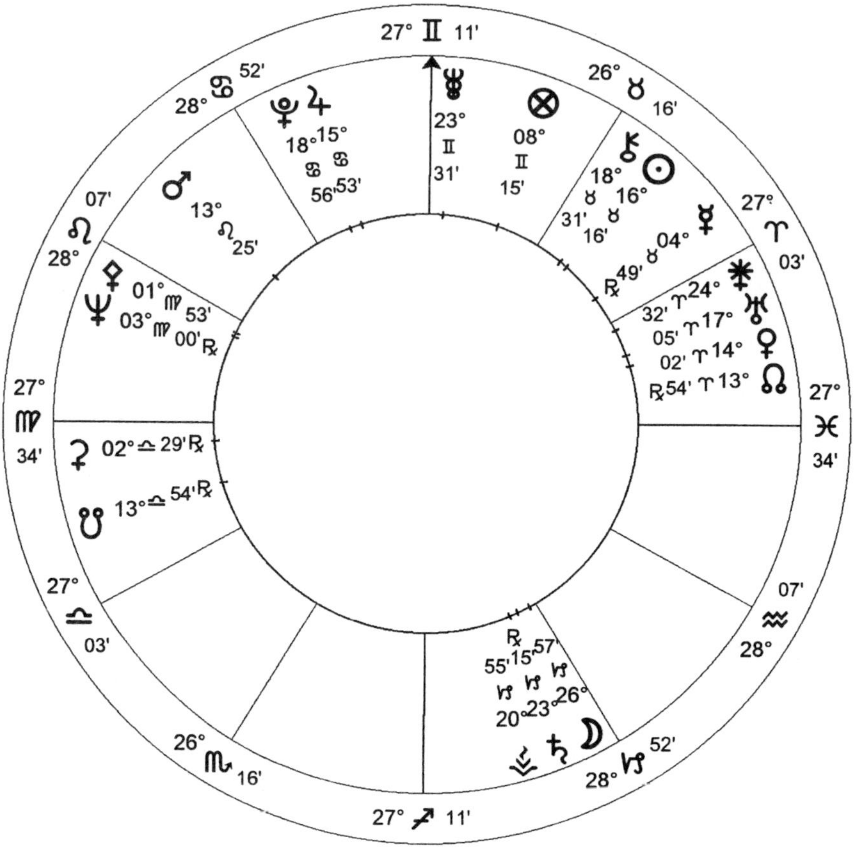

Jupiter/Saturn = Uranus and Pluto, direct—indicates erratic functioning of her liver and gall bladder, and the need for cleansing these organs

Transits and Progressions

In November 1992, when the ulcer was diagnosed, her progressed Sun was conjoined natal Jupiter; her progressed Moon was also conjunct Uranus. Transiting Pluto at 22 degrees Scorpio was on the Mars/Neptune midpoint

Midpoint Listing

Gastrointestinal • Woman • Natal Chart
In Planetery Sequence • Modulus 360°00'

☽	26°♑57	*☿*	04°♉49	♂/♆	23°♌12	*♅*	17°♈05	⚷/⛢	06°♊01
☽/☉	21°♓36	☿/♀	24°♈25	♂/♇	01°♌10	♅/♆	25°♊02	⚷/☊	01°♉13
☽/☿	15°♓53	☿/♂	24°♊07	♂/⚷	00°♋58	♅/♇	03°♊00	⚷/⊗	28°♉23
☽/♀	05°♓29	☿/♃	10°♊21	♂/⚳	02°♏10	♅/⚷	02°♉48	*⚳*	20°♑55
☽/♂	05°♏11	☿/♄	14°♓02	♂/⚴	22°♌39	♅/⚳	04°♓00	⚳/⚴	11°♏24
☽/♃	21°♈25	☿/♅	25°♈57	♂/⚵	18°♊58	♅/⚴	24°♊29	⚳/⚵	07°♓43
☽/♄	25°♑06	☿/♆	03°♋55	♂/⚶	07°♍57	♅/⚵	20°♈48	⚳/⚶	26°♏42
☽/♅	07°♓01	☿/♇	11°♊53	♂/⛢	18°♋28	♅/⚶	09°♋47	⚳/⛢	07°♈13
☽/♆	14°♏58	☿/⚷	11°♉40	♂/☊	13°♊39	♅/⛢	20°♉18	⚳/☊	02°♓25
☽/♇	22°♈57	☿/⚳	12°♓52	♂/⊗	10°♋50	♅/☊	15°♈29	⚳/⊗	29°♓35
☽/⚷	22°♓44	☿/⚴	03°♋21	*♃*	15°♋53	♅/⊗	12°♉40	*⚴*	01°♍53
☽/⚳	23°♑56	☿/⚵	29°♈40	♃/♄	19°♈34	*♆*	03°♍00	⚴/⚵	28°♊12
☽/⚴	14°♏25	☿/⚶	18°♋39	♃/♅	01°♊29	♆/♇	10°♌58	⚴/⚶	17°♍11
☽/⚵	10°♓44	☿/⛢	29°♉10	♃/♆	09°♌26	♆/⚷	10°♋46	⚴/⛢	27°♋42
☽/⚶	29°♏43	☿/☊	24°♈22	♃/♇	17°♋24	♆/⚳	11°♏58	⚴/☊	22°♊54
☽/⛢	10°♈14	☿/⊗	21°♉32	♃/⚷	17°♊12	♆/⚴	02°♍26	⚴/⊗	20°♋04
☽/☊	05°♓26	*♀*	14°♈02	♃/⚳	18°♈24	♆/⚵	28°♊46	*⚵*	24°♈32
☽/⊗	02°♈36	♀/♂	13°♊43	♃/⚴	08°♌53	♆/⚶	17°♍44	⚵/⚶	13°♋30
☉	16°♉16	♀/♃	29°♉57	♃/⚵	05°♊12	♆/⛢	28°♋15	⚵/⛢	24°♉01
☉/☿	10°♉33	♀/♄	03°♓39	♃/⚶	24°♌11	♆/☊	23°♊27	⚵/☊	19°♈13
☉/♀	00°♉09	♀/♅	15°♈33	♃/⛢	04°♋42	♆/⊗	20°♋37	⚵/⊗	16°♉23
☉/♂	29°♊50	♀/♆	23°♊31	♃/☊	29°♉54	*♇*	18°♋56	*⚶*	02°♎29
☉/♃	16°♊04	♀/♇	01°♊29	♃/⊗	27°♊04	♇/⚷	18°♊44	⚶/⛢	13°♌00
☉/♄	19°♓46	♀/⚷	01°♉16	*♄*	23°♑15	♇/⚳	19°♈56	⚶/☊	08°♋12
☉/♅	01°♉40	♀/⚳	02°♓28	♄/♅	05°♓10	♇/⚴	10°♌24	⚶/⊗	05°♌22
☉/♆	09°♋38	♀/⚴	22°♊57	♄/♆	13°♏08	♇/⚵	06°♊44	*⛢*	23°♊31
☉/♇	17°♊36	♀/⚵	19°♈17	♄/♇	21°♈06	♇/⚶	25°♌42	⛢/☊	18°♉43
☉/⚷	17°♉24	♀/⚶	08°♋15	♄/⚷	20°♓53	♇/⛢	06°♋13	⛢/⊗	15°♊53
☉/⚳	18°♓35	♀/⛢	18°♉46	♄/⚳	22°♑05	♇/☊	01°♊25	*☊*	13°♈54
☉/⚴	09°♋04	♀/☊	13°♈58	♄/⚴	12°♏34	♇/⊗	28°♊35	☊/⊗	11°♉05
☉/⚵	05°♉24	♀/⊗	11°♉08	♄/⚵	08°♓54	*⚷*	18°♉31	*⊗*	08°♊15
☉/⚶	24°♋22	*♂*	13°♌25	♄/⚶	27°♏52	⚷/⚳	19°♓43		
☉/⛢	04°♊53	♂/♃	29°♋39	♄/⛢	08°♈23	⚷/⚴	10°♋12		
☉/☊	00°♉05	♂/♄	03°♏20	♄/☊	03°♓35	⚷/⚵	06°♉31		
☉/⊗	27°♉15	♂/♅	15°♊15	♄/⊗	00°♈45	⚷/⚶	25°♋30		

and transiting Jupiter at 8 degrees Libra was on the indirect Mars/Neptune midpoint. Both Uranus and Neptune were opposite natal Jupiter and Pluto while Saturn was opposing natal Mars. The solar eclipse the following month, on December 24, was square her natal Ceres and sesquiquadrate her Sun Chiron conjunction.

In March 2000, when colitis was diagnosed, progressed Moon was opposite her Moon Saturn conjunction. Transiting Pluto was semi-square her natal Moon and trine her Mars. Neptune was square Mercury, Uranus was square the Sun, Saturn was conjoined her Sun, and Jupiter was conjoined Mercury. The lunar eclipse on January 20, 2000 was on her indirect Mars/Uranus midpoint; Mars/Uranus is related to the nervous system and colitis is a manifestation of the nervous system. On February 5, the solar eclipse was exactly square her Sun.

In April 2001, when both tests showed no gastritis or ulceration, transiting Pluto was trine Venus and the north node, Saturn was trine the Moon, and Jupiter was sesquiquadrate Saturn.

Case History #2

This young woman was diagnosed with Krohn's disease in January 1997. She was experiencing horrible pain, and in February 1997, had surgery in which a few feet of her colon were removed. She has been on medication since that time and has been very lethargic for many years. In late spring of 2001, she had an ulcer diagnosed.

Interpretation of Horoscope

Her Sun is in Taurus in the eighth house inconjunct the north node and sesquiquadrate Pluto. Her Taurus Moon is conjoined Chiron and Mercury, broadly opposite Uranus. Mercury opposite Uranus indicates a very sensitive nervous system; these planets are also in a T square with Saturn, relating to blockage. Jupiter is opposed Neptune, showing problems with the immune system and the liver. This could also indicate addiction to drugs or medications as well as alcohol. Mars and Venus are conjoined in the sixth house opposite Pluto in the twelfth. Pluto rules the colon and is in one of the health houses. The asteroid Vesta is on the MC; Vesta is associated with Virgo, which rules the digestive tract.

In terms of parallels of declination, her Moon is parallel Mercury, Pluto, and Pallas, which shows the connection with the colon. Venus is parallel Mars, and Jupiter is contra-parallel Neptune, indicating problems with the immune system and liver.

Midpoints

Saturn/Neptune = Pluto, direct—indicates chronic problems and could implicate the colon, ruled by Pluto

Mars/Uranus = nodes and MC, direct—shows a sensitive nervous system

Jupiter/Saturn = Pluto, direct—indicates the need for regeneration of the liver and gall bladder

Jupiter/Uranus = Sun, direct—shows the erratic functioning of the liver and the strong effect on her vitality

Transits and Progressions

In 1997, when Krohn's disease began, secondary progressed Venus and Mars were conjoined at the end of Aries. Her progressed Moon was in Capricorn, close to the fourth house cusp. Transiting Neptune was near the fourth house cusp as well, square the nodes, and conjoined the Mars Uranus midpoint. Jupiter and Uranus were in early Aquarius square her natal Mercury Chiron conjunction and her Moon, which may have indicated problems with her mother. On March 9, the solar eclipse in Pisces was square her natal Neptune, ruler of her sixth house.

In 2001, when her ulcer was diagnosed, secondary progressed Venus and Mars were conjoined on her natal Chiron. Transiting Pluto was almost on her Neptune, ruler of her sixth house, with Saturn opposite it. Uranus was square her Sun, indicating a lot of tension and stress, and Neptune was also square her Uranus. The lunar eclipse on July 5 was square her natal Pluto in the twelfth house.

RECOMMENDATIONS FOR AVOIDING GASTROINTESTINAL PROBLEMS

1. Acid foods create problems in the gastrointestinal system, especially on an empty stomach; starting the day with coffee or orange juice is not a good idea. It is preferable to start with some herb tea, some parsley tea, or potato broth, all of which are alkaline. This might be followed by a cooked whole grain cereal or bread, which also is alkaline, and will help to keep the blood sugar stable throughout the day.
2. Eat fruit alone, preferably in between meals, as it does not combine well with other foods.
3. Substitute lighter proteins such as fresh fish for heavier proteins such as red meats. Meat requires a lot of enzymes for digestion, and should not be combined with carbohydrates.
4. Cheese, milk, and other dairy products require a lot of pancreatic enzymes for digestion, and also are the source of food allergies. Goat milk products are better as well as rice milk.

Gastrointestinal—Woman 2
Natal Chart
May 15,1977, 5:07 PM CDT +5:00
Hinsdale
41N48 03 087W56 13

Geocentric
Tropical
Koch
True Node

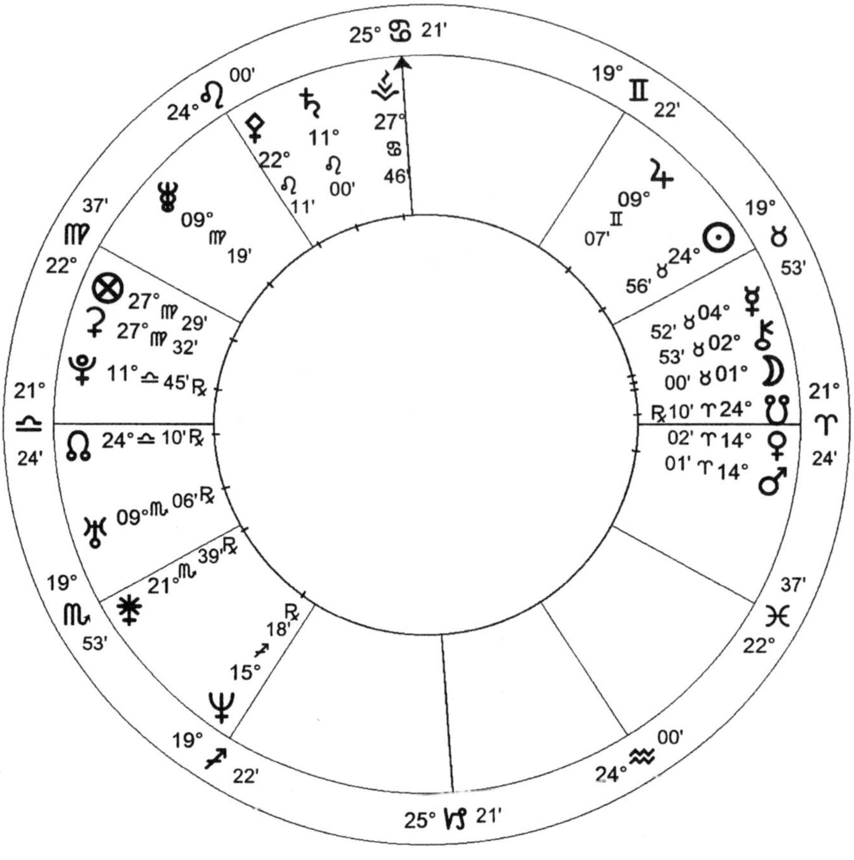

5. Dark green leafy vegetables aid the liver in its work, as well as providing lots of minerals and vitamins. They should be included twice a day at meals.
6. Exercising before meals and at intervals during the day is important in aiding digestion.
7. Frequent liquid fasts give the digestive tract a rest. At these times, a colonic irrigation or high enema can clean out old fecal matter from the colon.

Midpoint Listing

Gastrointestinal • Woman 2 • Natal Chart
In Planetery Sequence • Modulus 360°00'

☽	01°♉00	*☿*	04°♉52	♂/♆	14°♒39	*♅*	09°♏06	⚷/⚶	06°♋06
☽/☉	12°♉58	☿/♀	24°♈27	♂/♇	12°♋53	♅/♆	27°♏12	⚷/☊	28°♋32
☽/☿	02°♉56	☿/♂	24°♈26	♂/⚷	23°♈27	♅/♇	25°♎25	⚷/⊗	15°♋11
☽/♀	22°♈31	☿/♃	22°♉00	♂/⚳	05°♊53	♅/⚷	06°♒00	*⚳*	27°♋46
☽/♂	22°♈30	☿/♄	22°♊56	♂/⚴	18°♊06	♅/⚳	18°♍26	⚳/⚴	09°♌58
☽/♃	20°♉04	☿/♅	06°♒59	♂/⚵	02°♒50	♅/⚴	00°♎39	⚳/⚵	24°♍43
☽/♄	21°♊00	☿/♆	25°♒05	♂/⯚	05°♋46	♅/⚵	15°♏23	⚳/⯚	27°♌39
☽/♅	05°♒03	☿/♇	23°♋18	♂/⚶	26°♊40	♅/⯚	18°♎19	⚳/⚶	18°♌32
☽/♆	23°♒09	☿/⚷	03°♉53	♂/☊	19°♑05	♅/⚶	09°♎13	⚳/☊	10°♍58
☽/♇	21°♋23	☿/⚳	16°♊19	♂/⊗	05°♋45	♅/☊	01°♏38	⚳/⊗	27°♌37
☽/⚷	01°♉57	☿/⚴	28°♊32	*♃*	09°♊07	♅/⊗	18°♎18	*⚴*	22°♌11
☽/⚳	14°♊23	☿/⚵	13°♒16	♃/♄	10°♋04	*♆*	15°♐18	⚴/⚵	06°♎55
☽/⚴	26°♊36	☿/⯚	16°♋12	♃/♅	24°♌07	♆/♇	13°♏32	⚴/⯚	09°♍52
☽/⚵	11°♒20	☿/⚶	07°♋05	♃/♆	12°♓13	♆/⚷	24°♒06	⚴/⚶	00°♍45
☽/⯚	14°♋16	☿/☊	29°♋31	♃/♇	10°♌26	♆/⚳	06°♎32	⚴/☊	23°♍11
☽/⚶	05°♋10	☿/⊗	16°♋10	♃/⚷	21°♉00	♆/⚴	18°♎45	⚴/⊗	09°♍50
☽/☊	27°♋35	*♀*	14°♈02	♃/⚳	03°♋27	♆/⚵	03°♐29	*⚵*	21°♏39
☽/⊗	14°♋15	♀/♂	14°♈01	♃/⚴	15°♋39	♆/⯚	06°♏25	⚵/⯚	24°♎36
☉	24°♉56	♀/♃	11°♉35	♃/⚵	00°♍23	♆/⚶	27°♎19	⚵/⚶	15°♎29
☉/☿	14°♉54	♀/♄	12°♊31	♃/⯚	03°♌20	♆/☊	19°♏44	⚵/☊	07°♏55
☉/♀	04°♉29	♀/♅	26°♑34	♃/⚶	24°♋13	♆/⊗	06°♏24	⚵/⊗	24°♎34
☉/♂	04°♉28	♀/♆	14°♒40	♃/☊	16°♌39	*♇*	11°♎45	*⯚*	27°♍32
☉/♃	02°♊02	♀/♇	12°♋53	♃/⊗	03°♌18	♇/⚷	22°♋19	⯚/⚶	18°♍25
☉/♄	02°♋58	♀/⚷	23°♈28	*♄*	11°♌00	♇/⚳	04°♍45	⯚/☊	10°♎51
☉/♅	17°♌01	♀/⚳	05°♊54	♄/♅	25°♍03	♇/⚴	16°♍58	⯚/⊗	27°♍30
☉/♆	05°♓07	♀/⚴	18°♊07	♄/♆	13°♎09	♇/⚵	01°♏42	*⚶*	09°♍19
☉/♇	03°♌20	♀/⚵	02°♒51	♄/♇	11°♍22	♇/⯚	04°♎38	⚶/☊	01°♎45
☉/⚷	13°♉55	♀/⯚	05°♋47	♄/⚷	21°♊57	♇/⚶	25°♍32	⚶/⊗	18°♍24
☉/⚳	26°♊21	♀/⚶	26°♊41	♄/⚳	04°♌23	♇/☊	17°♎57	*☊*	24°♎10
☉/⚴	08°♋33	♀/☊	19°♑06	♄/⚴	16°♌36	♇/⊗	04°♎37	☊/⊗	10°♎50
☉/⚵	23°♌18	♀/⊗	05°♋46	♄/⚵	01°♎20	*⚷*	02°♉53	*⊗*	27°♍29
☉/⯚	26°♋14	*♂*	14°♈01	♄/⯚	04°♍16	⚷/⚳	15°♊20		
☉/⚶	17°♋07	♂/♃	11°♉34	♄/⚶	25°♌09	⚷/⚴	27°♊32		
☉/☊	09°♌33	♂/♄	12°♊30	♄/☊	17°♍35	⚷/⚵	12°♒16		
☉/⊗	26°♋12	♂/♅	26°♑33	♄/⊗	04°♍15	⚷/⯚	15°♋13		

8. Probiotics, including acidophilus and bifidus, are helpful in replacing intestinal bacteria.

SUPPLEMENT RECOMMENDATIONS FOR GASTROINTESTINAL PROBLEMS

Digestive enzymes are important. These include pancreatic enzymes, oxbile, papain and bromelain, taken after meals.

L-glutamine or glutamic acid helps in building the cells of the digestive tract. It is used in healing ulcers.

Probiotics, including many strands of intestinal bacteria, especially lactobacillus acidophilus and lactobacillus bifidus, re-implant friendly bacteria into the colon.

GLA found in evening primrose oil, borage oil, and black currant seed oil helps to protect the liver from alcohol and other irritating drugs and toxins.

Bioflavonoids or Vitamin P increase the strength of the capillaries, and also help protect against allergies, chemical sensitivities, and radiation. They are especially important for bleeding ulcers.

HERBAL RECOMMENDATIONS

Aloe vera gel or juice adds mucilage and helps the colon in elimination. If you have an aloe vera plant, eating the pulp from one or two leaves daily is a good way to obtain this.

Slippery elm is mucilaginous and soothes the digestive tract. It also helps the colon in elimination and should be used for any ulcers or gastritis.

Marshmallow root has a soothing demulcent effect on the mucous linings. For all inflammations of the digestive tract such as gastritis, colitis, enteritis, and ulcers, marshmallow root should be used in combination with comfrey root and golden seal.

Comfrey root contains allantoin, which helps heal wounds. It is also a strong demulcent making it ideal for healing gastritis, colitis, enteritis, and ulcers.

Golden seal powder is an excellent tonic for the mucous membranes of the digestive system and works well for all gastrointestinal problems.

CHAPTER 12

Cardiovascular Disease

CARDIOVASCULAR DISEASE IS THE LEADING CAUSE OF DEATH in the western world. Since the heart is the organ most crucial to life, we need to understand why we have so much cardiovascular disease, and how to nurture our hearts, physiologically, as well as psychologically. In underdeveloped countries, where people eat a more natural diet, there is a low incidence of cardiovascular disease. Diets high in fat and cholesterol, which include red meat, dairy products, and eggs are related to the high incidence of CVD.

Atherosclerosis, the hardening and clogging of the arteries, is at the base of CVD. Atherosclerosis involves the narrowing and thickening of our blood vessels, which occurs at a slow rate, but with certain factors, can happen very fast. Atherosclerosis can cause chest pain or angina pectoris. When this coronary artery disease progresses, it can result in a myocardial infarction (MI) or heart attack, the formation of dead cells in the heart muscle due to interruption of the blood supply to the area.

Hypertension or high blood pressure is behind CVD; high blood pressure weakens the vessel walls and causes plaque formation. If hypertension is untreated, it can lead to heart attacks and congestive heart failure, as well as to strokes.

High cholesterol is another factor in CVD. Current thinking is that high blood cholesterol with higher LDL cholesterol (the bad kind) and lower HDL cholesterol (the good kind, because it picks up used cholesterol and carries it back to the liver), is correlated with atherosclerosis and coronary heart disease. The cholesterol issue involves triglycerides, which comprise 95 per cent of the lipids in foods. Triglycerides include saturated fats, which are commonly found in animals and are hard at room temperature, and unsaturated fats, which include vegetable oils. Hydrogenated fats, like margarine and other spreads, are saturated and also raise the level of blood cholesterol. Eating saturated fats raises the LDL whereas the unsaturated fats such as vegetable oils and fish oils which contain EPA and DHA, raise the HDL.

Besides hypertension and high blood cholesterol, cigarette smoking, lack of exercise, and obesity also contribute to CVD. Cigarette smoking, through the effects of nicotine, stimulates the adrenal gland to overproduce aldosterone, epinephrine, and nor-epinephrine, which cause constriction of blood vessels. People who are overweight develop extra capillaries to nourish fat tissue. This makes the heart work harder to pump the blood through more veins. Exercise strengthens the smooth muscle of blood vessels, enabling them to assist circulation, thus increasing cardiac efficiency and output.

PSYCHOLOGICAL PATTERNS

Many of those with CVD fall into the category of Type A personalities. They are always working, need to accomplish many things, and yet never take the time to relax and enjoy life. Being strongly competitive personalities, they are also impatient and tend to be judgmental. Underneath their exterior self-assurance, they lack confidence. Type A personalities are also hostile, but they tend to keep this under control. These people have been written about by Drs. Friedmann and Rosemann in their book, *Type A Behavior and Your Heart*. In terms of research, this group was found to have a higher serum cholesterol, higher serum fat level, eat more foods high in cholesterol, smoke more cigarettes, and suffer more from high blood pressure than other groups.

Often those who have CVD tend to hold back their emotions and feelings. When a trauma occurs in their life, such as the breaking up of a relationship, or a death in the family, they can no longer hold back their feelings. The flood gates are open and the heart becomes vulnerable; chest pains may occur followed by a heart attack. One client, who was a well known and respected surgeon, had a heart attack after finding out his wife was having an affair.

ASTROLOGICAL PATTERNS

Astrologically, the heart is ruled by Leo and the Sun. Horoscopes of those with CVD have a fixed sign emphasis, especially the Moon. Fixed signs tend to hold back their emotions and are stubborn, set in their habit patterns. The Leo/Aquarius axis is involved with circulation and the Taurus/Scorpio axis governs cleansing. When there is a holding on to emotions, the throat (Taurus) and the colon (Scorpio) often become congested, and affect the rest of the fixed square by blocking circulation. Succedent houses are also strongly emphasized in these horoscopes.

With a blockage of the arteries or arteriosclerosis, Jupiter is often found in Leo or Aquarius, or the fifth and eleventh houses, with hard aspects from Saturn. Sometimes Jupiter is found in Capricorn, Saturn's sign.

In arhythmia of the heart or tachycardia (fast beat), Uranus is prominent, angular or conjoined the Sun, Moon, or ascendant, and often in hard aspect to Mars. Uranus governs the electrical conductivity system of the heart; those with strong Uranus, or under Uranus transits tend to be deficient in magnesium. With CVD, natal Uranus was often found in the sixth house. A woman was hospitalized with major chest pains; natally she had Uranus in 25 degrees Scorpio square Mars at 28 degrees Leo. Transiting Uranus was at 25 degrees Aquarius when the chest pains started.

MIDPOINTS

Of the general health midpoints, the most important one for CVD is Mars/Uranus, which relates to the activity and work of the heart. In addition to the general health midpoints, the following should be considered as well:

Sun/Uranus—corresponds to the rhythmic function of the cells

Moon/Uranus—indicates emotional tension and disturbances of blood pressure

Mars/Jupiter—rules the heart muscle

Saturn/Uranus—refers to heart block and disturbance of bodily rhythm

Cardiovascular—Man 1
Natal Chart
Feb 22, 1935, 8:50 PM MST +7:00
Santa Fe
35N41 13 105W56 14

Geocentric
Tropical
Koch
True Node

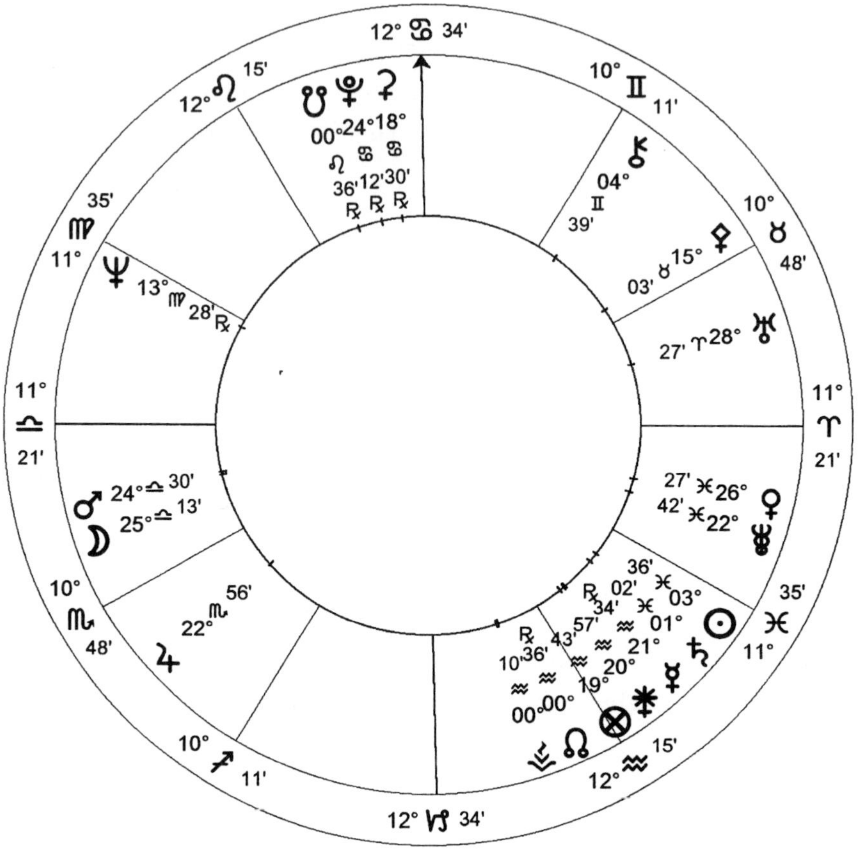

Uranus/Neptune—indicates heart failure and paralysis of the rhythmic processes

CASE HISTORIES

Case History #1

The health history of this man started with double pneumonia at the age of 4. He remembers having good health the rest of his childhood. He

Midpoint Listing

Cardiovascular • Man 1 • Natal Chart
In Planetery Sequence • Modulus 360°00'

☽	25°♎13	*☿*	21°♒34	♂/♆	03°♎59	*♅*	28°♈27	⚷/⯓	28°♈40
☽/☉	29°♐25	☿/♀	09°♓00	♂/♇	09°♍21	♅/♆	05°♋57	⚷/☊	02°♈38
☽/☿	23°♐24	☿/♂	23°♐02	♂/⚷	14°♌34	♅/♇	11°♊19	⚷/⊗	12°♈11
☽/♀	10°♑50	☿/♃	07°♑15	♂/⚶	12°♐20	♅/⚷	16°♉33	*⚶*	00°♒10
☽/♂	24°♎52	☿/♄	26°♒18	♂/⚴	04°♌46	♅/⚶	14°♓19	⚶/⚴	22°♓37
☽/♃	09°♏05	☿/♅	25°♓00	♂/⚵	22°♐44	♅/⚴	06°♉45	⚶/⚵	10°♒34
☽/♄	28°♐08	☿/♆	02°♐31	♂/⚳	06°♍30	♅/⚵	24°♓42	⚶/⚳	24°♈20
☽/♅	26°♋50	☿/♇	07°♉53	♂/⯓	08°♑36	♅/⚳	08°♊28	⚶/⯓	26°♒26
☽/♆	04°♎21	☿/⚷	13°♈06	♂/☊	12°♐33	♅/⯓	10°♈34	⚶/☊	00°♒23
☽/♇	09°♍43	☿/⚶	10°♒52	♂/⊗	22°♐06	♅/☊	14°♓31	⚶/⊗	09°♒57
☽/⚷	14°♌56	☿/⚴	03°♈18	*♃*	22°♏56	♅/⊗	24°♓05	*⚴*	15°♉03
☽/⚶	12°♐42	☿/⚵	21°♒16	♃/♄	11°♑59	*♆*	13°♍28	⚴/⚵	03°♈00
☽/⚴	05°♌08	☿/⚳	05°♉02	♃/♅	10°♒42	♆/♇	18°♌50	⚴/⚳	16°♊47
☽/⚵	23°♐05	☿/⯓	07°♓08	♃/♆	18°♎12	♆/⚷	24°♋04	⚴/⯓	18°♈52
☽/⚳	06°♍52	☿/☊	11°♒05	♃/♇	23°♍34	♆/⚶	21°♏49	⚴/☊	22°♓50
☽/⯓	08°♑58	☿/⊗	20°♒38	♃/⚷	28°♌48	♆/⚴	14°♋16	⚴/⊗	02°♈23
☽/☊	12°♐55	*♀*	26°♓27	♃/⚶	26°♐33	♆/⚵	02°♐13	*⚵*	20°♒57
☽/⊗	22°♐28	♀/♂	10°♑28	♃/⚴	19°♒00	♆/⚳	15°♌59	⚵/⚳	04°♉44
☉	03°♓36	♀/♃	24°♑42	♃/⚵	06°♑57	♆/⯓	18°♊05	⚵/⯓	06°♓50
☉/☿	27°♒35	♀/♄	13°♓44	♃/⚳	20°♍43	♆/☊	22°♏02	⚵/☊	10°♒47
☉/♀	15°♓01	♀/♅	12°♈27	♃/⯓	22°♑49	♆/⊗	01°♐36	⚵/⊗	20°♒20
☉/♂	29°♐03	♀/♆	19°♊58	♃/☊	26°♐46	*♇*	24°♋12	*⚳*	18°♋30
☉/♃	13°♑16	♀/♇	25°♉19	♃/⊗	06°♑20	♇/⚷	29°♊25	⚳/⯓	20°♉36
☉/♄	02°♓19	♀/⚷	00°♉33	*♄*	01°♓02	♇/⚶	27°♈11	⚳/☊	24°♈33
☉/♅	01°♈01	♀/⚶	28°♒19	♄/♅	29°♓44	♇/⚴	19°♊38	⚳/⊗	04°♉07
☉/♆	08°♐32	♀/⚴	20°♈45	♄/♆	07°♐15	♇/⚵	07°♉35	*⯓*	22°♓42
☉/♇	13°♉54	♀/⚵	08°♓42	♄/♇	12°♉37	♇/⚳	21°♋21	⯓/☊	26°♒39
☉/⚷	19°♈07	♀/⚳	22°♉29	♄/⚷	17°♈50	♇/⯓	23°♉27	⯓/⊗	06°♓12
☉/⚶	16°♒53	♀/⯓	24°♓34	♄/⚶	15°♒36	♇/☊	27°♈24	*☊*	00°♒36
☉/⚴	09°♈20	♀/☊	28°♒32	♄/⚴	08°♈03	♇/⊗	06°♉58	☊/⊗	10°♒10
☉/⚵	27°♒17	♀/⊗	08°♓05	♄/⚵	26°♒00	*⚷*	04°♊39	*⊗*	19°♒43
☉/⚳	11°♉03	*♂*	24°♎30	♄/⚳	09°♉46	⚷/⚶	02°♈25		
☉/⯓	13°♓09	♂/♃	08°♏43	♄/⯓	11°♓52	⚷/⚴	24°♉51		
☉/☊	17°♒06	♂/♄	27°♐46	♄/☊	15°♒49	⚷/⚵	12°♈48		
☉/⊗	26°♒40	♂/♅	26°♋28	♄/⊗	25°♒23	⚷/⚳	26°♊35		

worked for the Forest Service for many years, and also has been a jeweler. In the spring of 1970, at the age of 35, he went to a party and came home late, after drinking a bit. He fell to the ground, lost his balance, and was taken to the hospital where his condition was diagnosed as a stroke. He stayed in the hospital for 10 days and was given medication. At this time, he lost the feeling in the right side of his body, which has partially returned. He retired from the Forest Service when he was 55 at the end of

1990. In the spring of 1992, he was making jewelry. He felt very tired and could hardly mow his lawn. He went for a check up and was referred to a cardiologist; at first they thought he needed angioplasty (plastic repair of the blood vessels). Then they realized it was more serious. In fact, he had a quadruple by-pass of his heart. Now he is fully retired and in good health. He walks about four miles every morning, takes herbal supplements in capsules, and has massage and acupuncture treatments twice a month. However, he says he hasn't changed his diet and continues to eat meat, dairy products, and whatever else he chooses. He does take medication for his blood pressure.

Interpretation of Horoscope

His natal chart shows Saturn conjoined the Sun in Pisces, which portrays him as very responsible, but can also indicate blockages in the body. He has three planets, one asteroid, and the part of fortune in the fifth house. He has done creative work as a jeweler most of his life. The fifth house is the natural house of Leo, referring to the heart. His Moon in Libra is conjoined Mars and opposite Uranus; this shows a tendency to high blood pressure, a sensitive nervous system, and a speedy electrical conductivity of his heart. He needs a lot of physical exercise. This opposition forms a T square with Pluto in his tenth house; he is obviously a hard worker and could be compulsive about getting things done. Mercury is retrograde in Aquarius in the fifth house and exactly square Jupiter in Scorpio. The lungs (ruled by Mercury) are very affected by his liver (ruled by Jupiter). Mercury is also inconjunct Pluto in Cancer. Venus is in Pisces in the sixth house conjoined the asteroid Hygeia. Venus is in a grand trine with Jupiter in Scorpio and Pluto in Cancer, which exhibits his creative and intuitive gifts. The Moon Mars conjunction is inconjunct Venus and square Pluto. This could indicate a problem with blood sugar and metabolizing carbohydrates. Neptune in Virgo in his twelfth house is broadly opposite the Sun, showing his sensitivity, and is also exactly 135 degrees from Uranus, connecting his immune system with the electrical conductivity system. His south node is 0 degrees Leo in the tenth house; this can show a weakness in the heart area. His north node is 0 degrees Aquarius conjoined Vesta in the fourth house, indicating strong concerns with his family. The south node is 45 degrees from Neptune, showing the relationship of the immune system with the heart. Chiron is in the eighth house in Gemini, square his Sun Saturn conjunction, emphasizing the need to communicate his feelings and not hold back.

By declination, the Sun is parallel Mercury and Saturn, and contraparallel Uranus. This again shows potential problems with the electrical conductivity system.

Midpoints

Sun/Moon = Mars/Saturn, indicating blockages in vital energy

Mars/Uranus = Pluto, direct—chronic and long term problems with electrical conductivity system

Saturn/Neptune = Mars, indirect—lack of energy, depletion of adrenal glands

Uranus/Neptune = Mercury, indirect—sensitive nervous and respiratory systems

Transits and Progressions

In the spring of 1970, when he was 35 years old, he had a stroke. Progressed Moon was in Aquarius; it made an inconjunct to Neptune about the time (May) this occurred. Transiting Pluto was opposite sixth house Venus and sextile Pluto; transiting Neptune was square Saturn. Uranus was transiting the Uranus/Neptune midpoint at 5 degrees cardinal. Saturn was transiting the Saturn/Uranus indirect midpoint at 15 degrees fixed. Jupiter was exactly opposite natal Uranus. On February 21, on his birthday, there was a lunar eclipse at 2 degrees Virgo opposite his Sun Saturn conjunction. On March 7, there was a solar eclipse at 17 degrees Pisces opposite Neptune.

In the spring of 1992, when he was 57 years old, he had more problems and a quadruple by-pass surgery. Progressed Moon was in late Scorpio during this time period. Progressed Sun hit natal Uranus in 1990, when he retired from the Forest Service; in 1992, it was one degree away from progressed Uranus. Progressed Mars was within a degree of the natal ascendant. Transiting Pluto was exactly conjunct Jupiter in April, around the time of the surgery. The Uranus Neptune conjunction at 18 degrees Capricorn was opposite Ceres. Saturn at 17 degrees Aquarius was hitting the indirect midpoints of Mars/Neptune, Sun/Uranus, and Saturn/Uranus. Jupiter was exactly opposite the Sun. (Note the involvement of Jupiter, the liver, in both these time periods.) On June 15, the lunar eclipse was square Venus and inconjunct Pluto; on June 30, the solar eclipse was conjoined the MC and the Uranus/Neptune midpoint.

Cardiovascular—Man 2
Natal Chart
May 6, 1924, 7:45 PM CST +6:00
Mishawaka
41N39 43 086W09 31

Geocentric
Tropical
Koch
True Node

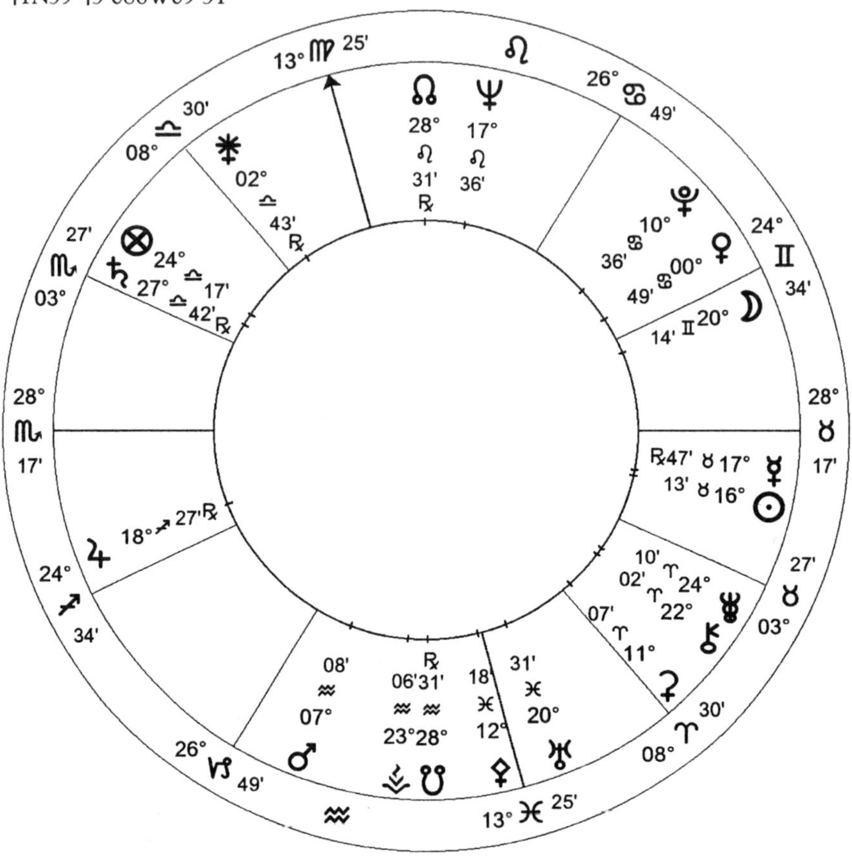

Case History #2

This man has had tachycardia for fifteen years and high cholesterol, but has been trying to take care of his health with some supplements and diet change. More recently, in 2001, he started a regular exercise program. He also has had psoriasis due to food allergies, and some arthritis on his right knee. In May of 1997, he had a hernia which required surgery. He has been taking flax seed oil and evening primrose oil for his essential fatty acids, magnesium and B complex for tachycardia, chromium for his blood sugar,

Midpoint Listing

Cardiovascular • Man 2 • Natal Chart
In Planetery Sequence • Modulus 360°00'

☽	20°♊14	*☿*	17°♉47	♂/♆	12°♏22	*♅*	20°♓31	⚷/⯓	23°♈06
☽/☉	03°♊13	☿/♀	09°♊18	♂/♇	23°♈52	♅/♆	04°♊03	⚷/☊	25°♊16
☽/☿	04°♊00	☿/♂	27°♓27	♂/⚷	14°♓35	♅/♇	15°♉33	⚷/⊗	23°♑09
☽/♀	25°♊32	☿/♃	03°♓07	♂/⚳	15°♒07	♅/⚷	06°♈16	*⚳*	23°♒06
☽/♂	13°♈41	☿/♄	07°♌44	♂/⚴	24°♒43	♅/⚳	06°♓49	⚳/⚴	02°♓42
☽/♃	19°♍20	☿/♅	19°♈09	♂/⚵	04°♐55	♅/⚴	16°♓24	⚳/⚵	12°♐55
☽/♄	23°♌58	☿/♆	02°♋41	♂/⚶	09°♓07	♅/⚵	26°♐37	⚳/⚶	17°♓07
☽/♅	05°♉22	☿/♇	14°♊11	♂/⯓	15°♓39	♅/⚶	00°♈49	⚳/⯓	23°♓38
☽/♆	18°♋55	☿/⚷	04°♉54	♂/☊	17°♏49	♅/⯓	07°♈21	⚳/☊	25°♏49
☽/♇	00°♋25	☿/⚳	05°♈27	♂/⊗	15°♐42	♅/☊	09°♊31	⚳/⊗	23°♐41
☽/⚷	21°♉08	☿/⚴	15°♈02	*♃*	18°♐27	♅/⊗	07°♑24	*⚴*	12°♓18
☽/⚳	21°♈40	☿/⚵	25°♋15	♃/♄	23°♏04	*♆*	17°♌36	⚴/⚵	22°♐31
☽/⚴	01°♉16	☿/⚶	29°♈27	♃/♅	04°♒29	♆/♇	29°♋06	⚴/⚶	26°♓43
☽/⚵	11°♌28	☿/⯓	05°♉59	♃/♆	18°♎01	♆/⚷	19°♊49	⚴/⯓	03°♈14
☽/⚶	15°♉40	☿/☊	08°♋09	♃/♇	29°♍31	♆/⚳	20°♉21	⚴/☊	05°♊24
☽/⯓	22°♉12	☿/⊗	06°♌02	♃/⚷	20°♒14	♆/⚴	29°♉57	⚴/⊗	03°♑17
☽/☊	24°♋22	*♀*	00°♋49	♃/⚳	20°♑47	♆/⚵	10°♍10	*⚵*	02°♎43
☽/⊗	22°♌15	♀/♂	18°♈58	♃/⚴	00°♒22	♆/⚶	14°♊22	⚵/⚶	06°♋55
☉	16°♉13	♀/♃	24°♍38	♃/⚵	10°♏35	♆/⯓	20°♊53	⚵/⯓	13°♋27
☉/☿	17°♉00	♀/♄	29°♌16	♃/⚶	14°♒47	♆/☊	23°♌04	⚵/☊	15°♍37
☉/♀	08°♊31	♀/♅	10°♉40	♃/⯓	21°♒19	♆/⊗	20°♍56	⚵/⊗	13°♎30
☉/♂	26°♓40	♀/♆	24°♋13	♃/☊	23°♎29	*♇*	10°♋36	*⚶*	11°♈07
☉/♃	02°♓20	♀/♇	05°♋43	♃/⊗	21°♏22	♇/⚷	01°♊19	⚶/⯓	17°♈39
☉/♄	06°♌57	♀/⚷	26°♉26	*♄*	27°♎42	♇/⚳	01°♉51	⚶/☊	19°♊49
☉/♅	18°♈22	♀/⚳	26°♈58	♄/♅	09°♑06	♇/⚴	11°♉27	⚶/⊗	17°♑42
☉/♆	01°♋54	♀/⚴	06°♉34	♄/♆	22°♍39	♇/⚵	21°♌39	*⯓*	24°♈10
☉/♇	13°♊24	♀/⚵	16°♌46	♄/♇	04°♍09	♇/⚶	25°♉51	⯓/☊	26°♊21
☉/⚷	04°♉07	♀/⚶	20°♉58	♄/⚷	24°♑52	♇/⯓	02°♊23	⯓/⊗	24°♑14
☉/⚳	04°♈40	♀/⯓	27°♉30	♄/⚳	25°♐24	♇/☊	04°♌33	*☊*	28°♌31
☉/⚴	14°♈15	♀/☊	29°♋40	♄/⚴	05°♑00	♇/⊗	02°♍26	☊/⊗	26°♍24
☉/⚵	24°♋28	♀/⊗	27°♌33	♄/⚵	15°♎12	*⚷*	22°♈02	*⊗*	24°♎17
☉/⚶	28°♈40	*♂*	07°♒08	♄/⚶	19°♑24	⚷/⚳	22°♓34		
☉/⯓	05°♉12	♂/♃	12°♑47	♄/⯓	25°♑56	⚷/⚴	02°♈10		
☉/☊	07°♋22	♂/♄	17°♐25	♄/☊	28°♍06	⚷/⚵	12°♋22		
☉/⊗	05°♌15	♂/♅	28°♒49	♄/⊗	25°♎59	⚷/⚶	16°♈34		

quercetin bioflavonoids for circulation, vitamins C and E as antioxidants, a good probiotic, and a few other supplements. He has cut out some of the fat and meat from his diet, but tends to eat a lot of his meals in restaurants where he cannot get good organic foods or many vegetables.

Interpretation of Horoscope

His Sun in Taurus is conjoined Mercury in the sixth house of health, forming a T square with Neptune in Leo and Mars in Aquarius. Mars squaring the

Sun Mercury conjunction can indicate a propensity to high blood pressure; Mars and south node in Aquarius refer to the cardiovascular system and circulation. Mars opposite Neptune can indicate allergies and the tendency to hypoglycemia, which he does have. The fixed signs are dominant with Scorpio rising, exactly square the nodes in Leo and Aquarius, which can also indicate problems with the cardiovascular system. His Gemini Moon is opposite Jupiter in Sagittarius and square Uranus in Pisces. Gemini Moon square Uranus speaks of a sensitive nervous system and shows a lack of magnesium, which can lead to spasms or other symptoms, including tachycardia. Jupiter in Sagittarius shows that the liver has a tendency to toxicity; this is a cause of both his allergies and arthritis. There are two grand trines here: one between Saturn, south node, and the Moon, and the other between Saturn, south node, and Venus. These have helped him to be disciplined in taking care of his health. Pluto, ruler of the chart, is broadly conjoined Venus in the eighth house and square Ceres; this motivates him to continue to transform and nurture himself.

In terms of declinations, Moon is parallel Mercury, his tendency to respiratory allergies, and Sun is parallel Neptune, showing a sensitive immune sytem.

Midpoints

Saturn/Neptune = Moon, direct—shows tendency to allergies

Mars/Saturn = Jupiter, direct—problems with liver function

Mars/Uranus = nodes, direct—tendency to high blood pressure, tachycardia

Mars/Pluto = Chiron, direct—the need to work on healing himself

Saturn/Uranus = Vesta, indirect—with Vesta in Aquarius, the need to heal some disturbance in the circulatory system

Mars/Jupiter = nodes and ascendant, indirect—the heart muscle is involved in problems with circulation

Transits and Progressions

In the fall of 1986, tachycardia began. Transiting Pluto was square natal Mars and on the Moon/Uranus midpoint. Transiting Uranus was conjoined

Jupiter and on the Mars/Saturn midpoint. Transiting Saturn was on the Sun/Moon midpoint as well as the Sun/Uranus midpoint (indirect). Transiting Jupiter was conjoined Uranus and on the Saturn/Neptune midpoint. On October 3, the solar eclipse squared his Pluto, and on Oct. 17, the lunar eclipse conjoined his Chiron and Hygeia while opposing Saturn.

In May 1997, when he had the hernia, transiting Pluto was on the Sun/Moon midpoint as well as the Sun/Uranus midpoint (indirect.) Transiting Neptune was square Saturn and inconjunct the north node. Transiting Uranus was conjoined Mars (a very significant transit for hernia). Transiting Saturn was on the Sun/Uranus midpoint, while transiting Jupiter was trine his Moon. On March 9, the solar eclipse squared his Jupiter exactly, and on March 24, the lunar eclipse made a sesquiquadrate to his Sun Mercury conjunction.

In May 2001, he began exercising for the first time and joined an exercise club. Secondary progressed Moon was conjoined Chiron. Transiting Pluto at 14 Sagittarius was close to his Jupiter, with transiting Jupiter opposing at 14 Gemini. Transiting Neptune was conjoined Mars; transiting Uranus was conjoined Vesta; and transiting Mars was exactly trine his north node. The solar eclipse of June 21 was conjoined his Venus while the lunar eclipse of July 5 was opposite his Pluto and square Ceres.

NATURAL TREATMENTS FOR CVD

To avoid hypertension and heart disease, the following guidelines are recommended.

1. Eat a diet low in cholesterol, saturated fats, and salt (use non-sodium seasonings).
2. Avoid all processed and refined foods such as white flour and sugar as well as all foods treated with preservatives and chemicals.
3. Eat only organic vegetables and fruits, organic poultry if desired.
4. Be careful with buying fish; choose wild ocean fish over farm raised fish, and avoid canned tuna fish, which is high in mercury.
5. Eat high fiber foods such as whole grains, whole grain cereals, and whole grain breads.
5. Exercise regularly, and include some aerobic exercise.
7. Avoid alcohol, smoking, and caffeinated beverages such as coffee, black tea, and cola drinks.

8. Eliminate all sources of metal poisoning such as aluminum and copper cooking utensils, and drinking tap water to which chlorine and other chemicals have been added.
9. Have regular acupuncture and massage treatments.
10. Practice some sort of meditation or breathing exercises, yoga, tai-chi, or chi gung.

SUPPLEMENT RECOMMENDATIONS FOR CVD

Potassium is an extremely important supplement for the heart; in people who have CVD, the sodium-potassium balance, which is the acid alkaline balance, is off. Include foods high in potassium as well as a potassium supplement.

Magnesium is the most essential mineral for the heart since it affects the electrical conductivity system. Dark green leafy vegetables are high in magnesium as is liquid chlorophyll, which is the magnesium ion. Magnesium can actually dilate the coronary arteries and reduce angina, as well as normalizing the heart beat. It also aids in blood pressure control. It should be taken with calcium and also as an additional supplement several times a day.

Bioflavonoids containing quercetin are necessary for circulation and bringing more oxygen to the heart. They also help with the acid alkaline balance.

B-Complex Vitamins are recommended for stress and work with magnesium in the electrical conductivity system. B complex should be used in a non yeast form, and may also be supplemented with additional B-6.

EPA and DHA—The Omega 3 fatty acids, found in fish oils and flaxseed oils, are very important in reducing lipid blood levels and plaque formation, thereby lessening atherosclerosis. These can be obtained through eating coldwater fish such as salmon, trout, herring, and sardines. If these types of fish are not eaten, then capsules should be taken several times a day. Flax seed oil should also be used daily.

Antioxidant nutrients—Vitamin E, Zinc, Selenium, Vitamin A—Vitamin E is a strong antioxidant, especially for preventing oxidation of fats. Selenium works with vitamin E to protect the cells and tissue linings. Zinc aids tissue healing and immune function, but too much zinc, over 100 mg. a day, may raise cholesterol levels. Vitamin A can improve oxygen utilization and reduce platelet clumping.

Co-Enzyme Q-10 helps with cardiac and lipid function.

L-Carnitine aids in fatty acid metabolism and may increase prostacyclin, a prostaglandin that dilates coronary arteries.

Chromium has been shown to lower LDL and raise HDL.

Vitamin C improves cholesterol metabolism, and can reduce cholesterol and LDL ratios.

HERBAL RECOMMENDATIONS

Garlic as a food or supplement can reduce triglycerides, cholesterol, and LDL, while raising HDL. Using 10-15 grams of garlic a day can reduce platelet stickiness and clotting.

Borage leaves make an excellent tea for strengthening the heart. Borage is high in magnesium, which nourishes the heart and nervous system.

Hawthorn berries are helpful in treating high and low blood pressure, rapid or arrhythmic heartbeat, inflammation of the heart muscle, and arteriosclerosis. Making a tea of the dried berries strengthens the heart muscle.

Motherwort is a good heart tonic combined with hawthorn berries. It helps in treating palpitations and preventing heart attacks. Motherwort is also useful for cramps and pain during menstruation, and nervous conditions such as insomnia and hysteria.

CHAPTER 13

Gynecological Problems

GYNECOLOGICAL PROBLEMS RUN THE GAMUT from PMS and menopause to difficulty conceiving, fibroid tumors in the reproductive system, miscarriages, and still births. Young girls reaching puberty often have many health problems from eating poor diets as well as being exposed to a lot of chemicals, both in their foods and from the environment.

Utilizing the astrological chart can be helpful in seeing where there are particular deficiencies so that these may be balanced with herbs and natural supplements. The horoscope is also an excellent tool in determining fertile cycles; there is a special cosmic fertility cycle, which is used in conjunction with the ovulation cycle for natural birth control. (Please see Appendix C for a discussion of Astrological Birth Control.)

Hormonal deficiencies are also common, especially in women who have used birth control pills and other medications. Balancing the levels of estrogen and progesterone are important for every woman, no matter what her age. Estrogen is released in the first half of the menstrual cycle with both estrogen and progesterone in the second half. These hormones decrease during menopausal years but can be supplemented with the proper foods and herbs.

Those who are infertile or who have experienced frequent miscarriages often have problems with the endocrine glands. A malfunctioning pituitary gland or low thyroid can interfere with the production of estrogen and progesterone. Obstruction of the fallopian tubes can also be a cause; this may be related to the use of diaphragms and other devices as well as various creams and foams.

PSYCHOLOGICAL FACTORS

There are many emotional problems that play a role in gynecological problems. Sexual abuse in childhood is one of the strongest. This often accounts for cramps and headaches related to menstruation. Many young girls need to learn how to honor their bodies and their womanhood. Puberty rituals are helpful for this. (See my book, Women's Medicine Ways for puberty rituals and suggestions.)

Problems in relationship lead to infertility and fears of becoming pregnant, especially if a woman thinks the marriage may end and she will be left alone with her child. A difficult relationship with one's mother also contributes to infertility; until this is worked through, pregnancy may not happen.

Many women also have anxieties about their age if they are in their late 30's or early 40's. Maintaining the body in good health through exercise, eating organic foods, using herbs and natural supplements, as well as positive thinking, can enable a woman to have a healthy pregnancy at any age. Finding a time period with supportive transits through astrology can be especially helpful.

Sometimes it is not a woman's role to have her own children, but to adopt children, teach, or take care of children. She may have other important work to do which will focus her maternal instincts.

ASTROLOGICAL PATTERNS

Women born at new and full Moon tend to have more difficulty conceiving than women born at other phases; they also have more problems during pregnancy. Those born during first and last quarter also have more problems (Sun square Moon). For women born during these phases, it is best to conceive at their ovulation time rather than during their cosmic fertility cycle, which is based on the lunar phase (see Appendix C).

Those who have difficulty conceiving often have Aquarius on the fifth house cusp, indicating that they may adopt children or work with children in some other way. Hard aspects from the Moon to Saturn can cause delay or difficulty in conceiving; this aspect suggests that there have been difficulties with one's own mother. A Capricorn Moon can also involve problems with conception. Hard aspects from the Moon to Mars may involve excessive bleeding at menstruation, miscarriages, or hemorrhage during delivery. Hard aspects from the Moon to Uranus often involve unexpected pregnancy; a woman with her natal Moon opposite Uranus conceived her first child at the age of 37 during a Uranus transit. Hard aspects from the Moon to Neptune may indicate unrealistic expectations about childbirth. A woman may want to conceive when her mate doesn't want a child, or when she is not ready to handle the responsibilities of becoming a mother. Hard aspects from Pluto can indicate miscarriage, abortion, or stillbirth.

MIDPOINTS

The general health midpoints, Saturn/Neptune and Mars/Saturn often equal Venus, possible holding back of love and also inhibited action of the thyroid gland, which is often a cause of not being able to conceive. Other important midpoints are the following:

Moon/Venus—is the ability to conceive

Moon/Mars—refers to hemorrhage, abortions, miscarriages

Moon/Venus = Saturn, inhibited glandular activity and malfunctioning thyroid

Moon/Venus = Neptune, abnormal glandular activity and imbalance with hormones, found most frequently in the charts of those who have difficulty conceiving

Moon/Venus = Uranus, can indicate erratic activity of the endocrine glands, especially the thyroid, and in some cases, unexpected pregnancy

Moon/Venus = Pluto, often found in the horoscopes of those who have miscarriages and stillbirths

Moon/Mars = Neptune, infection of the female organs

Moon/Mars = Pluto, often found in cases of miscarriage and stillbirth

CASE HISTORIES

Case History #1

The first case history is that of a woman who had two miscarriages but did end up adopting two children. While she was growing up, she did not have a lot of energy. She had some skin problems, and later, low blood sugar. She first became pregnant in April of 1992 when she was 41. Ten weeks later, in June 1992, she miscarried. She used herbs to rebalance her body, and later, in 1993, did an intense healing program including some pancha karma, which is the Ayurvedic system of cleansing. After this, her skin cleared up. In January 1994, her husband inherited some money and they began adoption procedures. In 1995, they had applied for a Korean child when she became pregnant for a second time. She conceived in April 1995, but miscarried in early June. On June 25, 1995, their Korean son arrived, who was thirteen months old. She felt stronger after the second miscarriage because she had gone back to eating meat. She had eliminated meat for a while, during which she had protein cravings and hypoglycemia. During her second pregnancy, she was tested for toxic minerals and was found to have a high copper toxicity. With the help of mineral and vitamin supplements and a new diet, she regained her energy. In 1998, she had her uterus adjusted, which had been tipped. In June 1998, she and her husband adopted a Vietnamese girl, who was six months old.

Interpretation of Horoscope

The Sun in Leo conjoined Pluto, forming a grand trine with an Aries ascendant and Chiron in Sagittarius, might appear to have lots of energy. However, Uranus exactly angular at the IC and Neptune angular at the 7th house cusp, make her extremely sensitive. The stellium in Virgo with Moon conjoined Mercury, Saturn, and south node, shows problems with the digestive system, as well as possible skin problems. Mars is in Scorpio square Venus in the last degree of Cancer, which also may point to skin problems. Mars in Scorpio shows good physical vitality, especially in a grand trine with Jupiter in Pisces, and Uranus in Cancer. Angular Neptune indicates a sensitive immune system, with a tendency to low blood sugar. Low blood sugar is also shown with Venus inconjunct Jupiter. With four planets in Virgo in the sixth house, she will put a lot of energy into her healing. This is also true with her Sun conjoined Pluto.

By declination, her Moon is parallel Mercury and contra parallel Neptune; this shows a sensitive nervous and immune system with possible

Gynecological—Woman 1
Natal Chart
Aug 15, 1950, 9:55 PM EDT +4:00
Cornwall, NY
41N27 074W01

Geocentric
Tropical
Koch
True Node

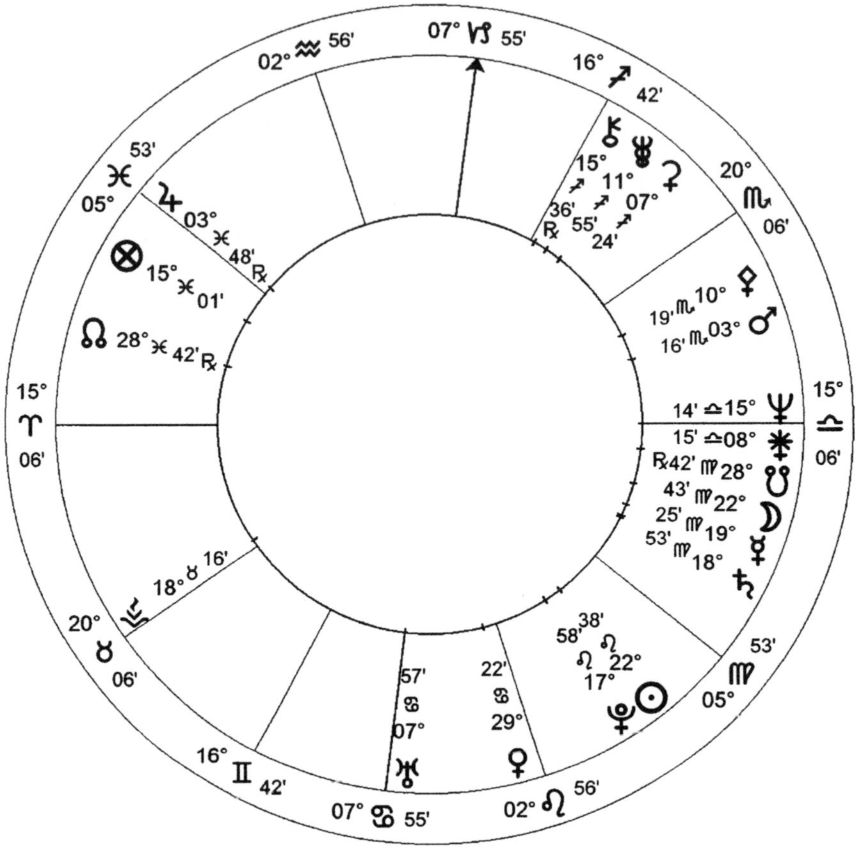

allergies. Her Sun is contra parallel Mars, while Uranus is parallel Pluto and contraparallel both Ceres and Hygeia. She has done a lot of healing on herself and works as a nutritionist, helping others with their healing.

Midpoints

Saturn/Neptune = Pluto and Vesta, indirect—long term healing and transformation of physical patterns

Midpoint Listing

Gynecological • Woman 1 • Natal Chart
In Planetery Sequence • Modulus 360°00'

☽	22°♍43	*☿*	19°♍25	♂/♆	24°♎15	*♅*	07°♋57	⚷/⚸	13°♐46
☽/☉	07°♍40	☿/♀	24°♌23	♂/♇	25°♍37	♅/♆	26°♌35	⚷/☊	07°♒09
☽/☿	21°♍04	☿/♂	11°♎20	♂/⚷	24°♏26	♅/♇	27°♋58	⚷/⊗	00°♒19
☽/♀	26°♌02	☿/♃	11°♐37	♂/⚳	10°♌46	♅/⚷	26°♍46	*⚳*	18°♉16
☽/♂	12°♎59	☿/♄	19°♍09	♂/⚴	06°♏47	♅/⚳	13°♊06	⚳/⚴	14°♌17
☽/♃	13°♐16	☿/♅	13°♌41	♂/⚵	20°♎45	♅/⚴	09°♍08	⚳/⚵	28°♋16
☽/♄	20°♍48	☿/♆	02°♎20	♂/⚶	20°♏20	♅/⚵	23°♌06	⚳/⚶	27°♒50
☽/♅	15°♌20	☿/♇	03°♍42	♂/⚸	22°♏35	♅/⚶	22°♍40	⚳/⚸	00°♓05
☽/♆	03°♎58	☿/⚷	02°♏31	♂/☊	15°♑59	♅/⚸	24°♍56	⚳/☊	23°♈29
☽/♇	05°♍21	☿/⚳	18°♋50	♂/⊗	09°♑08	♅/☊	18°♉20	⚳/⊗	16°♈39
☽/⚷	04°♏09	☿/⚴	14°♎52	*♃*	03°♓48	♅/⊗	11°♉29	*⚴*	10°♏19
☽/⚳	20°♋29	☿/⚵	28°♍50	♃/♄	11°♐21	*♆*	15°♎14	⚴/⚵	24°♎17
☽/⚴	16°♎31	☿/⚶	28°♎25	♃/♅	05°♉53	♆/♇	16°♍36	⚴/⚶	23°♏52
☽/⚵	00°♎29	☿/⚸	00°♏40	♃/♆	24°♐31	♆/⚷	15°♏25	⚴/⚸	26°♏07
☽/⚶	00°♏03	☿/☊	24°♊04	♃/♇	25°♉53	♆/⚳	01°♌45	⚴/☊	19°♑31
☽/⚸	02°♏19	☿/⊗	17°♐13	♃/⚷	24°♑42	♆/⚴	27°♎46	⚴/⊗	12°♑40
☽/☊	25°♊43	*♀*	29°♋22	♃/⚳	11°♈02	♆/⚵	11°♎45	*⚵*	08°♎15
☽/⊗	18°♐52	♀/♂	16°♍19	♃/⚴	07°♑04	♆/⚶	11°♏19	⚵/⚶	07°♏50
☉	22°♌38	♀/♃	16°♉35	♃/⚵	21°♐02	♆/⚸	13°♏35	⚵/⚸	10°♏05
☉/☿	06°♍01	♀/♄	24°♌07	♃/⚶	20°♑36	♆/☊	06°♑58	⚵/☊	03°♑29
☉/♀	11°♌00	♀/♅	18°♋39	♃/⚸	22°♑52	♆/⊗	00°♑08	⚵/⊗	26°♐38
☉/♂	27°♍57	♀/♆	07°♍18	♃/☊	16°♓15	*♇*	17°♌58	*⚶*	07°♐24
☉/♃	28°♉13	♀/♇	08°♌40	♃/⊗	09°♓25	♇/⚷	16°♎47	⚶/⚸	09°♐40
☉/♄	05°♍45	♀/⚷	07°♎29	*♄*	18°♍53	♇/⚳	03°♋07	⚶/☊	03°♒03
☉/♅	00°♌17	♀/⚳	23°♊49	♄/♅	13°♌25	♇/⚴	29°♍09	⚶/⊗	26°♑13
☉/♆	18°♍56	♀/⚴	19°♍50	♄/♆	02°♎04	♇/⚵	13°♍07	*⚸*	11°♐55
☉/♇	20°♌18	♀/⚵	03°♍49	♄/♇	03°♍26	♇/⚶	12°♎41	⚸/☊	05°♒19
☉/⚷	19°♎07	♀/⚶	03°♎23	♄/⚷	02°♏15	♇/⚸	14°♎57	⚸/⊗	28°♑28
☉/⚳	05°♋27	♀/⚸	05°♎39	♄/⚳	18°♋34	♇/☊	08°♊20	*☊*	28°♓42
☉/⚴	01°♎28	♀/☊	29°♉02	♄/⚴	14°♎36	♇/⊗	01°♊30	☊/⊗	21°♓52
☉/⚵	15°♍27	♀/⊗	22°♉12	♄/⚵	28°♍34	*⚷*	15°♐36	*⊗*	15°♓01
☉/⚶	15°♎01	*♂*	03°♏16	♄/⚶	28°♎09	⚷/⚳	01°♓56		
☉/⚸	17°♎17	♂/♃	03°♑32	♄/⚸	00°♏24	⚷/⚴	27°♏57		
☉/☊	10°♊40	♂/♄	11°♎04	♄/☊	23°♊48	⚷/⚵	11°♏56		
☉/⊗	03°♊50	♂/♅	05°♍36	♄/⊗	16°♐57	⚷/⚶	11°♐30		

Jupiter/Neptune = Moon, direct—tendency to low blood sugar and problems digesting carbohydrates

Transits and Progressions

In 1992, she conceived for the first time in April and then had a miscarriage in June. When she conceived, transiting Jupiter was opposite her natal Jupiter. By secondary progression, Mercury was conjoined Saturn and Venus was conjoined Mercury, both in the sixth house. Saturn at 18 degrees Aquarius was inconjunct natal Saturn in the sixth house. Uranus and Neptune were both trine her Saturn, which enabled her to regain her health through the use of herbs and supplements. The lunar eclipse on June 15 was square her natal Moon, ruling childbirth and motherhood. The solar eclipse on June 30 was conjunct natal Uranus in Cancer on her fourth house cusp.

In 1995, she conceived for the second time in April, miscarried in early June, and adopted her first child on June 25. By secondary progression, Mercury was on Saturn and Venus was conjoined her Moon. Her progressed Moon was exactly square Pluto in June. Transiting Saturn was squaring her Moon in June as well. Jupiter was conjoined the asteroid Hygeia when she miscarried, and conjoined the asteroid Ceres when her adopted son arrived. (Ceres is often involved when a woman becomes pregnant or delivers a child.) Transiting Uranus was exactly opposite fourth house Venus in Cancer. Transiting Pluto was trine Venus. Neptune was on her Mars/Neptune midpoint, (direct), and also on her Sun/Moon midpoint, (indirect.) This shows that her immune system was a cause of the miscarriage, but Neptune also indicates the spiritual blessing of having a child the same month she miscarried. The lunar eclipse on April 15 squared Venus and was conjoined the Mars/Neptune (direct) and Sun/Moon (indirect) midpoints. The solar eclipse on April 29 opposed her natal Mars in Scorpio.

In 1998, she had her uterus adjusted and also adopted her second child on June 25, the same date three years later that she got her first child. Secondary progressed Venus was conjunct her south node; it had been conjunct her Moon in 1995 when she first adopted. On June 25, the Sun is about 3 degrees Cancer, forming a grand trine with natal Mars, her chart ruler, and also natal Jupiter. Jupiter was transiting her north node in Pisces while Uranus was semi-square the node. Saturn was opposite natal Mars and Neptune was square Mars. Pluto at 6 degrees Sagittarius was almost conjoined Ceres, and also on the Mars/Uranus direct midpoint. The lunar eclipse on March 13 had been conjoined her natal Moon exactly.

Case History #2

This is a woman who has dealt with fibroid tumors in her uterus most of her life. She is a practitioner of Feng Shui, having worked and written about it for many years. In terms of her healing, she has undergone many types of treatments, been very careful of her diet, followed through on supplements, and done a lot of spiritual work. The fibroids are still with her. She has also had a low thyroid, for which she has taken both supplements and medication. Her fibroids became obvious after a bad automobile accident in 1983. The seat belt had wrenched her abdomen, and the place it was bruised was about where the first fibroid was found in early 1984. Doctors wanted to perform surgery and she was resistant to this. She came to see me as a client in November 1991. We worked with supplements, herbs, and homeopathy, as well as the psychological roots of the problem. We also did some deep session work in February of 1992, exploring her sexuality and her belief in healing herself.

In 2001, she wrote me the following statement, "The fibroids never completely disappeared; I am biding my time, hoping they shrink with the menopause I am now in. I did the supplements you suggested, began to feed myself better, did homeopathy, acupuncture, and herbs. Maybe these therapies slowed them down. I worried and prayed a lot that I wouldn't need surgery. I think you helped me the most to realize I could heal myself in my own way. You gave me the encouragement that if I didn't want to, I wouldn't have to play by western medicine's rules. It helped to rest my mind somewhat, knowing that I didn't have to be under the doctor's knife, which I was totally terrified of and still am."

Interpretation of Horoscope

The Sun is in Sagittarius conjoined Mercury and opposite Uranus, showing a strong communication theme and sensitive nervous system. The Sun and MC are ruled by Jupiter, focusing on the liver and pancreas. Jupiter is in Capricorn conjoined Mercury and trine Saturn. The Sun and Moon are exactly inconjunct. There is an energy drainage on an emotional level with the Cancer Moon and Pisces rising, which tends to take on other people's feelings. Venus is in Scorpio, the sign ruling the reproductive system; it is inconjunct Uranus, which points to an erratic thyroid. The south node is also in Scorpio, showing possible problems in the reproductive area. Mars is in Capricorn, which indicates good vitality, but it is square Neptune, which suggests that her energy dissipates. There are also indications for low blood sugar and a sensitive immune system with Pisces rising. Pluto, ruling the reproductive system, is in the sixth house and is square the asteroid Vesta in Scorpio.

By declination, the Moon is contra parallel Mercury, which tends to worry and anxiety. Mars is parallel Jupiter and contra parallel Uranus and

Gynecological—Woman 2
Natal Chart
Dec 18, 1948, 11:41 AM EST +5:00
Cleveland, OH
41N29 081W41

Geocentric
Tropical
Koch
True Node

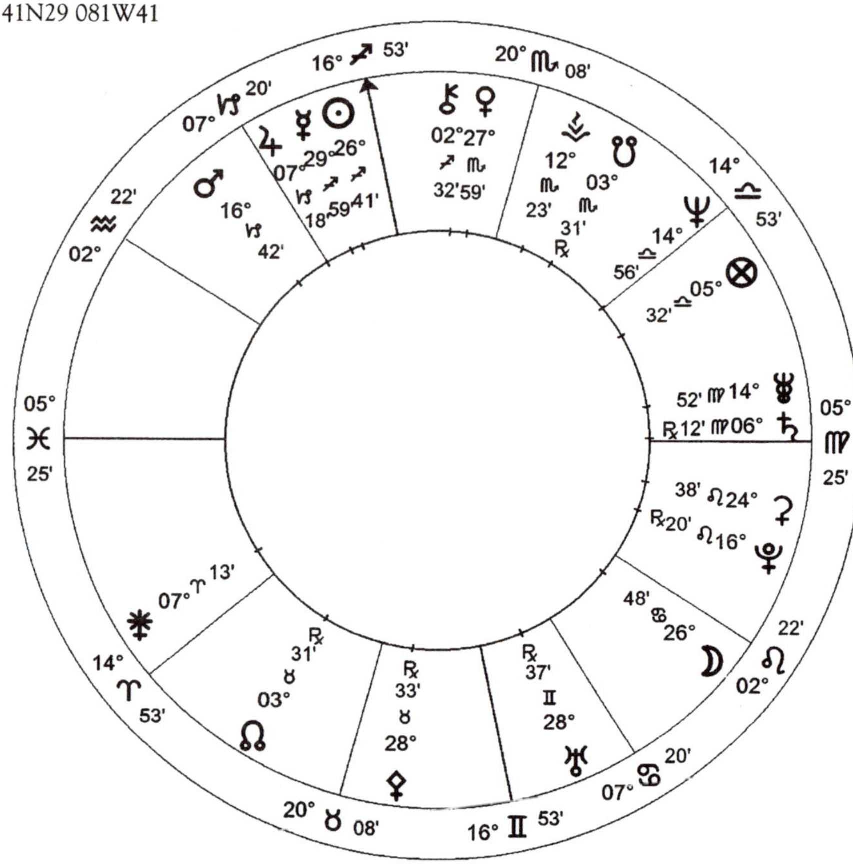

Pluto; Mars contra parallel Pluto can also indicate a need for healing the reproductive organs.

Midpoints

Sun/Moon = Venus, indirect—possible problems with thyroid; since Venus is in Scorpio, problems with reproductive organs

Mars/Saturn = Sun, indirect—blockages of energy within the body

Midpoint Listing

Gynecological• Woman 2 • Natal Chart
In Planetery Sequence • Modulus 360°00'

☽	26°♋48	*☿*	29°♐59	♂/♆	00°♐49	*♅*	28°♊37	⚷/⯰	23°♎42
☽/☉	11°♎45	☿/♀	13°♐59	♂/♇	01°♏31	♅/♆	21°♌46	⚷/☊	18°♒01
☽/☿	13°♎24	☿/♂	08°♑20	♂/⚷	24°♐37	♅/♇	22°♋28	⚷/⊗	04°♏02
☽/♀	27°♍24	☿/♃	03°♑38	♂/⚳	14°♐32	♅/⚷	15°♍34	*⚳*	12°♏23
☽/♂	21°♎45	☿/♄	03°♏05	♂/⚴	22°♓37	♅/⚳	05°♍30	⚳/⚴	20°♌28
☽/♃	17°♎03	☿/♅	29°♓18	♂/⚵	26°♒57	♅/⚴	13°♊35	⚳/⚵	24°♑48
☽/♄	16°♌30	☿/♆	22°♏28	♂/⚶	05°♏40	♅/⚵	17°♉55	⚳/⚶	03°♎30
☽/♅	12°♋43	☿/♇	23°♎10	♂/⯰	15°♏47	♅/⚶	26°♋37	⚳/⯰	13°♎38
☽/♆	05°♍52	☿/⚷	16°♐16	♂/☊	10°♓06	♅/⯰	06°♌44	⚳/☊	07°♒57
☽/♇	06°♌34	☿/⚳	06°♐11	♂/⊗	26°♏07	♅/☊	01°♊04	⚳/⊗	23°♎57
☽/⚷	29°♍40	☿/⚴	14°♓16	*♃*	07°♑18	♅/⊗	17°♌04	*⚴*	28°♉33
☽/⚳	19°♍36	☿/⚵	18°♒36	♃/♄	06°♏45	*♆*	14°♎56	⚴/⚵	02°♉53
☽/⚴	27°♊41	☿/⚶	27°♎18	♃/♅	02°♈57	♆/♇	15°♍38	⚴/⚶	11°♋35
☽/⚵	02°♊01	☿/⯰	07°♏26	♃/♆	26°♏07	♆/⚷	08°♏44	⚴/⯰	21°♋43
☽/⚶	10°♌43	☿/☊	01°♓45	♃/♇	26°♎49	♆/⚳	28°♎40	⚴/☊	16°♉02
☽/⯰	20°♌50	☿/⊗	17°♏45	♃/⚷	19°♐55	♆/⚴	06°♌44	⚴/⊗	02°♌02
☽/☊	15°♊09	*♀*	27°♏59	♃/⚳	09°♐50	♆/⚵	11°♑04	*⚵*	07°♈13
☽/⊗	01°♍10	♀/♂	22°♐20	♃/⚴	17°♓55	♆/⚶	19°♍47	⚵/⚶	15°♊55
☉	26°♐41	♀/♃	17°♐38	♃/⚵	22°♒15	♆/⯰	29°♍54	⚵/⯰	26°♊03
☉/☿	28°♐20	♀/♄	17°♎05	♃/⚶	00°♏58	♆/☊	24°♋13	⚵/☊	20°♈22
☉/♀	12°♐20	♀/♅	13°♍18	♃/⯰	11°♏05	♆/⊗	10°♎14	⚵/⊗	06°♋22
☉/♂	06°♑42	♀/♆	06°♏28	♃/☊	05°♓24	*♇*	16°♌20	*⚶*	24°♌38
☉/♃	01°♑59	♀/♇	07°♎10	♃/⊗	21°♏25	♇/⚷	09°♎26	⚶/⯰	04°♍45
☉/♄	01°♏26	♀/⚷	00°♐16	*♄*	06°♍12	♇/⚳	29°♍22	⚶/☊	29°♊04
☉/♅	27°♍39	♀/⚳	20°♏11	♄/♅	02°♌24	♇/⚴	07°♋27	⚶/⊗	15°♍05
☉/♆	20°♏49	♀/⚴	28°♌16	♄/♆	25°♍34	♇/⚵	11°♊47	*⯰*	14°♍52
☉/♇	21°♎31	♀/⚵	02°♒36	♄/♇	26°♌16	♇/⚶	20°♌29	⯰/☊	09°♋11
☉/⚷	14°♐37	♀/⚶	11°♎18	♄/⚷	19°♎22	♇/⯰	00°♍36	⯰/⊗	25°♍12
☉/⚳	04°♐32	♀/⯰	21°♎26	♄/⚳	09°♎17	♇/☊	24°♊55	*☊*	03°♉31
☉/⚴	12°♓37	♀/☊	15°♒45	♄/⚴	17°♋22	♇/⊗	10°♍56	☊/⊗	19°♋31
☉/⚵	16°♒57	♀/⊗	01°♏45	♄/⚵	21°♊42	*⚷*	02°♐32	*⊗*	05°♎32
☉/⚶	25°♎40	*♂*	16°♑42	♄/⚶	00°♍25	⚷/⚳	22°♏28		
☉/⯰	05°♏47	♂/♃	12°♑00	♄/⯰	10°♍32	⚷/⚴	00°♓32		
☉/☊	00°♓06	♂/♄	11°♏27	♄/☊	04°♋51	⚷/⚵	04°♒53		
☉/⊗	16°♏06	♂/♅	07°♈39	♄/⊗	20°♍52	⚷/⚶	13°♎35		

Jupiter/Neptune = Venus, direct—blood sugar problems and difficulty digesting carbohydrates

Transits and Progressions

In late 1983, she had an automobile accident. Secondary progressed Saturn was sitting exactly on her descendant with progressed Moon in Scorpio in the eighth house. Transiting Pluto was square her Moon. Neptune was conjoined the Sun Mercury and opposite Uranus. Saturn was on the south node, and the Jupiter Uranus conjunction was square natal Saturn and sesquiquadrate her Moon. The solar eclipse of December 1982 was conjunct her Sun, while the lunar eclipse in June 1983 hit her Mars/Uranus midpoint (direct) which often indicates accidents.

In early 1984, when her fibroids were diagnosed, Pluto was transiting her south node and the Jupiter Neptune conjunction was on her Mercury.

In November of 1991, when we had our first session, the transiting Uranus Neptune conjunction was square her natal Neptune. Saturn was square her nodes, and Jupiter had just conjoined her natal Saturn. The lunar eclipse of December 1991 conjoined her Uranus and opposed Mercury; the solar eclipse of January 1992 squared Neptune. In our first deep healing session in February 1992, the Uranus Neptune conjunction was square her natal Neptune.

SUGGESTIONS FOR WOMEN WITH PMS, DIFFICULTY CONCEIVING, OR MENOPAUSE

1. Increased exercise is important, especially yoga postures, which stimulate the thyroid and pituitary, helping to balance the energy to the reproductive organs. Increasing circulation through aerobic exercise such as dancing, walking, and swimming is also important..
2. Cleansing the colon through colonic irrigations has proven very helpful.
3. Detoxifying the liver is essential; olive oil and lemon in hot water may be used certain mornings as well as certain herbs.
4. It is essential to get rid of candida, yeast, and herpes through eliminating sugars, fruits, fruit juices, cows milk products, and wheat. Maintaining the proper acid alkali balance by a fairly yang diet—grains, vegetables, and proteins is also essential.
5. Lots of minerals are needed. Obtain minerals through dark green leafy vegetables rich in calcium and magnesium and include kelp, kombu, dulse, and other sea vegetables high in iodine and iron. Eat whole grains which are rich in B vitamins; use nuts, seeds, and cold pressed oils containing linoleic and linolenic acids, which are helpful for hormone production.
6. It is very helpful to obtain one's constitutional homeopathic remedy, which cn help balance emotions as well as raise the vital force.
7. Bach flower remedies and other flower remedies that deal with emotional states in combating fears and anxieties are often used.
8. Working with therapies such as acupressure, Jin Shinn, and polarity therapy help unblock meridians and increase "chi" or vital energy.

9. Visualization exercises that allow us to see the body as healthy and in balance work for many women.
10. Doing rituals and ceremonies to celebrate each stage of life is an important ingredient in maintaining health of the female organs.

SUPPLEMENT RECOMMENDATIONS FOR GYNECOLOGICAL PROBLEMS

GLA such as evening primrose oil or borage oil for the prostaglandin E-1 series balances the hormones.

EPA and DHA which are found in fish and fish oils for prostaglandin series 3 are also necessary for hormonal balance.

Bioflavonoids help circulation, protect the immune system, and increase the strength of the capillaries during bleeding.

A **Calcium/Magnesium** supplement several times a day aids mineral balance, helps prevent cramping during menstrual cycle, osteoporosis, and other bone problems.

B-6 taken 5 days before and during menstrual cycle helps nervousness, headaches, and irritability.

Magnesium, in addition to calcium/magnesium, taken 5 days before cycle, helps with cramping and restlessness.

Potassium taken 5 days before menstruation helps with low blood sugar and irritability.

Probiotics promotes good intestinal health and helps to clear up candida problems.

HERBAL RECOMMENDATIONS

Raspberry leaf is a good toner for female system, also high in magnesium.

Sarsaparilla root is an important herb when beginning menopause; it balances estrogen, and is a good blood purifier.

Nettles is high in iron and other minerals.

Horsetail is the best source of silica, which is necessary to assimilate calcium in the body.

Alfalfa contains most of the minerals and amino acids; it helps to alkalize the body and can be mixed with nettles and horsetail.

Golden seal leaf is a good herb to detoxify the liver and helps with hot flashes during menopause.

Kelp capsules, which contain all the minerals in addition to iodine, help to regulate the thyroid.

CHAPTER 14

Eye Disorders

OUR EYES ARE ONE OF OUR MOST IMPORTANT ORGANS; they reflect what is going on in the rest of our body. Many people wear glasses or contact lenses in order to see. Some have developed cataracts or glaucoma, which can lead to blindness. Our vision is often affected during periods of stress, anxiety, and emotional upheaval. Those who develop serious eye problems at an early age are often protecting themselves from something they have not wanted to see.

The eyes are affected by toxins in the body. Cataracts often occur when the liver is very toxic and the diet is heavy in dairy products and other animal fats, which contribute to cholesterol build up in the arteries.

When a cataract forms, the crystalline lens of the eye becomes clouded or opaque. As opacity is increased, vision is diminished. During surgery the crystalline lens is removed.

An increase of pressure within the eye occurs in glaucoma, which interferes with vision. This is due to a disturbance in the drainage of fluid that fills the interior of the eye in front of the lens. Too much fluid may be produced or the normal amount may not drain properly. Eyedrops constrict the pupil to allow more space for the fluid; they also help the fluid to flow through the walls of the canal. Unfortunately, these drops have many side effects. They distort the vision for the first thirty to forty minutes after they are used, as well as making it difficult to perceive colors clearly.

The lack of certain nutrients is also related to eye disorders. Vitamin B-2 or riboflavin has a preventive function in dealing with cataracts. Riboflavin is important in the utilization of vitamin A. Sufficient amounts of natural vitamin D are also essential. Vitamin D from synthetic sources is difficult to utilize but vitamin D from sunlight is absorbed by the eyes. Wearing of sunglasses, except when driving or when absolutely necessary, is best avoided.

PSYCHOLOGICAL FACTORS

Stress is a key factor in eye disorders. After emotional upsets, the eyes can become blurry and vision can be distorted. Stress controlling techniques such as autogenics, biofeedback, and visualization have been helpful, particularly in working with glaucoma.

Not wanting to be aware of or acknowledge something in our lives also affects the eyes. When this occurs, we need to ask ourselves what patterns we are unwilling to see. Once we have explored this, our physical vision will usually improve.

Often those who have the ability for clairvoyance develop eye problems. This is sometimes due to fear of using this ability, and other times, it is necessary to become physically blind in order to develop one's inner vision. A friend of mine was totally blind for four and a half years with glaucoma. When she finally had surgery, her sight was miraculously restored. During the time period she was blind, she developed her inner sight, which enabled her to do deeper work as a spiritual counselor.

ASTROLOGICAL FACTORS

Eye problems are related to the signs Aries and Libra. Aries rules the area of the head and thus the eyes; Libra governs the kidneys. Malfunctioning kidneys often manifest in eye problems. Dr. William Davidson, in his *Lectures on Medical Astrology*, says the following, "The reciprocalness between Aries and Libra and the consequent reflex influence from kidneys to eyes is well known, but not understood in medicine. But this knowledge is very helpful in refraction, the fitting of glasses. Many doctors are confounded and condemned because the glasses don't fit. It is really due to the changing condition of the kidney function."

Since Neptune rules the pineal gland or 'third eye', and so many eye problems relate to inner vision, Neptune is often found conjoined the Sun,

Moon, or other planets. Neptune also governs the immune system; when there are problems with the immune system, the eyes often are affected.

Certain prominent fixed stars are often found on the angles of the horoscope, or conjoined the Sun, Moon, or another planet. These stars seem to influence the planet when they are within a one degree orb—especially the hard aspects. In Helen Keller's horoscope, the Pleiades conjoin her Pluto and oppose her ascendant. John Milton, the blind poet, had Antares conjunct his ascendant and opposite Uranus, with the Pleiades conjoined the Moon in his sixth house.

Fixed Stars which affect the eyes most are the Pleiades at 29 Taurus, the Hyades at 5 Gemini, the Aselli at 6 and 7 Leo, Antares at 9 Sagittarius, and Spiculum at 29 Sagittarius.

MIDPOINTS

Particular midpoints to look at in studying eye disorders are:

Saturn/Neptune—known as the health axis, it also relates to blockages in the function of the immune system

Mars/Neptune—shows toxicity and susceptibility to infection

Sun/Neptune—shows fluid concentration in the cells

Moon/Neptune—points to over accumulation of water in the tissues of the body and hyper-sensitivity

CASE HISTORIES

Case History #1

The first case history involves a man who had some very traumatic circumstances in childhood with his eyes. At the age of 5, he tripped on a shoelace and put a scissors through his eye. His eye was operated upon and removed. When he was 11, he got into a fight with another boy; the boy took a sling shot and shot a paper clip into his remaining eye. When he was 17, in 1954, he had surgery and regained partial vision in that eye but then blood clots formed and he became totally blind. He got a complete scholarship to college, where he majored in physics and did very well. Most of his life he worked as a computer operator but he also was an amateur radio operator. When he was 35, he married and later had

Eye Disorders—Man
Natal Chart
Sep 18, 1937, 11:32 AM CST +6:00
Margaret, Texas
34N02 58 099W39 03

Geocentric
Tropical
Koch
True Node

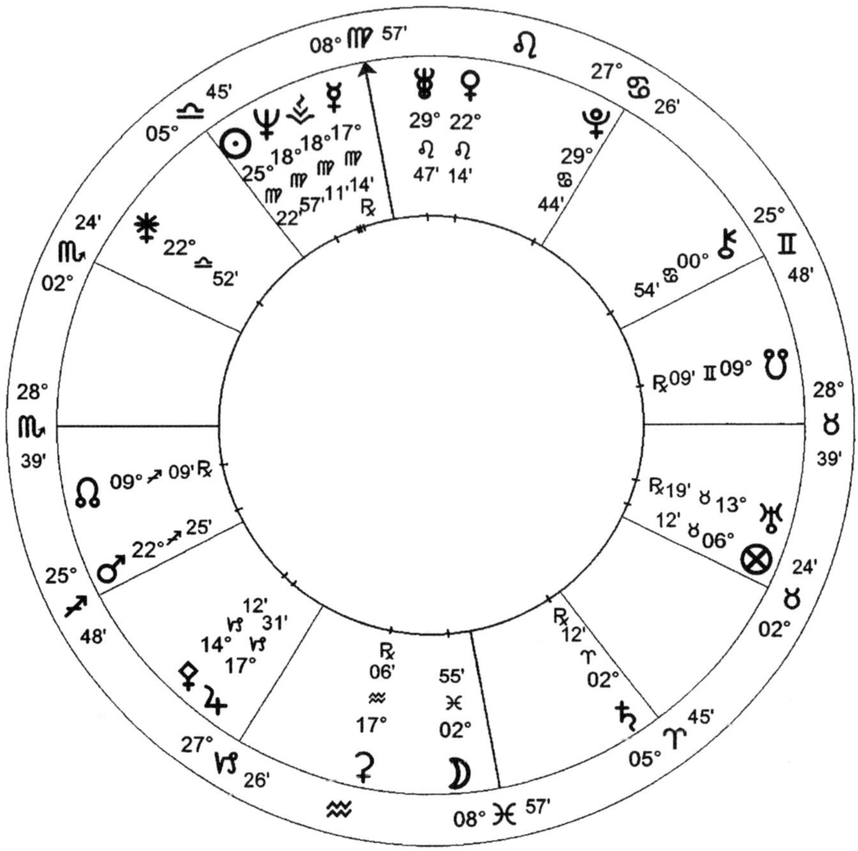

one daughter. At the age of 46, he developed cancer of the colon and died shortly afterward.

Interpretation of Horoscope

His Virgo Sun is conjoined Neptune, Mercury, and Vesta in the tenth house, showing deep intuition and psychic ability. The exact square to Mars shows his propensity to accidents. His Moon in Pisces, another Neptune

Midpoint Listing

Eye Disorders • Man • Natal Chart
In Planetery Sequence • Modulus 360°00'

☽	02°♓55	*☿*	17°♍14	♂/♆	05°♏41	*♅*	13°♉19	⚷/⚶	00°♌21
☽/☉	14°♐08	☿/♀	04°♍44	♂/♇	11°♎04	♅/♆	16°♋08	⚷/☊	20°♍02
☽/☿	10°♐04	☿/♂	04°♏50	♂/⚷	26°♍39	♅/♇	21°♊31	⚷/⊗	03°♊33
☽/♀	27°♉34	☿/♃	17°♏22	♂/⚳	05°♏18	♅/⚷	07°♊06	*⚳*	18°♍11
☽/♂	27°♑40	☿/♄	24°♊43	♂/⚴	03°♑18	♅/⚳	15°♋45	⚳/⚴	16°♏11
☽/♃	10°♒13	☿/♅	15°♋17	♂/⚵	22°♏39	♅/⚴	13°♓46	⚳/⚵	05°♎31
☽/♄	17°♓33	☿/♆	18°♍05	♂/⚸	19°♑45	♅/⚵	03°♌06	⚳/⚸	02°♐38
☽/♅	08°♈07	☿/♇	23°♌29	♂/⚶	26°♎06	♅/⚸	00°♈13	⚳/⚶	08°♍59
☽/♆	10°♐56	☿/⚷	09°♌04	♂/☊	15°♐47	♅/⚶	06°♋33	⚳/☊	28°♎40
☽/♇	16°♉19	☿/⚳	17°♍42	♂/⊗	29°♒19	♅/☊	26°♒14	⚳/⊗	12°♋11
☽/⚷	01°♉54	☿/⚴	15°♏43	*♃*	17°♑31	♅/⊗	09°♉46	*⚴*	14°♑12
☽/⚳	10°♐33	☿/⚵	05°♎03	♃/♄	24°♒51	*♆*	18°♍57	⚴/⚵	03°♐32
☽/⚴	08°♒33	☿/⚸	02°♐10	♃/♅	15°♓25	♆/♇	24°♌20	⚴/⚸	00°♒39
☽/⚵	27°♐53	☿/⚶	08°♍31	♃/♆	18°♏14	♆/⚷	09°♌55	⚴/⚶	07°♏00
☽/⚸	25°♒00	☿/☊	28°♎12	♃/♇	23°♎37	♆/⚳	18°♍34	⚴/☊	26°♐41
☽/⚶	01°♊21	☿/⊗	11°♋43	♃/⚷	09°♈12	♆/⚴	16°♏34	⚴/⊗	10°♓12
☽/☊	21°♑02	*♀*	22°♌14	♃/⚳	17°♏51	♆/⚵	05°♎54	*⚵*	22°♎52
☽/⊗	04°♈33	♀/♂	22°♎19	♃/⚴	15°♑51	♆/⚸	03°♐01	⚵/⚸	19°♐59
☉	25°♍22	♀/♃	04°♏52	♃/⚵	05°♐11	♆/⚶	09°♍22	⚵/⚶	26°♍20
☉/☿	21°♍18	♀/♄	12°♊13	♃/⚸	02°♒18	♆/☊	29°♎03	⚵/☊	16°♏01
☉/♀	08°♍48	♀/♅	02°♋46	♃/⚶	08°♏39	♆/⊗	12°♋34	⚵/⊗	29°♋32
☉/♂	08°♏53	♀/♆	05°♍35	♃/☊	28°♐20	*♇*	29°♋44	*⚸*	17°♒06
☉/♃	21°♏26	♀/♇	10°♌59	♃/⊗	11°♓51	♇/⚷	15°♋19	⚸/⚶	23°♏27
☉/♄	28°♊47	♀/⚷	26°♋34	*♄*	02°♈12	♇/⚳	23°♌57	⚸/☊	13°♑08
☉/♅	19°♋20	♀/⚳	05°♍12	♄/♅	22°♈45	♇/⚴	21°♎58	⚸/⊗	26°♓39
☉/♆	22°♍09	♀/⚴	03°♏13	♄/♆	25°♊34	♇/⚵	11°♍18	*⚶*	29°♌47
☉/♇	27°♌33	♀/⚵	22°♍33	♄/♇	00°♊58	♇/⚸	08°♉25	⚶/☊	19°♎28
☉/⚷	13°♌08	♀/⚸	19°♏40	♄/⚷	16°♉33	♇/⚶	14°♌46	⚶/⊗	03°♋00
☉/⚳	21°♍46	♀/⚶	26°♌01	♄/⚳	25°♊11	♇/☊	04°♎26	*☊*	09°♐09
☉/⚴	19°♏47	♀/☊	15°♎41	♄/⚴	23°♒12	♇/⊗	17°♊58	☊/⊗	22°♒41
☉/⚵	09°♎07	♀/⊗	29°♊13	♄/⚵	12°♑32	*⚷*	00°♋54	*⊗*	06°♉12
☉/⚸	06°♐14	*♂*	22°♐25	♄/⚸	09°♓39	⚷/⚳	09°♌32		
☉/⚶	12°♍34	♂/♃	04°♑58	♄/⚶	16°♊00	⚷/⚴	07°♈33		
☉/☊	02°♏15	♂/♄	12°♒18	♄/☊	05°♒41	⚷/⚵	26°♌53		
☉/⊗	15°♋47	♂/♅	02°♓52	♄/⊗	19°♈12	⚷/⚸	24°♈00		

theme, is inconjunct Pluto and square the nodes. Late Scorpio rising places the Pleiades on his seventh house cusp. Saturn in Aries is in his fourth house, squaring Chiron in the eighth and opposite his Sun. He did have problems with his father which he had to work out. Venus in Leo in his ninth house is exactly trine his Mars. Jupiter is in Capricorn in his second house, trining Mercury, Vesta, Neptune, and Sun in Virgo as well as Uranus in Taurus, which gives him good practical abilities. His north node is on the fixed star Antares, while his Sun is on the fixed star Copula, which can also cause eye damage.

In terms of parallels of declination, the Sun is parallel Mercury and contra parallel the asteroid Juno. Jupiter is parallel the north node and contra parallel Pluto. This strong Jupiter Pluto connection shows his ability to heal and adapt to his situation.

Midpoints

Saturn/Neptune = Sun, direct—possibility of major health problems as well as healing ability

Mars/Uranus = Moon, direct—sensitive nervous system, possible accidents

Mars/Saturn = Uranus, direct—unexpected accidents that affect the body

Sun/Neptune = Mars, direct—strong intuitive ability, weak life force

Moon/Neptune = nodes, direct—problems with fluids in the body, problems that could affect the vision

Transits and Progressions

On September 10, 1942, when he had his first accident, secondary progressed Mars was square his natal Sun, while Venus was square the ascendant. Transiting Pluto was semi-square Mars. Uranus was square his Moon. Saturn was semi-square Pluto. Jupiter was opposite Jupiter. Mars was conjoined the Sun and the Sun was conjunct Mercury. On August 12, the solar eclipse was conjoined Venus, while on August 26, the lunar eclipse was exactly conjunct his Moon.

On October 9, 1948, when the paper clip went into his eye, secondary progressed Mercury was conjunct Neptune and Vesta, while Mars was inconjunct Pluto. Transiting Pluto was square Uranus. Neptune was conjoined the Mars/Pluto midpoint (direct). Uranus was conjunct Chiron. Saturn was opposing his Moon, and Jupiter was conjunct Mars. On October 18, the lunar eclipse was square his Pluto.

On June 1, 1954, when he had his surgery, progressed Mercury was conjoined his Sun and the progressed Moon was on the asteroid Juno. Transiting Pluto was conjoined Venus and trine Mars. Neptune was transiting Juno. Saturn was trine his Moon. Jupiter was conjoined Chiron and trine his Moon. The lunar eclipse on July 16 was square Juno, which is also his Jupiter-Pluto midpoint. The Jupiter Pluto midpoint indicates regeneration of the organs.

On Feb. 19, 1983, when he died from colon cancer, he had a progressed new Moon in Scorpio, with his progressed Sun and Moon at 10 degrees, opposing his sixth house Uranus. Transiting Pluto was square natal Pluto and sextile Hygeia. Neptune was sesquiquadrate Uranus, inconjunct Pluto, and trine Hygeia. Uranus and Jupiter were conjoined at 8 degrees Sagittarius on his north node. Saturn was semi-square Mercury, Vesta, and Neptune. The transiting north node was exactly trine his Moon. The day he died, there was a Venus Mars conjunction in 25 degrees Pisces, exactly opposite his Sun. The solar eclipse of December 15, 1982 was conjoined his Mars, while the lunar eclipse of December 30 was semi-square his Venus.

Case History #2

This is the case of a woman whose right eye was bad since the 1970's; it developed scar tissue and she had trouble seeing out of it. Meanwhile, her left eye was diagnosed with macular degeneration in 1991. In June of that year, her left eye also developed a cataract. In 1999, she had cataract surgery on both eyes, but still can not see out of her right eye. In 2001, she had a laser treatment which helped to stop the bleeding in the left eye. However, she has no central vision and says that she feels she is looking through a plastic film. She has not used any alternative therapies or special supplements in dealing with her eyes.

Interpretation of Horoscope

Her chart shows a Moon in Cancer near the ascendant conjoined Pluto, squaring both her Sun in Libra and Chiron in Aries. This could suggest problems with fluid balance as well as with digestion. Mars is in Sagittarius square Saturn in Virgo, which indicates problems with digestion and the liver. Jupiter in Virgo opposite Uranus in Pisces and semi-square the ascendant also suggests liver problems. Venus is in Scorpio conjoined the north node and square Neptune; there are problems assimilating carbohydrates and probably low blood sugar. Venus and the north node are also semi-square Mars in Sagittarius.

In terms of parallels of declination, Mercury is parallel Uranus, Venus, and the north node; this suggests allergies. The Moon is parallel Neptune, showing sensitivity with the eyes and immune system.

Eye Disorders—Woman
Natal Chart
Oct 4, 1920, 11:22 PM CST +6:00
Iowa City, Iowa
41N39 40 091W31 48

Geocentric
Tropical
Koch
True Node

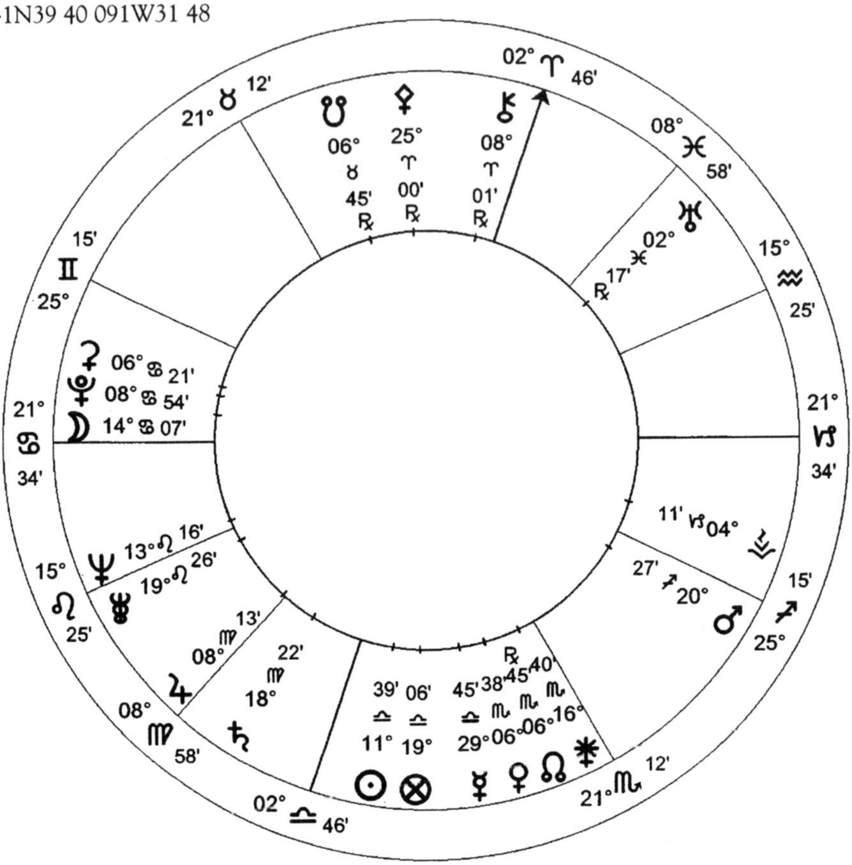

Midpoints

Saturn/Neptune = Uranus, direct—possible problems with nervous system

Mars/Neptune = Uranus, indirect—connection between immune system and nervous system

Moon/Neptune = Mercury, direct—possible problems with vision and respiratory allergies

Midpoint Listing

Eye Disorders • Woman • Natal Chart
In Planetery Sequence • Modulus 360°00'

☽	14°♋07	*☿*	29°♎45	♂/♆	16°♎51	*♅*	02°♓17	⚷/⚶	13°♊44
☽/☉	27°♌53	☿/♀	03°♏11	♂/♇	29°♍41	♅/♆	22°♉47	⚷/☊	22°♑23
☽/☿	06°♍56	☿/♂	25°♏06	♂/⚷	14°♒14	♅/♇	05°♉36	⚷/⊗	13°♑34
☽/♀	10°♍23	☿/♃	03°♎59	♂/⚳	27°♐19	♅/⚷	20°♓09	*⚳*	04°♑11
☽/♂	02°♎17	☿/♄	09°♎03	♂/⚴	22°♒43	♅/⚳	03°♒14	⚳/⚴	29°♒36
☽/♃	11°♌10	☿/♅	01°♑01	♂/⚵	03°♐33	♅/⚴	28°♓39	⚳/⚵	10°♐25
☽/♄	16°♌14	☿/♆	21°♍30	♂/⯚	28°♍24	♅/⚵	09°♑29	⚳/⯚	05°♎16
☽/♅	08°♉12	☿/♇	04°♍19	♂/⚶	19°♎56	♅/⯚	04°♉19	⚳/⚶	26°♎49
☽/♆	28°♋41	☿/⚷	18°♑53	♂/☊	28°♏36	♅/⚶	25°♉52	⚳/☊	05°♐28
☽/♇	11°♋31	☿/⚳	01°♐58	♂/⊗	19°♏46	♅/☊	04°♑31	⚳/⊗	26°♏39
☽/⚷	26°♉04	☿/⚴	27°♑22	*♃*	08°♍13	♅/⊗	25°♐42	*⚴*	25°♈00
☽/⚳	09°♎09	☿/⚵	08°♏12	♃/♄	13°♍17	*♆*	13°♌16	⚴/⚵	05°♒50
☽/⚴	04°♊34	☿/⯚	03°♍03	♃/♅	05°♐15	♆/♇	26°♋05	⚴/⯚	00°♊41
☽/⚵	15°♍23	☿/⚶	24°♍35	♃/♆	25°♌44	♆/⚷	10°♊39	⚴/⚶	22°♊13
☽/⯚	10°♋14	☿/☊	03°♏15	♃/♇	08°♌34	♆/⚳	23°♎43	⚴/☊	00°♒53
☽/⚶	01°♌47	☿/⊗	24°♎25	♃/⚷	23°♊07	♆/⚴	19°♊08	⚴/⊗	22°♋03
☽/☊	10°♍26	*♀*	06°♏38	♃/⚳	06°♏12	♆/⚵	29°♍58	*⚵*	16°♏40
☽/⊗	01°♍36	♀/♂	28°♏33	♃/⚴	01°♋36	♆/⯚	24°♋48	⚵/⯚	11°♍30
☉	11°♎39	♀/♃	07°♎26	♃/⚵	12°♎26	♆/⚶	16°♌21	⚵/⚶	03°♎03
☉/☿	20°♎42	♀/♄	12°♎30	♃/⯚	07°♌17	♆/☊	25°♍00	⚵/☊	11°♏43
☉/♀	24°♎09	♀/♅	04°♑28	♃/⚶	28°♌49	♆/⊗	16°♍11	⚵/⊗	02°♏53
☉/♂	16°♏03	♀/♆	24°♍57	♃/☊	07°♎29	*♇*	08°♋54	*⯚*	06°♋21
☉/♃	24°♍56	♀/♇	07°♍46	♃/⊗	28°♍39	♇/⚷	23°♉28	⯚/⚶	27°♋54
☉/♄	00°♎01	♀/⚷	22°♑20	*♄*	18°♍22	♇/⚳	06°♎33	⯚/☊	06°♍33
☉/♅	21°♐58	♀/⚳	05°♐25	♄/♅	10°♐20	♇/⚴	01°♊57	⯚/⊗	27°♌44
☉/♆	12°♍28	♀/⚴	00°♒49	♄/♆	00°♍49	♇/⚵	12°♍47	*⚶*	19°♌26
☉/♇	25°♌17	♀/⚵	11°♏39	♄/♇	13°♌38	♇/⯚	07°♋38	⚶/☊	28°♍06
☉/⚷	09°♑50	♀/⯚	06°♍30	♄/⚷	28°♊12	♇/⚶	29°♋10	⚶/⊗	19°♍16
☉/⚳	22°♏55	♀/⚶	28°♍02	♄/⚳	11°♏16	♇/☊	07°♍50	*☊*	06°♏45
☉/⚴	18°♋20	♀/☊	06°♏42	♄/⚴	06°♋41	♇/⊗	29°♌00	☊/⊗	27°♎56
☉/⚵	29°♎10	♀/⊗	27°♎52	♄/⚵	17°♎31	*⚷*	08°♈01	*⊗*	19°♎06
☉/⯚	24°♌00	*♂*	20°♐27	♄/⯚	12°♌21	⚷/⚳	21°♒06		
☉/⚶	15°♍33	♂/♃	29°♎20	♄/⚶	03°♍54	⚷/⚴	16°♈31		
☉/☊	24°♎12	♂/♄	04°♏24	♄/☊	12°♎34	⚷/⚵	27°♑21		
☉/⊗	15°♎23	♂/♅	26°♑22	♄/⊗	03°♎44	⚷/⯚	22°♉11		

Transits and Progressions

In June 1991, when the cataracts began, secondary progressed Mars was opposite Neptune. Transiting Neptune and Uranus were opposing her Moon. Saturn was square Venus and the north node. Jupiter was conjunct Neptune. On June 27, the lunar eclipse was conjoined her sixth house Vesta; on July 11, the solar eclipse was conjoined the Moon.

In May 1999, when she had cataract surgery, progressed Venus was opposite Neptune. Transiting Pluto was square her Jupiter. Neptune was square Venus and the nodes. Saturn was conjoined the south node. The July 28 lunar eclipse was square her nodes and Venus.

In August 2001, when she had laser surgery which helped her left eye, transiting Pluto was sextile her Sun. Neptune was square her Venus and nodes. Mars was square Saturn.

SUPPLEMENT RECOMMENDATIONS FOR EYE DISORDERS

Vitamin A is one of the most important nutrients for the eyes. Preformed vitamin A, known as retinol, is found in animal products with its highest concentration in liver and fish liver oils. Beta carotene or provitamin A is found in yellow and orange colored vegetables and fruits, and also green leafy vegetables. Both sources should be taken through foods and in capsules.

Vitamin B-2 or Riboflavin helps the cells utilize oxygen and is important in maintaining good vision as well as in healthy hair, skin, and nails. Riboflavin is produced from intestinal bacteria, so it is important to take a good probiotic as well. It is found in high amounts in organic liver, other organ meats, oily fish such as mackerel, trout, and sardines, as well as in dark leafy green vegetables.

Vitamin D or Calciferol is manufactured in the human skin when it is in contact with the sun's ultraviolet rays. Taking vitamin D along with vitamin A has helped in studies regarding cataracts and other visual problems. D-3 or natural vitamin D is found in fish liver oil, eggs, butter, organic liver, and oily fish such as mackerel, salmon, and sardines. Plant foods are low in vitamin D so vegetarians need to get it from the sun. Supplementation with cod liver oil or other vitamin D and A capsules is important.

Bioflavonoids or Vitamin P support the immune system and circulation as well as protect the body from radiation. Bioflavonoids help with chemical substances in the air, which often affect the eyes, as do other allergic reactions. Bioflavonoids are found in citrus fruit, rose hips, and the grain buckwheat, which is a good source of rutin. There are many supplements which have bioflavonoids, especially quercitin, which is important for allergies.

Vitamin B Complex is manufactured in the large intestine from intestinal bacteria. The B vitamins are important in the normal functioning of the nervous system; they help relax those who are under stress. Since so many eye conditions are caused by stress, having adequate B complex is important.

HERBAL RECOMMENDATIONS

Alfalfa is a very nutritious herb and contains the essential amino acids. It is also high in vitamin A and chlorophyll, and has a very alkaline effect on the body.

Eyebright is used both internally and as a compress for stinging eyes, conjunctivitis, and other allergic conditions of the eyes. Internally, it is often mixed with golden seal powder and elder flower; for allergic conditions it is combined with ephedra. As a compress, eyebright may be mixed with golden seal powder.

CHAPTER 15

Arthritis

ARTHRITIS HAS BECOME ONE OF THE CHIEF causative factors of chronic disability in the world. Many arthritis sufferers have found release in recent years by working with biological medicine, including cleansing, diet, and herbs; as a result, they have been able to regain their health rather than be in constant pain. For those who are using cortisone and gold treatments, unfortunately, there havc been difficult side effects.

Arthritis refers to over one hundred different types of joint diseases, though **osteoarthritis** and **rheumatoid arthritis** have become the most widespread. Rheumatism refers to any pain in the joints or muscles. The joints become inflamed, enlarged, and swollen; the cartilage loses its elasticity, becoming dry and brittle while the ligaments and muscles which surround the joint may also become inflamed. Swelling and pain also increases during motion.

Rheumatoid arthritis is a disease of the auto-immune system, where the system attacks itself. This is the most painful and crippling form of arthritis where one or more joints become swollen or inflamed. Later, there can be degeneration of the joint with possible deformity and immobility. Osteoarthritis is much less crippling because it does not cause the two bone surfaces to fuse and immobilize the joint.

Other common types of arthritis include:

Lupus, a disease of the connective tissue producing changes in the structure and function of the skin, joints, and internal organs; **Spondylitis**, which is caused by an inflammation of the joints of one or more vertebrae; **Gout**, which results from a defect in body chemistry that leads to high blood levels of uric acid and forms needle-like crystals in the joint; **Bursitis**, which is the inflammation of a bursa, the sac like structure resembling a joint, located between the skin and bone in places where the skin rubs over the bone.

Among the factors leading to arthritis are prolonged periods of stress. These periods lead to adrenal exhaustion as well as malfunctioning of other glands of the endocrine system. When the glands are no longer able to produce sufficient hormones, a severe imbalance results. This hormonal imbalance, in combination with a very acidic body and toxins that are not being discharged by the liver, affects the structure of various tissues.

PSYCHOLOGICAL FACTORS

Many arthritis patients have difficulty expressing their anger; they turn their anger inward and it often manifests as pain. One arthritic client mentioned that her physical therapist used to insult her while he was working on her so that she would release her anger.

Often these individuals feel a strong sense of duty and responsibility. A friend who has lupus was supporting her daughter, since her ex-husband did not make enough money; she was also called upon to help support her father, which she felt compelled to do, even though her two brothers could have helped.

Another trait is an exaggerated sense of orderliness, tidiness, and precision. They are not very flexible and sometimes have trouble adapting to new people and circumstances.

The arthritic personality has a strong sense of service; they may go to extremes of self sacrifice in order to serve others. A client with osteoarthritis lives with her ninety year old mother and takes care of her in the evenings, though she does have some help during the day.

Many arthritis patients have had a difficult childhood; often the father was extremely authoritarian and cold, resulting in a strong attachment to the mother. Sometimes the mother was also distant. There was much anxiety in adolescence and sexuality was often inhibited. Both women and men experienced sexual problems in their marriage.

Although these characteristics may be present for many years, it usually takes a catalyst such as the death of a loved one, (especially the mother), difficulty in one's marriage, problems at work, increased responsibilities, and other stressful situations for the physical symptoms of arthritis to begin.

Once the disease begins to manifest, other psychological complications appear. Feelings of inferiority connected with the body increase as well as dependency on others due to limited mobility. Depending on others for food and transportation also leads to a loss of self esteem. Getting sufficient physical exercise, which relieves tension, becomes more difficult as well as the ability to express emotions through the body, such as jumping for joy.

ASTROLOGICAL FACTORS

Many arthritis patients have a strong Saturn in their charts; it is often angular, or conjoined the Sun or Moon. Several planets in Capricorn may also be present. One client who has had osteoarthritis for many years has a Moon conjoined Saturn in Capricorn.

Another theme is the Virgo-Pisces theme—strong service and self sacrifice. Often these signs are found on the angles, or several planets may be in these signs. Neptune is often angular as well, since Neptune rules the immune system, which is related particularly to rheumatoid arthritis. There is often an interchange between the planets Mars, Saturn, and Neptune. All three may be involved in a T square or Neptune may equal the Mars/Saturn midpoint, Saturn the Mars/Neptune midpoint, or Mars the Saturn/Neptune midpoint. These combinations tend to emphasize the tendency to be self sacrificing as well as the quality of frustration.

MIDPOINTS

Important midpoints to consider for arthritis are the following general health midpoints:

Saturn/Neptune—is considered the cardinal point of disease, but is also related to the immune system

Mars/Saturn—refers to the body's structure, as well as to the inhibition or restriction of some bodily function

Mars/Neptune—refers to toxic conditions within the body, allergies, chemical sensitivities, and is also related to the immune system

CASE HISTORIES

Case History #1

This is a woman who has been dealing with rheumatoid arthritis for about six years now, but by using various alternative healing methods, is learning to control her symptoms. In 1995, she started having pain in her shoulders. She was diagnosed as having a somewhat elevated RH factor. At this same time, she was also diagnosed as having an interstitial lung illness, which gave her a chronic cough. She worked with Chinese herbs, acupuncture, and then had some lymph drainage done. A few years later, she worked with a naturopathic doctor who found she had parasites and some yeast. She did some cleansing and took supplements, which helped to rid her of parasites. Her arthritis has given her some difficulty walking. In the winter of 2001, she developed a bad case of pneumonia and had to use antibiotics. She also developed a chronic cough from the pneumonia. Currently, she is using herbs, getting B-12 shots weekly, and taking supplements for her immune system and low thyroid.

Interpretation of Horoscope

This chart shows Gemini rising with the ruler Mercury conjoined her Sagittarian Sun in the seventh house. Sun and Mercury are also square her Moon Neptune in Virgo, which indicates not only a very sensitive immune system, but also problems with the respiratory system. Mars is exactly square Pluto, which could give her the tendency to anemia. Venus is conjoined the north node in the sixth house and opposite Uranus, which shows an erratic thyroid. Saturn is semi-square Jupiter, indicating that there may be some restrictions on her liver functioning. She has several grand trines in earth with Moon Neptune in Virgo, Uranus, Ceres, and south node in Taurus, and Vesta in Capricorn. She is an avid gardener, grows a lot of vegetables and herbs, and spends some of her time in community service.

In terms of declination, her Sun is parallel Mercury, and Venus is contra-parallel Uranus and Chiron. Sun parallel Mercury again indicates weak lungs and respiratory problems. Venus contra parallel Uranus points to erratic thyroid functioning.

Midpoints

Saturn/Neptune = nodes and Venus, indirect—possible problems with thyroid and blood sugar

Arthritis—Woman 1
Natal Chart
Dec 13, 1938, 4:03 PM EST +5:00
Williamsport
41N14 28 077W00 05

Geocentric
Tropical
Koch
True Node

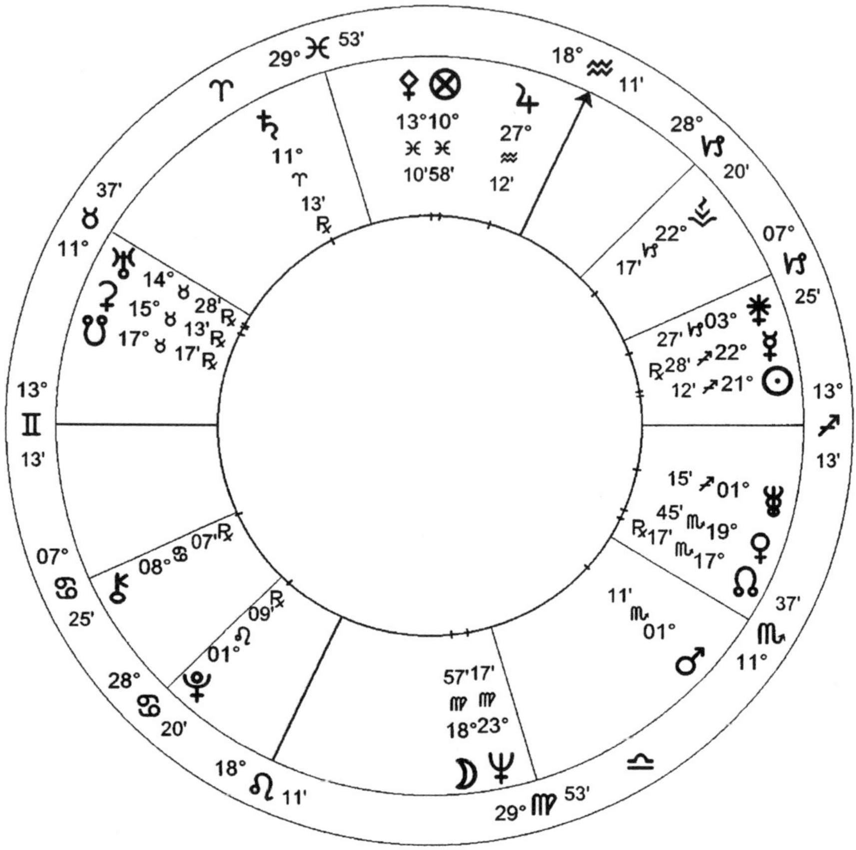

Mars/Neptune = Saturn, direct and Jupiter, indirect—immune system deficiencies and liver toxicity

Mars/Saturn = Vesta, direct—possible problems with digestive system

Transits and Progressions

In 1995, when her symptoms first started, transiting Pluto was exactly square

Midpoint Listing

Arthritis • Woman 1 • Natal Chart
In Planetery Sequence • Modulus 360°00'

☽	18°♍57	*☿*	22°♐28	♂/♆	12°♎14	*♅*	14°♉28	⚷/⚸	19°♍41
☽/☉	05°♏05	☿/♀	06°♐06	♂/♇	16°♍10	♅/♆	18°♋53	⚷/☊	12°♍42
☽/☿	05°♏43	☿/♂	26°♏49	♂/⚷	04°♍39	♅/♇	22°♊49	⚷/⊗	09°♉32
☽/♀	19°♎21	☿/♃	24°♑50	♂/⚳	11°♐44	♅/⚷	11°♊18	*⚳*	22°♑17
☽/♂	10°♎04	☿/♄	16°♒51	♂/⚴	07°♑11	♅/⚳	18°♓23	⚳/⚴	17°♒44
☽/♃	08°♐04	☿/♅	03°♓28	♂/⚵	02°♐19	♅/⚴	13°♈49	⚳/⚵	12°♑52
☽/♄	00°♋05	☿/♆	07°♏53	♂/⚶	08°♌12	♅/⚵	08°♓58	⚳/⚶	18°♓45
☽/♅	16°♋43	☿/♇	11°♎49	♂/⚸	16°♏13	♅/⚶	14°♉50	⚳/⚸	26°♐46
☽/♆	21°♍07	☿/⚷	00°♎17	♂/☊	09°♏14	♅/⚸	22°♒52	⚳/☊	19°♐47
☽/♇	25°♌03	☿/⚳	07°♑22	♂/⊗	06°♑04	♅/☊	15°♒53	⚳/⊗	16°♒37
☽/⚷	13°♌32	☿/⚴	02°♒49	*♃*	27°♒12	♅/⊗	12°♈43	*⚴*	13°♓10
☽/⚳	20°♏37	☿/⚵	27°♐58	♃/♄	19°♓12	*♆*	23°♍17	⚴/⚵	08°♒19
☽/⚴	16°♐04	☿/⚶	03°♓50	♃/♅	05°♈50	♆/♇	27°♌13	⚴/⚶	14°♈12
☽/⚵	11°♏12	☿/⚸	11°♐52	♃/♆	10°♐14	♆/⚷	15°♌42	⚴/⚸	22°♑13
☽/⚶	17°♋05	☿/☊	04°♐53	♃/♇	14°♉10	♆/⚳	22°♏47	⚴/☊	15°♑14
☽/⚸	25°♎06	☿/⊗	01°♒43	♃/⚷	02°♉39	♆/⚴	18°♐14	⚴/⊗	12°♓04
☽/☊	18°♎07	*♀*	19°♏45	♃/⚳	09°♒44	♆/⚵	13°♏22	*⚵*	03°♑27
☽/⊗	14°♐58	♀/♂	10°♏28	♃/⚴	05°♓11	♆/⚶	19°♋15	⚵/⚶	09°♓20
☉	21°♐12	♀/♃	08°♑28	♃/⚵	00°♒19	♆/⚸	27°♎16	⚵/⚸	17°♐21
☉/☿	21°♐50	♀/♄	00°♒29	♃/⚶	06°♈12	♆/☊	20°♎17	⚵/☊	10°♐22
☉/♀	05°♐29	♀/♅	17°♒07	♃/⚸	14°♑13	♆/⊗	17°♐07	⚵/⊗	07°♒12
☉/♂	26°♏12	♀/♆	21°♎31	♃/☊	07°♑14	*♇*	01°♌09	*⚶*	15°♉13
☉/♃	24°♑12	♀/♇	25°♍27	♃/⊗	04°♓05	♇/⚷	19°♋38	⚶/⚸	23°♒14
☉/♄	16°♒13	♀/⚷	13°♍56	*♄*	11°♈13	♇/⚳	26°♎43	⚶/☊	16°♒15
☉/♅	02°♓50	♀/⚳	21°♐01	♄/♅	27°♈51	♇/⚴	22°♉10	⚶/⊗	13°♈05
☉/♆	07°♏15	♀/⚴	16°♑28	♄/♆	02°♋15	♇/⚵	17°♎18	*⚸*	01°♐15
☉/♇	11°♎11	♀/⚵	11°♐36	♄/♇	06°♊11	♇/⚶	23°♊11	⚸/☊	24°♏16
☉/⚷	29°♍39	♀/⚶	17°♒29	♄/⚷	24°♉40	♇/⚸	01°♎12	⚸/⊗	21°♑06
☉/⚳	06°♑44	♀/⚸	25°♏30	♄/⚳	01°♓45	♇/☊	24°♍13	*☊*	17°♏17
☉/⚴	02°♒11	♀/☊	18°♏31	♄/⚴	27°♓12	♇/⊗	21°♉03	☊/⊗	14°♑08
☉/⚵	27°♐20	♀/⊗	15°♑21	♄/⚵	22°♒20	*⚷*	08°♋07	*⊗*	10°♓58
☉/⚶	03°♓12	*♂*	01°♏11	♄/⚶	28°♈13	⚷/⚳	15°♈12		
☉/⚸	11°♐14	♂/♃	29°♐11	♄/⚸	06°♒14	⚷/⚴	10°♉39		
☉/☊	04°♐15	♂/♄	21°♑12	♄/☊	29°♑15	⚷/⚵	05°♎47		
☉/⊗	01°♒05	♂/♅	07°♌50	♄/⊗	26°♓06	⚷/⚶	11°♊40		

her Jupiter, indicating the need to cleanse her liver. Uranus was opposite her Pluto and square her Mars. Saturn was square her Sun and Mercury, relating to the lung problems. Neptune was conjoined Vesta, which is her Mars/Saturn midpoint. Neptune on this midpoint refers to the immune system and body structure. The lunar eclipse on October 8 was conjoined natal Saturn, while the solar eclipse on October 24 was conjoined Mars and square Pluto.

In February 2001, when she got pneumonia badly in the winter, transiting Pluto was conjoined her seventh house and opposite her ascendant. Neptune was sesquiquadrate her Sun Mercury conjunction, affecting both her immune system and lungs. Uranus was square her Venus and nodes. Saturn was square Jupiter, showing some possible problems with the liver. The solar eclipse of December 25, 2000, was semisquare her Venus north node conjunction, while the lunar eclipse of January 9, 2001 was conjoined the Mars/Saturn midpoint.

Case History #2

This case is that of a woman with osteoarthritis whose arthritic symptoms started in her early 60's. Her right knee was particularly bad for a long time and she took various types of pain relievers. She also has had other health problems involving her digestive system, and her lungs, with frequent congestion and coughing as well as respiratory allergies. In 2000, her back got very bad; she took a series of cortisone injections for six weeks which seemed to help. In 2001, her shoulder started bothering her. She does take a few vitamin and mineral supplements along with her medications and on occasion, sees a chiropractor.

Interpretation of Horoscope

Her Virgo Sun is opposite Uranus in Pisces, which is exactly on the MC. This indicates a very sensitive nervous system with a lot of electrical energy running through the body, which could also affect the heart. (In fact, she had some heart problems a few years ago that doctors thought was a minor heart attack.) The Sagittarius Moon is in the sixth house conjoined Mars and is in a T-square with Mercury and the nodes. This shows problems with the respiratory system as well as with the liver and digestive system. There is a tendency here, as well, for allergies from inhalants such as pollens. The liver can become very toxic with the Moon and Mars in Sagittarius in the sixth house; it would be important to cleanse the liver in order to avoid allergies. The Moon is also sesquiquadrate Neptune, indicating a very sensitive immune system. Cancer is rising with the planet Pluto not far from the ascendant. Cancer rising also indicates a sensitive stomach, and with all the Virgo influence, the digestive system needs constant care. Pluto is square Saturn in Libra, and also more broadly, the Chiron Jupiter opposition in Aries and Libra, which shows challenges and lessons through relationship. Saturn is conjoined the north node, and closely square the ascendant, which can indicate the need for a lot of calcium, and the tendency to arthritis. Venus is conjoined Jupiter in Libra, pointing to a very creative nature as well as low blood sugar, which she does have. The Venus Jupiter conjunction is opposite Chiron and sextile both Neptune and the Moon Mars conjunction. In addition to creativity, this also shows a lot of support and harmony from her family.

In terms of parallels of declination, the Sun is parallel Chiron and Juno, while being contra parallel to Venus, Jupiter, and Uranus. This shows her sensitive nervous system, tendency to low blood sugar, and liver toxicity. The Moon is contra-parallel Vesta, pointing to possible digestive problems.

Midpoints

Saturn/Neptune = Uranus, direct—problems with nervous system and electrical conductivity system

Mars/Saturn = Neptune, direct—weak vitality and few resources to combat toxins that might affect the immune system

Mars/Neptune = Jupiter, direct—difficulties digesting carbohydrates, problems with the liver

Mars/Pluto = ascendant, direct, and Neptune, indirect—the need to regenerate the immune system

Transits and Progressions

In the early spring of 1983, her arthritis began with a knee problem. At the time her secondary progressed Moon was conjoined natal Uranus in Pisces. Transiting Pluto was sesquiquadrate Uranus and sextile her Moon. Neptune was conjoined her natal Moon and exactly square the nodes. Uranus was square her Sun. Saturn was hitting her Mars/Uranus midpoint (direct). Jupiter was square both Uranus and her Sun. The solar eclipse of December 15, 1982 was conjoined her Mars while the lunar eclipse on December 30 was hitting her natal Pluto.

In January 2000, when her back started bothering her, secondary progressed Vesta was conjoined her Sun while progressed Venus was square her Sun. Transiting Pluto was square Uranus. Neptune was

Arthritis—Woman 2
Natal Chart
Aug 31, 1922, 0:35 AM CST +6:00
Kansas City
39N05 59 094W34 42

Geocentric
Tropical
Koch
True Node

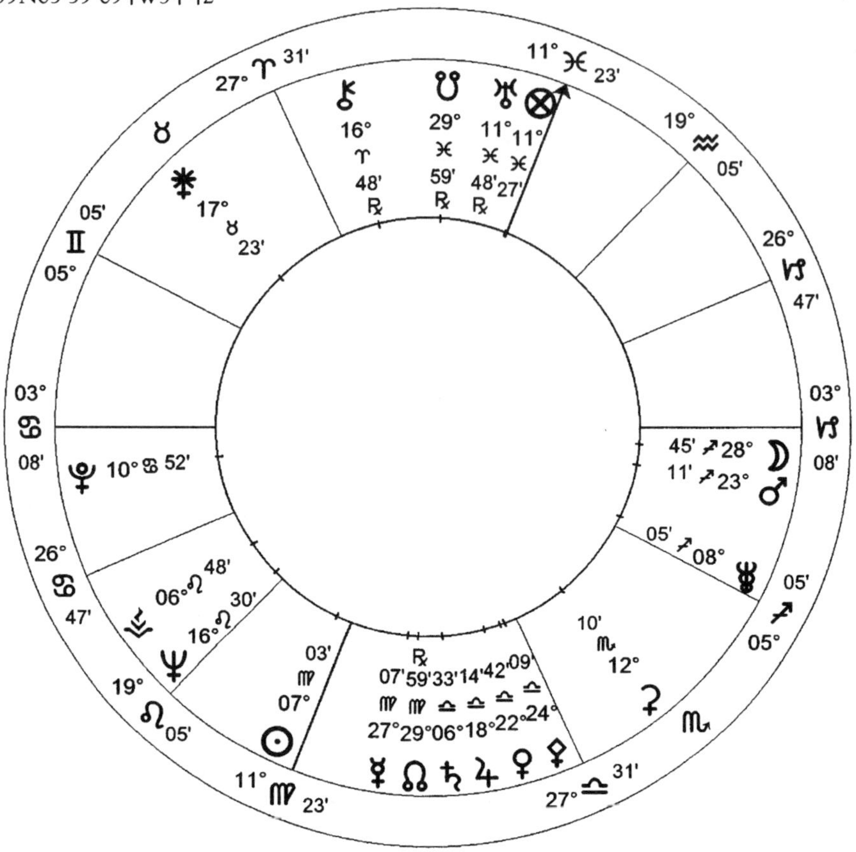

hitting the Mars/Uranus midpoint (direct). Uranus was opposite Neptune. Saturn was opposite Ceres and sextile Pluto. Jupiter was inconjunct Mercury. The solar eclipse of February 5 was exactly opposite her natal Neptune.

TREATMENTS FOR ARTHRITIS

1. The most important treatment for arthritis is cleansing. To get rid of toxic wastes and strengthen the immune system, colonic irrigations and

Midpoint Listing

Arthritis • Woman 2 • Natal Chart

In Planetery Sequence • Modulus 360°00'

☽	28°♐45	*☿*	27°♍07	♂/♆	19°♎50	*♅*	11°♓48	⚷/⚶	12°♒27
☽/☉	02°♏54	☿/♀	09°♎55	♂/♇	02°♎01	♅/♆	29°♉09	⚷/☊	08°♋23
☽/☿	12°♏56	☿/♂	10°♏09	♂/⚷	19°♒59	♅/♇	11°♉20	⚷/⊗	29°♓07
☽/♀	25°♏44	☿/♃	07°♎40	♂/⚳	14°♎59	♅/⚷	29°♓18	*⚳*	06°♌48
☽/♂	25°♐58	☿/♄	01°♎50	♂/⚴	23°♏40	♅/⚳	24°♉18	⚳/⚴	15°♍29
☽/♃	23°♏30	☿/♅	19°♐27	♂/⚵	05°♓17	♅/⚴	02°♑59	⚳/⚵	27°♊06
☽/♄	17°♏39	☿/♆	06°♍48	♂/?	02°♐40	♅/⚵	14°♈35	⚳/?	24°♍29
☽/♅	05°♒16	☿/♇	19°♌00	♂/⚶	15°♐38	♅/?	11°♑59	⚳/⚶	07°♎27
☽/♆	22°♎38	☿/⚷	06°♋57	♂/☊	11°♏35	♅/⚶	24°♑56	⚳/☊	03°♍23
☽/♇	04°♎49	☿/⚳	01°♍58	♂/⊗	02°♒19	♅/☊	20°♐53	⚳/⊗	24°♉07
☽/⚷	22°♒46	☿/⚴	10°♎38	*♃*	18°♎14	♅/⊗	11°♓37	*⚴*	24°♎09
☽/⚳	17°♎47	☿/⚵	22°♋15	♃/♄	12°♎24	*♆*	16°♌30	⚴/⚵	05°♌46
☽/⚴	26°♏27	☿/?	19°♎39	♃/♅	00°♑01	♆/♇	28°♋41	⚴/?	03°♏10
☽/⚵	08°♓04	☿/⚶	02°♏36	♃/♆	17°♍22	♆/⚷	16°♊39	⚴/⚶	16°♏07
☽/?	05°♐28	☿/☊	28°♍33	♃/♇	29°♌33	♆/⚳	11°♌39	⚴/☊	12°♎04
☽/⚶	18°♐25	☿/⊗	19°♐17	♃/⚷	17°♑31	♆/⚴	20°♍20	⚴/⊗	02°♑48
☽/☊	14°♏22	*♀*	22°♎42	♃/⚳	12°♍31	♆/⚵	01°♋56	*⚵*	17°♉23
☽/⊗	05°♒06	♀/♂	22°♏56	♃/⚴	21°♎12	♆/?	29°♍20	⚵/?	14°♌47
☉	07°♍03	♀/♃	20°♎28	♃/⚵	02°♌48	♆/⚶	12°♎18	⚵/⚶	27°♒44
☉/☿	17°♍05	♀/♄	14°♎38	♃/?	00°♏12	♆/☊	08°♍14	⚵/☊	23°♋41
☉/♀	29°♍53	♀/♅	02°♑15	♃/⚶	13°♏10	♆/⊗	28°♉58	⚵/⊗	14°♈25
☉/♂	00°♏07	♀/♆	19°♍36	♃/☊	09°♎06	*♇*	10°♋52	*?*	12°♏10
☉/♃	27°♍39	♀/♇	01°♍47	♃/⊗	29°♐50	♇/⚷	28°♉50	?/⚶	25°♏08
☉/♄	21°♍48	♀/⚷	19°♑45	*♄*	06°♎33	♇/⚳	23°♋50	?/☊	21°♎05
☉/♅	09°♊26	♀/⚳	14°♍45	♄/♅	24°♐10	♇/⚴	02°♍31	?/⊗	11°♑48
☉/♆	26°♌47	♀/⚴	23°♎26	♄/♆	11°♍32	♇/⚵	14°♊08	*⚶*	08°♐05
☉/♇	08°♌58	♀/⚵	05°♌03	♄/♇	23°♌43	♇/?	11°♍31	⚶/☊	04°♏02
☉/⚷	26°♊56	♀/?	02°♏26	♄/⚷	11°♋40	♇/⚶	24°♍29	⚶/⊗	24°♑46
☉/⚳	21°♌56	♀/⚶	15°♏24	♄/⚳	06°♍41	♇/☊	20°♌26	*☊*	29°♍59
☉/⚴	00°♎36	♀/☊	11°♎21	♄/⚴	15°♎21	♇/⊗	11°♉09	☊/⊗	20°♐43
☉/⚵	12°♋13	♀/⊗	02°♑04	♄/⚵	26°♋58	*⚷*	16°♈48	*⊗*	11°♓27
☉/?	09°♎37	*♂*	23°♐11	♄/?	24°♎22	⚷/⚳	11°♊48		
☉/⚶	22°♎34	♂/♃	20°♏42	♄/⚶	07°♏19	⚷/⚴	20°♑29		
☉/☊	18°♍31	♂/♄	14°♏52	♄/☊	03°♎16	⚷/⚵	02°♉05		
☉/⊗	09°♊15	♂/♅	02°♒29	♄/⊗	24°♐00	⚷/?	29°♑29		

high enemas are important, as well as saunas, particularly infra red saunas which help to clear toxic metals such as mercury and lead.

2. One of the major physiological problems of the arthritis patient is an extremely acidic body. There is a strong need to make the body more alkaline. A broth made of potato peels is very alkalinizing as is parsley tea. There are several supplements that also help to alkalinize the body; these contain potassium and sodium bicarbonate and are called Pleo-alkala, Alkala base, and similar names.

3. Occasional liquid fasts for a few days with soup broths, vegetable juices, and herb teas will aid the cleansing process. Fruit juices should not be used as they are too acidic.
4. Exercises for the joints and limbs are necessary to increase mobility and loosen the muscles. Swimming is excellent for the arthritic patient as water is very relaxing. Yoga exercises are also good since they work with the breath and relaxation.
5. Physical therapies that break up old patterns of body armoring and crystallization are helpful.
6. Soaking the limbs in a hot epsom salts solution is helpful (one half pound of epsom salts in a large basin). Also, rubbing a mixture of peanut oil and jojoba oil on sore joints aids in dissolving some of the crystallized material. Castor oil packs, made by heating the castor oil and dipping a flannel cloth in it, can be applied to the affected area.

SUPPLEMENT RECOMMENDATIONS FOR ARTHRITIS

Calcium/Magnesium is most important, preferably in a liquid or powdered form that will assimilate in the body. Capsules may be opened. Calcium/Magnesium should be taken in generous doses three times a day, but not with meals—early morning, mid-afternoon, and before bed are good times.

Bioflavonoids help circulation, which is extremely important for arthritis patients. They also work with the immune system and would be used in significant amounts by those with rheumatoid arthritis.

B-complex helps to balance the nervous system and is important for stress. It is also necessary in producing intestinal bacteria.

Pantothenic Acid is an important supplement for the adrenals. The adrenal glands produce cortisone and other adrenal hormones to combat stress.

Niacin or B-3 stimulates circulation and is helpful with stimulating blood flow in the capillaries. Depending on the individual's reaction to niacin, it should be taken in small amounts at first.

Vitamin E is a strong antioxidant; it helps to prevent free radicals that lead to chronic inflammation, and also increases stamina.

L-phenylalanine—The D and DL forms of phenylalanine, which are good for depression, also work as pain relievers. For pain, DL phenylalanine should be taken several times a day.

Evening Primrose oil is a source of GLA; GLA helps the immune system and also has an anti-inflammatory effect.

Zinc is very important for the immune system; it can increase the production of T lymphocytes.

MSM is a sulfur compound that has anti-inflammatory and antioxidant properties.

Chondroitin Sulfate and **Glucosamine Sulfate** help alleviate joint problems; they also aid in reducing potential inflammation. Chondrotin and glucosamine should be used in combination.

HERBAL RECOMMENDATIONS

Devil's claw is helpful in cases where there is inflammation and pain as it acts as an anti-inflammatory.

Wintergreen and **willow** contain salicylic acid which aids in relieving pain.

Comfrey and **borage** are high in calcium and magnesium and can be made in mixtures with **alfalfa**, which contains all the amino acids and helps to alkalinize the body.

Sarsaparilla root is helpful for rheumatoid arthritis.

CHAPTER 16

Alcoholism and Drug Addiction

ALCOHOLICS AND DRUG ADDICTS SUFFER from similar problems, both physiologically and psychologically. They often come from broken homes where one or more parents have been alcoholic or addicted to some substance. Most of them have not received any nurturing in life and have had to face the world alone. Alcohol or some substance often makes this seem easier.

Biochemically, they have certain imbalances. Alcoholics are hypoglycemic; they have low blood sugar and require certain nutrients which enable them to secrete the necessary hormones to maintain their blood sugar level. If they don't get these nutrients, they crave alcohol. Once they stop using alcohol, they usually crave sugar, unless their bodies are being balanced with the correct nutrients.

In his book, *Alcoholism and Nutrition*, Dr. Roger Williams speaks of the genetotrophic problems. "A genetotrophic difficulty is one that stems from the possession of some unusually high nutritional requirement of genetic origin coupled with the failure to meet the need. The deficiency which results from using significant amounts of alcohol weakens the regulatory tissues in the hypothalamus and enhances the poisoning effect of alcohol on these tissues. This, in turn, impairs the appetite controlling centers.

Besides creating nutritional deficiencies, the liver and other organs can be severely damaged by the use of alcohol and drugs. As alcohol and drugs are absorbed through the stomach, they go through the bloodstream to the liver. By attempting to convert them to harmless substances, the liver becomes very toxic.

Habit forming drugs like cocaine, heroin, morphine, amphetamines, nicotine, and caffeine make the body feel good through being "high" or ecstatic, eliminating pain, getting quick energy, or sedating the nervous system. Drug addicts, like alcoholics, eat little food and gradually develop extreme deficiencies of vitamins, minerals, and essential hormones.

PSYCHOLOGICAL FACTORS

Most alcoholics and drug addicts are depressed individuals who feel alone in the world and are unable to develop relationships with others. They also feel alienated from society and have a great deal of anxiety and insecurity. In many cases, they have not received much stability from their families. Alcohol or a drug enables them to withdraw into their own worlds, where they become unrealistic and dream of possibilities that do not exist for them.

Illness often leads to alcoholism or drug addiction. When pain is involved, morphine or another pain killing drug may be used, whose side effects are so pleasant that it becomes addictive.

Sensitive emotional people often turn to drugs for a numbing effect. In time, they no longer feel their emotional pain and have diverted their energy to obtaining drugs that help them stay numb.

Poverty is another contributing factor since many, who are not trained vocationally and who have been poor, turn to drug dealing as a way of making money. They also become heavy users through dealing. Alcoholics and drug addicts share qualities of impatience and an inability to endure difficult times. They often lack discipline and have anger directed against family, friends, or society. They may feel that their talents have not been recognized and wallow in self-pity.

ASTROLOGICAL PATTERNS

Alcoholics and drug addicts share a strong Neptunian influence. Neptune may be angular, conjoined the Sun or Moon, or there may be several Pisces or twelfth house planets. Hard aspects between the Moon and Neptune are prevalent, which indicate a sensitive nature, lack of emotional clarity, and also low blood sugar. A Moon Neptune hard aspect may also indicate a mother who was alcoholic or addicted to drugs. Saturn Neptune hard aspects also appear in many cases; Neptune makes the Saturnian boundaries fuzzy and more challenging in dealing with realistic situations.

Jupiter and Neptune hard aspects are also common; Jupiter expands the Neptunian effect and also rules the liver and pancreas. This aspect can indicate hypoglycemia, as well as the tendency of the liver to become toxic. It also can relate to allergies as well as to chemical sensitivities. Hard aspects between Venus and Neptune are found in these charts as well. Venus Neptune is often under emotional illusions, which likes sweet foods and substances that make them feel good. In addition, Venus Neptune relates to low blood sugar.

About one third of the horoscopes studied have hard aspects between Mars and Neptune, Mercury and Neptune, and Sun and Neptune. Mars Neptune hard aspects can indicate trouble with manifesting goals, a sense of inferiority, and lowered vitality. On the other hand, those with Mars Neptune are often very psychically attuned, good musicians and poets, photographers, and artists. Mercury Neptune hard aspects may relate to muddled thinking, having unrealistic ideas, and also being very sensitive to various allergens. With Mercury Neptune, one can be very intuitive and perceptive. Sun Neptune hard aspects may indicate an alcoholic father or family background. They may also show a lack of vitality. Sometimes an individual with this aspect works hard to integrate spirituality into her life; sometimes one becomes a martyr or victim with alcohol or drugs providing an escape.

In addition to Neptune, Pluto is often angular. A strong Plutonian theme is found in the horoscopes of those who are drug dealers or drug users. Drug dealing has its underworld mafia type associations. Many drug users are often seeking deep transformations.

Jupiter is also emphasized by being angular or conjoined the Sun, Moon, or another planet. Jupiter rules the liver and pancreas, which are the organs most affected by alcohol and drugs, especially as these individuals usually have low blood sugar and lack pancreatic enzymes. Jupiter also relates to excess.

Other characteristics these horoscopes share are a predominance of Moon and ascendant in fixed signs. Since the Moon has to do with habit patterns, this implies habits that are deep rooted and difficult to break.

Degree areas given by Charles Carter on alcoholism include 9 degrees and 25 degrees of the fixed signs and 11 degrees of the cardinals. These degrees were found in about half of the horoscopes studied with the Sun, Moon, and Saturn in one of these degrees.

MIDPOINTS

In addition to the midpoints generally used in health conditions, it is important to check out the following:

Sun/Neptune—indicates craving for drugs and narcotic stimulants as well as fluid concentration in the cells

Moon/Neptune—may point to illusions and self-deception as well as over accumulation of water in the fluids of the body

Jupiter/Neptune—suggests a conflict between reality and illusion as well as lack of tone in the organs of the body

Midpoint combinations most frequently seen are:

Saturn/Neptune = Sun—indicates a weak vitality and sensitive physical vehicle

Saturn/Neptune = Moon—shows both emotional sensitivity and depression

Saturn/Neptune = Jupiter—suggests problems with the liver and pancreas

Jupiter/Neptune = Sun, Moon, or ascendant—may point to a very idealistic nature, a tendency to live in a somewhat unreal world, and malfunctioning of the liver and pancreas

Mars/Neptune = Mercury—points to nervous conditions resulting from alcohol or drugs

Mars/Neptune = ascendant—usually manifests as low energy or difficulty in asserting oneself

CASE HISTORIES

Case History #1

This woman started drinking when she was 13 years old and by the time she was a junior in high school, was drinking heavily and using speed.

Alcoholic—Woman
Natal Chart
Jan 7, 1960, 10:50 AM EST +5:00
Herkimer
43N01 32 074W59 11

Geocentric
Tropical
Koch
True Node

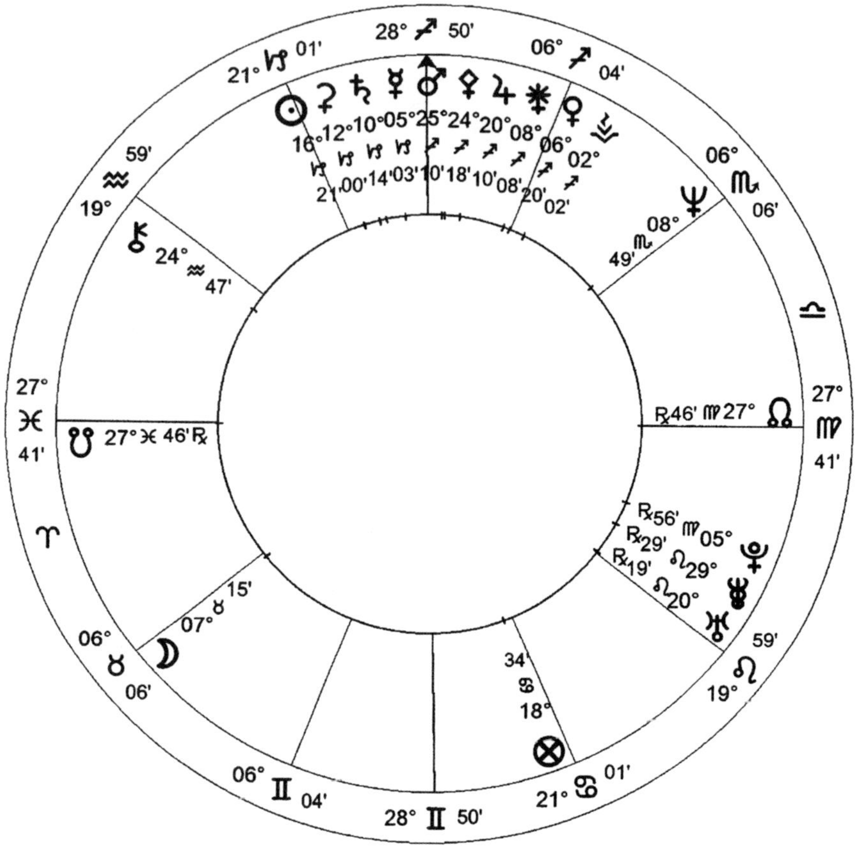

During her senior year, she experimented with LSD and other drugs as well. She always managed to keep a job while she was drinking. In 1987 and 1988, she was in an abusive relationship and drinking heavily. Her partner hit her in the head with a steel rod and she had a major concussion. She finally got into AA and by 1994, was totally sober. She has not touched a drop of alcohol since that time. When she first stopped drinking, she ate a lot of Reese's peanut butter cups as well as other chocolate bars. She stopped

Midpoint Listing

Alcoholic • Woman • Natal Chart
In Planetery Sequence • Modulus 360°00'

☽	07°♉15	*☿*	05°♑03	♂/♆	02°♐00	*♅*	20°♌19	⚷/⚸	27°♏08
☽/☉	11°♓48	☿/♀	20°♐41	♂/♇	00°♏33	♅/♆	29°♍34	⚷/☊	11°♐17
☽/☿	06°♓09	☿/♂	00°♑07	♂/⚷	24°♑59	♅/♇	28°♌08	⚷/⊗	06°♉40
☽/♀	21°♒47	☿/♃	27°♐37	♂/⚳	13°♐36	♅/⚷	22°♉33	*⚳*	02°♐02
☽/♂	01°♓12	☿/♄	07°♑38	♂/⚴	24°♐44	♅/⚳	11°♎11	⚳/⚴	13°♐10
☽/♃	28°♒42	☿/♅	27°♎41	♂/⚵	16°♐39	♅/⚴	22°♎19	⚳/⚵	05°♐05
☽/♄	08°♓44	☿/♆	06°♐56	♂/⚶	03°♑35	♅/⚵	14°♎14	⚳/⚶	22°♐01
☽/♅	28°♊47	☿/♇	05°♏29	♂/⚸	27°♎20	♅/⚶	01°♏10	⚳/⚸	15°♎45
☽/♆	08°♒02	☿/⚷	29°♑55	♂/☊	11°♏28	♅/⚸	24°♌54	⚳/☊	29°♎54
☽/♇	06°♋35	☿/⚳	18°♐32	♂/⊗	06°♎52	♅/☊	09°♍03	⚳/⊗	25°♍18
☽/⚷	01°♈01	☿/⚴	29°♐40	*♃*	20°♐10	♅/⊗	04°♌27	*⚴*	24°♐18
☽/⚳	19°♒38	☿/⚵	21°♐36	♃/♄	00°♑12	*♆*	08°♏49	⚴/⚵	16°♐13
☽/⚴	00°♓46	☿/⚶	08°♑32	♃/♅	20°♎15	♆/♇	07°♎23	⚴/⚶	03°♑09
☽/⚵	22°♒41	☿/⚸	02°♏16	♃/♆	29°♏30	♆/⚷	01°♑48	⚴/⚸	26°♎53
☽/⚶	09°♓37	☿/☊	16°♏25	♃/♇	28°♎03	♆/⚳	20°♏25	⚴/☊	11°♏02
☽/⚸	03°♋22	☿/⊗	11°♎48	♃/⚷	22°♑29	♆/⚴	01°♐34	⚴/⊗	06°♎26
☽/☊	17°♋31	*♀*	06°♐20	♃/⚳	11°♐06	♆/⚵	23°♏29	*⚵*	08°♐08
☽/⊗	12°♊54	♀/♂	15°♐45	♃/⚴	22°♐14	♆/⚶	10°♐25	⚵/⚶	25°♐04
☉	16°♑21	♀/♃	13°♐15	♃/⚵	14°♐09	♆/⚸	04°♎09	⚵/⚸	18°♎48
☉/☿	10°♑42	♀/♄	23°♐17	♃/⚶	01°♑05	♆/☊	18°♎18	⚵/☊	02°♏57
☉/♀	26°♐21	♀/♅	13°♎20	♃/⚸	24°♎50	♆/⊗	13°♍42	⚵/⊗	28°♍21
☉/♂	05°♑46	♀/♆	22°♏35	♃/☊	08°♏58	*♇*	05°♍56	*⚶*	12°♑00
☉/♃	03°♑16	♀/♇	21°♎08	♃/⊗	04°♎22	♇/⚷	00°♐21	⚶/⚸	05°♏44
☉/♄	13°♑18	♀/⚷	15°♑33	*♄*	10°♑14	♇/⚳	18°♎59	⚶/☊	19°♏53
☉/♅	03°♏20	♀/⚳	04°♐11	♄/♅	00°♏17	♇/⚴	00°♏07	⚶/⊗	15°♎17
☉/♆	12°♐35	♀/⚴	15°♐19	♄/♆	09°♐32	♇/⚵	22°♎02	*⚸*	29°♌29
☉/♇	11°♏09	♀/⚵	07°♐14	♄/♇	08°♏05	♇/⚶	08°♏58	⚸/☊	13°♍38
☉/⚷	05°♒34	♀/⚶	24°♐10	♄/⚷	02°♒30	♇/⚸	02°♍42	⚸/⊗	09°♌01
☉/⚳	24°♐12	♀/⚸	17°♎54	♄/⚳	21°♐08	♇/☊	16°♍51	*☊*	27°♍46
☉/⚴	05°♑20	♀/☊	02°♏03	♄/⚴	02°♑16	♇/⊗	12°♌15	☊/⊗	23°♌10
☉/⚵	27°♐15	♀/⊗	27°♍27	♄/⚵	24°♐11	*⚷*	24°♒47	*⊗*	18°♋34
☉/⚶	14°♑11	*♂*	25°♐10	♄/⚶	11°♑07	⚷/⚳	13°♑24		
☉/⚸	07°♏55	♂/♃	22°♐40	♄/⚸	04°♏51	⚷/⚴	24°♑32		
☉/☊	22°♏04	♂/♄	02°♑42	♄/☊	19°♏00	⚷/⚵	16°♑28		
☉/⊗	17°♎28	♂/♅	22°♎45	♄/⊗	14°♎24	⚷/⚶	03°♒24		

the chocolate after three years. Currently, she takes a few basic vitamins, Prozac for depression, and has some acupuncture and massage treatments. She feels she has been spiritually blessed with the help she has been given and is very open to helping other alcoholics. She worked as a bookkeeper for many years. Then she worked for a short time at a shelter for domestic violence with some of the children, but feels she was too sensitive for that kind of work. Now she has her own business cleaning houses.

Interpretation of Horoscope

Sun in Capricorn is conjoined both Ceres and Saturn, showing a responsible and nurturing nature. Sun conjoined Saturn can incline her to depression. Mercury is also conjoined Saturn, indicating a mind capable of organizing details. All the Capricorn planets are trine the Moon in Taurus. The Moon is exactly opposite Neptune, a combination that exhibits great sensitivity, as well as the propensity for drugs or alcohol as an escape mechanism. Mars is at the MC in Sagittarius conjoined both Pallas and Jupiter. Mars in Sagittarius here manifests strong will and good physical energy; Jupiter indicates possible problems with the liver. These planets are also trine Uranus in Leo. She has Pisces rising with the south node exactly on the ascendant in Pisces. This shows her very sensitive nature, and along with Neptune opposite the Moon, signifies the potential for alcohol or drug use as well as the need for a strong spiritual life to satisfy her Piscean nature. Venus is in Sagittarius conjunct both Juno and Vesta and square Pluto in Virgo in the sixth house. Relationships have been a challenge for her, but she has a strong desire to serve people.

Her Sun is parallel Mars, Jupiter, and Saturn and contra-parallel Pluto. The Jupiter theme regarding her liver is again present while the Mars and Saturn connections indicate a strong will. Pluto shows the possibility of strong transformation in her life.

MIDPOINTS

Mars/Neptune = Sun, indirect—which shows a sensitive immune system, low blood sugar, and difficulty metabolizing carbohydrates

Mars/Uranus = Venus, indirect—which indicates possible thyroid problems

Moon/Neptune = Mars, indirect—shows psychic sensitivity and potential for alcohol or drug abuse

Jupiter/Neptune = Sun—indirect, indicates liver toxicity

Transits and Progressions

In June of 1973, the summer she started drinking, secondary progressed Mars was conjoined Mercury, while progressed Venus and progressed Jupiter were conjunct. Transiting Neptune was conjoined Venus, and Saturn was opposite Mars. The lunar eclipse on June 15 was conjoined Mars, while the solar eclipse on June 30 was opposite Saturn.

At the end of 1987 and 1988, she was drinking heavily, in an abusive relationship, and suffered a concussion as a result of being hit with a steel pole. Secondary progressed Jupiter was conjoined Mars, progressed Venus was conjoined Saturn, and progressed Mars was conjunct her Sun. Transiting Pluto was on her Neptune while Neptune was on natal Mercury. Uranus was transiting Mars, and Saturn was on Jupiter. The solar eclipse in September 1987 was conjoined her north node, while the lunar eclipse in early October was exactly square her Sun, Ceres, and Saturn.

When she began her recovery, on February 12, 1994, progressed Venus was one degree past her natal Sun, while progressed Jupiter was two degrees away from her MC. Transiting Pluto was sextile her north node and conjoined the Jupiter/ Neptune midpoint. Transiting Neptune and Uranus at 22 and 24 Capricorn were on the Saturn/ Neptune indirect midpoint, the health axis. Saturn was square Vesta and on the Mars/Neptune midpoint. Jupiter was sextile the Sun. On November 29, 1993, the lunar eclipse had opposed her natal Venus.

Case History #2

This man has been using a variety of drugs since he was a teen-ager, including speed and cocaine, which he both snorts and injects. His drug addiction started early when he experienced drug induced psychosis from LSD. He is very shy with low self-esteem; using both the drugs and alcohol help him to feel more attractive. His psychosis kept him out of the military. He would work as a mechanic, take people's cars apart, and use the money they gave him for parts to buy more drugs. Then he would have trouble putting the cars back together. Recently, he was living in a homeless shelter and then in a transitional apartment in 2000, where he did a year of therapy. In 2001, he tested positive for Hepatitis C. In June 2001, he was taken to a sweat lodge by his therapist, and was very moved by the spiritual experience he had.

Interpretation of Horoscope

This chart is very mutable with a Pisces Sun and Pisces ascendant square a Gemini Moon. It is difficult for this person to focus on anything for a long time. His Sun is also exactly inconjunct Neptune, both in 29 degrees. This could indicate alcoholism or drug addiction, as well as low blood sugar

Drug Addict—Man
Natal Chart
Mar 19. 1956, 6:09 AM MST +7:00
Belen
34N39 46 106W46 33

Geocentric
Tropical
Koch
True Node

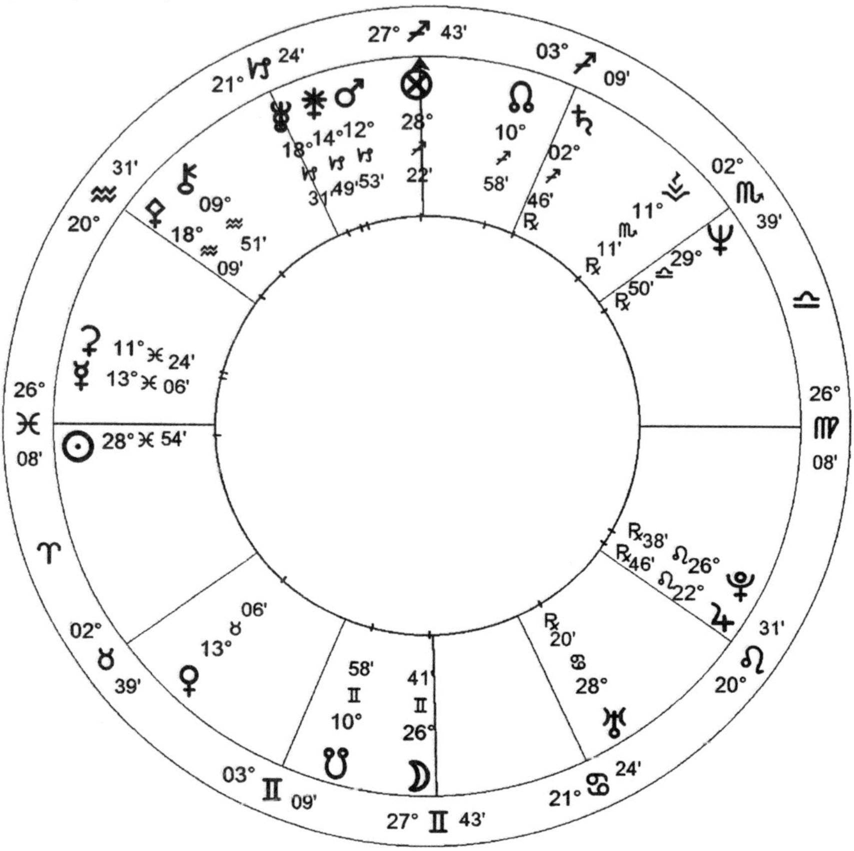

and a tendency to be unrealistic. Mercury is in Pisces in the twelfth house conjoined Ceres and square the nodes in Sagittarius and Gemini; it is also sextile both Venus and Mars. Mercury in Pisces square the nodes can indicate allergies as well as low blood sugar. Jupiter is in the sixth house in Leo conjoined Pluto; both are inconjunct the Pisces Sun and ascendant as well as sextile Neptune, forming a yod with these. Jupiter expands his Plutonian habits, and in a yod with the Sun and Neptune, shows problems

Midpoint Listing

Drug Addict • Man • Natal Chart
In Planetery Sequence • Modulus 360°00'

☽	26°♊41	*☿*	13°♓06	♂/♆	06°♐22	*♅*	28°♋20	⚷/⚶	29°♑11
☽/☉	12°♉48	☿/♀	13°♈06	♂/♇	04°♏46	♅/♆	14°♍05	⚷/☊	10°♑25
☽/☿	04°♉53	☿/♂	12°♒59	♂/⚷	26°♑22	♅/♇	12°♌29	⚷/⊗	19°♑06
☽/♀	04°♊54	☿/♃	02°♊56	♂/⚳	12°♐02	♅/⚷	04°♉06	*⚳*	11°♏11
☽/♂	04°♈47	☿/♄	22°♑56	♂/⚴	00°♒31	♅/⚳	19°♍46	⚳/⚴	29°♐40
☽/♃	24°♋43	☿/♅	20°♉43	♂/⚵	13°♑51	♅/⚴	08°♉15	⚳/⚵	13°♐00
☽/♄	14°♍43	☿/♆	06°♑28	♂/⯚	12°♒09	♅/⚵	21°♎35	⚳/⯚	11°♑18
☽/♅	12°♋31	☿/♇	04°♊52	♂/⚶	15°♑42	♅/⯚	19°♉52	⚳/⚶	14°♐51
☽/♆	28°♌15	☿/⚷	26°♒28	♂/☊	26°♐56	♅/⚶	23°♎26	⚳/☊	26°♏05
☽/♇	26°♋39	☿/⚳	12°♑08	♂/⊗	05°♑38	♅/☊	04°♎39	⚳/⊗	04°♐47
☽/⚷	18°♈16	☿/⚴	00°♓37	*♃*	22°♌46	♅/⊗	13°♎21	*⚴*	18°♒09
☽/⚳	03°♍56	☿/⚵	13°♒57	♃/♄	12°♎46	*♆*	29°♎50	⚴/⚵	01°♒29
☽/⚴	22°♈25	☿/⯚	12°♓15	♃/♅	10°♌33	♆/♇	28°♍14	⚴/⯚	29°♒47
☽/⚵	05°♈45	☿/⚶	15°♒48	♃/♆	26°♍18	♆/⚷	19°♐51	⚴/⚶	03°♒20
☽/⯚	04°♉03	☿/☊	27°♑02	♃/♇	24°♌42	♆/⚳	05°♏31	⚴/☊	14°♑34
☽/⚶	07°♈36	☿/⊗	05°♒44	♃/⚷	16°♏19	♆/⚴	24°♐00	⚴/⊗	23°♑16
☽/☊	18°♍50	*♀*	13°♉06	♃/⚳	01°♎59	♆/⚵	07°♐20	*⚵*	14°♑49
☽/⊗	27°♓31	♀/♂	13°♓00	♃/⚴	20°♏28	♆/⯚	05°♑37	⚵/⯚	13°♒07
☉	28°♓54	♀/♃	02°♋56	♃/⚵	03°♏48	♆/⚶	09°♐11	⚵/⚶	16°♑40
☉/☿	21°♓00	♀/♄	22°♒56	♃/⯚	02°♊05	♆/☊	20°♏24	⚵/☊	27°♐54
☉/♀	21°♈00	♀/♅	20°♊43	♃/⚶	05°♏39	♆/⊗	29°♏06	⚵/⊗	06°♑35
☉/♂	20°♒54	♀/♆	06°♌28	♃/☊	16°♎52	*♇*	26°♌38	*⯚*	11°♓24
☉/♃	10°♊50	♀/♇	04°♋52	♃/⊗	25°♎34	♇/⚷	18°♏14	⯚/⚶	14°♒58
☉/♄	00°♒50	♀/⚷	26°♓29	*♄*	02°♐46	♇/⚳	03°♎55	⯚/☊	26°♑11
☉/♅	28°♉37	♀/⚳	12°♌09	♄/♅	00°♎33	♇/⚴	22°♏24	⯚/⊗	04°♒53
☉/♆	14°♑22	♀/⚴	00°♈38	♄/♆	16°♏18	♇/⚵	05°♏43	*⚶*	18°♑31
☉/♇	12°♊46	♀/⚵	13°♓58	♄/♇	14°♎42	♇/⯚	04°♊01	⚶/☊	29°♐45
☉/⚷	04°♓23	♀/⯚	12°♈15	♄/⚷	06°♑18	♇/⚶	07°♏35	⚶/⊗	08°♑27
☉/⚳	20°♑03	♀/⚶	15°♓49	♄/⚳	21°♏58	♇/☊	18°♎48	*☊*	10°♐58
☉/⚴	08°♓32	♀/☊	27°♒02	♄/⚴	10°♑27	♇/⊗	27°♎30	☊/⊗	19°♐40
☉/⚵	21°♒52	♀/⊗	05°♓44	♄/⚵	23°♐47	*⚷*	09°♒51	*⊗*	28°♐22
☉/⯚	20°♓09	*♂*	12°♑53	♄/⯚	22°♑05	⚷/⚳	25°♐31		
☉/⚶	23°♒43	♂/♃	02°♏50	♄/⚶	25°♐38	⚷/⚴	14°♒00		
☉/☊	04°♒56	♂/♄	22°♐49	♄/☊	06°♐52	⚷/⚵	27°♑20		
☉/⊗	13°♒38	♂/♅	20°♎37	♄/⊗	15°♐34	⚷/⯚	25°♒38		

with the pancreas, liver, low blood sugar, and toxicity from drugs or chemicals. Saturn in early Sagittarius is in a grand trine with Uranus in late Cancer and the Sun in late Pisces. This could provide some discipline as well as indicate mechanical ability.

In terms of the parallels of declination, the Moon is parallel Pluto and Uranus, while being contra parallel Mars and the node. Venus is contra parallel Saturn. Moon parallel Uranus shows his erratic quality while the parallel to Pluto shows he has the ability to change his habit patterns. Moon contra parallel Mars shows a highly emotional nature and the tendency to excess in habit patterns. Venus contra parallel Saturn can indicate a lack of affection from his parents, as well as the tendency to have a low thyroid.

Midpoints

Sun/Moon = Venus, direct—indicates a creative nature as well as problems with blood sugar and possible thyroid problem.

Sun/Neptune = Mars, direct—shows low energy, feeling "spaced out," difficulty metabolizing carbohydrates.

Moon/Neptune = Mars, indirect—may indicate psychic abilities and the desire to experience ecstatic states of consciousness.

Transits and Progressions

In the beginning of 2000, when he went into therapy, secondary progressed Venus was one degree from his Moon and his progressed Sun was one degree from Venus. Transiting Pluto was on his north node. Uranus was squaring Venus and both Jupiter and Saturn in Taurus transited his natal Venus during the year. He had a very good connection with his therapist, a woman, who later brought him to the sweat lodge in June of 2001. In January of 2000, the lunar eclipse at 0 degrees Leo conjoined his Uranus while the solar eclipse in February 2000, conjoined Pallas and squared Venus.

In June of 2001, progressed Sun was exactly conjoined natal Venus, and progressed Venus was conjoined natal Moon. Transiting Pluto was inconjunct natal Venus. Uranus was trine his natal Moon while Neptune was almost conjoined his Chiron. Saturn was close to his south node, and Jupiter was on his Moon. The solar eclipse at 0 degrees Cancer was conjunct his Moon, while the lunar eclipse of July 5 conjoined his Mars in Capricorn.

SUPPLEMENT RECOMMENDATIONS FOR ALCOHOLISM AND DRUG ADDICTION

Probiotics including various strands of intestinal bacteria are very important in re-implanting friendly bacteria into the colon and will help to produce more vitamin B.

Green Drinks containing barley, alfalfa, and wheat grasses are an important source of chlorophyll, minerals, and certain vitamins. Alcoholics and drug addicts are extremely deficient and need strong sources of these nutrients.

L-Glutamine reduces the craving for both alcohol and sugar. It is also helpful for drug addicts in re-balancing their bodies.

Pancreas glandular helps those with low blood sugar and aids digestion by providing pancreatic enzymes. All alcoholics and drug addicts are hypoglycemic and need the pancreas glandular after meals.

Bioflavonoids with Quercetin help the immune system and are also important for circulation and aiding the kidneys. The kidneys may be damaged after using alcohol and drugs.

Vitamin C in an ascorbate form supports the adrenals so that the body can handle stress. Large doses of vitamin C will help to detoxify the body.

B-Complex is important in balancing the nervous system.

Calcium/Magnesium helps with the hormonal balance, especially for women, and also the nervous system, which needs lots of support in all types of addictions.

Zinc helps the liver to detoxify alcohol and is also used for detoxifying chemicals in the blood.

Potassium aids the alkalinity of the body, which has become extremely acidic in the case of both alcoholics and drug addicts. The kidneys, which are often damaged, control the acid alkaline balance.

GLA oil such as evening primrose oil, borage oil, and black currant seed oil helps protect the liver from alcohol and other irritating drugs.

EPA and DHA oils, which are found in fish oils and flaxseed oil, are important in re-balancing the prostaglandins and hormones.

HERBAL RECOMMENDATIONS

Aloe vera gel from the plant or in a bottle helps clean out the colon as well as cleanse the liver and kidneys. For the first month, about one half a cup or the insides of three large leaves should be taken every other day, After that, one quarter of a cup. It is helpful to use this before bedtime.

Parsley tea made by simmering fresh organic parsley in a few cups of water will help to clear the kidneys and alkalinize the body. This should be drunk every other morning.

Herbs that are liver tonics such as **golden seal leaf, Oregon grape root**, and **wild yam** should be used daily for a few months. A liver flush with hot water, two tablespoons of cold pressed olive oil, and one quarter of a lemon should be taken on arising for one week every three months.

Nutritional herbs such as **alfalfa leaves, nettle leaves, horsetail, dandelion leaves,** and **comfrey** should be used to help re-balance the body.

CHAPTER 17

Cancer

THE GROWTH AND SPREAD OF THE DISEASES known as cancer reflects the complexity of our lives in this technological era and our struggle to live a healthy life style in the midst of environmental toxins, genetically modified foods, and contaminated water. These challenges, in addition to electromagnetic pollution, which creates havoc in our nervous systems, and our personal emotional traumas, cause cellular changes in our bodies affecting our DNA.

Cancer is characterized by uncontrolled growth of cells. There are two large groups—**carcinomas** and **sarcomas**. **Carcinomas** are the most common cancers; they are malignant tumors that occur in the epithelial cells covering tissues and body cavities and in glandular organs such as the breast, stomach, uterus, skin, and tongue. **Sarcomas**, less common but highly malignant, form in connective tissues, muscle, bone, and cartilage. **Leukemias**, in which abnormal leukocytes are produced in enormous quantity, are commonly considered cancers and respond to the same types of treatment.

Cell mutation may be caused by chemical damage to cell membranes or by damaged DNA. A pre-cancerous cell is a mutated cell that may lead to a full fledged cancer, unless the mutated cells are recognized by the immune system and destroyed. The cell membrane is the protective outer skin of a cell that is responsible for the transport of nutrients into the cell as well as the removal of waste products. If the cell membrane is damaged, uncontrolled growth may result.

Many conditions are responsible for the change in the physiology of a cell, which are referred to as cancer cells or malignant cells. It is possible that a virus, bacteria, or parasite can change the cells and deplete the immune system. Environmental toxins, especially radiation in the atmosphere and from cell phones and microwave ovens, may catalyze changes in cells. Emotional states and traumatic conditions also have the power to change cell structure. Visualization exercises and meditative techniques have been used to change the malignant cells to normal cells. Stephanie and Carl Simonton, in their book, *Getting Well Again*, were the first to explore techniques of visualization where the mind can visualize the body as whole and healthy.

For some of the children who develop cancer at an early age, visualization techniques have proven extremely helpful. Their suffering and dealing with the death of their peers in children's cancer groups may train them to become healers and therapists at a later stage in their lives. In some cases, hormonal preparations were given to the mothers of these children. One of them, DES, or Diethylstilbestrol, was a preparation prescribed as a contraceptive. The daughters of some of these women developed vaginal cancer as a result.

PSYCHOLOGICAL FACTORS

Some cancer patients have been rejected by their families; they have felt unwanted since their childhood. Others have had difficulty dealing with one or more parents. Cancer patients are often extremely sensitive and vulnerable to outside forces. They do not know how to protect themselves emotionally from the feelings of others. Their vulnerability psychologically also makes them particularly sensitive to pollutants in the environment. A therapist in Michigan told me that when he regressed his cancer patients back to the fetal state, they all felt unwanted.

Many of those with cancer have repressed their anger and resentment over the years. Since the emotion anger corresponds to the liver in Traditional Chinese Medicine, the liver then becomes toxic and cannot do its part in helping the immune system.

Some cancer patients have been very fixed in their habit patterns; it has been observed that many of them have their Moon in a fixed sign and a predominance of fixed sign planets in their horoscopes. The process of healing forces them to break up these rigid patterns. Some have also played the role of victims and feel victimized by society.

ASTROLOGICAL PATTERNS

Neptune is often found angular or conjoined the Sun or Moon; sometimes there are several planets in Pisces. Besides ruling the immune system, Neptune also governs the lymphatic system and the lymphocytes, which are responsible for immunity. Those with strong Neptune are super sensitive and may feel like victims.

Fixed sign Moons are also pre-dominant, showing habit patterns that are difficult to break. Sun and ascendant are often in fixed signs as well as the nodes of the Moon, which relate to the emotional patterning through many incarnations. There are often hard aspects to the Moon, indicating problems to be worked out with the family.

The planet Jupiter, which rules the liver and the pancreas, as well as tumors, is often angular, or conjoined the Sun, Moon, or another planet. Most cancer patients have a history of hypoglycemia, which involves the pancreas. Many theories on cancer treat it as a metabolic disease. Jupiter also rules unrestrained growth.

Since cancer involves the mutation of cells that happen in an underground fashion, the planet Pluto and the sign Scorpio are usually prominent in the chart, and often by transit or progression when cancer is diagnosed. A strong Plutonian personality can keep issues hidden and they may fester underground. A Plutonian also faces the issue of death and dying, as well as the continuous process of transformation. Many Scorpio type individuals are also being trained to heal others.

MIDPOINTS

In addition to the midpoints for general health, the following midpoints are important in the horoscopes of cancer patients:

Moon/Neptune—indicates hyper-sensitivity and the over-accumulation of water in the tissues

Mars/Jupiter—governs the relationship between the liver and adrenals as well as increased metabolic changes

Jupiter/Saturn—shows the restrictive action of the liver and pancreas

Jupiter/Uranus—refers to unexpected cell growth and change

Jupiter/Neptune—indicates toxic conditions of the liver and pancreas

Jupiter/Pluto—refers to expansion of cellular growth and regeneration of the organs

Midpoint patterns commonly found in the horoscopes of those with Cancer are the following:

Saturn/Neptune = Pluto—This combination indicates a chronic condition or one where the body undergoes a strong regenerative process

Moon/Neptune = Pluto—This suggests emotional upheaval and catharsis, as well as changing the balance of liquids in the body

Jupiter/Neptune = Moon—This shows problems with metabolism, often found in the charts of those with hypoglycemia and allergies

Jupiter/Pluto = ascendant—With the ascendant representing the physical body, this grouping emphasizes the regenerative quality of the body organs, especially the liver and pancreas

Jupiter/Pluto = Venus—Since Venus refers to the blood sugar, this combination indicates incomplete carbohydrate metabolism

Jupiter/Neptune = Venus—This also refers to faulty carbohydrate metabolism and abnormal sugar level in the blood

CASE HISTORIES

Case History #1

This case history is of a woman who had breast cancer diagnosed in August of 1983, and shortly after had a mastectomy. In June of 1983, her husband died of heart failure, when he was 52, due to a genetic defect. Prior to this, she had given birth to a son in 1965, whom she gave up for adoption. Then she had three miscarriages between the years of 1971-73, when she was ready to have a child. Before November 1975, she had been an alcoholic for a short time period, but has been sober since then. She had also smoked cigarettes from the age of 21. When the cancer was diagnosed, she cut down her work load as a therapist. In addition, she did some intense dream therapy and some shamanic work, as well as some work with movement. She left the New Jersey-New York area and moved to New Mexico, where the pace of her life became a lot slower. She did not take a lot of additional supplements or herbs. Her cancer has been in remission since 1986.

Interpretation of Horoscope

This chart has a T square between Neptune, Saturn, and the Moon on the angles; the Sun is also square Neptune and Saturn, and opposite her Chiron south node conjunction, making it a grand square. With Saturn in Pisces opposite Neptune and square both a Sagittarius Moon and Sun, the immune system is greatly compromised; there is hypoglycemia and possibly diabetes, with serious problems involving the liver and pancreas. Virgo is also rising which indicates a sensitive digestive system. With the nodes in Sagittarius and Gemini, there could be both food and respiratory allergies. Mercury, ruler of the chart, is in Capricorn, conjoined Ceres and Jupiter, ruler of the Sun and Moon signs. This shows the studying of various philosophies, possibly teaching or counseling, as well as respiratory allergies. Venus is in Aquarius in the fifth house, square Uranus, opposite Pluto, and semi-square both Pallas and Saturn. This indicates problems with child bearing and sudden miscarriages. Venus in Aquarius square Uranus also represents the son she gave up for adoption, as well as erratic functioning of the thyroid. Mars is in Libra, inconjunct Saturn but sextile Pallas, the Moon, and Sun, as well as square Vesta. Mars inconjunct Saturn does not have a lot of physical vitality.

In terms of declination, her Sun is parallel her Moon, Venus, Jupiter, node, and contra parallel Pluto. This can indicate a tendency to overweight, which is also seen with the Sun and north node broadly conjoined Jupiter. Blood sugar problems with Venus and Jupiter parallel the Moon are evident.

Midpoints

Saturn/Neptune = Venus, indirect—problems with thyroid and blood sugar

Mars/Neptune = Mercury, indirect—possible respiratory allergies

Moon/Neptune = Venus, direct, Saturn, indirect—problems with blood sugar, difficulties in child birth

Cancer—Woman 1
Natal Chart
Dec 12, 1936, 11:15 PM CST +6:00
Minneapolis
44N58 48 093W15 49

Geocentric
Tropical
Koch
True Node

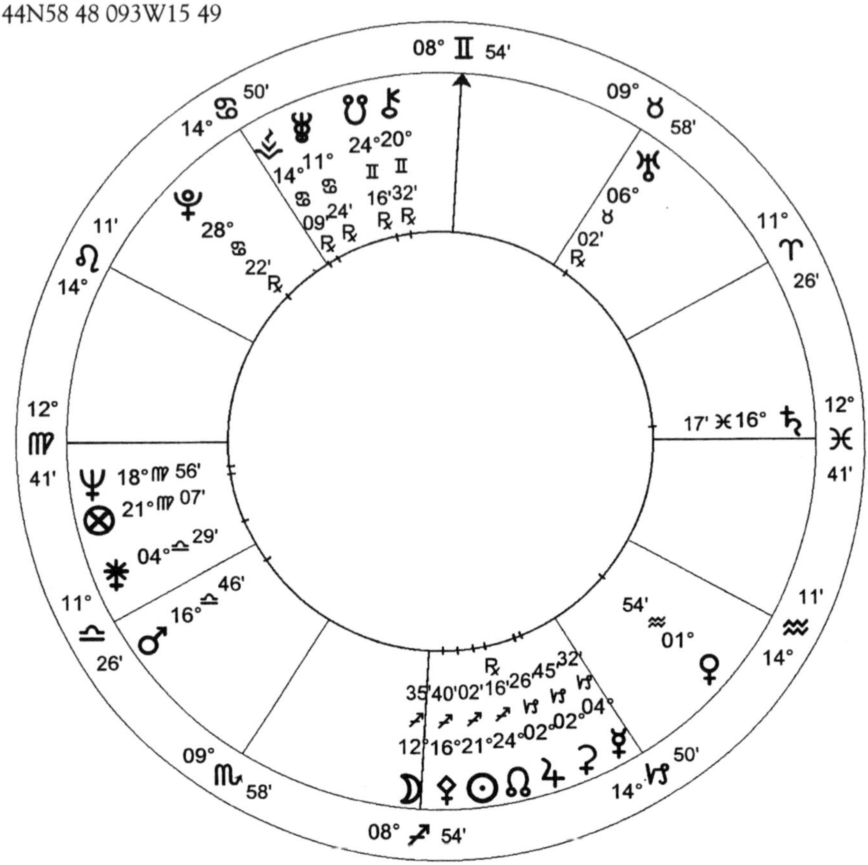

Jupiter/Neptune = north node in Sagittarius, indirect—problems with liver and immune system

Jupiter/Saturn = north node in Sagittarius, indirect—restricted functioning of the liver

Transits and Progressions
In June 1983, when her husband died, transiting Pluto was square Pluto.

Midpoint Listing

Cancer • Woman 1 • Natal Chart
In Planetery Sequence • Modulus 360°00'

☽	12°♐35	*☿*	04°♑32	♂/♆	02°♎51	*♅*	06°♉02	⚷/⛢	00°♋58
☽/☉	16°♐49	☿/♀	18°♑13	♂/♇	07°♍34	♅/♆	12°♋29	⚷/☊	22°♓24
☽/☿	23°♐34	☿/♂	25°♏39	♂/⚷	18°♌39	♅/♇	17°♊12	⚷/⊗	05°♌49
☽/♀	07°♑15	☿/♃	03°♑29	♂/⚳	00°♍27	♅/⚷	28°♉17	*⚳*	14°♋09
☽/♂	14°♏41	☿/♄	10°♒24	♂/⚴	16°♏43	♅/⚳	10°♊05	⚳/⚴	00°♎24
☽/♃	22°♐31	☿/♅	05°♓17	♂/⚵	10°♎38	♅/⚴	26°♒21	⚳/⚵	24°♌19
☽/♄	29°♑26	☿/♆	11°♏44	♂/⚶	24°♏45	♅/⚵	20°♋16	⚳/⚶	08°♎27
☽/♅	24°♒19	☿/♇	16°♎27	♂/⛢	29°♌05	♅/⚶	04°♓23	⚳/⛢	12°♋46
☽/♆	00°♏46	☿/⚷	27°♓32	♂/☊	20°♏31	♅/⛢	08°♊43	⚳/☊	04°♎12
☽/♇	05°♎29	☿/⚳	09°♎20	♂/⊗	03°♎57	♅/☊	00°♓09	⚳/⊗	17°♌38
☽/⚷	16°♍34	☿/⚴	25°♐36	*♃*	02°♑26	♅/⊗	13°♋35	*⚴*	16°♐40
☽/⚳	28°♍22	☿/⚵	19°♏30	♃/♄	09°♒21	*♆*	18°♍56	⚴/⚵	10°♏35
☽/⚴	14°♐38	☿/⚶	03°♑38	♃/♅	04°♓14	♆/♇	23°♌39	⚴/⚶	24°♐42
☽/⚵	08°♏32	☿/⛢	07°♎58	♃/♆	10°♏41	♆/⚷	04°♌44	⚴/⛢	29°♍02
☽/⚶	22°♐40	☿/☊	29°♐24	♃/♇	15°♎24	♆/⚳	16°♌32	⚴/☊	20°♐28
☽/⛢	27°♍00	☿/⊗	12°♏49	♃/⚷	26°♓29	♆/⚴	02°♏48	⚴/⊗	03°♏54
☽/☊	18°♐26	*♀*	01°♒54	♃/⚳	08°♎17	♆/⚵	26°♍43	*⚵*	04°♎29
☽/⊗	01°♏51	♀/♂	09°♐20	♃/⚴	24°♐33	♆/⚶	10°♏50	⚵/⚶	18°♏37
☉	21°♐02	♀/♃	17°♑10	♃/⚵	18°♏28	♆/⛢	15°♌10	⚵/⛢	22°♌57
☉/☿	27°♐47	♀/♄	24°♒05	♃/⚶	02°♑35	♆/☊	06°♏36	⚵/☊	14°♏23
☉/♀	11°♑28	♀/♅	18°♓58	♃/⛢	06°♎55	♆/⊗	20°♍02	⚵/⊗	27°♍48
☉/♂	18°♏54	♀/♆	25°♏25	♃/☊	28°♐21	*♇*	28°♋22	*⚶*	02°♑45
☉/♃	26°♐44	♀/♇	00°♉08	♃/⊗	11°♏47	♇/⚷	09°♋27	⚶/⛢	07°♎04
☉/♄	03°♒39	♀/⚷	11°♈13	*♄*	16°♓17	♇/⚳	21°♋15	⚶/☊	28°♐30
☉/♅	28°♒32	♀/⚳	23°♈01	♄/♅	11°♈09	♇/⚴	07°♎31	⚶/⊗	11°♏56
☉/♆	04°♏59	♀/⚴	09°♑17	♄/♆	17°♐37	♇/⚵	01°♍25	*⛢*	11°♋24
☉/♇	09°♎42	♀/⚵	03°♐12	♄/♇	22°♉19	♇/⚶	15°♎33	⛢/☊	02°♎50
☉/⚷	20°♓47	♀/⚶	17°♑19	♄/⚷	03°♉24	♇/⛢	19°♋53	⛢/⊗	16°♌16
☉/⚳	02°♎35	♀/⛢	21°♈39	♄/⚳	15°♉13	♇/☊	11°♎19	*☊*	24°♐16
☉/⚴	18°♐51	♀/☊	13°♑05	♄/⚴	01°♒28	♇/⊗	24°♌44	☊/⊗	07°♏42
☉/⚵	12°♏46	♀/⊗	26°♏31	♄/⚵	25°♐23	*⚷*	20°♊32	*⊗*	21°♍07
☉/⚶	26°♐53	*♂*	16°♎46	♄/⚶	09°♒31	⚷/⚳	02°♋20		
☉/⛢	01°♎13	♂/♃	24°♏36	♄/⛢	13°♉50	⚷/⚴	18°♍36		
☉/☊	22°♐39	♂/♄	01°♑32	♄/☊	05°♒16	⚷/⚵	12°♌30		
☉/⊗	06°♏05	♂/♅	26°♋24	♄/⊗	18°♐42	⚷/⚶	26°♓38		

Uranus was inconjunct Uranus in her eighth house, and Saturn was square Pluto. In September, when she had her surgery, Pluto was also semi-square her Moon, and ascendant. Uranus and Jupiter were inconjunct natal Uranus, while Saturn was sesquiquadrate Saturn and square Venus. Neptune was also 2 degrees past her north node, relating to the immune system, as well as showing the shamanic and spiritual work she did at this time. The solar eclipse on June 11 was conjoined Chiron and opposite her Sun, while the lunar eclipse on June 25 was conjoined Jupiter, Ceres, and Mercury.

Cancer—Woman 2
Natal Chart
Nov 5, 1940, 7:15 AM MST +7:00
Santa Fe
35N41 13 105W56 14

Geocentric
Tropical
Koch
True Node

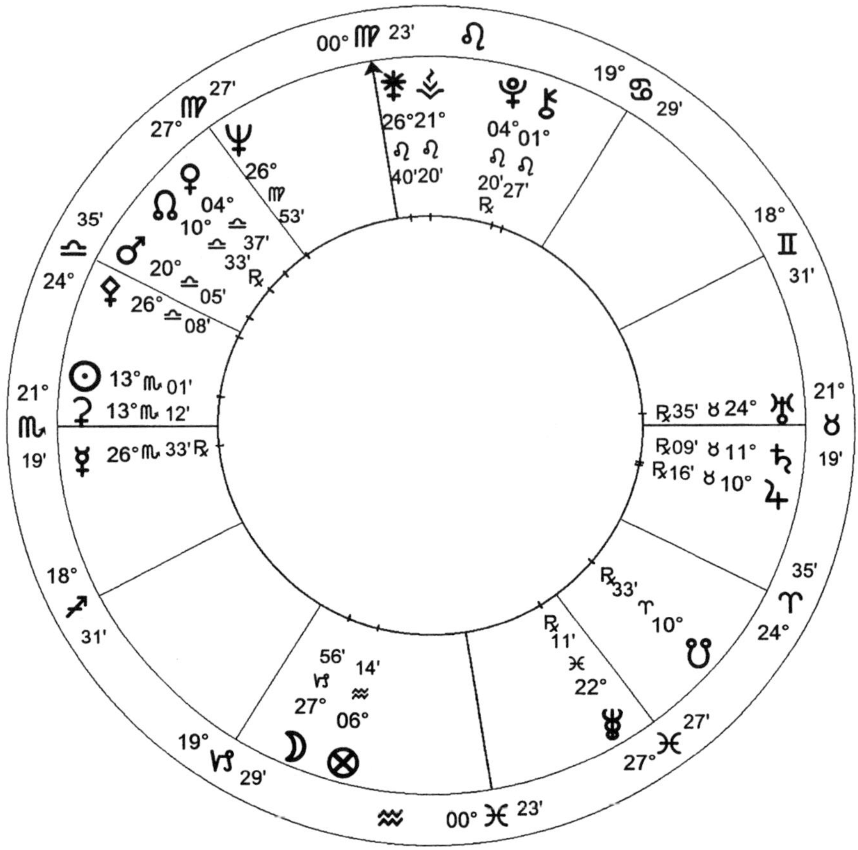

Case History #2

This horoscope is that of a woman who had cancer of the uterus diagnosed when she was 38 years old. She subsequently had a hysterectomy and is in good health today. At the time the cancer was diagnosed, she was living in Detroit and training as a Waldorf school teacher. Her life style was quite healthy; she ate organic foods and always had a large garden. She grew up in New Mexico and had spent most of her life there. She had four children

Midpoint Listing

Cancer • Woman 2 • Natal Chart

In Planetery Sequence • Modulus 360°00'

☽	27°♑56	*☿*	26°♏33	♂/♆	08°♎29	*♅*	24°♉35	⚷/⛢	26°♉49
☽/☉	20°♐29	☿/♀	00°♏35	♂/♇	12°♍12	♅/♆	25°♋44	⚷/☊	06°♍00
☽/☿	27°♐15	☿/♂	08°♏19	♂/⚷	10°♍46	♅/♇	29°♊27	⚷/⊗	03°♉50
☽/♀	01°♐17	☿/♃	18°♒25	♂/⚳	20°♍43	♅/⚷	28°♊01	*⚳*	21°♌20
☽/♂	09°♐01	☿/♄	18°♒51	♂/⚴	23°♎07	♅/⚳	07°♋57	⚳/⚴	23°♍44
☽/♃	19°♓06	☿/♅	25°♒34	♂/⚵	23°♍22	♅/⚴	10°♌22	⚳/⚵	24°♌00
☽/♄	19°♓33	☿/♆	26°♎43	♂/⚶	01°♏39	♅/⚵	10°♋37	⚳/⚶	02°♎16
☽/♅	26°♓16	☿/♇	00°♎27	♂/⛢	06°♑08	♅/⚶	18°♌54	⚳/⛢	06°♊46
☽/♆	27°♏25	☿/⚷	29°♍00	♂/☊	15°♎19	♅/⛢	23°♈23	⚳/☊	15°♍57
☽/♇	01°♏08	☿/⚳	08°♎57	♂/⊗	13°♐10	♅/☊	02°♌34	⚳/⊗	13°♏47
☽/⚷	29°♎42	☿/⚴	11°♏21	*♃*	10°♉16	♅/⊗	00°♈25	*⚴*	26°♎08
☽/⚳	09°♏38	☿/⚵	11°♎36	♃/♄	10°♉43	*♆*	26°♍53	⚴/⚵	26°♍24
☽/⚴	12°♐02	☿/⚶	19°♏53	♃/♅	17°♉25	♆/♇	00°♍36	⚴/⚶	04°♏40
☽/⚵	12°♏18	☿/⛢	24°♑22	♃/♆	18°♋35	♆/⚷	29°♌10	⚴/⛢	09°♑10
☽/⚶	20°♐34	☿/☊	03°♏33	♃/♇	22°♊18	♆/⚳	09°♍07	⚴/☊	18°♎21
☽/⛢	25°♒04	☿/⊗	01°♑24	♃/⚷	20°♊51	♆/⚴	11°♎31	⚴/⊗	16°♐11
☽/☊	04°♐15	*♀*	04°♎37	♃/⚳	00°♋48	♆/⚵	11°♍46	*⚵*	26°♌40
☽/⊗	02°♒05	♀/♂	12°♎21	♃/⚴	03°♌12	♆/⚶	20°♎03	⚵/⚶	04°♎56
☉	13°♏01	♀/♃	22°♋26	♃/⚵	03°♋28	♆/⛢	24°♐32	⚵/⛢	09°♊26
☉/☿	19°♏47	♀/♄	22°♋53	♃/⚶	11°♒44	♆/☊	03°♎43	⚵/☊	18°♍37
☉/♀	23°♎49	♀/♅	29°♋36	♃/⛢	16°♈14	♆/⊗	01°♐34	⚵/⊗	16°♏27
☉/♂	01°♏33	♀/♆	00°♎45	♃/☊	25°♋25	*♇*	04°♌20	*⚶*	13°♏12
☉/♃	11°♒39	♀/♇	04°♍28	♃/⊗	23°♓15	♇/⚷	02°♌53	⚶/⛢	17°♑42
☉/♄	12°♒05	♀/⚷	03°♍02	*♄*	11°♉09	♇/⚳	12°♌50	⚶/☊	26°♎53
☉/♅	18°♌48	♀/⚳	12°♍58	♄/♅	17°♉52	♇/⚴	15°♍14	⚶/⊗	24°♐43
☉/♆	19°♎57	♀/⚴	15°♎23	♄/♆	19°♋01	♇/⚵	15°♌30	*⛢*	22°♓11
☉/♇	23°♍40	♀/⚵	15°♍38	♄/♇	22°♊45	♇/⚶	23°♍46	⛢/☊	01°♑22
☉/⚷	22°♍14	♀/⚶	23°♎55	♄/⚷	21°♊18	♇/⛢	28°♉16	⛢/⊗	29°♒13
☉/⚳	02°♎11	♀/⛢	28°♐24	♄/⚳	01°♋15	♇/☊	07°♍27	*☊*	10°♎33
☉/⚴	04°♏35	♀/☊	07°♎35	♄/⚴	03°♌39	♇/⊗	05°♉17	☊/⊗	08°♐24
☉/⚵	04°♎50	♀/⊗	05°♐26	♄/⚵	03°♋55	*⚷*	01°♌27	*⊗*	06°♒14
☉/⚶	13°♏07	*♂*	20°♎05	♄/⚶	12°♒11	⚷/⚳	11°♌23		
☉/⛢	17°♑36	♂/♃	00°♌11	♄/⛢	16°♈40	⚷/⚴	13°♍47		
☉/☊	26°♎47	♂/♄	00°♌37	♄/☊	25°♋51	⚷/⚵	14°♌03		
☉/⊗	24°♐38	♂/♅	07°♌20	♄/⊗	23°♓42	⚷/⚶	22°♍19		

from two different marriages; at the time of the diagnosis, her youngest child was two years old. During Christmas vacation of 1979, she underwent a hysterectomy, and they also removed her ovaries, to which she had not agreed. She did not use any hormonal support and did experience hot flashes. She relied on natural herbs and a few supplements. In May 2001, she had pre-cancerous cells in her pap smear; she started using various supplements including liquid chlorophyll, CO Q-10, folic acid, and evening primrose oil, as well as some other supplements and herbs to cleanse her liver. Within six months, her pap smear was normal.

Interpretation of Horoscope

Her chart shows a strong emphasis in the fixed signs. Sun, Ceres, Mercury and ascendant are in Scorpio. The Sun Ceres conjunction is opposite Jupiter and Saturn in Taurus in her sixth house of health. Mercury is opposite Uranus in Taurus, indicating a sensitive nervous system. Pluto is in Leo conjoined Chiron, square Jupiter and Saturn, and broadly squaring the Sun Ceres conjunction. This emphasizes the colon and the reproductive system, especially since Pluto is the ruler of the chart and the other planets in the T square are in the health houses. Vesta and Juno are conjoined in Leo near the MC; healing and service work are important to her. Her Moon is in Capricorn and is part of a grand trine with Neptune in Virgo and Uranus in Taurus. This gives her good practical skills as well as the ability to teach. Mars is in Libra in the eleventh house square her Moon and inconjunct Uranus, indicating a need for physical exercise to work with any body tension. Venus is in Libra conjoined the north node, also in the eleventh house; Venus is semi-square the ascendant and sextile Pluto. These Libra planets in the eleventh house emphasize work with groups.

In terms of parallels of declination, the Sun is parallel the Moon and contra parallel Vesta, again emphasizing the theme of service. Jupiter is parallel Saturn, which like the conjunction, shows some restrictions with liver functioning.

Midpoints

Sun/Moon = Pluto, indirect—emphasizes the colon and reproductive system, as well as many deep transformations in her life

Saturn/Neptune = Mars, direct—adrenals can become depleted; with Mars in Libra, the necessity of checking the acid-alkaline balance

Mars/Neptune = nodes, direct—possible problems with low blood sugar and carbohydrate assimilation

Jupiter/Neptune = Mars, direct—problems with carbohydrate assimilation and pancreas, need for liver cleansing

Moon/Neptune = Mercury, direct—possible respiratory allergies and sensitive nervous system

Mars/Jupiter = Chiron, direct—healing the liver and adrenals

Transits and Progressions

In December 1979, when she had her hysterectomy, her secondary progressed Moon was inconjunct her ascendant. Transiting Pluto was conjoined Mars. Neptune was sextile Mars and transiting the Mars/Uranus indirect midpoint (surgeries) as well as the progressed Sun. Uranus was opposite natal Uranus and close to the ascendant. Saturn was conjoined natal Neptune; Jupiter was trine the Saturn Jupiter conjunction in the sixth house and inconjunct the south node, while Chiron was transiting Jupiter. The solar eclipse of August 22 was square Uranus and Mercury while the lunar eclipse of September 6 was trine her Sun.

In May 2001, when her pap smear showed pre-cancerous cells, secondary progressed Moon was conjoined her south node. The transiting node was square her natal nodes; the Pluto Jupiter opposition was transiting her Mars Jupiter midpoint (indirect), which did show some problems with her liver and adrenals. Neptune was square the Jupiter Saturn conjunction, Uranus was square Uranus, and Saturn was semi-square Mars. The solar eclipse of June 21 was square her Venus, while the lunar eclipse of July 5 was squaring her nodes.

TREATMENTS FOR CANCER

1. Complete physiological cleansing will rid the body of toxic material and build up the immune system. Colonic irrigations and enemas are most important. There are many variations on these treatments; wheat grass implants after an enema are often done, as well as coffee enemas. A liquid fast is also advisable, from a few days to several weeks, depending on the individual. The fast should include predominantly vegetable juices, soup broths, herb teas, but little fruit juice. The juice from organic beef liver has also been used, especially for those with leukemia and those needing large amounts of iron. After the fast, a light diet of steamed and raw vegetables should be followed for a few weeks. Some people will also need some easy to digest protein such as baked or steamed fish. Grains may be added at a later time.

2. During the cleansing, a liver flush is necessary. Adding 2 tablespoons of cold pressed olive oil plus one quarter of a lemon to a cup of hot water in the morning may be done for a week, several times during the year.
3. Ozone and oxygenation therapies are helpful in re-building the immune system.
4. Chelation therapy, to remove toxic metals, is often necessary as well.
5. Lymphatic massage works to cleanse the lymph system. Other types of body work are also helpful in stimulating circulation and energy flow.
6. Visualization techniques, introduced by Drs. Carl and Stephanie Simonton, (see their book, *Getting Well Again*) are helpful in achieving a healthy integration of mind and body.
7. Making changes and adaptations in one's life style are absolutely necessary.

SUPPLEMENT RECOMMENDATIONS FOR CANCER

Organic pancreas glandular assists the pancreas and provides extra pancreatic enzymes. It should be taken four times daily, after meals and mid-day. (for vegetarians, substitute chromium four times a day and vegetarian enzymes.)

Organic thymus glandular supports the thymus gland and immune system. It should be taken several times daily.

Vitamin C in ascorbate form is an antioxidant and helps to reduce the effect of toxic materials. It also activates white blood cells and increases the production of lymphocytes. Vitamin C may be used effectively in dosages of 10 grams or more, slowly dripped into the blood to reach optimum tissue level before excretion.

Bioflavonoids or Vitamin P help to absorb Vitamin C; they also offer protection against radiation and other toxic substances. They should be taken several times a day in doses of at least 500 mg.

B-complex is helpful in grounding the nervous system for those who are stressed or fatigued. It works with enzymes to convert carbohydrates to glucose, as well as being important in fat and protein metabolism.

Organo-germanium is an antioxidant which has an effect on the immune system in restoring the function of T-cells and stimulating interferon production. In Japan, 3-6 grams daily is used in treating cancer.

N Acetyl Cysteine binds with heavy metals such as lead, cadmium, and mercury, to aid in eliminating them from the body. A dose of 500mg. several times a day may be taken.

Vitamin A is an antioxidant that helps to fight off environmental toxins. It is best taken along with vitamin D.

Zinc is a mineral which can help to increase the production of T lymphocytes. Several 25 mg. capsules may be used a day.

EPA and DHA are found in fish oils. For those who are not eating fish, a capsule of salmon oil or another fish oil should be used a few times a day. Flax seed oil is also a good source of the Omega 3 fatty acids.

GLA oil is found in evening primrose oil and other oils; it protects the liver from toxins and helps the immune system. A capsule of evening primrose oil, which usually contains about 500 mg., may be used several times daily.

Probiotics—Various strands of intestinal bacteria help to produce immunity in the body. A good probiotics supplement should be used three times a day, preferably in powder form for assimilation.

HERBAL RECOMMENDATIONS

Chaparral tea is an excellent blood purifier and will help to re-build the immune system. Spearmint or peppermint may be added to help with the bitter taste. A combination of chaparral and red clover is excellent. Simmer three teaspoons of chaparral and three teaspoons of red clover in four cups of water for 10-15 minutes. Drink three cups daily or alternate days.

Other good blood purifiers that help to balance the immune system are **echinacea root, yarrow**, and **violet**.

Golden seal leaf, Oregon grape root, and **wild yam** are excellent herbs to detoxify the liver. Drinking several cups on alternate days is helpful. (It is good to alternate with the chapparal/red clover mixture.)

Wheatgrass juice helps the liver and also is an additional source of iron. It can be drunk alternate days, 2 ounces in water or in vegetable juice.

Aloe vera gel should be taken before bed at least every other evening. It will help to cleanse the colon and mucosal linings of the body. About $^1/_4$ cup of the gel should be used or the gel from 2 large leaves.

Thyme may be used on food; it helps the thymus gland.

CHAPTER 18

AIDS and HIV Virus

AIDS (Acquired Immune Deficiency Syndrome) and ARC (Aids Related Complex) refer to a group of symptoms caused by several viruses including the HIV virus. The viruses, bacteria, and fungi involved in the opportunistic infections include cytomegalovirus, cryptosporidia, Epstein-Barr virus, herpes virus, candida albicans, pneumocystis carini, and others. These viruses weaken the immune system so that it becomes invaded by forms of cancer such as Kaposi's sarcoma and pneumocystis carinii pneumonia. In addition, nutritional deficiencies, toxic chemicals in our environment and on our food, and emotional stress furthur deplete the immune system.

Much research has been conducted as to the causes of AIDS. Since World War II and especially since the 1970's, there has been an increased incidence of all the neuro-systemic degenerative diseases with the arrival of previously unheard of diseases like chronic fatigue syndrome and AIDS. Biological warfare, which started in 1942, paved the way to creating viruses and vaccines which would infect humans. Experimental infection with these genetically engineered hybrid viruses was reported to cause leukemia, lymphoma, and sarcoma. Donald W. Scott and

William L.C. Scott in Canada have documented government papers and medical journals in their books (see *The Brucellosis Triangle*, Chelmsford Publishers, Ontario, Canada) and in the Journal of Degenerative Diseases published by the Common Cause Medical Research Foundation. In this country, Leonard Horowitz has also documented these facts in his book, *Emerging Viruses: Aids and Ebola*, Tetrahedron Publishing.

The transmission of hybrid viruses from contaminated animals and laboratories involved in vaccine production might also explain the simultaneous outbreak of the first cases of AIDS in Africa and in New York in the late 1970's, as well as the peculiar epidemiology of AIDS, which initially affected white homosexual men in the United States and black heterosexual Africans. These outbreaks occurred shortly after hepatitis B vaccines were given to gay men in New York and to black men in Africa. The disease erupted in the United States in the gay community, among IV drug users, and among hemophiliacs who require blood transfusions; it also spread like wildfire throughout the African continent.

There are many medications that have served to keep the HIV virus in check, and to suppress the symptoms associated with AIDS related diseases. The most helpful treatments for AIDS may be those listed at the end of this chapter that work to keep the immune system healthy.

PSYCHOLOGICAL FACTORS

Since AIDS is a sexually transmitted disease, it affects relationships and gives rise to fears of sexual involvement. Often one holds back the expression of love and then feels more alone and inhibited. There has also been a stigma in our society regarding homosexual relationships; sometimes one's knowledge of having AIDS forces him to reveal his sexual identity. This has increased the stress level for many.

When one is under any kind of stress, the thymus gland shrinks (the thymus regulates the immune system), and white blood cells decrease. Depression, fear, and worry increase as one feels more lethargic.

Many individuals with AIDS had a sense of insecurity from childhood and problems with acceptance from their parents.

ASTROLOGICAL FACTORS

When the first cases of AIDS were discovered, Pluto was in Libra, the sign of relationships. In March 1981, with the first cases of Kaposi's sarcoma in

New York and Los Angeles, there was a Jupiter/Saturn conjunction at 8 degrees of Libra.

Many of those who developed AIDS in the beginning have fixed signs dominant in their horoscopes, especially Scorpio, which suggests that there is a blockage of emotions and also of toxins held in the body as Scorpio rules the colon and excretory system. Neptune tends to be prominent or several planets in Pisces, indicating a sensitive immune system as well as being psychically sensitive. These individuals may also be musicians, writers, or artists who in some cases have used psycho-active drugs and depleted their immune systems. Jupiter is also prominent in many of these horoscopes; Jupiter rules the liver and pancreas. If these are not functioning in optimum fashion, there are problems getting rid of toxic substances. In addition, Jupiter rules excesses in drinking and eating. Pluto is also strong in these horoscopes; the themes of confronting death as well as transforming sexuality are certainly indicated here.

In terms of planetary signatures, those who were first diagnosed with AIDS have Uranus in Cancer, suggesting a new way of relating emotionally as well as breaking bonds with families. They also have Neptune in Libra, a sign ruled by Venus, indicating a focus on the arts and also a more spiritual way of looking at relationships. Pluto is in Leo, showing the need to find one's power and transform individual egos.

MIDPOINTS

Saturn/Neptune—is the health axis but also deals with the immune functions

Mars/Neptune—relates to toxicity and the immune system

Jupiter/Neptune—indicates liver toxicity, sensitivity to alcohol and drugs

Venus/Neptune suggests weakened glandular functions and blood sugar problems

Frequent patterns in these charts were the following:

Saturn/Neptune = Sun, ascendant, Mars, or Pluto

Mars/Neptune = Sun, ascendant, or Pluto

HIV Positive—Woman
Natal Chart
Jul 16, 1959, 11:50 PM EDT +4:00
Bangor, Maine
44N48 04 068W46 42

Geocentric
Tropical
Koch
True Node

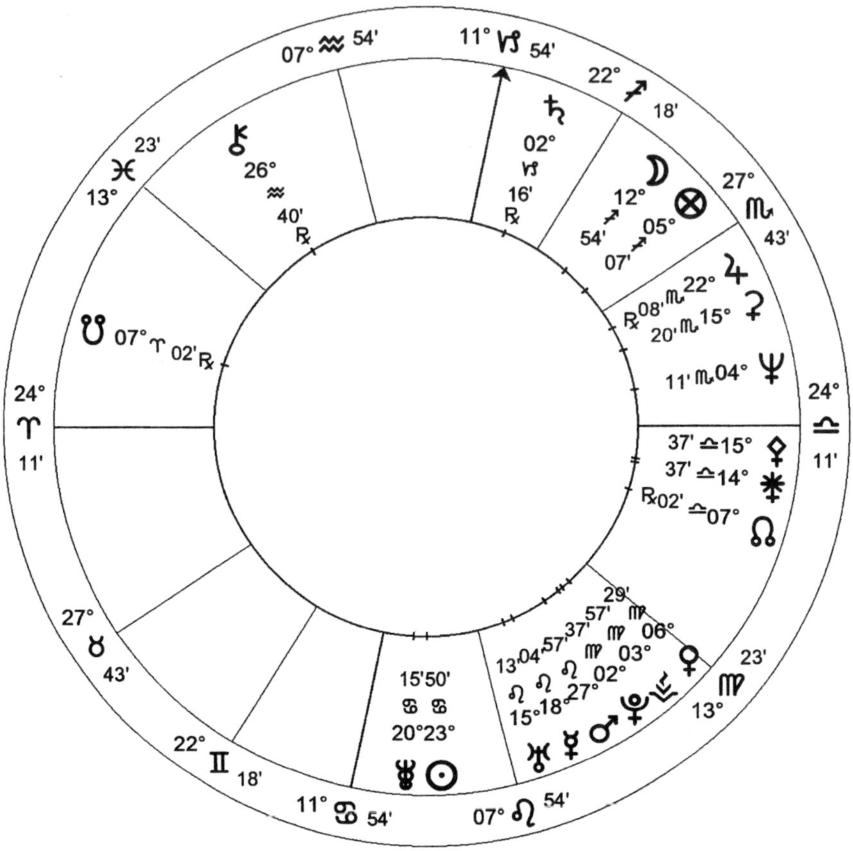

CASE HISTORIES

Case History #1

The first case history is that of a young woman who discovered she had HIV in April of 1995. A few weeks later she was diagnosed with AIDS. She was told she was only going to live for a few more years. She realized that the virus had been transmitted to her by a man, with whom she had been in relationship in 1986-7, but she was unaware of this until 1995. However, she is

Midpoint Listing

HIV Positive • Woman • Natal Chart

In Planetery Sequence • Modulus 360°00'

☽	12°♐54	*☿*	18°♌04	♂/♆	01°♎04	*♅*	15°♌13	⚷/⚶	08°♉27
☽/☉	03°♎22	☿/♀	27°♌16	♂/♇	00°♍17	♅/♆	24°♍42	⚷/☊	16°♐51
☽/☿	15°♎29	☿/♂	23°♌00	♂/⚷	27°♏18	♅/♇	23°♌55	⚷/⊗	15°♑53
☽/♀	24°♎41	☿/♃	05°♎06	♂/⚳	00°♍57	♅/⚷	20°♉57	*⚳*	03°♍57
☽/♂	20°♎25	☿/♄	25°♎10	♂/⚴	21°♍47	♅/⚳	24°♌35	⚳/⚴	24°♍47
☽/♃	02°♐31	☿/♅	16°♌38	♂/⚵	21°♍17	♅/⚴	15°♍25	⚳/⚵	24°♍17
☽/♄	22°♐35	☿/♆	26°♍07	♂/⚸	06°♎39	♅/⚵	14°♍55	⚳/⚸	09°♎39
☽/♅	14°♎03	☿/♇	25°♌20	♂/⚶	09°♌06	♅/⚸	00°♎17	⚳/⚶	12°♌06
☽/♆	23°♏32	☿/⚷	22°♉22	♂/☊	17°♍29	♅/⚶	02°♌44	⚳/☊	20°♍29
☽/♇	22°♎45	☿/⚳	26°♌00	♂/⊗	16°♎32	♅/☊	11°♍08	⚳/⊗	19°♎32
☽/⚷	19°♑47	☿/⚴	16°♍50	*♃*	22°♏08	♅/⊗	10°♎10	*⚴*	15°♎37
☽/⚳	23°♎25	☿/⚵	16°♍20	♃/♄	12°♐12	*♆*	04°♏11	⚴/⚵	15°♎07
☽/⚴	14°♏15	☿/⚸	01°♎42	♃/♅	03°♎41	♆/♇	03°♎24	⚴/⚸	00°♏29
☽/⚵	13°♏45	☿/⚶	04°♌09	♃/♆	13°♏09	♆/⚷	00°♑25	⚴/⚶	02°♍56
☽/⚸	29°♏07	☿/☊	12°♍33	♃/♇	12°♎22	♆/⚳	04°♎04	⚴/☊	11°♎19
☽/⚶	01°♎34	☿/⊗	11°♎35	♃/⚷	09°♑24	♆/⚴	24°♎54	⚴/⊗	10°♏22
☽/☊	09°♏58	*♀*	06°♍29	♃/⚳	13°♎02	♆/⚵	24°♎24	*⚵*	14°♎37
☽/⊗	09°♐00	♀/♂	02°♍13	♃/⚴	03°♏52	♆/⚸	09°♏46	⚵/⚸	29°♎59
☉	23°♋50	♀/♃	14°♎19	♃/⚵	03°♏22	♆/⚶	12°♍13	⚵/⚶	02°♍26
☉/☿	05°♌57	♀/♄	04°♏23	♃/⚸	18°♏44	♆/☊	20°♎36	⚵/☊	10°♎49
☉/♀	15°♌10	♀/♅	25°♌51	♃/⚶	21°♍11	♆/⊗	19°♏39	⚵/⊗	09°♏52
☉/♂	10°♌53	♀/♆	05°♎20	♃/☊	29°♎35	*♇*	02°♍37	*⚸*	15°♏20
☉/♃	22°♍59	♀/♇	04°♍33	♃/⊗	28°♏37	♇/⚷	29°♏38	⚸/⚶	17°♍48
☉/♄	13°♎03	♀/⚷	01°♐35	*♄*	02°♑16	♇/⚳	03°♍17	⚸/☊	26°♎11
☉/♅	04°♌32	♀/⚳	05°♍13	♄/♅	23°♎45	♇/⚴	24°♍07	⚸/⊗	25°♏14
☉/♆	14°♍00	♀/⚴	26°♍03	♄/♆	03°♐13	♇/⚵	23°♍37	*⚶*	20°♋15
☉/♇	13°♌13	♀/⚵	25°♍33	♄/♇	02°♏26	♇/⚸	08°♎59	⚶/☊	28°♌38
☉/⚷	10°♉15	♀/⚸	10°♎55	♄/⚷	29°♑28	♇/⚶	11°♌26	⚶/⊗	27°♍41
☉/⚳	13°♌53	♀/⚶	13°♌22	♄/⚳	03°♏06	♇/☊	19°♍49	*☊*	07°♎02
☉/⚴	04°♍43	♀/☊	21°♍46	♄/⚴	23°♏57	♇/⊗	18°♎52	☊/⊗	06°♏04
☉/⚵	04°♍13	♀/⊗	20°♎48	♄/⚵	23°♏26	*⚷*	26°♒40	*⊗*	05°♐07
☉/⚸	19°♍35	*♂*	27°♌57	♄/⚸	08°♐48	⚷/⚳	00°♐18		
☉/⚶	22°♋02	♂/♃	10°♎02	♄/⚶	11°♎15	⚷/⚴	21°♐08		
☉/☊	00°♍26	♂/♄	00°♏07	♄/☊	19°♏39	⚷/⚵	20°♐38		
☉/⊗	29°♍28	♂/♅	21°♌35	♄/⊗	18°♐42	⚷/⚸	06°♑00		

doing quite well today with the help of both medications and alternative treatments. In 1996, she started on medications that had just been released for HIV and did well at first, but then had side effects including depression and weight gain. She switched medications in May of 2000, and had other side effects including chest pain and anxiety. I also worked with her at that time adding some minerals, vitamins, and dietary suggestions. She is a singer and songwriter, and has been very active in the AIDS community, speaking and educating in the schools. Her medications were switched again in the summer of 2001, and she had side effects of candida and yeast in the back of her throat and lungs. She is ready to work with homeopathy and more alternative treatments now. On the positive side, the virus has not been detected, though she would like to strengthen her immune system.

Interpretation of Horoscope

This chart shows a Cancer Sun in the fourth house trine Jupiter in Scorpio in the seventh and exactly square an Aries ascendant. The Sun is conjoined the asteroid Hygeia, which shows an emphasis on healing. Mars, the ruler of the chart is in Leo conjoined Pluto, indicating a strong vital force and the ability to transform her energy. There are five planets in the fifth house emphasizing creativity. Her Moon is in Sagittarius in the eighth house trine the Mercury Uranus conjunction in Leo and square Venus in Virgo. The eighth house Moon also points to a strong theme of transformation on the emotional and spiritual levels. Mercury conjoined Uranus indicates a sensitive nervous system and lungs; with the square to Jupiter, the liver also can become toxic. Neptune is in her seventh house sextile the Venus Pluto conjunction and sextile Saturn in Capricorn in the ninth. Saturn is square the nodes, which are in the sixth and twelfth houses of healing; it is also sesquiquadrate the Mercury Uranus conjunction, which can indicate problems with the lungs.

By declination, the Sun is parallel Pluto and contra parallel Saturn, again emphasizing the theme of working on her body and strong transformation. The Moon is parallel Jupiter, referring to the liver, and contra parallel Uranus, her sensitive nervous system.

Midpoints

Sun/Moon = Saturn, direct, and Mercury, Uranus, indirect—possible problems with bones, joints, nervous system, and lungs

Mars/Neptune = Saturn, direct, and Mercury, Uranus, indirect—sensitive immune system, lungs particularly susceptible

Venus/Neptune = nodes, direct—tendency to blood sugar irregularities

Jupiter/Saturn = Moon, direct—restrictive functioning of the liver and gall bladder

Transits and Progressions

At the end of 1986, when her partner transmitted the HIV virus to her, the secondary progressed Moon was almost conjoined her natal Moon. By transit, Pluto was on her Neptune, ruling the immune system, and Neptune was conjunct Saturn. Transiting Uranus was trine her Mercury Uranus conjunction while Saturn was conjoining her Saturn/Neptune midpoint, the health axis. In October 1986, the solar eclipse hit her north node in the sixth house, while the lunar eclipse conjoined her ascendant.

In April 1995, when she discovered she was HIV positive and AIDS was diagnosed, her secondary progressed Moon was close to her south node in the twelfth house. Transiting Pluto was square her Pluto Vesta conjunction, Neptune was square her ascendant, and Uranus was inconjunct Pluto and Vesta. Saturn was inconjunct Mercury, and Jupiter was trine Mercury and Uranus. The lunar eclipse on April 15 was exactly opposite her ascendant.

Case History #2

This case is that of a man who was a very well know musician but passed away in July 1984. In January of 1982, he felt exhausted and took a six month leave to tour Australia and Hawaii. Although he was only 35, he felt tired and burned out. He was not diagnosed with AIDS until February of 1984, but he thought he had AIDS symptoms several months before. When I saw him in 1982, he was recovering from shingles in late November-December 1981, and also had strept throat. His nervous system was overly sensitive and he needed to focus on getting some nutritious food and good supplements into his body. Before he passed over, he had been in and out of a rehabilitation center for six months.

Interpretation of Horoscope

This chart shows a Taurus Sun in the eighth house broadly conjoined Mercury and opposite Jupiter in Scorpio. The Sun is also square Pluto, again emphasizing the eighth house themes of healing, confronting death, and deep transformation. His Moon in Sagittarius in the third house is conjoined the south node and trine both Saturn and Pluto in Leo. The Moon in the third house shows traveling and communications, especially in Sagittarius. He also had some issues with his family to work out, as seen by the south node and Moon conjunction. Libra is rising with Neptune close to the ascendant and opposed to his ruler Venus; this shows his strong affinity for music, and also his hypoglycemic tendencies and psychic

AIDS—Man
Natal Chart
May 6, 1947, 3:53 PM CST +6:00
Concordia
39N34 15 097W39 44

Geocentric
Tropical
Koch
True Node

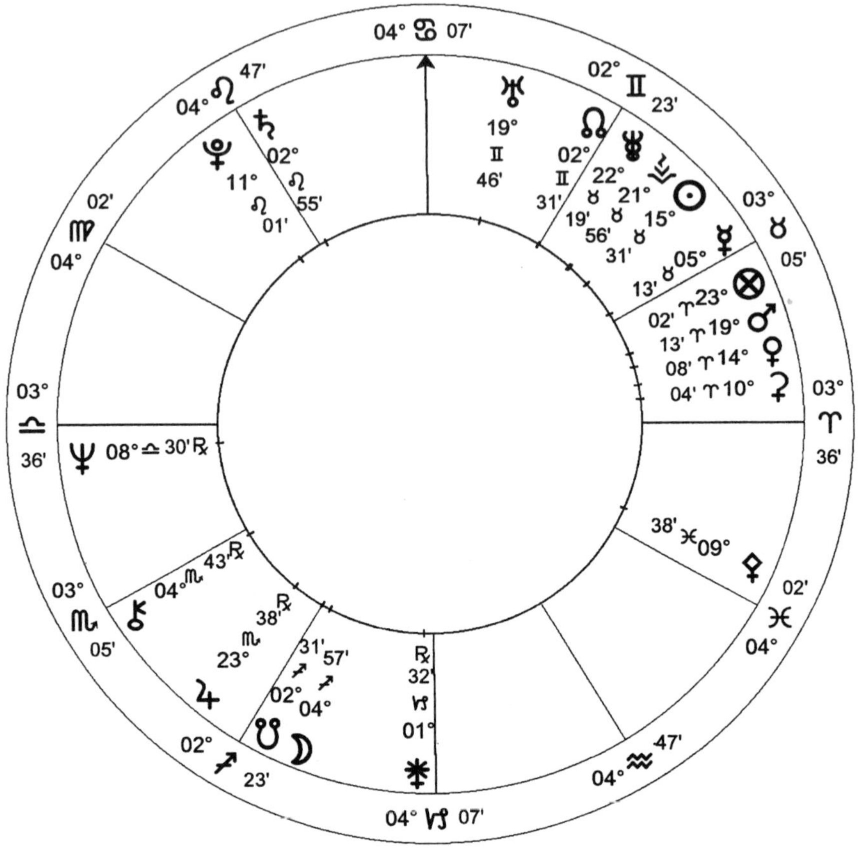

sensitivity. With Venus conjoined Mars in the seventh house, relationships were very important to him; the Venus Mars conjunction is sextile Uranus in his ninth house and trine Pluto in Leo. His Moon and south node in Sagittarius show a tendency to a weak liver; Neptune on the ascendant, his sensitive immune system. With Mercury square Saturn and inconjunct his Moon and south node, there is also the possibility of weak lungs and nervous system.

Midpoint Listing

AIDS • Man • Natal Chart
In Planetery Sequence • Modulus 360°00'

☽	04°♐57	*☿*	05°♉13	♂/♆	13°♋52	*♅*	19°♊46	⚷/⚸	13°♌31
☽/☉	25°♒14	☿/♀	24°♈40	♂/♇	15°♊07	♅/♆	14°♌08	⚷/☊	18°♌37
☽/☿	20°♒05	☿/♂	27°♈13	♂/⚷	26°♑58	♅/♇	15°♋23	⚷/⊗	28°♑53
☽/♀	09°♒32	☿/♃	14°♒25	♂/⚳	05°♉35	♅/⚷	27°♌14	*⚳*	21°♉56
☽/♂	12°♒05	☿/♄	19°♊04	♂/⚴	29°♓25	♅/⚳	05°♊51	⚳/⚴	15°♈47
☽/♃	29°♏17	☿/♅	27°♉29	♂/⚵	25°♒23	♅/⚴	29°♈42	⚳/⚵	11°♓44
☽/♄	03°♎56	☿/♆	21°♋52	♂/⚶	14°♈39	♅/⚵	25°♓39	⚳/⚶	01°♉00
☽/♅	12°♍21	☿/♇	23°♊07	♂/⚸	05°♉46	♅/⚶	14°♉55	⚳/⚸	22°♉08
☽/♆	06°♏44	☿/⚷	04°♌58	♂/☊	10°♉52	♅/⚸	06°♊03	⚳/☊	27°♉14
☽/♇	07°♎59	☿/⚳	13°♉35	♂/⊗	21°♈08	♅/☊	11°♊08	⚳/⊗	07°♉29
☽/⚷	19°♏50	☿/⚴	07°♈25	*♃*	23°♏38	♅/⊗	21°♉24	*⚴*	09°♓38
☽/⚳	28°♒27	☿/⚵	03°♓23	♃/♄	28°♍16	*♆*	08°♎30	⚴/⚵	05°♒35
☽/⚴	22°♑17	☿/⚶	22°♈39	♃/♅	06°♍42	♆/♇	09°♍45	⚴/⚶	24°♓51
☽/⚵	18°♐15	☿/⚸	13°♉46	♃/♆	01°♏04	♆/⚷	21°♎36	⚴/⚸	15°♈59
☽/⚶	07°♒31	☿/☊	18°♉52	♃/♇	02°♎19	♆/⚳	00°♌13	⚴/☊	21°♈05
☽/⚸	28°♒38	☿/⊗	29°♈08	♃/⚷	14°♏10	♆/⚴	24°♐04	⚴/⊗	01°♈20
☽/☊	03°♓44	*♀*	14°♈08	♃/⚳	22°♒47	♆/⚵	20°♏01	*⚵*	01°♑32
☽/⊗	14°♒00	♀/♂	16°♈40	♃/⚴	16°♑38	♆/⚶	09°♋17	⚵/⚶	20°♒48
☉	15°♉31	♀/♃	03°♒53	♃/⚵	12°♐35	♆/⚸	00°♌25	⚵/⚸	11°♓56
☉/☿	10°♉22	♀/♄	08°♊31	♃/⚶	01°♒51	♆/☊	05°♌31	⚵/☊	17°♓02
☉/♀	29°♈49	♀/♅	16°♉57	♃/⚸	22°♒59	♆/⊗	15°♋46	⚵/⊗	27°♒17
☉/♂	02°♉22	♀/♆	11°♋19	♃/☊	28°♌04	*♇*	11°♌01	*⚶*	10°♈04
☉/♃	19°♒34	♀/♇	12°♊34	♃/⊗	08°♒20	♇/⚷	22°♍52	⚶/⚸	01°♉12
☉/♄	24°♊13	♀/⚷	24°♑25	*♄*	02°♌55	♇/⚳	01°♋29	⚶/☊	06°♉18
☉/♅	02°♊38	♀/⚳	03°♉02	♄/♅	11°♋20	♇/⚴	25°♉19	⚶/⊗	16°♈33
☉/♆	27°♋00	♀/⚴	26°♓53	♄/♆	05°♍43	♇/⚵	21°♎17	*⚸*	22°♉19
☉/♇	28°♊16	♀/⚵	22°♒50	♄/♇	06°♌58	♇/⚶	10°♊32	⚸/☊	27°♉25
☉/⚷	10°♌07	♀/⚶	12°♈06	♄/⚷	18°♍49	♇/⚸	01°♋40	⚸/⊗	07°♉41
☉/⚳	18°♉43	♀/⚸	03°♉14	♄/⚳	27°♊26	♇/☊	06°♋46	*☊*	02°♊31
☉/⚴	12°♈34	♀/☊	08°♉19	♄/⚴	21°♉16	♇/⊗	17°♊02	☊/⊗	12°♉47
☉/⚵	08°♓32	♀/⊗	18°♈35	♄/⚵	17°♎14	*⚷*	04°♏43	*⊗*	23°♈02
☉/⚶	27°♈47	*♂*	19°♈13	♄/⚶	06°♊30	⚷/⚳	13°♌20		
☉/⚸	18°♉55	♂/♃	06°♒25	♄/⚸	27°♊37	⚷/⚴	07°♑10		
☉/☊	24°♉01	♂/♄	11°♊04	♄/☊	02°♋43	⚷/⚵	03°♐08		
☉/⊗	04°♉16	♂/♅	19°♉29	♄/⊗	12°♊59	⚷/⚶	22°♑23		

In terms of parallels of declination, his Sun is contra parallel Jupiter, again referring to his liver, while his Moon is contra parallel Saturn and the north node, indicating issues with his family.

Midpoints

Sun/Moon = Jupiter, direct, possible weakness and toxicity with the liver

Saturn/Neptune = Moon, direct, emotional sensitivity and depression

Mars/Neptune = Venus, direct, problems with blood sugar, difficulty digesting carbohydrates

Transits and Progressions

In January 1982, when he was feeling "burned out" and traveled to Australia, secondary progressed Mars was conjoined his Sun, progressed Sun was conjoined Uranus in his ninth house, and the progressed Moon was squaring his natal Moon. Transiting Neptune was sesquiquadrate Pluto, Uranus was conjoined his Sagittarian Moon, and Jupiter was conjoined Chiron. The lunar eclipse of January 9 was sesquiquadrate his Moon, while the solar eclipse on January 25 was opposite Saturn, square Mercury and Chiron.

In February 1984, when AIDS was diagnosed, the secondary progressed Sun was conjoined progressed Uranus. Transiting Pluto was square Saturn, and beginning to conjoin Chiron and oppose Mercury. Transiting Neptune was sesquiquadrate his Sun. Uranus was trine his Venus, while Saturn was opposite his Sun. Jupiter was conjoined the fourth house cusp, trine Mercury, and beginning to square Neptune. The lunar eclipse of December 20, 1983 was semi-square his Sun.

On July 15, 1984, when he passed over, transiting Pluto was still squaring Saturn. Neptune was sesquiquadrate his Sun, while Uranus was trine Pluto Saturn was square Pluto and Jupiter was on his fourth house cusp. The lunar eclipse of June 13 was opposite his Uranus.

SUGGESTIONS FOR MAINTAINING A HEALTHY IMMUNE SYSTEM

1. Cleanse the colon through colonic irrigations, enemas with wheatgrass implants, coffee enemas, supplements such as aloe vera juice, psyllium seed, and bentonite clay. Liquid fasts with vegetable juices, wheatgrass juice, vegetable broths, and herb teas are helpful as well.
2. Cleanse the skin through infra red saunas, which help get rid of toxic metals.
3. Cleanse the liver by using various herbs, as well as one half a cup of hot water with 2 T. olive oil and one quarter of a lemon upon rising. This should be done every few months, particularly the week prior to having a colonic.
4. Cleanse the kidneys by drinking parsley tea each morning for a week every few months.

5. Eat lightly, with only organic foods, emphasizing dark green leafy vegetables, such as collard greens, arugula, mustard greens, dandelion greens, and kale. Eliminate animal fats and dairy products, sweeteners, and acidic foods such as most fruits, vinegar, brewer's yeast, cranberries, tomatoes, green pepper, and raw spinach. Use fresh ocean fish such as Alaskan salmon, not farm raised fish, which have been given genetically engineered foods. Use cooked whole grains such as buckwheat, barley, quinoa, brown rice, millet, amaranth, and oats, but not wheat as it is mucous forming. Use root vegetables such as turnips, potatoes, squash, and carrots. Later, organic liver and poultry may be added to the diet. Use cold pressed vegetable oils, especially flax seed oil and olive oil.
6. Acupuncture is helpful in working with the "chi" energy and in tonifying the liver, spleen, lungs, and kidneys. Body therapies that work with the meridian system such as jin shinn do and shiatsu should also be incorporated.
7. It is important to obtain one's constitutional homeopathic remedy to boost the vital force.

SUPPLEMENT RECOMMENDATIONS FOR AIDS AND HIV

Bioflavonoids with Quercetin several times a day. Quercetin has strong anti-viral properties.

Vitamin C ascorbate (in powdered or crystalline form) increases interferon production and can activate the immune response to viruses.

Pantothenic Acid or Vitamin B-5 helps the adrenal glands to produce cortisone and other adrenal hormones to counteract stress.

Probiotics promote intestinal bacteria that grow in the colon. They replace intestinal bacteria that may have been killed by any pharmaceutical drugs; they also help the immune system.

Green drink containing barley, alfalfa, and wheat grasses. This is an important source of chlorophyll, minerals, and certain vitamins.

Zinc is the most important mineral for the immune system, improving antibody response, and regulating the function of the white blood cells.

Vitamin E is used for its antioxidant properties.

Vitamin A is a strong antioxidant, which helps to fight off environmental toxins. It may be used with vitamin D.

Coenzyme Q-10 or Ubiquinone is an antioxidant and immune stimulant, which has proven helpful in the treatment of AIDS.

Glutathione and L-cysteine are antioxidants which help to protect against environmental toxins, heavy metals, cigarette smoke, and radiation exposure by detoxifying these chemicals into less toxic forms. Glutathione is obtained from L-cysteine or N-acetyl cysteine.

Lipoic Acid is a strong antioxidant that is manufactured in trace amounts in the body. It increases the level of glutathione, the most important antioxidant compound in the body.

GLA oil (Gamma linolenic acid) protects the liver from irritating drugs and toxins, and helps the immune system.

Adrenal glandulars are helpful for fatigue and stress.

HERBAL RECOMMENDATIONS

Garlic is antiviral and antifungal. It contains the bioflavonoid Quercetin and should be used fresh in cooking every day.

Chaparral is one of the best natural antibiotics and works well in treating bacterial and viral infections. Since it is a very bitter herb, it also works to detoxify the liver and is often mixed with other herbs such as the mints to make it more palatable.

Echinacea root helps to purify the blood and the lymph. It can increase the white blood cell count and stimulate the production of T cells.

Goldenseal leaf is an excellent herb to detoxify the liver and clear the whole digestive system.

CHAPTER 19

Neuromuscular Diseases: Multiple Sclerosis

NEUROMUSCULAR DISEASES INCLUDE MULTIPLE SCLEROSIS, muscular dystrophy, and myasthenia gravis. MS is the most common neuromuscular disease diagnosed in people between the ages of 20 and 50. It affects women almost three times more than men and generally appears more common in people in a higher socio-economic class. The immune system in those with MS reacts abnormally; it fails to recognize myelin as its own and attacks it as if it were foreign tissue.

Multiple sclerosis (MS) is a disease of the central nervous system in which a vital insulating material called myelin is destroyed or damaged. When this occurs, the messages from the brain's "thinking" cells to the "doing cells" and spinal cord are short circuited. The range of symptoms depends on where the short circuiting occurs. Symptoms range from extreme fatigue, decreased or blurred vision, numbness, tingling, dizziness, tremors, loss of bladder and bowel control, faulty speech, and paralysis in specific areas.

Traditional Chinese Medicine looks at MS, muscular dystrophy, and myasthenia gravis—all dealing with muscle feebleness or flaccidity, as having two basic categories of causes—external pathogens and internal organ dysfunction. Pathogens are toxins from viral, bacterial, or yeast infections, exposure to chemicals, pesticides, or preservatives. These toxins accumulate and create an invasion of external damp heat into the body. Internal disorders which block "chi" energy to the muscles are attributed to a deficiency of the spleen and stomach, or of the liver and kidneys. Spleen and stomach deficiency can be caused by long term illness, digestive disturbances due to anti-acids and spicy foods, as well as by medications such as antibiotics, anti-inflammatories, or pain killers. Medications which are immunosuppressive such as chemotherapeutic agents can kill blood cells and also lead to spleen or stomach deficiency.

Deficiency of spleen or stomach leads to nutritional malabsorption. When the nervous system and blood are not replenished nutritionally, there is a liver blood deficiency and a kidney "chi" deficiency, which causes the withering of muscles (flaccidity) and bone marrow deficiency.

External toxins or pathogens most commonly enter through inhalation (the lungs) or by ingestion (the digestive tract). If the lung and digestive systems do not expel the pathogens, they invade the blood stream. The liver and kidney systems can filter toxins from the blood and dump them through the digestive tract, skin, or urinary tract. If these are not expelled, they allow heat and dampness to accumulate.

The liver is responsible for cleaning the toxins out of the blood and tissues; it also circulates "chi" to the muscles, tendons, skin, and nails. The liver system can be weakened by excess sweets, alcohol, fats, drugs (including medications), a serious viral infection such as hepatitis, or excessive expression of anger.

The kidney builds healthy bone and bone marrow, nurtures the brain and spinal cord, controls minerals and the chemical balance of the body for all organs, maintains fluid balance, and hormone balance. The kidney controls the use of "chi"(the central nervous system). Without "chi," blood cannot be lead to muscle. Without fluids, muscles cannot be adequately lubricated. Without minerals, muscles cannot contract. This deficiency of "chi," fluids, and minerals can create muscle flaccidity.

PSYCHOLOGICAL FACTORS

Psychologically, individuals with MS may be inflexible and rigid. They need to let go of control and flow with the universal energy. They also tend to be over achievers and take on too much. Some of these individuals were very vulnerable as children, but had little opportunity to express their emotions.

ASTROLOGICAL FACTORS

A sensitive nervous system is always involved. There may be several planets in Aquarius or Gemini. The Sun or Moon may be conjunct Mercury. Mars may be in Gemini or Aquarius. Mars may be making a hard aspect to Mercury or Uranus.

There is also a strong Saturn theme relating to body structure—Mars conjoined, opposite, or square Saturn, Sun conjoined Saturn, Capricorn Moon, or south node in Capricorn, are some of the ways this is expressed.

A weak immune system is also prevalent. This is sometimes manifest as a Pisces Sun or Moon; Mars in Pisces; Moon conjoined Neptune; Sun, Mars, or Jupiter conjoined Neptune.

MIDPOINTS

Of the general health midpoints, Saturn/Neptune, Mars/Neptune, Mars/Uranus, and Mars/Saturn are important to check out. Other midpoints are:

Mercury/Uranus—relates to the spinal cord and disturbances of equilibrium

Mercury/Neptune—indicates the paralysis of the nerves, nervous weakness, and the loss of feeling or sensing

CASE HISTORIES

Case History #1

This is a woman who has had problems since 1983, and is now bedridden. She was living in Seattle when she had a bad back injury, from which she didn't heal. In 1994, she was diagnosed with MS; she had been working as a nurse for thirty years but had to quit work in June 1995 and go on disability. In 1996, she could still walk with a walker. Since 1998, she has been confined to bed except for going to the bathroom. In July 2001, she fell and could no longer get out of bed. She had to move out of her home, where her 85 year old mother was taking care of her, to a nursing home. She has done a lot of alternative healing— working with a chiropractor for years, studying and using Ayurvedic herbs for her digestive system, having acupuncture and massage treatments, as well as using many good nutritional supplements.

MS—Woman 1
Natal Chart
Jan 22, 1947, 8:35 AM EST +5:00
New York
40N42 51 074W00 23

Geocentric
Tropical
Koch
True Node

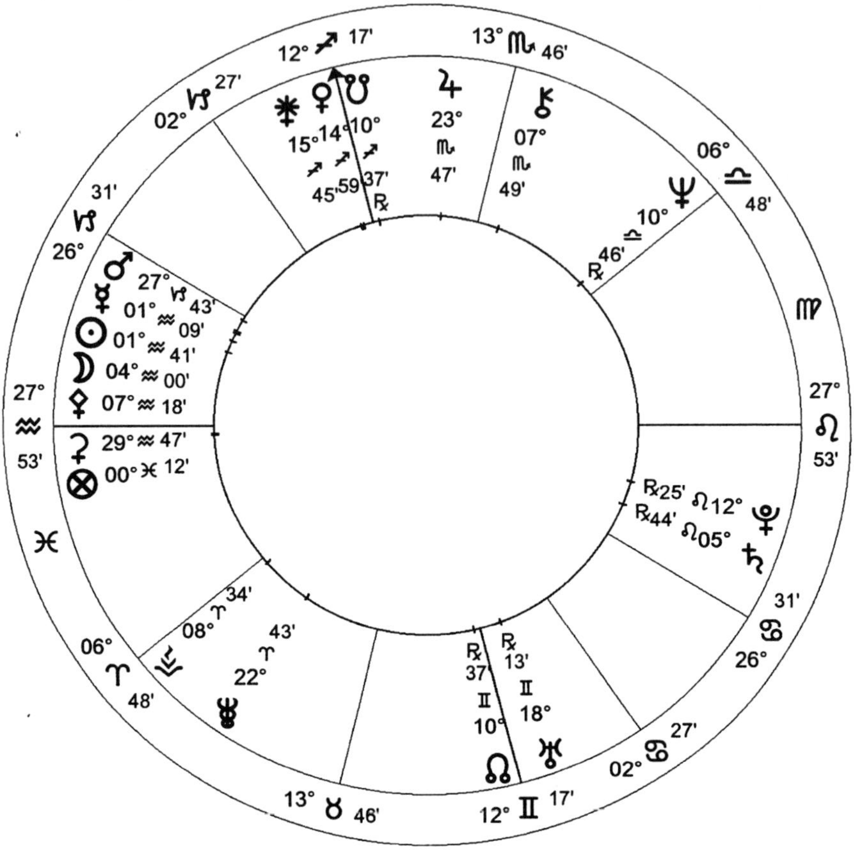

Interpretation of Horoscope

The Aquarian element is very strong in this chart with Sun, Mercury, Moon, and ascendant in Aquarius, as well as the asteroids Pallas and Ceres. They are all in the twelfth house, except Ceres, with the Sun and Mercury sesquiquadrate Uranus. Saturn is opposing them from the sixth house; with Saturn conjoined Pluto, there is even more of a challenge to the nervous system. The fact that she was a nurse who studied many systems of

Midpoint Listing

MS • Woman 1 • Natal Chart
In Planetery Sequence • Modulus 360°00'

☽	04°♒00	*☿*	01°♒09	♂/♆	04°♐15	*♅*	18°♊13	⚷/⯚	00°♒16
☽/☉	02°♒51	☿/♀	08°♑04	♂/♇	05°♏04	♅/♆	14°♌30	⚷/☊	24°♌13
☽/☿	02°♒35	☿/♂	29°♑26	♂/⚷	17°♐46	♅/♇	15°♋19	⚷/⊗	04°♑01
☽/♀	09°♑30	☿/♃	27°♐28	♂/⚶	03°♓09	♅/⚷	28°♌01	*⚶*	08°♈34
☽/♂	00°♒52	☿/♄	03°♏26	♂/⚴	02°♒30	♅/⚶	13°♉24	⚶/⚴	07°♓56
☽/♃	28°♐54	☿/♅	09°♈41	♂/⚵	06°♑44	♅/⚴	12°♈45	⚶/⚵	12°♒10
☽/♄	04°♏52	☿/♆	05°♐57	♂/⚳	13°♒45	♅/⚵	16°♍59	⚶/⚳	19°♓11
☽/♅	11°♈07	☿/♇	06°♏47	♂/⯚	10°♓13	♅/⚳	24°♈00	⚶/⯚	15°♈39
☽/♆	07°♐23	☿/⚷	19°♐29	♂/☊	04°♈10	♅/⯚	20°♉28	⚶/☊	09°♉36
☽/♇	08°♏13	☿/⚶	04°♓52	♂/⊗	13°♒58	♅/☊	14°♊25	⚶/⊗	19°♓23
☽/⚷	20°♐55	☿/⚴	04°♒13	*♃*	23°♏47	♅/⊗	24°♈13	*⚴*	07°♒18
☽/⚶	06°♓17	☿/⚵	08°♑27	♃/♄	29°♍45	*♆*	10°♎46	⚴/⚵	11°♑32
☽/⚴	05°♒39	☿/⚳	15°♒28	♃/♅	06°♍00	♆/♇	11°♍36	⚴/⚳	18°♒32
☽/⚵	09°♑53	☿/⯚	11°♓56	♃/♆	02°♏17	♆/⚷	24°♎18	⚴/⯚	15°♓01
☽/⚳	16°♒54	☿/☊	05°♈53	♃/♇	03°♎06	♆/⚶	09°♑40	⚴/☊	08°♈58
☽/⯚	13°♓22	☿/⊗	15°♒40	♃/⚷	15°♏48	♆/⚴	09°♐02	⚴/⊗	18°♒45
☽/☊	07°♈19	*♀*	14°♐59	♃/⚶	01°♒11	♆/⚵	13°♏16	*⚵*	15°♐45
☽/⊗	17°♒06	♀/♂	06°♑21	♃/⚴	00°♑32	♆/⚳	20°♐16	⚵/⚳	22°♑46
☉	01°♒41	♀/♃	04°♐23	♃/⚵	04°♐46	♆/⯚	16°♋45	⚵/⯚	19°♒14
☉/☿	01°♒25	♀/♄	10°♎22	♃/⚳	11°♑47	♆/☊	10°♌42	⚵/☊	13°♓11
☉/♀	08°♑20	♀/♅	16°♍36	♃/⯚	08°♒15	♆/⊗	20°♐29	⚵/⊗	22°♑59
☉/♂	29°♑42	♀/♆	12°♏53	♃/☊	02°♍12	*♇*	12°♌25	*⚳*	29°♒47
☉/♃	27°♐44	♀/♇	13°♎42	♃/⊗	12°♑00	♇/⚷	25°♍07	⚳/⯚	26°♓15
☉/♄	03°♏43	♀/⚷	26°♏24	*♄*	05°♌44	♇/⚶	10°♊30	⚳/☊	20°♈12
☉/♅	09°♈57	♀/⚶	11°♒47	♄/♅	11°♋58	♇/⚴	09°♏52	⚳/⊗	29°♒59
☉/♆	06°♐14	♀/⚴	11°♑09	♄/♆	08°♍15	♇/⚵	14°♎05	*⯚*	22°♈43
☉/♇	07°♏03	♀/⚵	15°♐22	♄/♇	09°♌05	♇/⚳	21°♉06	⯚/☊	16°♉40
☉/⚷	19°♐45	♀/⚳	22°♑23	♄/⚷	21°♍46	♇/⯚	17°♊34	⯚/⊗	26°♓28
☉/⚶	05°♓08	♀/⯚	18°♒51	♄/⚶	07°♊09	♇/☊	11°♋31	*☊*	10°♊37
☉/⚴	04°♒30	♀/☊	12°♓48	♄/⚴	06°♉31	♇/⊗	21°♉19	☊/⊗	20°♈25
☉/⚵	08°♑43	♀/⊗	22°♑36	♄/⚵	10°♎45	*⚷*	07°♏49	*⊗*	00°♓12
☉/⚳	15°♒44	*♂*	27°♑43	♄/⚳	17°♉45	⚷/⚶	23°♑12		
☉/⯚	12°♓12	♂/♃	25°♐45	♄/⯚	14°♊14	⚷/⚴	22°♐33		
☉/☊	06°♈09	♂/♄	01°♏43	♄/☊	08°♋11	⚷/⚵	26°♏47		
☉/⊗	15°♒57	♂/♅	07°♈58	♄/⊗	17°♉58	⚷/⚳	03°♑48		

alternative healing can be seen here. The chart shows a very sensitive nervous system, as well as problems with respiratory allergies. Jupiter is in Scorpio exactly square the ascendant, which indicates possible problems with the liver. This is accentuated by the south node in Sagittarius conjoined Venus, which also shows a tendency to low blood sugar. Venus is opposite Uranus, indicating potential problems with the thyroid as well. Mars is in the twelfth house in Capricorn, semi-square Venus, and the south node, and broadly opposite Saturn. There is a grand trine in air between Neptune in Libra, the north node in Gemini, and the Aquarian Moon, showing her talents in communication and writing. She wants to write a book on her experiences if gets her health back. Currently, she is not able to write.

In terms of parallels of declination, everything is very close together. The Moon is parallel Mercury and Mars, while contra parallel to Uranus, Pluto, and the north node. This again shows her sensitive nervous system and proneness to respiratory allergies. The Sun is parallel Venus, Jupiter, and Ceres, while contra parallel Saturn. This points to possible problems with the liver and low blood sugar.

Midpoints

Mars/Saturn = Sun and Mercury, direct; Uranus, indirect—blockages in the neurological system

Mars/Uranus = Jupiter, indirect—possible liver problems affecting the nervous system

Mars/Pluto = Moon, direct—need for emotional transformation, potential long term illness

Mercury/Uranus = Neptune, direct; ascendant, indirect—connection between the immune system and nervous system

Transits and Progressions

In 1983, when she had the accident, secondary progressed Mars was almost on her ascendant. Transiting Pluto and Saturn were square her natal Mars. Neptune was semi-square her Pluto. Uranus was trine Saturn, sextile her Moon, and conjoined the Mercury/Neptune midpoint.

In 1994, when MS was diagnosed, the secondary progressed Moon was in Scorpio, square her Aquarius and Leo planets. Transiting Pluto was conjunct Jupiter and square the ascendant, Neptune and Uranus were transiting the indirect Saturn/Neptune midpoint. Saturn was square the nodes while Jupiter was squaring both the Moon and Saturn. The solar eclipse of May 10 opposed her Jupiter.

In July 2001, progressed Mercury was conjunct progressed Mars, and her progressed Moon was conjunct natal Sun. Transiting Pluto was on her MC, while transiting Saturn was conjoined her fourth house cusp. Neptune was opposing Saturn and Uranus was square Jupiter, almost conjunct her ascendant. The lunar eclipse of July 5 squared Neptune.

Case History #2

This woman experienced her first symptoms at the age of 21, when she had severe vertigo and had to be hospitalized. That was at the time of her first year of teaching; she was also working on a Master's degree. She taught for 11 years and always felt tired, but kept pushing herself. At this time, she started her own business as a communications consultant, working long hours with individual companies. She maintained this business for 9 years, finally leaving in June 1992, due to her failing health. Her main symptoms were a weakness in her right leg and increasing fatigue. This forced her to stop jogging and dancing; she rented a cottage in the Berkshires with her husband to rest. Then she had trouble lifting her right arm above her head. She finally sought out a neurologist, who gave her tests for MS, which proved positive. When she first consulted with me in 1997, she was in training for Psychosynthesis and transformational psychology. Her symptoms included spasticity in the legs, optic neuritis in the left eye, some slurring of speech, overall weakness of muscles, and some urinary and digestive problems. She was able to control most of her symptoms through frequent visits to a chiropractor and massage therapist, along with some mild exercise, nutritional supplements, and Chinese herbs. After our consultation, she did some colonics, liver cleansing, and worked to get her body more alkaline. She also used some herbs and made some dietary adjustments.

Interpretation of Horoscope

Her Pisces Sun is in the tenth house inconjunct Saturn in Libra. Mercury is in Aquarius in the tenth opposite a Moon Pluto conjunction in Leo and squaring the asteroid Vesta. This shows possible problems with the nervous system and circulation, with a tendency to deficiencies in magnesium and the B vitamins. Jupiter, north node, Mars, and Venus are conjunct in Pisces in addition to her Sun, indicating a very sensitive immune system. Jupiter and the north node are also inconjunct Neptune, and inconjunct the Moon Pluto conjunction in Leo, forming a Yod formation. Since Jupiter rules the liver and is the focal point of the Yod, there is the tendency to have a toxic liver. Uranus in Cancer is trine her Sun, but square Saturn, opposite Chiron, and inconjunct the MC, focusing again on the nervous system.

MS—Woman 2
Natal Chart
Feb 20, 1951, 10:30 AM EST +5:00
Brooklyn, NY
40N38 073W56

Geocentric
Tropical
Koch
True Node

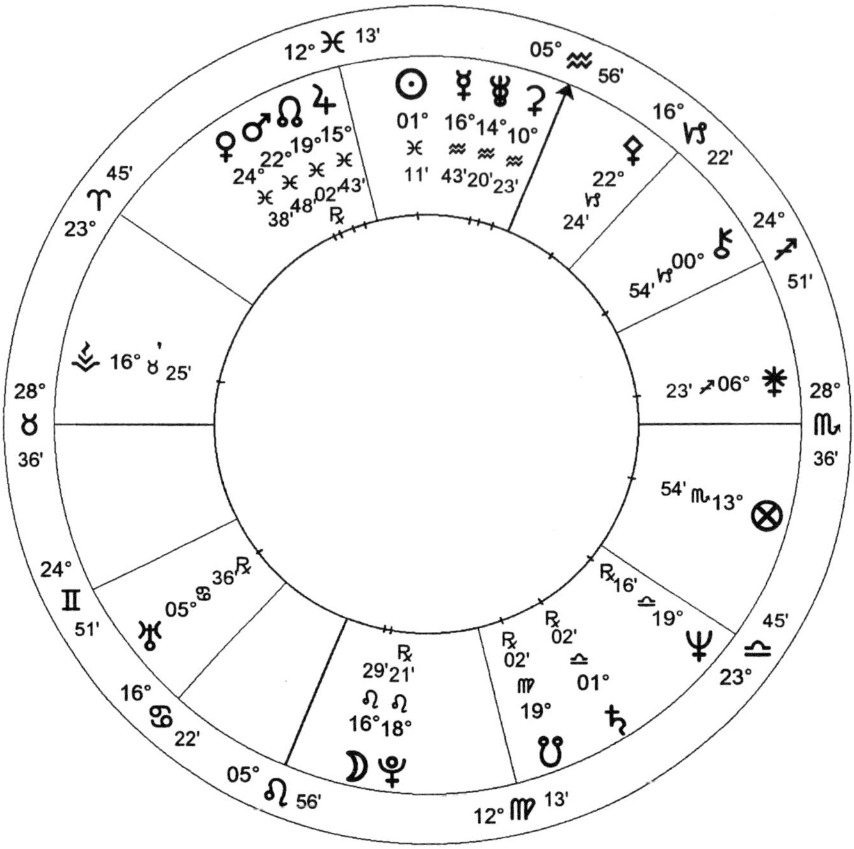

In terms of parallels of declination, the Moon is contra parallel Mercury and Chiron, again indicating the sensitive nervous system. Venus is parallel Mars and the north node, which could indicate low blood sugar.

Midpoints

Mars/Uranus = Mercury and Moon, direct—problems with the nervous system and circulation

Midpoint Listing

MS • Woman 2 • Natal Chart
In Planetery Sequence • Modulus 360°00'

☽	16°♌29	*☿*	16°♒43	♂/♆	06°♑02	*♅*	05°♋36	⚷/⚶	22°♑37
☽/☉	23°♉50	☿/♀	05°♓41	♂/♇	05°♊35	♅/♆	27°♌26	⚷/☊	09°♒58
☽/☿	16°♉36	☿/♂	04°♓46	♂/⚷	11°♒51	♅/♇	26°♋59	⚷/⊗	07°♐24
☽/♀	05°♊33	☿/♃	01°♓13	♂/⚸	19°♈37	♅/⚷	03°♎15	*⚸*	16°♉25
☽/♂	04°♊38	☿/♄	08°♐52	♂/⚴	22°♒36	♅/⚸	11°♊01	⚸/⚴	19°♓25
☽/♃	01°♊06	☿/♅	26°♈10	♂/⚵	29°♑35	♅/⚴	14°♈00	⚸/⚵	26°♒24
☽/♄	08°♍45	☿/♆	18°♐00	♂/⚳	01°♓35	♅/⚵	21°♍00	⚸/⚳	28°♓24
☽/♅	26°♋03	☿/♇	17°♏32	♂/⚶	03°♓34	♅/⚳	23°♈00	⚸/⚶	00°♈23
☽/♆	17°♍53	☿/⚷	23°♑48	♂/☊	20°♓55	♅/⚶	24°♈58	⚸/☊	17°♈43
☽/♇	17°♌25	☿/⚸	01°♈34	♂/⊗	18°♑21	♅/☊	12°♉19	⚸/⊗	15°♌10
☽/⚷	23°♎41	☿/⚴	04°♒34	*♃*	15°♓43	♅/⊗	09°♍45	*⚴*	22°♑24
☽/⚸	01°♋27	☿/⚵	11°♑33	♃/♄	23°♐22	*♆*	19°♎16	⚴/⚵	29°♐23
☽/⚴	04°♏26	☿/⚳	13°♒33	♃/♅	10°♉40	♆/♇	18°♍49	⚴/⚳	01°♒23
☽/⚵	11°♎26	☿/⚶	15°♒32	♃/♆	02°♑30	♆/⚷	25°♏05	⚴/⚶	03°♒22
☽/⚳	13°♏26	☿/☊	02°♓52	♃/♇	02°♊02	♆/⚸	02°♌51	⚴/☊	20°♒43
☽/⚶	15°♏25	☿/⊗	00°♑19	♃/⚷	08°♒18	♆/⚴	05°♐50	⚴/⊗	18°♐09
☽/☊	02°♊45	*♀*	24°♓38	♃/⚸	16°♈04	♆/⚵	12°♏50	*⚵*	06°♐23
☽/⊗	00°♎12	♀/♂	23°♓43	♃/⚴	19°♒04	♆/⚳	14°♐50	⚵/⚳	08°♑23
☉	01°♓11	♀/♃	20°♓11	♃/⚵	26°♑03	♆/⚶	16°♐48	⚵/⚶	10°♑22
☉/☿	23°♒57	♀/♄	27°♐50	♃/⚳	28°♒03	♆/☊	04°♑09	⚵/☊	27°♑42
☉/♀	12°♓54	♀/♅	15°♉07	♃/⚶	00°♓02	♆/⊗	01°♏35	⚵/⊗	25°♏08
☉/♂	11°♓59	♀/♆	06°♑57	♃/☊	17°♓23	*♇*	18°♌21	*⚳*	10°♒23
☉/♃	08°♓27	♀/♇	06°♊30	♃/⊗	14°♑49	♇/⚷	24°♎37	⚳/⚶	12°♒22
☉/♄	16°♐06	♀/⚷	12°♒46	*♄*	01°♎02	♇/⚸	02°♋23	⚳/☊	29°♒42
☉/♅	03°♉24	♀/⚸	20°♈32	♄/♅	18°♌19	♇/⚴	05°♏23	⚳/⊗	27°♐08
☉/♆	25°♐14	♀/⚴	23°♒31	♄/♆	10°♎09	♇/⚵	12°♎22	*⚶*	14°♒20
☉/♇	24°♉46	♀/⚵	00°♒30	♄/♇	09°♍41	♇/⚳	14°♏22	⚶/☊	01°♓41
☉/⚷	01°♒02	♀/⚳	02°♓30	♄/⚷	15°♏58	♇/⚶	16°♏21	⚶/⊗	29°♐07
☉/⚸	08°♈48	♀/⚶	04°♓29	♄/⚸	23°♋43	♇/☊	03°♊41	*☊*	19°♓02
☉/⚴	11°♒47	♀/☊	21°♓50	♄/⚴	26°♏43	♇/⊗	01°♎08	☊/⊗	16°♑28
☉/⚵	18°♑47	♀/⊗	19°♑16	♄/⚵	03°♏42	*⚷*	00°♑54	*⊗*	13°♏54
☉/⚳	20°♒47	*♂*	22°♓48	♄/⚳	05°♐42	⚷/⚸	08°♓39		
☉/⚶	22°♒46	♂/♃	19°♓16	♄/⚶	07°♐41	⚷/⚴	11°♑39		
☉/☊	10°♓06	♂/♄	26°♐55	♄/☊	25°♐02	⚷/⚵	18°♐38		
☉/⊗	07°♑33	♂/♅	14°♉12	♄/⊗	22°♎28	⚷/⚳	20°♑38		

Mercury/Neptune = nodes, direct—connection between nervous system and immune system

Transits and Progressions

In 1972, when she first experienced vertigo, transiting Pluto was conjoined her Saturn and inconjunct her Sun. Neptune was semi-square Neptune, while Uranus was conjoined Neptune. Saturn was on her ascendant, and

Jupiter was square her north node, Mars, and Venus. The solar eclipse on January 16 was conjoined the Mercury Uranus midpoint, while the lunar eclipse on January 30 was sesquiquadrate Venus and Mars.

In June 1992, when she left her job, her progressed Moon had just gone into Pisces, conjoining her Sun and inconjunct Saturn. Transiting Pluto was square Pluto. Neptune and Uranus were square Neptune, and Saturn was conjoined Mercury. On June 15, the lunar eclipse was square her nodes, Venus, and Mars, while on June 30 the solar eclipse was conjoined Uranus.

TREATMENTS FOR MS AND OTHER NEUROMUSCULAR DISEASES

1. Physical therapies such as exercise, massage, and other body therapies relax muscles and increase circulation to affected limbs.
2. Hydrotherapy, which includes hot mineral baths as well as hot and cold showers, stimulates and relaxes the nervous system.
3. Chelation therapy helps to get rid of toxic metals, which can bind with candida and use up the body's nutrients.
4. Colonics and liver cleanses help the liver and colon, allowing better assimilation of nutrients.
5. Acupuncture and Chinese herbs work with deficiencies of spleen and stomach, as well as liver and kidneys, helping to unblock "chi" energy to the muscles.
6. Using ozone and oxygen therapy is very helpful. In England, hyperbaric oxygen (a chamber used by deep sea divers) is the primary treatment for MS.
7. An intravenous form of calcium known as calcium AEP helps tremendously. However, it is very expensive since it has to be obtained from Europe and administered by an MD.

SUPPLEMENT RECOMMENDATIONS FOR MS

Calcium/Magnesium should be taken in a powdered form in high doses throughout the day on an empty stomach.

Quercetin Bioflavonoids help with circulation and the immune system and should be taken several times during the day.

Super B complex is most important to balance the nervous system; often B complex is given intravenously along with vitamin C and magnesium.

Magnesium is helpful given intravenously as well as through capsules, and by drinking liquid chlorophyll, which provides the magnesium ion.

B-12 and **folic acid** injections should be given once or twice a week. In addition, a sub-lingual supplement may be used.

EPA and **DHA**, which are found in fish oils, generate Series 3 prostaglandins and have some anti-inflammatory effects. If fish is a part of the diet, they may not be needed as much as in a vegetarian diet.

Evening Primrose Oil contains GLA, which stimulates certain prostaglandins and is anti-inflammatory. GLA also helps nerve conduction and immune support.

Phosphatydyl Serine is a brain food that helps with all neurological problems; it is also an anti-aging supplement.

Pancreas Glandular (organic) helps with digestion and keeps up the blood sugar. For vegetarians, chromium may be taken instead.

Octacosanol brings more oxygen to the lungs and muscles and thus works well for neuromuscular disorders.

MSM has antioxidant properties and is helpful in treating neuromuscular disorders.

HERBAL RECOMMENDATIONS

Echinacea root is a powerful herb for the immune system. It can stimulate the production of T cells and increase the white blood cell count. It is also a strong blood purifier.

Astragalus is a Chinese herb which is very potent for the immune system; it is often used in combination with other herbs, particularly Chinese licorice, which helps bring the energy to all the meridians.

Rehmannia is a Chinese herb that works to energize the kidney; it is used in formulas along with other herbs.

Golden seal leaf helps to detoxify the liver and clear the digestive system.

Alfalfa, Nettles and Horsetail provide an excellent way to get more minerals into the body, as alfalfa contains many minerals and amino acids, nettles is high in iron, and horsetail is high in silica. Alfalfa is also alkalinizing to the body.

CHAPTER 20

Neurodegenerative Diseases: Parkinson's and Altzheimer's

PARKINSON'S DISEASE

Parkinson's disease is a progressive disorder of the central nervous system. It is characterized by a loss of spontaneous movements, gait difficulty, rigidity, and tremor. In Parkinson's, there is a degeneration of neurons in the *substantia nigra* of the brain resulting in decreased dopamine availability. Causes of Parkinson's have been attributed to a virus, to carbon monoxide poisoning, and other toxic substances, and in older patients, to cerebral arteriosclerosis.

Recently, researchers have found that environmental conditions can interact with a genetic predisposition to create toxicity that occurs in the *substantia nigra*. The genetic predisposition relates to an enzyme dysfunction that helps to detoxify the liver. Iron concentration was found to be high in many cases of those who had Parkinson's disease; this leads to free radical accumulation and consequently to cell destruction. There are now available treatments in alternative medicine that can work with these root causes. For many years, the medication, levodopa, has been the standard treatment for Parkinson's. This drug changes to dopamine before reaching the brain and often produces unpleasant side effects.

PSYCHOLOGICAL FACTORS

Many with Parkinson's have a desire to control people and a fear of letting go of control. They also tend to be inflexible and rigid in their thinking.

ASTROLOGICAL PATTERNS

In terms of astrological patterns, the signs Gemini and Sagittarius are seen frequently as well as Aquarius. There are often hard aspects between Mars and Uranus or Mercury and Uranus. Sometimes there are combinations such as Mars in Aquarius, Mercury in Aquarius, and Uranus in Gemini with hard aspects. Uranus often makes a hard aspect to a personal planet. Neptune is also strong, sometimes making a hard aspect to the Sun, Moon, or ascendant, and often square Saturn.

MIDPOINTS

Of the specific health midpoints, Sun/Moon, Saturn/Neptune, Mars/Neptune, and Mars/Uranus are used. Mars/Uranus often equals the Sun, Moon, or Mercury. Saturn/Neptune or Sun/Moon may equal Uranus.

Other midpoints to look at are:

Sun/Uranus—indicates rhythmic function of the cells and body

Sun/Neptune—relates to sluggish and weak cells

Mercury/Uranus—refers to the spinal cord and disturbances of equilibrium

Mercury/Neptune—indicates the paralysis of the nerves, nervous weakness, and the loss of feeling or sensing

CASE HISTORIES

Case History #1

This is the case of a woman who had tremors in her right leg beginning in 1983. She had acupuncture treatments and went to a naturopathic doctor, but there was little improvement. Finally she took the medication L-Dopa, and that helped her to walk. She also took some herbs for the side effects the medicine created. Earlier in her life, at the age of 27, she had cataracts; there was a fluid leak in her left eye and she required an operation. She sees a neurologist and an alternative practitioner, who uses different supplements and herbs with her, depending upon what she needs. She still has side effects from the medication which involve involuntary spasms of her head and limbs.

Interpretation of Horoscope

In her natal horoscope, the Sun and Jupiter are conjoined in Sagittarius in the seventh house. Sun Jupiter point to her liver, as does the sign Sagittarius. The Sun is making a broad opposition to Uranus in Gemini, showing a sensitive nervous system and possible circulatory problems. Her Moon is in Libra in the fifth house conjoined Neptune and square Venus in Capricorn. This indicates a sensitive immune system and possible problems with blood sugar as well as a strong creative talent. The 29th degree of Taurus is rising (the Pleiades) which refers to eye problems. Mercury is exactly opposite at 29 Scorpio. Mercury is also inconjunct Uranus, which shows the vulnerability of her nervous system. The nodes at 23 Taurus and Scorpio are in the twelfth and sixth houses, exactly square Saturn in the fourth. She did have problems with both her parents. Saturn is also conjoined Pluto and square Chiron in the sixth. Pluto is trine her Sun and Jupiter, which indicates a good potential for healing the body. Mars is in Virgo in the fourth house trine Venus and opposite Pallas in the tenth.

In terms of parallels of declination, the Sun is parallel Jupiter, pointing to problems with her liver. It is contra-parallel Uranus and Pluto, showing her sensitive nervous system. Saturn is contra parallel Chiron and Juno; this can indicate a strong need to heal herself.

Midpoints

Sun/Moon = Uranus, indirect—sensitive nervous system and circulatory problems

Mars/Uranus = Sun, indirect—neurological system will be the focus of health problems

Sun/Neptune = Pluto, direct—problems with immune system can be long term

Mercury/Uranus = Sun, direct—along with Mars/Uranus, indicates neurological problems

Parkinson's—Woman
Natal Chart
Dec 6, 1947, 3:31 PM EST +5:00
New York
40N42 51 074W00 23

Geocentric
Tropical
Koch
True Node

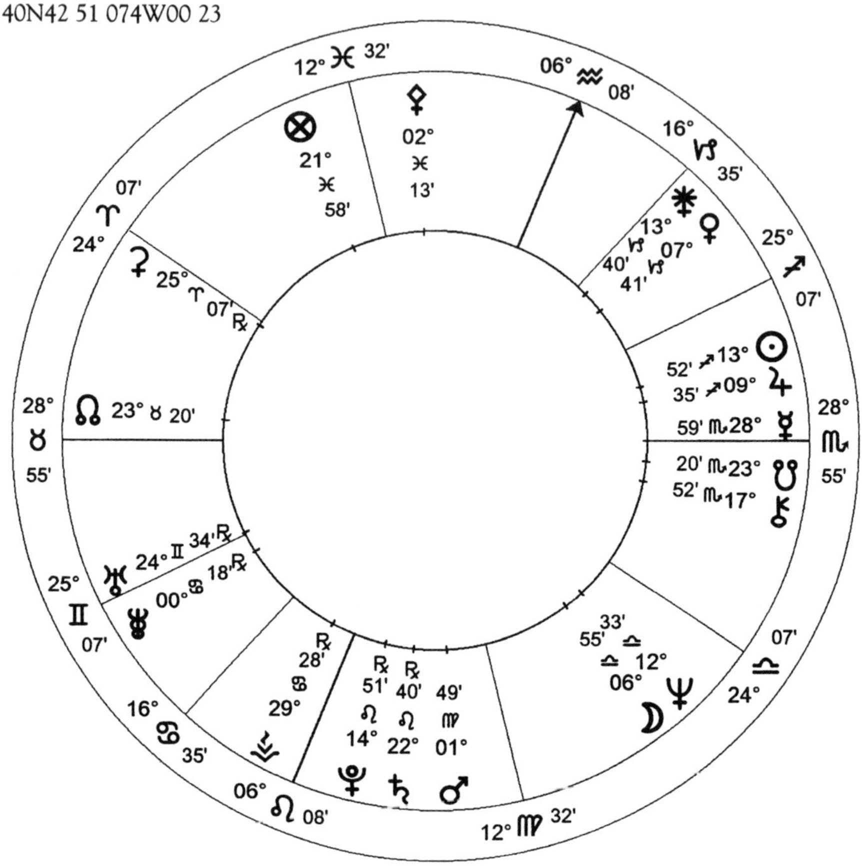

Transits and Progressions

In August 1974, when she had the cataract surgery, her secondary progressed Moon was trine her ascendant and sextile Mercury. Transiting Pluto was conjoined her Moon. Neptune was conjunct Jupiter. Uranus was trine natal Uranus and inconjunct the north node. Saturn was square Neptune. Jupiter was square her Sun and conjoined her Saturn/ Neptune midpoint, the health axis. The lunar eclipse on June 4 was exactly on her Sun while the solar eclipse on June 20 was conjoined Uranus.

Midpoint Listing

Parkinson's • Woman • Natal Chart
In Planetery Sequence • Modulus 360°00'

☽	06°♎55	*☿*	28°♏59	♂/♆	22°♍11	*♅*	24°♊34	⚷/⯓	09°♍05
☽/☉	10°♏24	☿/♀	18°♐20	♂/♇	23°♌20	♅/♆	18°♌33	⚷/☊	20°♌36
☽/☿	02°♏57	☿/♂	15°♎24	♂/⚷	09°♎50	♅/♇	19°♋42	⚷/⊗	19°♑55
☽/♀	22°♏18	☿/♃	04°♐17	♂/⚳	15°♌38	♅/⚷	06°♍13	*⚳*	29°♋28
☽/♂	19°♍22	☿/♄	10°♎50	♂/⚴	02°♊01	♅/⚳	12°♋01	⚳/⚴	15°♉50
☽/♃	08°♏15	☿/♅	11°♍46	♂/⚵	07°♏44	♅/⚴	28°♈23	⚳/⚵	21°♎34
☽/♄	14°♍47	☿/♆	05°♏46	♂/⚶	28°♊28	♅/⚵	04°♈07	⚳/⚶	12°♊18
☽/♅	15°♌44	☿/♇	06°♎55	♂/⯓	01°♌03	♅/⚶	24°♉50	⚳/⯓	14°♋53
☽/♆	09°♎44	☿/⚷	23°♏26	♂/☊	12°♋34	♅/⯓	27°♊26	⚳/☊	26°♊24
☽/♇	10°♍53	☿/⚳	29°♍14	♂/⊗	11°♊53	♅/☊	08°♊57	⚳/⊗	25°♉43
☽/⚷	27°♎23	☿/⚴	15°♑36	*♃*	09°♐35	♅/⊗	08°♉16	*⚴*	02°♓13
☽/⚳	03°♍11	☿/⚵	21°♐20	♃/♄	16°♎07	*♆*	12°♎33	⚴/⚵	07°♒56
☽/⚴	19°♐34	☿/⚶	12°♒03	♃/♅	17°♍04	♆/♇	13°♍42	⚴/⚶	28°♓40
☽/⚵	25°♏18	☿/⯓	14°♍39	♃/♆	11°♏04	♆/⚷	00°♏13	⚴/⯓	01°♉15
☽/⚶	16°♋01	☿/☊	26°♒10	♃/♇	12°♎13	♆/⚳	06°♍01	⚴/☊	12°♈46
☽/⯓	18°♌37	☿/⊗	25°♑29	♃/⚷	28°♏43	♆/⚴	22°♐23	⚴/⊗	12°♓05
☽/☊	00°♌08	*♀*	07°♑41	♃/⚳	04°♎31	♆/⚵	28°♏07	*⚵*	13°♑40
☽/⊗	29°♐26	♀/♂	04°♏45	♃/⚴	20°♑54	♆/⚶	18°♋50	⚵/⚶	04°♓24
☉	13°♐52	♀/♃	23°♐38	♃/⚵	26°♐37	♆/⯓	21°♌26	⚵/⯓	06°♈59
☉/☿	06°♐26	♀/♄	00°♏10	♃/⚶	17°♒21	♆/☊	02°♌57	⚵/☊	18°♓30
☉/♀	25°♐47	♀/♅	01°♈07	♃/⯓	19°♍56	♆/⊗	02°♑16	⚵/⊗	17°♒49
☉/♂	22°♎51	♀/♆	25°♏07	♃/☊	01°♓27	*♇*	14°♌51	*⚶*	25°♈07
☉/♃	11°♐43	♀/♇	26°♎16	♃/⊗	00°♒46	♇/⚷	01°♎22	⚶/⯓	27°♉43
☉/♄	18°♎16	♀/⚷	12°♐46	*♄*	22°♌40	♇/⚳	07°♌10	⚶/☊	09°♉14
☉/♅	19°♍13	♀/⚳	18°♎34	♄/♅	23°♋37	♇/⚴	23°♉32	⚶/⊗	08°♈33
☉/♆	13°♏13	♀/⚴	04°♒57	♄/♆	17°♍36	♇/⚵	29°♎16	*⯓*	00°♋18
☉/♇	14°♎22	♀/⚵	10°♑40	♄/♇	18°♌46	♇/⚶	19°♊59	⯓/☊	11°♊49
☉/⚷	00°♐52	♀/⚶	01°♓24	♄/⚷	05°♎16	♇/⯓	22°♋35	⯓/⊗	11°♉08
☉/⚳	06°♎40	♀/⯓	03°♈59	♄/⚳	11°♌04	♇/☊	04°♋06	*☊*	23°♉20
☉/⚴	23°♑03	♀/☊	15°♓30	♄/⚴	27°♉26	♇/⊗	03°♊25	☊/⊗	22°♈39
☉/⚵	28°♐46	♀/⊗	14°♒49	♄/⚵	03°♏10	*⚷*	17°♏52	*⊗*	21°♓58
☉/⚶	19°♒30	*♂*	01°♍49	♄/⚶	23°♊54	⚷/⚳	23°♍40		
☉/⯓	22°♍05	♂/♃	20°♎42	♄/⯓	26°♋29	⚷/⚴	10°♑02		
☉/☊	03°♓36	♂/♄	27°♌14	♄/☊	08°♋00	⚷/⚵	15°♐46		
☉/⊗	02°♒55	♂/♅	28°♋11	♄/⊗	07°♊19	⚷/⚶	06°♒30		

In 1983, when the tremors began in her right leg, the progressed Moon was in Capricorn. In June 1983, she had a progressed new Moon with both the Sun and Moon at 20 degrees. Transiting Pluto and Saturn were conjoined in late Libra, exactly inconjunct her ascendant and on the Mars/Uranus midpoint. Neptune was also inconjunct the ascendant and opposite Uranus. Uranus was transiting natal Jupiter while Jupiter was square Mars. On June 11, the solar eclipse hit her Uranus while the lunar eclipse on June 25 was conjoined her eighth house Venus.

Parkinson's—Man
Natal Chart
Jul 17, 1948, 3:47 AM PDT +7:00
Carmel
36N33 18 121W55 06

Geocentric
Tropical
Koch
True Node

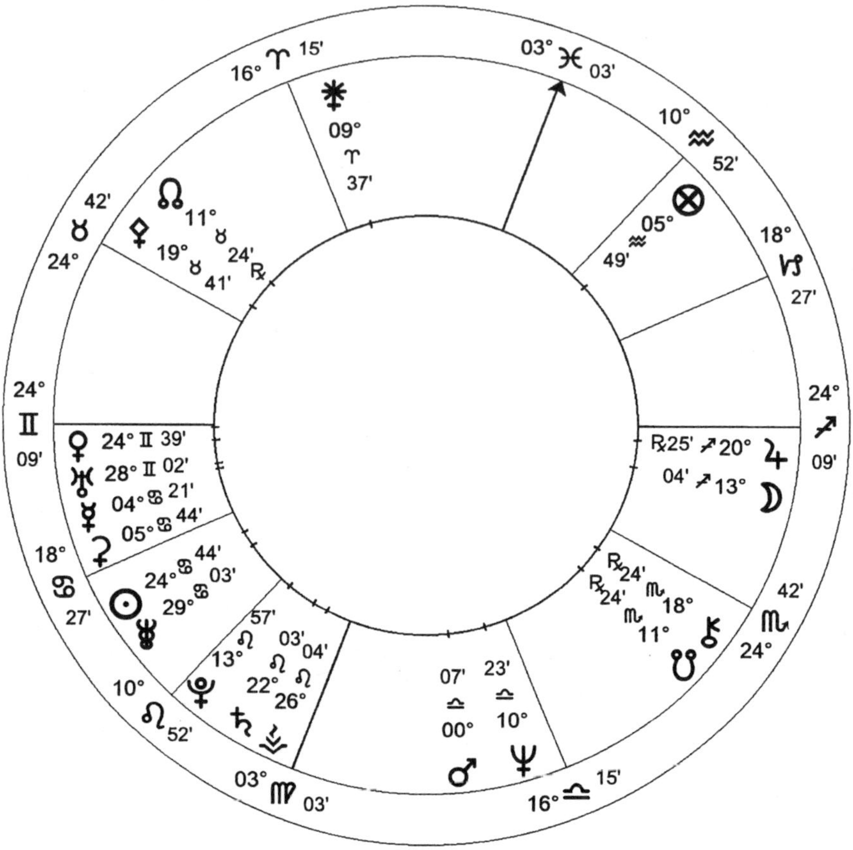

Case History #2

This man's symptoms started in 1993, with tremors on the right side of his body. It was not diagnosed as Parkinson's disease until many years later. He had been exposed to an insecticide that was sprinkled in his house for termites, shortly before his symptoms started. He did some acupuncture and other treatments, but nothing helped and he became very depressed. He also had a severe thyroid problem and was taking some medication for

Midpoint Listing

Parkinson's • Man • Natal Chart
In Planetery Sequence • Modulus 360°00'

☽	13°♐04	*☿*	04°♋21	♂/♆	05°♎15	*♅*	28°♊02	⚷/⯰	23°♍43
☽/☉	03°♎54	☿/♀	29°♊30	♂/♇	07°♍02	♅/♆	19°♌13	⚷/☊	14°♒54
☽/☿	23°♍43	☿/♂	17°♌14	♂/⚷	24°♎15	♅/♇	20°♋59	⚷/⊗	27°♐06
☽/♀	18°♍52	☿/♃	27°♍23	♂/⚶	13°♍06	♅/⚷	08°♍13	*⚶*	26°♌04
☽/♂	06°♏36	☿/♄	28°♋12	♂/⚴	24°♋54	♅/⚶	27°♋03	⚶/⚴	07°♋53
☽/♃	16°♐44	☿/♅	01°♋12	♂/⚵	04°♋52	♅/⚴	08°♊52	⚶/⚵	17°♊51
☽/♄	17°♎34	☿/♆	22°♌22	♂/⚳	17°♌56	♅/⚵	18°♉49	⚶/⚳	00°♌54
☽/♅	20°♍33	☿/♇	24°♋09	♂/⯰	29°♌35	♅/⚳	01°♋53	⚶/⯰	12°♌34
☽/♆	11°♏44	☿/⚷	11°♍22	♂/☊	20°♋46	♅/⯰	13°♋32	⚶/☊	03°♋44
☽/♇	13°♎30	☿/⚶	00°♌13	♂/⊗	02°♐58	♅/☊	04°♊43	⚶/⊗	15°♏57
☽/⚷	00°♐44	☿/⚴	12°♊01	*♃*	20°♐25	♅/⊗	16°♈55	*⚴*	19°♉41
☽/⚶	19°♎34	☿/⚵	21°♉59	♃/♄	21°♎14	*♆*	10°♎23	⚴/⚵	29°♈39
☽/⚴	01°♓23	☿/⚳	05°♋03	♃/♅	24°♍13	♆/♇	12°♍10	⚴/⚳	12°♊43
☽/⚵	11°♒20	☿/⯰	16°♋42	♃/♆	15°♏24	♆/⚷	29°♎23	⚴/⯰	24°♊22
☽/⚳	24°♍24	☿/☊	07°♊53	♃/♇	17°♎11	♆/⚶	18°♍14	⚴/☊	15°♉33
☽/⯰	06°♎03	☿/⊗	20°♈05	♃/⚷	04°♐24	♆/⚴	00°♌02	⚴/⊗	27°♓45
☽/☊	27°♒14	*♀*	24°♊39	♃/⚶	23°♎15	♆/⚵	10°♑00	*⚵*	09°♈37
☽/⊗	09°♑26	♀/♂	12°♌23	♃/⚴	05°♓03	♆/⚳	23°♌04	⚵/⚳	22°♉41
☉	24°♋44	♀/♃	22°♍32	♃/⚵	15°♒01	♆/⯰	04°♍43	⚵/⯰	04°♊20
☉/☿	14°♋33	♀/♄	23°♋21	♃/⚳	28°♍05	♆/☊	25°♋54	⚵/☊	25°♈31
☉/♀	09°♋42	♀/♅	26°♊21	♃/⯰	09°♎44	♆/⊗	08°♐06	⚵/⊗	07°♓43
☉/♂	27°♌26	♀/♆	17°♌31	♃/☊	00°♓54	*♇*	13°♌57	*⚳*	05°♋44
☉/♃	07°♎34	♀/♇	19°♋18	♃/⊗	13°♑07	♇/⚷	01°♎10	⚳/⯰	17°♋24
☉/♄	08°♌24	♀/⚷	06°♍31	*♄*	22°♌03	♇/⚶	20°♌00	⚳/☊	08°♊34
☉/♅	11°♋23	♀/⚶	25°♋22	♄/♅	25°♋03	♇/⚴	01°♋49	⚳/⊗	20°♈47
☉/♆	02°♍33	♀/⚴	07°♊10	♄/♆	16°♍13	♇/⚵	11°♊47	*⯰*	29°♋03
☉/♇	04°♌20	♀/⚵	17°♉08	♄/♇	18°♌00	♇/⚳	24°♋50	⯰/☊	20°♊13
☉/⚷	21°♍34	♀/⚳	00°♋12	♄/⚷	05°♎14	♇/⯰	06°♌30	⯰/⊗	02°♉26
☉/⚶	10°♌24	♀/⯰	11°♋51	♄/⚶	24°♌04	♇/☊	27°♊40	*☊*	11°♉24
☉/⚴	22°♊13	♀/☊	03°♊02	♄/⚴	05°♋52	♇/⊗	09°♏53	☊/⊗	23°♓37
☉/⚵	02°♊10	♀/⊗	15°♈14	♄/⚵	15°♊50	*⚷*	18°♏24	*⊗*	05°♒49
☉/⚳	15°♋14	*♂*	00°♎07	♄/⚳	28°♋54	⚷/⚶	07°♎14		
☉/⯰	26°♋53	♂/♃	10°♏16	♄/⯰	10°♌33	⚷/⚴	19°♌02		
☉/☊	18°♊04	♂/♄	11°♍05	♄/☊	01°♋44	⚷/⚵	29°♑00		
☉/⊗	00°♉16	♂/♅	14°♌05	♄/⊗	13°♏56	⚷/⚳	12°♍04		

his thyroid. In the spring of 2000, he called me for a consultation. Two months before, the tremors had spread to his left side; he had also lost his voice for a while. He was still teaching school but was about to lose his driver's license. Shortly after we consulted, he found a doctor nearby who worked with alternative therapies. This doctor started giving him injections of glutathione three times a week; his left side improved soon after. He was also given some supplements for his liver, as well as ginko biloba extract, NAC (N-acetyl cysteine), vitamin E, special enzymes, and other supplements. All of these things seemed to help him quite a bit, although the symptoms are still with him.

Interpretation of Horoscope

His Cancer Sun in the second house is conjoined the asteroid Hygeia, sesquiquadrate the nodes, and inconjunct Jupiter in the sixth. Moon and Jupiter conjunct in the sixth, especially in Sagittarius, indicates problems with liver toxicity. Jupiter is also opposite the Venus Uranus conjunction in Gemini. This shows that there will be challenges with the blood sugar. The Venus Uranus conjunction also points to his thyroid problems. With Uranus so close to the ascendant, a highly sensitive nervous system is indicated. Mercury is in Cancer conjoined the asteroid Ceres and square both Mars and Neptune. Mercury square Neptune refers to possible respiratory allergies and environmental sensitivities. Mars is also square the Venus Uranus conjunction. There is a lot of electrical energy here that needs to be grounded. Saturn is conjunct Pluto in Leo trine the Moon Jupiter conjunction. Pluto is square the nodes, indicating the potential for healing. With the nodes in Taurus and Scorpio, colon cleansing is needed. There is also a problem with circulation involving Saturn Pluto in Leo square the nodes.

In terms of the parallels of declination, the Sun is parallel Mercury and Pluto but contra parallel Jupiter. This shows a sensitive nervous system and liver problems.

Midpoints

Sun/Moon = Saturn, indirect—blockage of energy to vital organs

Mars/Uranus = Pluto, direct—long term problems with the nervous system

Mars/Neptune = Saturn, indirect—possible problems with the immune system

Mercury/Neptune = Saturn, direct—respiratory allergies and sensitivity of respiratory system

Sun/Uranus = Neptune, direct—connection between nervous system and immune system

Transits and Progressions

In 1993, when his symptoms started, secondary progressed Moon was conjoined his Sun. Transiting Pluto was square natal Saturn and trine the Sun. Uranus and Neptune were opposing his Sun, Saturn was inconjunct Mars, and Jupiter was square the Mercury Ceres conjunction. The lunar eclipse on June 4 was exactly on his Moon.

In 2000, when he began the new therapies and got some relief, secondary progressed Moon was conjoined the progressed south node. Transiting Pluto was on his Moon. Neptune was inconjunct Mercury. Uranus was opposite Saturn. Saturn was opposite Chiron and square natal Saturn. Jupiter was on the north node. The solar eclipse on February 5 was square Chiron and opposite Pluto.

TREATMENTS FOR PARKINSON'S DISEASE

1. Chelation therapy is very important; the chelating agent EDTA has a strong affinity for unbound iron. EDTA reduces the production of free radicals. Other chelating agents may also be used. (Assessment of hepatic detoxification competence can be done through Great Smokies Laboratory Diagnostic Profile). High doses of antioxidant supplements can slow the destruction of cells.
2. Regular colonics and colon cleansing help to get rid of the toxic substances and promote assimilation of nutrients.
3. Physical therapies that work with muscular structure are important. Deep bodywork, such as rolfing and bioenergetics, helps to break up crystallization in the psyche as well as in the body.
4. Regular daily exercise to increase circulation to the brain and heart should be done. Water therapies such as water aerobics are helpful. Yoga postures combined with deep breathing are extremely good.
5. It is absolutely essential that all foods eaten be organic and free from pesticides, chemicals, and additives. The liver has a difficult time detoxifying these substances and this puts an even greater strain on it.
6. Certain herbs work well for circulation and for the nervous system.
7. Obtaining one's constitutional homeopathic remedy can benefit the nervous system and help the "chi" energy.

ALTZHEIMER'S DISEASE

In Altzheimer's disease, there are excess amyloid plaques or sticky fibers in the brain. These are fragments of protein which accrue like tangled spaghetti around dead and dying cells. In Traditional Chinese Medicine, one would speak of a spleen deficiency which creates phlegm and mucus in the system; the phlegm plugs up the channels. A spleen that functions well would take the food and transfer it into energy. There is also liver "chi" stagnation; the liver traditionally stores the blood.

Symptoms of Altzheimer's include memory loss and a gradual loss of basic abilities, which enable one to function in the world. Sometimes the person becomes very angry and strikes out at people; sometimes they become very moody and withdrawn. In the later stages of Altzheimer's, the patient is unable to engage in conversation and loses bladder and bowel control. Often, they also lose their ability to speak and can only make sounds.

PSYCHOLOGICAL PATTERNS

As one gets older and certain faculties such as eyesight and hearing weaken, there is a fear of rejection, which leads to unconsciousness and dependency.

ASTROLOGICAL PATTERNS

There is a strong Uranus and Aquarius theme, which shows a sensitive nervous system. Neptune may be angular or conjoined the Sun or Moon; there may also be several planets in Pisces or the twelfth house. These are indications of a weak immune system; perhaps the person has had allergies or MCS or some type of toxic condition from the environment.

MIDPOINTS

The same midpoints that are used for Parkinson's Disease are relevant for Altzheimer's.

CASE HISTORIES

Case History #1

This chart is of a woman who has had a lot of health problems throughout her life. After many years of college, graduate school, and working at nights during the depression, she had a nervous breakdown at 23. She received electroshock therapy during this time. In addition, she was quite anemic and also had a hypo-thyroid condition, for which she took thyroid medication. She got B-12 shots for her anemia. When she was 44 years old, her husband died, leaving her with two children. She went back to teaching, which she had done much earlier in her life. A few years later, she re-married and continued substitute teaching for a while. Later, she developed arthritis and used medication for that, plus medication for sleeping, which was a perennial problem. She also broke a hip at one point and needed a walker. When she was 86, she fell and broke her ribs. While she was recuperating, her husband passed away. She was placed in an assisted living home, where she did well for a few months, but then began having problems relating to people and functioning. She went through many stages with what was diagnosed as Altzheimer's, becoming incontinent when she was 88. At 89, she lost the ability to speak and could only move her tongue. She could still watch people with her eyes, but mostly slept. She passed away soon after her 91st birthday.

Interpretation of Horoscope

Her Sun is conjoined Uranus and Mercury in the third house and opposite Moon and Neptune; these are squared by her sixth house Saturn Vesta conjunction. Jupiter is in the twelfth conjoined the south node and near the ascendant. Mars is in Sagittarius, broadly opposite Pluto, and forming a yod with Neptune and the north node; this shows the tendency to anemia. Venus is in Aquarius square Jupiter, indicating a desire for sweets and along with the Neptune Moon conjunction, low blood sugar and potential thyroid problems. Mercury is in Capricorn exactly opposite her Moon, trine the north node, and sextile Jupiter, the ascendant, and south node. She did a lot of writing and majored in journalism and English at college. Pluto is in the eighth house in Gemini (she lost two husbands), inconjunct her Sun and Uranus, trine Chiron, and sextile Saturn.

In terms of parallels of declination, her Sun is parallel Venus and Uranus, while being contra parallel Neptune. The parallel between Venus and Uranus indicates the thyroid problem. Pluto is parallel the north node which shows strong transformation and healing in her life.

Midpoints

Saturn/Neptune = Moon, Mercury, indirect—problems with nervous system

Mars/Saturn = MC, direct—possible arthritis and bone problems

Mars/Neptune = nodes, indirect—weak immune system

Mercury/Uranus = Neptune, direct—sensitive nervous system

Alzheimer's—Woman 1
Natal Chart
Jan 14, 1911, 2:10 AM EST +5:00
Brooklyn, NY
40N38 073W56

Geocentric
Tropical
Koch
True Node

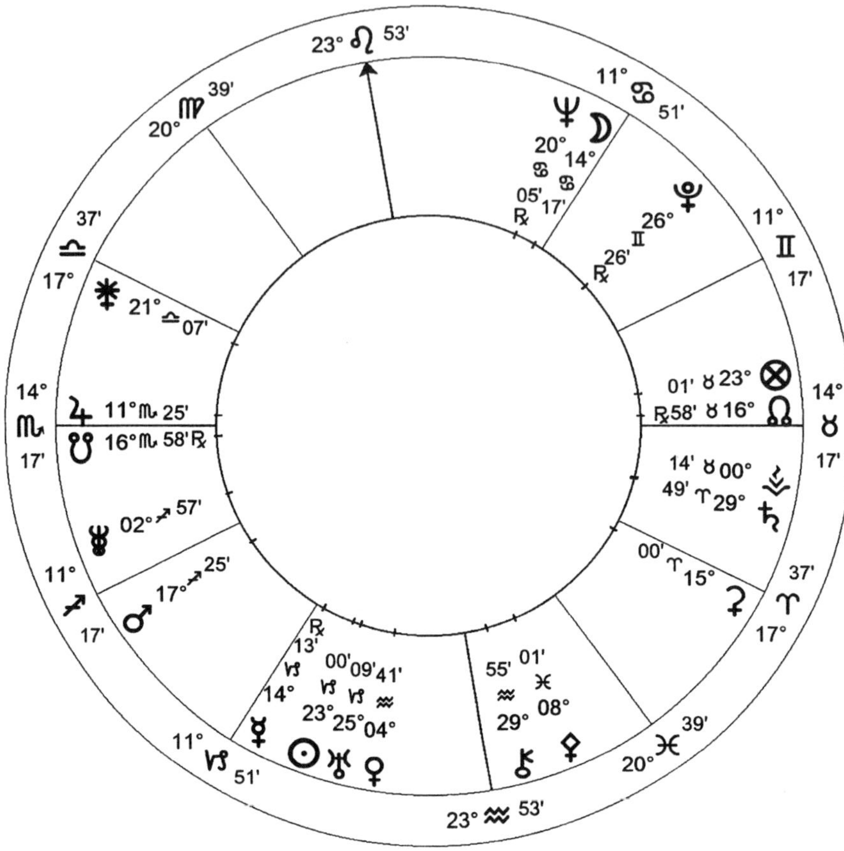

Transits and Progressions

In 1934, when she had a nervous breakdown, her secondary progressed Sun was square the nodes. Transiting Pluto was opposite her Sun. Neptune was semi-square her Sun Uranus conjunction. Uranus was also square her Sun Uranus. Saturn was square her ascendant and north node. Jupiter was square her Sun. The lunar eclipse on January 30 was square her Jupiter, while the solar eclipse on February 14 was conjoined her fourth house cusp.

Midpoint Listing

Alzheimer's • Woman 1 • Natal Chart
In Planetery Sequence • Modulus 360°00'

☽	14°♋17	*☿*	14°♑13	♂/♆	03°♎45	*♅*	25°♑09	⚷/⚶	16°♑26
☽/☉	18°♈39	☿/♀	24°♑27	♂/♇	21°♍55	♅/♆	22°♈37	⚷/☊	08°♈27
☽/☿	14°♎15	☿/♂	00°♑49	♂/⚷	23°♑40	♅/♇	10°♈47	⚷/⊗	11°♈28
☽/♀	24°♈29	☿/♃	12°♐49	♂/⚳	23°♒49	♅/⚷	12°♒32	*⚳*	00°♉14
☽/♂	00°♎51	☿/♄	07°♓01	♂/⚴	27°♑43	♅/⚳	12°♓41	⚳/⚴	04°♈07
☽/♃	12°♍51	☿/♅	19°♑41	♂/⚵	19°♏16	♅/⚴	16°♒35	⚳/⚵	25°♋40
☽/♄	07°♊03	☿/♆	17°♎09	♂/⚸	16°♒12	♅/⚵	08°♐08	⚳/⚸	22°♈37
☽/♅	19°♈43	☿/♇	05°♈19	♂/⚶	10°♐11	♅/⚸	05°♓04	⚳/⚶	16°♒35
☽/♆	17°♋11	☿/⚷	07°♒04	♂/☊	02;♓11	♅/⚶	29°♐03	⚳/☊	08°♉36
☽/♇	05°♋21	☿/⚳	07°♓13	♂/⊗	05°♓13	♅/☊	21°♓04	⚳/⊗	11°♉37
☽/⚷	07°♉06	☿/⚴	11°♒07	*♃*	11°♏25	♅/⊗	24°♓05	*⚴*	08°♓01
☽/⚳	07°♊15	☿/⚵	02°♐40	♃/♄	05°♒37	*♆*	20°♋05	⚴/⚵	29°♐34
☽/⚴	11°♉09	☿/⚸	29°♒36	♃/♅	18°♐17	♆/♇	08°♋15	⚴/⚸	26°♓30
☽/⚵	02°♍42	☿/⚶	23°♐35	♃/♆	15°♍45	♆/⚷	10°♉00	⚴/⚶	20°♑29
☽/⚸	29°♉38	☿/☊	15°♓35	♃/♇	03°♍55	♆/⚳	10°♊10	⚴/☊	12°♈29
☽/⚶	23°♍37	☿/⊗	18°♓37	♃/⚷	05°♑40	♆/⚴	14°♉03	⚴/⊗	15°♈31
☽/☊	15°♊38	*♀*	04°♒41	♃/⚳	05°♒49	♆/⚵	05°♍36	*⚵*	21°♎07
☽/⊗	18°♊39	♀/♂	11°♑03	♃/⚴	09°♑43	♆/⚸	02°♊33	⚵/⚸	18°♑03
☉	23°♑00	♀/♃	23°♐03	♃/⚵	01°♏16	♆/⚶	26°♍31	⚵/⚶	12°♏02
☉/☿	18°♑37	♀/♄	17°♓15	♃/⚸	28°♑12	♆/☊	18°♊32	⚵/☊	04°♌02
☉/♀	28°♑51	♀/♅	29°♑55	♃/⚶	22°♏11	♆/⊗	21°♊33	⚵/⊗	07°♌04
☉/♂	05°♑13	♀/♆	27°♈23	♃/☊	14°♌11	*♇*	26°♊26	*⚸*	15°♈00
☉/♃	17°♐12	♀/♇	15°♈33	♃/⊗	17°♌13	♇/⚷	28°♈11	⚸/⚶	08°♒58
☉/♄	11°♓25	♀/⚷	17°♒18	*♄*	29°♈49	♇/⚳	28°♉20	⚸/☊	00°♉59
☉/♅	24°♑05	♀/⚳	17°♓27	♄/♅	12°♓29	♇/⚴	02°♉13	⚸/⊗	04°♉00
☉/♆	21°♈33	♀/⚴	21°♒21	♄/♆	09°♊57	♇/⚵	23°♌46	*⚶*	02°♐57
☉/♇	09°♈43	♀/⚵	12°♐54	♄/♇	28°♉07	♇/⚸	20°♉43	⚶/☊	24°♒58
☉/⚷	11°♒28	♀/⚸	09°♓50	♄/⚷	29°♓52	♇/⚶	14°♍41	⚶/⊗	27°♒59
☉/⚳	11°♓37	♀/⚶	03°♑49	♄/⚳	00°♉01	♇/☊	06°♊42	*☊*	16°♉58
☉/⚴	15°♒31	♀/☊	25°♓50	♄/⚴	03°♈55	♇/⊗	09°♊43	☊/⊗	19°♉59
☉/⚵	07°♐04	♀/⊗	28°♓51	♄/⚵	25°♋28	*⚷*	29°♒55	*⊗*	23°♉01
☉/⚸	04°♓00	*♂*	17°♐25	♄/⚸	22°♈25	⚷/⚳	00°♈05		
☉/⚶	27°♐59	♂/♃	29°♏25	♄/⚶	16°♒23	⚷/⚴	03°♓58		
☉/☊	19°♓59	♂/♄	23°♒37	♄/☊	08°♉24	⚷/⚵	25°♐31		
☉/⊗	23°♓01	♂/♅	06°♑17	♄/⊗	11°♉25	⚷/⚸	22°♓28		

At the end of November 1997, when she first became disoriented, her secondary progressed Sun was square Neptune, while progressed Mercury was conjoined progressed Saturn and progressed north node. Transiting Pluto was sesquiquadrate Neptune. Neptune was conjoined Uranus while Uranus was conjoined Venus. Saturn was conjoined Ceres, inconjunct the ascendant and south node. Jupiter was square Jupiter, the nodes, and ascendant. The solar eclipse of September 1 was sesquiquadrate her Sun

Uranus conjunction while the lunar eclipse of September 16 was square her Pluto.

Towards the end of 1999, when her condition became worse, secondary progressed Sun was square her natal Sun. Transiting Pluto was semi-square her Sun. Neptune was conjoined Venus while Uranus was square Jupiter. Saturn was conjoined her north node and opposite her Jupiter and ascendant. Jupiter was conjunct Saturn. The lunar eclipse of July 28 was on her Venus, while the solar eclipse of August 11 was square her nodes and ascendant.

Case History #2

This woman taught piano, did clay sculpture, and other types of art work. She also studied Italian and opera in her late 50's. She had terrible migraines all her life; she would be in bed for 2-3 days and vomit continuously. She didn't take medication for her migraines, only used ice packs or hot packs. This condition may have been brought on by having been hit in the head when young by a wooden swing. She loved to walk and hike and had a juicer back in the 30's, making carrot juice as well as taking lecithin, wheat germ oil, and lots of vitamins. She also avoided aluminum and cooked in stainless steel pots. At the age of 73, she began stuttering to get her words out. She also had trouble spelling simple words and she had always been a good speller. Within two years, she was in a wheelchair, had to be fed by her husband, have her diapers changed, and was totally helpless. She died in September, 1992, at the age of 79.

Interpretation of Horoscope

Her fourth house Sun is opposite Ceres in Scorpio in the tenth. Her Scorpio Moon is very closely conjoined the MC, showing a very sensitive nature. The Moon is opposite Venus and Mercury, as well as squaring Uranus. Uranus is conjoined Vesta and in the twelfth house close to her ascendant in Aquarius, indicating a sensitive nervous system as well as deficiencies in magnesium and B-complex vitamins, which caused the severe migraines. Mercury is in Taurus in the fourth opposite her Moon and square Uranus, again emphasizing her nervous system. Venus is square Neptune . Jupiter is opposite Neptune, showing her artistic skills as well as low blood sugar. Mars is in Aries conjoined the north node and sextile both Uranus and Saturn. Saturn in the fourth house in Gemini is in a grand trine with Uranus, the ascendant in Aquarius and the south node in

Libra. She obviously had a gift in communicating. Pluto in the fifth house in the last degree of Gemini is trine Pallas in Libra near the MC and square the nodes;

In terms of parallels of declination, the Moon is contra parallel Mercury, showing her sensitive nervous system. Saturn is parallel Neptune and contra parallel Jupiter, indicating toxicity with her liver.

Midpoints

Sun/Moon = Vesta, direct and Pluto, indirect—good ability to regenerate vital force

Saturn/Neptune = Pluto, direct and Vesta, indirect—possible long term illness

Mars/Uranus = Saturn, direct—tension in her body and possible high blood pressure

Mars/Saturn = Uranus, direct—tension in her body and problems with nervous system

Sun/Neptune = Mercury, indirect—sensitive nervous and immune systems

Mercury/Neptune = Moon, indirect—possible problems with blood sugar

Transits and Progressions

In 1986, when her symptoms began, her secondary progressed Sun was opposite Uranus. Transiting Pluto was square Uranus. Neptune was squaring the nodes. Uranus was semi-square her Moon, while Saturn was opposite her natal Saturn. The lunar eclipse of April 24 was conjoined her Moon.

In 1988, when she became incontinent and confined to a wheel chair, her secondary progressed Moon was in the sixth house conjunct both natal and progressed Neptune. Transiting Pluto was opposite Mercury. Neptune was square Mars, and both Uranus and Saturn were square the nodes. The March 3 lunar eclipse was opposite Chiron, while the solar eclipse of March 18 was square Pluto.

Alzheimer's—Woman 2
Natal Chart
May 13 ,1913, 9:52 PM NZ -11:30
Napier
39S29 176E55

Geocentric
Tropical
Koch
True Node

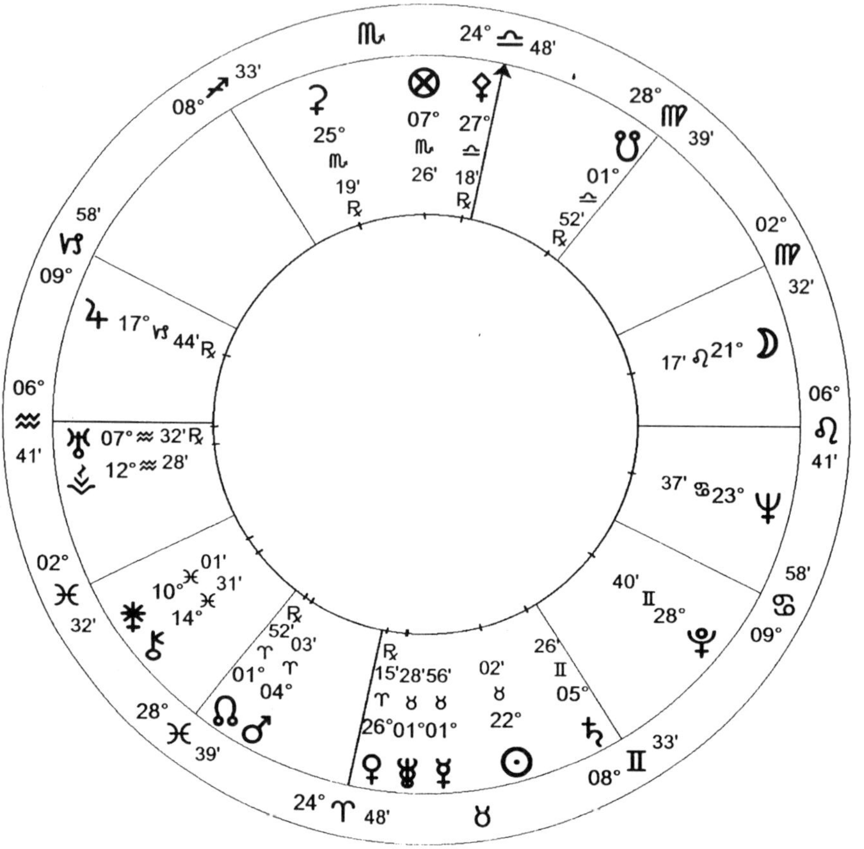

On September 28, 1992, when she died, secondary progressed Mercury was on her seventh house cusp, while the progressed Moon was square natal Pluto. Transiting Pluto was trine Neptune and beginning to oppose her Sun. Neptune and Uranus were conjoined Jupiter. Saturn was conjunct the ascendant while Jupiter was square Pluto. Mars was square Mars, and Venus was conjoined her Moon. The lunar eclipse of June 15 was opposite Pluto, while the solar eclipse of June 30 was square Mars.

Midpoint Listing

Alzheimer's • Woman 2 • Natal Chart
In Planetery Sequence • Modulus 360°00'

☽	21°♌17	*☿*	01°♉56	♂/♆	28°♉50	*♅*	07°♒32	⚷/⛢	07°♈59
☽/☉	06°♋39	☿/♀	29°♈05	♂/♇	16°♉21	♅/♆	00°♉35	⚷/☊	23°♓12
☽/☿	26°♊36	☿/♂	18°♈00	♂/⚷	24°♓17	♅/♇	18°♈06	⚷/⊗	10°♑59
☽/♀	23°♊46	☿/♃	09°♓50	♂/⚳	08°♓15	♅/⚷	26°♒02	*⚳*	12°♒28
☽/♂	12°♊40	☿/♄	18°♉41	♂/⚴	15°♑41	♅/⚳	10°♒00	⚳/⚴	19°♐53
☽/♃	04°♏30	☿/♅	19°♓44	♂/⚵	22°♓02	♅/⚴	17°♐25	⚳/⚵	26°♒14
☽/♄	13°♋22	☿/♆	12°♊47	♂/⚶	29°♑41	♅/⚵	23°♒47	⚳/⚶	03°♑53
☽/♅	14°♏25	☿/♇	00°♊18	♂/⛢	17°♈45	♅/⚶	01°♑26	⚳/⛢	21°♓58
☽/♆	07°♌27	☿/⚷	08°♈14	♂/☊	02°♈58	♅/⛢	19°♓30	⚳/☊	07°♓10
☽/♇	24°♋58	☿/⚳	22°♓12	♂/⊗	20°♑45	♅/☊	04°♓42	⚳/⊗	24°♐57
☽/⚷	02°♊54	☿/⚴	29°♋37	*♃*	17°♑44	♅/⊗	22°♐29	*⚴*	27°♎18
☽/⚳	16°♏52	☿/⚵	05°♈59	♃/♄	26°♓35	*♆*	23°♋37	⚴/⚵	03°♑40
☽/⚴	24°♍18	☿/⚶	13°♒38	♃/♅	27°♑38	♆/♇	11°♋09	⚴/⚶	11°♏19
☽/⚵	00°♊39	☿/⛢	01°♉42	♃/♆	20°♎41	♆/⚷	19°♉04	⚴/⛢	29°♋23
☽/⚶	08°♎18	☿/☊	16°♈54	♃/♇	08°♈12	♆/⚳	03°♉02	⚴/☊	14°♑35
☽/⛢	26°♊22	☿/⊗	04°♒41	♃/⚷	16°♒08	♆/⚴	10°♍28	⚴/⊗	02°♏22
☽/☊	11°♊35	*♀*	26°♈15	♃/⚳	00°♒06	♆/⚵	16°♉49	*⚵*	10°♓01
☽/⊗	29°♍22	♀/♂	15°♈09	♃/⚴	07°♐31	♆/⚶	24°♍28	⚵/⚶	17°♑40
☉	22°♉02	♀/♃	06°♓59	♃/⚵	13°♒53	♆/⛢	12°♊33	⚵/⛢	05°♈44
☉/☿	11°♉59	♀/♄	15°♉51	♃/⚶	21°♐32	♆/☊	27°♉45	⚵/☊	20°♓57
☉/♀	09°♉08	♀/♅	16°♓54	♃/⛢	09°♓36	♆/⊗	15°♍32	⚵/⊗	08°♑44
☉/♂	28°♈02	♀/♆	09°♊56	♃/☊	24°♒48	*♇*	28°♊40	*⚶*	25°♏19
☉/♃	19°♓53	♀/♇	27°♉27	♃/⊗	12°♐35	♇/⚷	06°♉36	⚶/⛢	13°♒23
☉/♄	28°♉44	♀/⚷	05°♈23	*♄*	05°♊26	♇/⚳	20°♈34	⚶/☊	28°♑36
☉/♅	29°♓47	♀/⚳	19°♓21	♄/♅	06°♈29	♇/⚴	27°♌59	⚶/⊗	16°♏23
☉/♆	22°♊50	♀/⚴	26°♑47	♄/♆	29°♊32	♇/⚵	04°♉21	*⛢*	01°♉28
☉/♇	10°♊21	♀/⚵	03°♈08	♄/♇	17°♊03	♇/⚶	11°♍59	⛢/☊	16°♈40
☉/⚷	18°♈16	♀/⚶	10°♒47	♄/⚷	24°♈59	♇/⛢	00°♊04	⛢/⊗	04°♒27
☉/⚳	02°♈15	♀/⛢	28°♈51	♄/⚳	08°♈57	♇/☊	15°♉16	*☊*	01°♈52
☉/⚴	09°♌40	♀/☊	14°♈04	♄/⚴	16°♌22	♇/⊗	03°♍03	☊/⊗	19°♑39
☉/⚵	16°♈02	♀/⊗	01°♒51	♄/⚵	22°♈44	*⚷*	14°♓31	*⊗*	07°♏26
☉/⚶	23°♒40	*♂*	04°♈03	♄/⚶	00°♍23	⚷/⚳	28°♒29		
☉/⛢	11°♉45	♂/♃	25°♒54	♄/⛢	18°♉27	⚷/⚴	05°♑55		
☉/☊	26°♈57	♂/♄	04°♉45	♄/☊	03°♉39	⚷/⚵	12°♓16		
☉/⊗	14°♌44	♂/♅	05°♓48	♄/⊗	21°♌26	⚷/⚶	19°♑55		

TREATMENTS FOR ALTZHEIMER'S DISEASE

1. Chelation therapy is very helpful to clear out toxic metals as well as other toxic material.
2. High doses of vitamin E which is a strong antioxidant.
3. Some exercise is essential. Even though older people may not be able to walk much, small walks around a nursing home help the circulation.

4. Acupuncture treatments can be given frequently to support the "chi" energy and help detoxify the liver.
5. Massage and body work will help to relax the body and is good for circulation.
6. Obtaining one's constitutional homeopathic remedy helps the vital force and is an aid in working with emotional balance.
7. Eating only organic foods and foods free from chemicals is essential. Unfortunately, most nursing homes and assisted living homes follow a standard American diet, which is full of pesticides and chemical additives. Making healthy liquid "smoothies" with fruit and rice milk or goat yogurt, as well as added minerals and vitamins is one way to get some nutrition into older people.

SUPPLEMENT RECOMMENDATIONS FOR PARKINSON'S AND ALTZHEIMER'S

Vitamin C is a very strong antioxidant; high doses are recommended.

Vitamin E is another strong antioxidant; and should be taken daily.

Quercetin Bioflavonoids aid the immune system and the other bioflavonoids are extremely important for circulation.

Lipoic Acid is a strong antioxidant that contains sulfur; it increases the level of glutathione, the most important antioxidant compound in the body.

Probiotics, including acidophilus and bifidus, help to produce immunity in the body as well as assist in producing vitamin B.

NADH (Nicotinamide Adenine Dinucleotide Hydrogen) provides the cells with energy; a healthy body can make it from niacinamide, but those with neurodegenerative diseases are not able to.

Phosphatydyl Serine is a brain food that helps with all neurological problems.

Super B complex is an important vitamin to help balance the nervous system. It is often given intravenously with magnesium and vitamin C.

Magnesium is needed for the circulation and heart, as well as for the nervous system, to help control the tremors. This may be taken intravenously, as well as through drinking liquid chlorophyll and in capsules.

HERBAL RECOMMENDATIONS

Golden seal leaf tea is a bitter herb that works well to clear and detoxify the liver. Spearmint may be added to cut the bitter taste.

Oregon grape root tea is a bitter root that needs to be simmered in water to make a tea. It is excellent for the liver and gall bladder.

Gingko Biloba extract was found very useful for detoxifying the body and helping the neurological system.

Herbs that relax the nervous system such as **vervain, hops, scullcap, camomile, catnip,** and **spearmint** are also helpful.

CHAPTER 21

Attention Deficit Disorder

IN RECENT YEARS, WE ARE HEARING MORE about ADD, Attention Deficit Disorder, both in children and adults. Hyperactivity affects two to four per cent of school children who exhibit varying degrees of restlessness, inattention, and impulsiveness, which often lead to serious behavior problems. These symptoms may persist into adulthood as well. There seems to be a genetic factor in this condition, as often children with ADD have parents who experienced the same type of symptoms.

Researchers have found that those with ADD have a low brain metabolism in the part of the brain that controls voluntary movement and attention. This means that the rate at which the brain uses glucose, its main energy source, is eight per cent lower in a group of adults with hyperactivity than in a similar group who do not have this condition.

Western medicine treats hyperactivity with anti-depressants such as Ritalin or stimulants to correct the neurotransmitter flaws that cause the disorder. Often the patient is given exercises to lengthen her or his attention span and hone organizational skills.

Traditional Chinese Medicine views hyperactivity as a disturbance in the functions of the heart and liver system. Excess "fire" may be present in the heart channel which is due to deficient heart yin. Manifestations are disturbed sleep with excess dreaming, night sweats, impatience, irritability, redness or soreness at the tip of the tongue, and dryness of the mouth. The heart is disturbed by excess "fire" in the blood which develops as a result of the liver's inability to filter heat or "fire" out of the blood.

The liver's function is to regulate the flow of "chi" and blood. It filters the blood by removing toxins, pathogens, heat, and mucus. When it is congested, the liver cannot accomplish these activities. With an excess intake of alcohol, sugar, animal fats, medications, or any bacterial, viral, and fungal infections, the liver becomes congested. Symptoms of liver congestion are a yellow coating on the tongue, anger, uneasiness, headaches, red eyes, neck aches, nightmares, and sleepwalking.

The diet in the United States with its emphasis on sugar, preservatives, and food additives, has been contributing to this problem, which didn't appear until the 1970's. In addition, the increased use of antibiotics has led to other problems, including poor digestion and absorption of nutrients, since antibiotics wipe out intestinal bacteria. A sufficient amount of probiotics, the various strands of intestinal bacteria such as acidophilus, help to manufacture B complex vitamins in the colon.

PSYCHOLOGICAL FACTORS

Children who are hyperactive have difficulty concentrating in school and therefore are underachievers. This creates low self esteem which they may carry throughout their lives. They often get into trouble with teachers due to their impulsiveness, which contributes to poor relationships as they grow older. Often their parents have these same symptoms and have not given them boundaries, or sufficient ways to discipline themselves and focus their energy.

ASTROLOGICAL PATTERNS

Uranus may be angular or making hard aspects to Mercury, Mars, or Jupiter, which rules the liver. Saturn and Uranus are often in hard aspect in longitude or declination. Uranus is the rebellious energy breaking out of a mold. Saturn is boundaries or restrictions. The signs Aquarius, Gemini, and Sagittarius are often prominent. Hard aspects from Mercury to Mars and Mercury to Uranus, as well as hard aspects from Uranus to the Sun or Moon, are frequently seen.

MIDPOINTS

Of the specific health midpoints, Sun/Moon, Saturn/Neptune, Mars/ Saturn, Mars/Uranus, and Mars/Neptune are used

Other midpoints to look at are:

Mercury/Uranus—refers to the spinal cord and disturbances of equilibrium, which impact the neurological system

Sun/Uranus—indicates rhythmic functions of the cells and body and relates to the nervous system

Saturn/Uranus—indicates irritability and inhibition, as well as tension in the body. It can refer to blockages in the heart.

Often Mercury/Uranus equals an important point in the chart such as the nodes, Pluto, or the ascendant. Mars/Uranus often equals another planet or an angle.

CASE HISTORIES

Case History #1

This is the chart of a young man who has had ADD along with learning disabilities, obsessive compulsive disorder, anxiety, and fears of people. These symptoms started when he was about three years old. He has poor circulation and his temperature runs low, indicating hypothyroidism. When he was growing up, his father was physically abusive; when he was 19, his mother divorced. He has one younger brother with whom he gets along well. He had been taking several medications including ritalin for ADD, luvox for the obsessive compulsive disorder, and adavan for anxiety. During high school, he had a lot of speech therapy. When he begins to speak, he often cannot find the correct words. He had never taken any nutritional supplements. In January 2000, I did a consultation with his mother. It was suggested that he undergo some liver cleansing and work with a good Naturopathic physician to replace his medications with mineral and vitamin supplements. I suggested niacin, vitamin C, quercetin bioflavonoids, B-6, zinc, and magnesium to start with. It was also suggested that he work with a good homeopathic doctor. He is currently taking some of the nutritional supplements; his medications have been cut down, and he is doing better.

Interpretation of Horoscope

His Pisces Sun is conjoined Mercury and Venus, showing a sensitive immune system; these are in a grand trine with Uranus in Scorpio and Mars in

Cancer. Sun conjoined Mercury relates to the nervous system; this is square his Moon Neptune conjunction in Sagittarius, which also indicates a very sensitive immune system and problems with a toxic liver. The Moon is exactly inconjunct Mars, showing an extremely emotional nature. His Scorpio ascendant is semi-square his Moon and trine his Sun. Uranus is close to the ascendant and square Saturn in Leo in his tenth house, indicating body tension and frustration. Saturn is trine his Pallas, Neptune, Moon, Hygeia stellium. Pluto is in his twelfth house in Libra and square Mars; this may indicate the physical abuse he experienced. The nodes are in Libra and Aries; with the south node in Aries, he could have experienced a head injury from the physical abuse.

In terms of parallels of declination, the Sun is parallel Mercury, pointing to the nervous system. Saturn is contra parallel Vesta, which can also show that it is difficult for him to discipline himself.

Midpoints

Mars/Saturn = ascendant, direct, and Moon, indirect—emotional restrictions and possible fears

Mars/Uranus = Neptune, direct—link between neurological and immune system

Mars/Neptune = nodes, direct—sensitive immune system and problems with carbohydrate digestion and low blood sugar

Mercury/Uranus = Pluto, direct—possible problems with compulsive behavior

Saturn/Uranus = nodes, direct—body tension, possible stuttering or problems with nervous system

Sun/Uranus = Pluto, direct—need for healing the nervous system

Transits and Progressions

When he was three years old and his symptoms began, his secondary progressed Sun conjoined natal Mercury. The progressed Moon was in Aquarius. Transiting Pluto was exactly square Mars, which may have indicated the physical abuse. Neptune was conjoined his Moon, Uranus

ADD—Boy
Natal Chart
Mar 2, 1978, 10:32 PM EST +5:00
Bronx, New York
40N51 073W54

Geocentric
Tropical
Koch
True Node

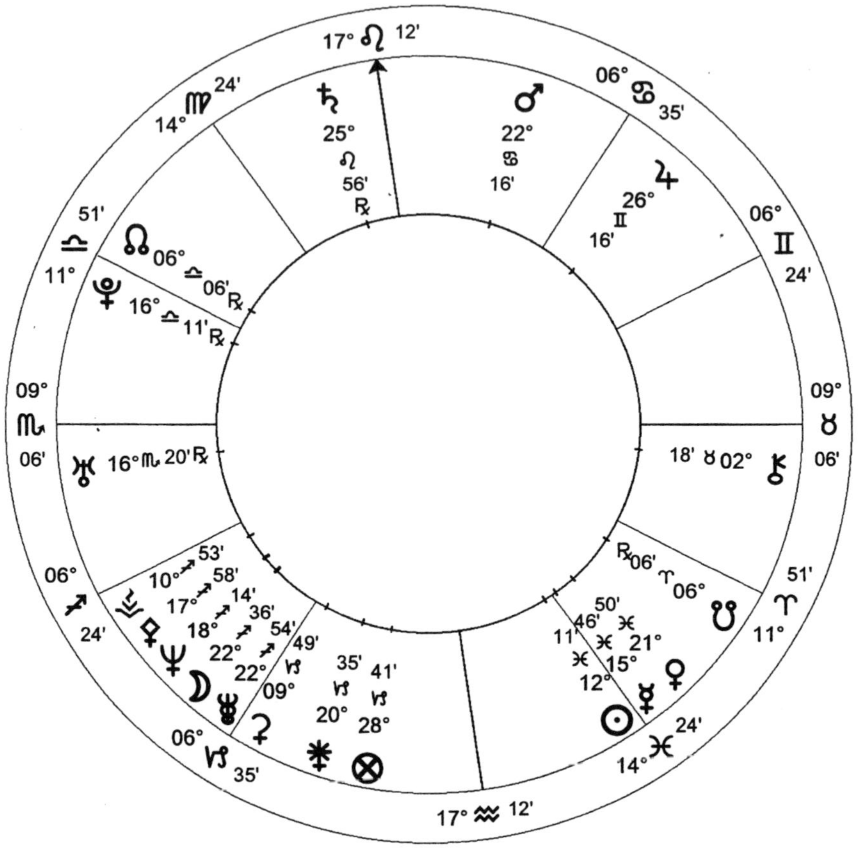

was square Saturn, and Saturn was conjoined his north node. In January 1981, the lunar eclipse was sesquiquadrate his Neptune, and in February, the solar eclipse was exactly square Uranus.

When he was almost 22 and began to take some nutritional supplements and pursue alternative therapies, the progressed Moon was conjoined his north node. Transiting Pluto was hitting Vesta. Neptune was semi-square Venus. Uranus was square Uranus. Saturn was conjoined his seventh

Midpoint Listing

ADD • Boy • Natal Chart

In Planetery Sequence • Modulus 360°00'

☽	22°♐36	*☿*	15°♓46	♂/♆	05°♎15	*♅*	16°♏20	⚷/Vx	27°♒36
☽/☉	02°♒24	☿/♀	18°♓48	♂/♇	04°♍14	♅/♆	02°♐17	⚷/☊	19°♋12
☽/☿	04°♒11	☿/♂	19°♉01	♂/⚷	12°♊17	♅/♇	01°♏16	⚷/⊗	15°♓30
☽/♀	07°♒13	☿/♃	06°♉01	♂/⚳	01°♎34	♅/⚷	09°♒19	*⚳*	10°♐53
☽/♂	07°♎26	☿/♄	05°♊51	♂/⚴	05°♎07	♅/⚳	28°♏36	⚳/⚴	14°♐25
☽/♃	24°♍26	☿/♅	16°♑03	♂/⚵	21°♎26	♅/⚴	02°♐09	⚳/⚵	00°♑44
☽/♄	24°♎16	☿/♆	02°♒00	♂/⚶	16°♎02	♅/⚵	18°♐28	⚳/⚶	25°♐21
☽/♅	04°♐28	☿/♇	00°♑58	♂/Vx	07°♎35	♅/⚶	13°♐04	⚳/Vx	16°♐53
☽/♆	20°♐25	☿/⚷	09°♈02	♂/☊	29°♌11	♅/Vx	04°♐37	⚳/☊	08°♏29
☽/♇	19°♏23	☿/⚳	28°♑19	♂/⊗	25°♈29	♅/☊	26°♎13	⚳/⊗	04°♑47
☽/⚷	27°♒27	☿/⚴	01°♒52	*♃*	26°♊16	♅/⊗	22°♐31	*⚴*	17°♐58
☽/⚳	16°♐44	☿/⚵	18°♒11	♃/♄	26°♋06	*♆*	18°♐14	⚴/⚵	04°♑16
☽/⚴	20°♐17	☿/⚶	12°♒47	♃/♅	06°♍18	♆/♇	17°♏12	⚴/⚶	28°♐53
☽/⚵	06°♑35	☿/Vx	04°♒20	♃/♆	22°♍15	♆/⚷	25°♒16	⚴/Vx	20°♐26
☽/⚶	01°♑12	☿/☊	25°♐56	♃/♇	21°♌13	♆/⚳	14°♐33	⚴/☊	12°♏02
☽/Vx	22°♐45	☿/⊗	22°♒14	♃/⚷	29°♉17	♆/⚴	18°♐06	⚴/⊗	08°♑19
☽/☊	14°♏21	*♀*	21°♓50	♃/⚳	18°♍34	♆/⚵	04°♑24	*⚵*	20°♑35
☽/⊗	10°♑38	♀/♂	22°♉03	♃/⚴	22°♍07	♆/⚶	29°♐01	⚵/⚶	15°♑12
☉	12°♓11	♀/♃	09°♉03	♃/⚵	08°♈25	♆/Vx	20°♐34	⚵/Vx	06°♑45
☉/☿	13°♓59	♀/♄	08°♊53	♃/⚶	03°♈02	♆/☊	12°♏10	⚵/☊	28°♏20
☉/♀	17°♓01	♀/♅	19°♑05	♃/Vx	24°♍35	♆/⊗	08°♑27	⚵/⊗	24°♑38
☉/♂	17°♉14	♀/♆	05°♒02	♃/☊	16°♌11	*♇*	16°♎11	*⚶*	09°♑49
☉/♃	04°♉14	♀/♇	04°♑01	♃/⊗	12°♈29	♇/⚷	24°♋14	⚶/Vx	01°♑21
☉/♄	04°♊04	♀/⚷	12°♈04	*♄*	25°♌56	♇/⚳	13°♏32	⚶/☊	22°♏57
☉/♅	14°♑16	♀/⚳	01°♒21	♄/♅	06°♎08	♇/⚴	17°♏04	⚶/⊗	19°♑15
☉/♆	00°♒12	♀/⚴	04°♒54	♄/♆	22°♎05	♇/⚵	03°♐23	*Vx*	22°♐54
☉/♇	29°♐11	♀/⚵	21°♒13	♄/♇	21°♍03	♇/⚶	28°♏00	Vx/☊	14°♏30
☉/⚷	07°♈15	♀/⚶	15°♒49	♄/⚷	29°♊07	♇/Vx	19°♏33	Vx/⊗	10°♑48
☉/⚳	26°♑32	♀/Vx	07°♒22	♄/⚳	18°♎24	♇/☊	11°♎08	*☊*	06°♎06
☉/⚴	00°♒04	♀/☊	28°♐58	♄/⚴	21°♎57	♇/⊗	07°♐26	☊/⊗	02°♐23
☉/⚵	16°♒23	♀/⊗	25°♒16	♄/⚵	08°♏16	*⚷*	02°♉18	*⊗*	28°♑41
☉/⚶	11°♒00	*♂*	22°♋16	♄/⚶	02°♏52	⚷/⚳	21°♒35		
☉/Vx	02°♒33	♂/♃	09°♋16	♄/Vx	24°♎25	⚷/⚴	25°♒08		
☉/☊	24°♐08	♂/♄	09°♌06	♄/☊	16°♍01	⚷/⚵	11°♓26		
☉/⊗	20°♒26	♂/♅	19°♍18	♄/⊗	12°♏19	⚷/⚶	06°♓03		

house cusp and semi-square Jupiter. The lunar eclipse of January 21 was sesquiquadrate his Neptune, while the solar eclipse of February 5 was square Uranus.

Case History #2

This is a young girl who began to manifest some symptoms of hyperactivity at the age of two, when she started walking. She had a lot of ear

ADD—Girl
Natal Chart
Dec 26, 1994, 4:17 PM PST +8:00
Pasadena
34N08 52 118W08 37

Geocentric
Tropical
Koch
True Node

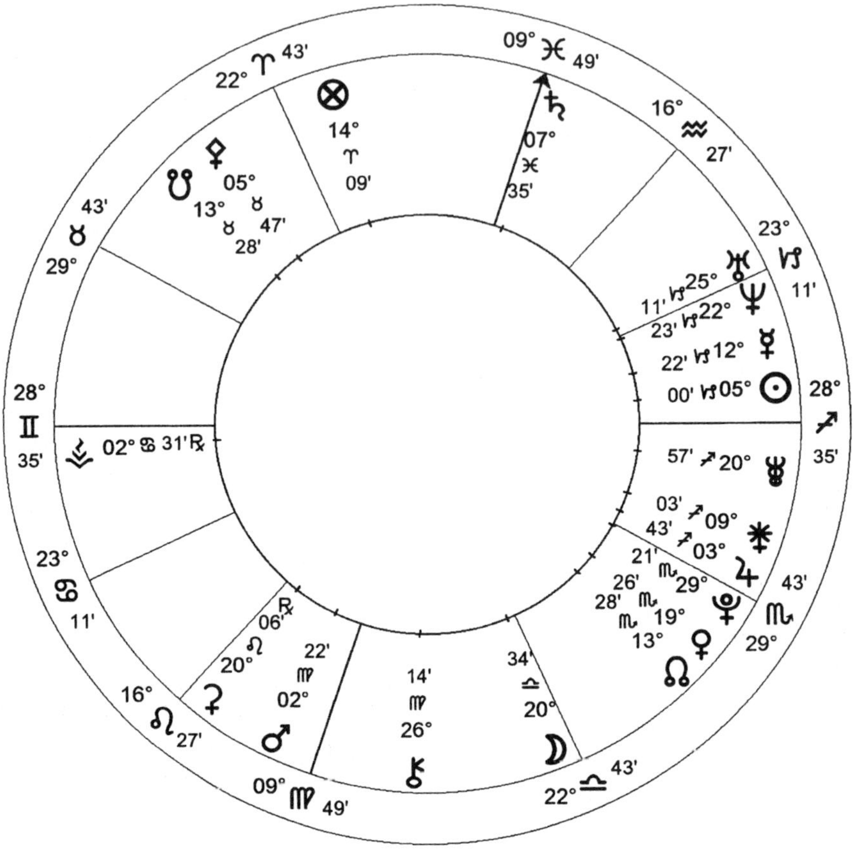

---

infections between the ages of one and three, and was given many antibiotics. Her hearing was affected, and she ended up having surgery on her ear drum when she was about two and a half. She also had a speech problem, but after some speech therapy, she is fine and reads well. She does have a short attention span, but becomes totally absorbed when watching television. At the age of seven now, her symptoms seem to have abated.

Midpoint Listing

ADD • Girl • Natal Chart

In Planetery Sequence • Modulus 360°00'

☽	20°♎34	*☿*	12°♑22	♂/♆	12°♏22	*♅*	25°♑11	⚷/⚶	08°♏36
☽/☉	27°♏47	☿/♀	15°♐54	♂/♇	15°♎51	♅/♆	23°♑47	⚷/☊	19°♎51
☽/☿	01°♐28	☿/♂	07°♏22	♂/⚷	14°♍18	♅/♇	27°♐16	⚷/⊗	05°♋11
☽/♀	05°♏00	☿/♃	23°♐02	♂/⚘	02°♌26	♅/⚷	25°♏42	*⚘*	02°♋31
☽/♂	26°♍28	☿/♄	09°♒58	♂/⚴	04°♋04	♅/⚘	13°♈51	⚘/⚴	04°♊09
☽/♃	12°♏08	☿/♅	18°♑46	♂/⚵	20°♎42	♅/⚴	15°♓29	⚘/⚵	20°♍47
☽/♄	29°♐04	☿/♆	17°♑22	♂/⚳	26°♌14	♅/⚵	02°♑07	⚘/⚳	26°♋18
☽/♅	07°♐52	☿/♇	20°♐51	♂/⚶	26°♎40	♅/⚳	07°♏38	⚘/⚶	26°♍44
☽/♆	06°♐28	☿/⚷	19°♏18	♂/☊	07°♎55	♅/⚶	08°♑04	⚘/☊	08°♍00
☽/♇	09°♏57	☿/⚘	07°♈26	♂/⊗	23°♊15	♅/☊	19°♐20	⚘/⊗	23°♉20
☽/⚷	08°♎24	☿/⚴	09°♓04	*♃*	03°♐43	♅/⊗	04°♓40	*⚴*	05°♉47
☽/⚘	26°♌32	☿/⚵	25°♐42	♃/♄	20°♑39	*♆*	22°♑23	⚴/⚵	22°♒25
☽/⚴	28°♋10	☿/⚳	01°♏14	♃/♅	29°♐27	♆/♇	25°♐52	⚴/⚳	27°♊56
☽/⚵	14°♏48	☿/⚶	01°♑39	♃/♆	28°♐03	♆/⚷	24°♏18	⚴/⚶	28°♒22
☽/⚳	20°♍20	☿/☊	12°♐55	♃/♇	01°♐32	♆/⚘	12°♈27	⚴/☊	09°♒38
☽/⚶	20°♏46	☿/⊗	28°♒15	♃/⚷	29°♎58	♆/⚴	14°♓05	⚴/⊗	24°♈58
☽/☊	02°♏01	*♀*	19°♏26	♃/⚘	18°♍07	♆/⚵	00°♑43	*⚵*	09°♐03
☽/⊗	17°♑21	♀/♂	10°♎54	♃/⚴	19°♒45	♆/⚳	06°♏14	⚵/⚳	14°♎34
☉	05°♑00	♀/♃	26°♏34	♃/⚵	06°♐23	♆/⚶	06°♑40	⚵/⚶	15°♐00
☉/☿	08°♑41	♀/♄	13°♑31	♃/⚳	11°♎54	♆/☊	17°♐56	⚵/☊	26°♏16
☉/♀	12°♐13	♀/♅	22°♐18	♃/⚶	12°♐20	♆/⊗	03°♓16	⚵/⊗	11°♒36
☉/♂	03°♏41	♀/♆	20°♐54	♃/☊	23°♏36	*♇*	29°♏21	*⚳*	20°♌06
☉/♃	19°♐21	♀/♇	24°♏23	♃/⊗	08°♒56	♇/⚷	27°♎47	⚳/⚶	20°♎31
☉/♄	06°♒17	♀/⚷	22°♎50	*♄*	07°♓35	♇/⚘	15°♍56	⚳/☊	01°♎47
☉/♅	15°♑05	♀/⚘	10°♍58	♄/♅	16°♒23	♇/⚴	17°♒34	⚳/⊗	17°♊07
☉/♆	13°♑41	♀/⚴	12°♒36	♄/♆	14°♒59	♇/⚵	04°♐12	*⚶*	20°♐57
☉/♇	17°♐10	♀/⚵	29°♏14	♄/♇	18°♑28	♇/⚳	09°♎43	⚶/☊	02°♐13
☉/⚷	15°♏37	♀/⚳	04°♎46	♄/⚷	16°♐54	♇/⚶	10°♐09	⚶/⊗	17°♒33
☉/⚘	03°♈45	♀/⚶	05°♐12	♄/⚘	05°♉03	♇/☊	21°♏25	*☊*	13°♏28
☉/⚴	05°♓23	♀/☊	16°♏27	♄/⚴	06°♈41	♇/⊗	06°♒45	☊/⊗	28°♑49
☉/⚵	22°♐01	♀/⊗	01°♒47	♄/⚵	23°♑19	*⚷*	26°♍14	*⊗*	14°♈09
☉/⚳	27°♎33	*♂*	02°♍22	♄/⚳	28°♉50	⚷/⚘	14°♌22		
☉/⚶	27°♐59	♂/♃	18°♎02	♄/⚶	29°♑16	⚷/⚴	16°♋00		
☉/☊	09°♐14	♂/♄	04°♊58	♄/☊	10°♑32	⚷/⚵	02°♏38		
☉/⊗	24°♒34	♂/♅	13°♏46	♄/⊗	25°♓52	⚷/⚳	08°♍10		

Interpretation of Horoscope

Her Capricorn Sun is conjoined Mercury, which is the ruler of her chart. Mercury is also broadly conjoined Neptune, square the Moon, and semi-square Pluto. She certainly has a volatile nervous system with all the Mercury activity and also Gemini rising. The Libra Moon is square the Uranus Neptune conjunction, semi-square Mars and Jupiter, and sesqui-quadrate Saturn. She could be very moody and spaced out with the

Moon square Neptune, and also very hyper with the square to Uranus. Mars, Saturn, and Jupiter are in a T square with Jupiter in Sagittarius. This can indicate some congestion in the liver, and Jupiter in its own sign does tend toward liver toxicity. Jupiter is also conjoined Pluto, the need to cleanse the liver. Venus is in Scorpio, conjoined the north node, broadly conjoined Pluto, square Ceres in Leo, and sextile the Uranus Neptune conjunction. This suggests a good deal of creative energy and may indicate some problems with the reproductive system at some time in her life. Vesta is close to the ascendant in Cancer, opposite her Sun, trine Saturn, and sextile Mars. Vesta in this position indicates strong service work.

In terms of parallels of declination, the Sun is parallel Mercury, which indicates a sensitive nervous system. The north node is parallel Venus and contra parallel Mars, this could point to blood sugar problems. Uranus is parallel Neptune and contra parallel Vesta; this relates to her nervous system and may also indicate a weak immune system.

Midpoints

Sun/Moon = Pluto, direct and Mercury, indirect—sensitive nervous system and problems with respiratory system

Mars/Uranus = ascendant, indirect—tendency to be hyper and get excited easily

Mars/Neptune = node, direct—sensitive immune system, problems digesting carbohydrates and low blood sugar

Mars/Saturn = Jupiter, direct—congestion and restrictions with liver functioning

Mercury/Uranus = Jupiter, indirect—erratic functioning of liver

Sun/Uranus = Pluto, indirect—need for healing the nervous system

Transits and Progressions

When she was about two and a half years old, her symptoms began; she also had surgery on her ears. Pluto was transiting her Jupiter, indicating there were problems with her liver and a need to cleanse the liver. Neptune was inconjunct her Mars, suggesting her immune system was very vulnerable. Saturn was opposing her Moon and on her Mercury/Uranus midpoint, indicating blockages in the nervous system. In September 1997, there was a solar eclipse opposite her Saturn.

TREATMENTS FOR ADD

1. Avoid any chemical additives in foods, pesticide sprayed vegetables and fruits, sugar and sweeteners. Avoid hot spicy foods that tend to aggravate liver heat.
2. Avoid fluorescent lighting and household chemicals used for cleaning.
3. Eat a balanced diet with emphasis on whole grains for B complex vitamins, and dark green vegetables for their natural chlorophyll, which is the magnesium ion.
4. Use chelation therapy to get rid of heavy metals such as mercury, cadmium, lead, and aluminum.
5. Ozone treatments are very helpful for clearing the liver and getting rid of toxic material.
6. Supplementation with important minerals and nutritional factors is very important. In research with ADD children, deficiencies in the essential fatty acids and in zinc were common.
7. Acupuncture and magnet therapy are helpful. Certain acupuncture points work to calm the spirit, as do magnets applied to the inside of the elbow and the inside of the wrists.
8. Finding the homeopathic constitutional remedy is very important.
9. Color therapy has worked well to relax the nervous system. Sound therapy has worked very well to balance the spirit and supply tones that may be missing from the individual's range.

SUPPLEMENT RECOMMENDATIONS FOR ADD

GLA is one of the EFA's (essential fatty acids) which is found in evening primrose oil, borage oil and black currant seed oil.

EPA and DHA are the Omega 3 long chain fatty acids that are found in fish oils. They are particularly helpful for those with allergies and chemical sensitivities.

Zinc helps the body in cases of chemical detoxification. It is very important for the immune system and regulates the function of the white blood cells.

Magnesium a key mineral for the nervous system and helps in the assimilation of calcium as well. It can be supplemented through liquid chlorophyll, as well as through capsules.

Manganese helps the nervous system and also helps in blood sugar disorders.

B Complex vitamins are important for stress and for the normal functioning of the nervous system. Deficiencies can contribute to depression, insomnia, and irritability.

Bioflavonoids with Quercitin help the immune system and are important in protecting from allergic substances and chemical sensitivities. They also are necessary in circulation and in manufacturing vitamin C in the body.

Vitamin E is a strong antioxidant which helps to prevent the breakdown of nutrients.

Glutathione and L-cysteine—Glutathione is an antioxidant; it helps protect against environmental toxins and heavy metals by detoxifying these chemicals. It is obtained from L-cysteine or N-acetyl cysteine.

Probiotics are very important in producing the B vitamins in the body; they also help with food assimilation. They may be taken in powdered or capsule form.

HERBAL RECOMMENDATIONS

Nervine herbs including **hops, camomile, scullcap, catnip, lavender,** and **spearmint** are very helpful as teas.

Alfalfa tea is good for making the body more alkaline and balancing the blood sugar.

Parsley tea made from fresh organic parsley simmered in water alkalinizes he body and clears the kidneys.

CHAPTER 22

Bipolar Disorder

BIPOLAR DISORDER, ALSO KNOWN AS MANIC DEPRESSION, affects more and more people in our society. Researchers have discovered that food allergies, as well as untreated endocrine problems, may cause severe mood disorders. In addition, periods of stress or tension may exacerbate symptoms of mood disorders.

Diagnostic criteria from the American Psychiatric Association define bipolar disorder as including both manic episodes and depressive episodes that occur almost every day for at least a one week period. These mood disturbances are severe enough to cause impairment in occupational functioning, social activities or relationships with others, or to necessitate hospitalization to prevent harm to one's self or others. Symptoms are not due to direct physiological effects of a substance such as a drug or medication, or a general medical condition.

Criteria for major depressive episodes include a depressed mood most of the day; diminished interest or pleasure in almost all activities; fatigue or loss of energy daily; feelings of worthlessness or inappropriate guilt nearly every day; diminished ability to think or concentrate; indecisiveness; recurrent thoughts of death with the idea of suicide, but no specific plan for committing suicide; insomnia or hypersomnia; and often significant weight loss or weight gain.

Criteria for manic episodes include a period of elevated, expansive, or irritable mood, lasting at least a week; inflated self-esteem or grandiosity; decreased need for sleep; more talkative than usual; distractibility; increase in goal directed activity either socially, at work or school, or sexually; excessive involvement in pleasurable activities that have a potential for painful consequences (foolish business investments, unrestrained buying sprees, strange sexual liasons.)

In the past, bipolar disorder has been treated through various medications including lithium and other antidepressants. Now many doctors agree that the pharmaceuticals available to patients are not always satisfactory. Many patients find that there are serious side effects to the medications; they have to choose between those side effects and learning to manage severe mood swings. Many bipolar women who want to have children, face the choice of undergoing extreme mood swings during pregnancy or risking birth defects in their children, since all of the medications are suspected of being harmful to developing fetuses.

Alternative methods to managing bipolar disorder tend to work in several ways. Some therapies are similar to pharmaceuticals, but with fewer side effects. For example, the herb St. John's Wort can function as an antidepressant. Some alternative methods look to other explanations for what psychiatrists have labeled as manic depression, for example, severe food allergies. Certain treatments attempt to improve the overall health so that this will allow the body to effectively fight off mood problems. When all the organs in the body are properly functioning, and the liver and colon are cleansed, it is more difficult to have reactions from food and other substances that cause mood swings. Most manic depressive patients tend to have problems with candida in their intestinal tract and need to do some cleansing and work with diet.

Excessive stress often depletes the zinc and B-6 in the body so that the person becomes "pyroluric" and has excessive mood swings. (Urinary excretion of pyrroles was first connected with psychosis in 1958, when various doctors doing research noted a new substance in the urine of patients undergoing experimental LSD model psychosis. This same substance was also found in the urine of many psychiatric patients who had never taken LSD or other drugs. Since the extracted urine made a lavender color when treated with certain reagents, it was referred to as the "mauve factor." Later, a

Canadian physician found that the mauve factor was the chemical kryptopyrrole. Because kryptopyrrole produces severe deficiencies of B-6 and zinc, those patients with the "mauve factor" were treated with both B-6 and zinc and responded very well. The term "pyroluria" was then coined.)

Women who are premenstrual often become very tense as well as depressed. Before menstruation, blood copper is highest and blood zinc lowest. Copper is a stimulant to the brain, while zinc has an anti-anxiety effect. With adequate zinc and B-6, pre-menstrual tension and depression can be alleviated.

PSYCHOLOGICAL FACTORS

Those who are bipolar often lack self confidence. They have difficulty sticking to a job or profession in which they could become successful. They also have problems with emotional relationships because of their excessive mood swings. This can make them feel very isolated in society unless they receive adequate treatment.

ASTROLOGICAL FACTORS

In examining the horoscopes of those with bipolar disorder, we often find Uranus angular, which suggests a very hyper or wired condition. Sometimes Neptune can be angular as well; an angular Neptune can make one very moody and super- sensitive. Mercury is also strong, either angular or conjoined the Sun or Moon. The signs Gemini and Sagittarius show up most frequently, as they are related to the nervous system; those with strong placements in these signs can be very scattered and tend to experience their emotions at both ends of the spectrum. Jupiter also seems very prominent; often it is conjoined the Sun, and sometimes conjoined the Moon or ascendant. Jupiter rules the liver; those with tendencies to bipolarity seem to have toxic livers and are more affected by allergic reactions. Jupiter also rules the pancreas, which is related to blood sugar; low blood sugar seems to accompany this condition. There is often an emphasis on the sign Libra with the Sun, Moon, or ascendant being in Libra. Libra is the balance and sometimes the scales of balance tip to one side or the other. These horoscopes have few planets in earth or water signs.

MIDPOINTS

Of the specific health midpoints, patterns that were found are the following:

Sun/Moon = Uranus or Mercury, sometimes Neptune—this shows a highly sensitive nervous system or immune system

Saturn/Neptune = Uranus or Mercury—problems caused by the nervous system

Mars/Uranus = Mercury, Sun, or Moon—may be very nervous and hyper, anxiety prone

Mars/Neptune = Jupiter—problems with liver and blood sugar

Other midpoints that might equal a planet or angle are:

Mercury/Mars—rashness, tendency to exaggerate or magnify, nervousness, nerve irritation

Mercury/Uranus—disturbances of equilibrium, tendency to scatter one's energies, confusion

Mercury/Neptune—nervous weakness, loss of feeling or sensing, confused ideas and perceptions, self-deception

CASE HISTORIES

Case History #1

The first case is that of a man who has had a difficult time with depression and anxiety for many years, as well as experiencing phases where he felt very high. At the age of 21, when he was in college, he attempted suicide by taking a bunch of pills. He was placed in a mental institution for three months, but not given much therapy or medications. Then he was taken out and sent back to college, where he was quite unhappy. He spent part of his childhood in Italy, where his mother lives, but he never got along well with his mother. In 1986 and 87, he was married, but things were not going well. Again, he attempted suicide but apparently "botched up." He has one son from that marriage and another son from another relationship. In 1991, he was living in Italy and having a lot of problems with his mother. He started drinking a lot and had a bad automobile accident on Easter Sunday. That got him out of Italy and back to the United States. In 1993, he re-met a woman whom he had known many years earlier; they had had a child together (his other son), and they have been in relationship since then. He does some work in the community, helping elders and also juveniles with problems, but never feels satisfied with the work he is doing. He has tried different forms of creative expression, but has not felt fulfilled in any of them. Currently, he has not been using any medications, though he did try some in the past. In December 2001, he obtained his constitutional remedy from a homeopathic physician; this helped him to give up marijuana, which he had used for anxiety. I also recommended several supplements to him, which seem to be helping. He is currently taking quercetin bioflavonoids, magnesium, niacinamide, and another supplement called Embalance, which has several amino acids and B vitamins in it.

Interpretation of Horoscope

This chart is mostly made up of the fire element with the Sun conjoined Jupiter in Sagittarius in the twelfth house. The Sun is square Mars in late Leo, and inconjunct the Moon in late Aries, making him very impulsive. His Moon is conjoined the asteroid Ceres, which shows nurturing women in his life; this is true of his partner. The Aries Moon shows a very dominant mother, with whom he has had a difficult time. His Moon is also part of a grand trine with Saturn and Mars in Leo and Venus in Sagittarius, indicating a strong creative and spiritual nature. Mars conjoined Saturn in a fire sign can be challenging, as Saturn tends to hold Mars back, so he can become impatient and frustrated. Pluto is also in Leo conjoined Saturn, trine Jupiter, and ascendant. Mercury in Scorpio is exactly square Pluto; along with Pluto conjoined Saturn, it can tend toward depression. Mercury conjuncts Chiron and the south node, so there is a need to understand and work with healing. Venus in the first house in Sagittarius is exactly opposite Uranus in the seventh. This can indicate changes in relationship, as well as a more unusual manifestation of creative energy. Uranus is angular and sextile both the Moon and the Mars Saturn conjunction. It is also inconjunct the south node. He needs to focus his energy through Saturn and Mars to ground Uranus. Neptune is in Libra in the eleventh house and semi-square Mars, which gives him the tendency to space out. Neptune is also sextile Pluto, as well as Jupiter and the ascendant; this could make him become too expansive and fantasize unrealistic projects.

In terms of parallels of declination, the Sun is parallel Jupiter and the south node; it is contra parallel Vesta. This shows liver toxicity and also lack of discipline. Venus is contra parallel Uranus and Pluto; this indicates

Bipolar Disorder—Man 1
Natal Chart
Nov 25,1947, 7:25 AM MST +7:00
El Paso, Texas
31N45 31 106W29 11

Geocentric
Tropical
Koch
True Node

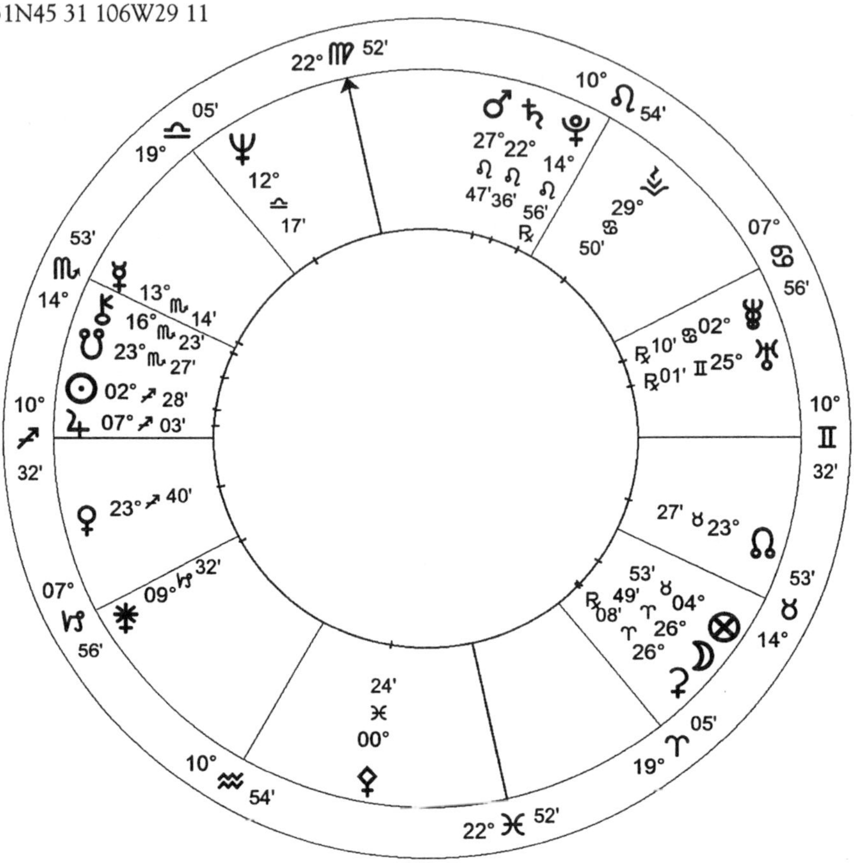

changes in relationship as well as the need to transform relationships; it can also show erratic thyroid functioning.

Midpoints
Sun/Moon = Mercury and Pluto, direct—quick mind, possible allergies, and tendency to depression

Mars/Uranus = Moon, direct—can become wired and emotionally volatile

Midpoint Listing

Bipolar Disorder • Man 1 • Natal Chart

In Planetery Sequence • Modulus 360°00'

☽	26°♈49	*☿*	13°♏14	♂/♆	20°♍02	*♅*	25°♊01	⚷/⯰	09°♍16		
☽/☉	14°♒38	☿/♀	03°♐27	♂/♇	21°♌21	♅/♆	18°♌39	⚷/☊	19°♌55		
☽/☿	05°♒01	☿/♂	05°♎31	♂/⚷	07°♎05	♅/♇	19°♋58	⚷/⊗	10°♒38		
☽/♀	25°♒14	☿/♃	25°♏08	♂/⚶	13°♌48	♅/⚷	05°♍42	*⚶*	29°♋50		
☽/♂	27°♊18	☿/♄	02°♎55	♂/⚴	29°♉06	♅/⚶	12°♋25	⚶/⚴	15°♉07		
☽/♃	16°♒56	☿/♅	04°♍07	♂/⚵	03°♏40	♅/⚴	27°♈42	⚶/⚵	19°♎41		
☽/♄	24°♊42	☿/♆	27°♎45	♂/⚳	26°♊58	♅/⚵	02°♈16	⚶/⚳	12°♊59		
☽/♅	25°♉55	☿/♇	29°♍05	♂/⯰	29°♋59	♅/⚳	25°♉35	⚶/⯰	16°♋00		
☽/♆	19°♋33	☿/⚷	14°♏48	♂/☊	10°♋37	♅/⯰	28°♊35	⚶/☊	26°♊38		
☽/♇	20°♊52	☿/⚶	21°♍32	♂/⊗	01°♋20	♅/☊	09°♊14	⚶/⊗	17°♊21		
☽/⚷	06°♒36	☿/⚴	06°♑49	*♃*	07°♐03	♅/⊗	29°♉57	*⚴*	00°♓24		
☽/⚶	13°♊19	☿/⚵	11°♐23	♃/♄	14°♎49	*♆*	12°♎17	⚴/⚵	04°♒58		
☽/⚴	28°♓36	☿/⚳	04°♒41	♃/♅	16°♍02	♆/♇	13°♍36	⚴/⚳	28°♓16		
☽/⚵	03°♓11	☿/⯰	07°♍42	♃/♆	09°♏40	♆/⚷	29°♎20	⚴/⯰	01°♉17		
☽/⚳	26°♈29	☿/☊	18°♌20	♃/♇	10°♎59	♆/⚶	06°♍03	⚴/☊	11°♈55		
☽/⯰	29°♉29	☿/⊗	09°♒03	♃/⚷	26°♏43	♆/⚴	21°♐21	⚴/⊗	02°♈39		
☽/☊	10°♉08	*♀*	23°♐40	♃/⚶	03°♎26	♆/⚵	25°♏55	*⚵*	09°♑32		
☽/⊗	00°♉51	♀/♂	25°♎43	♃/⚴	18°♑44	♆/⚳	19°♋13	⚵/⚳	02°♓50		
☉	02°♐28	♀/♃	15°♐21	♃/⚵	23°♐18	♆/⯰	22°♌14	⚵/⯰	05°♈51		
☉/☿	22°♏51	♀/♄	23°♎08	♃/⚳	16°♒36	♆/☊	02°♌52	⚵/☊	16°♓30		
☉/♀	13°♐04	♀/♅	24°♍20	♃/⯰	19°♍37	♆/⊗	23°♋35	⚵/⊗	07°♓13		
☉/♂	15°♎08	♀/♆	17°♏58	♃/☊	00°♓15	*♇*	14°♌56	*⚳*	26°♈08		
☉/♃	04°♐46	♀/♇	19°♎18	♃/⊗	20°♒58	♇/⚷	00°♎39	⚳/⯰	29°♉09		
☉/♄	12°♎32	♀/⚷	05°♐01	*♄*	22°♌36	♇/⚶	07°♌23	⚳/☊	09°♉48		
☉/♅	13°♍44	♀/⚶	11°♎45	♄/♅	23°♋48	♇/⚴	22°♉40	⚳/⊗	00°♉31		
☉/♆	07°♏23	♀/⚴	27°♑02	♄/♆	17°♍26	♇/⚵	27°♎14	*⯰*	02°♋10		
☉/♇	08°♎42	♀/⚵	01°♑36	♄/♇	18°♌46	♇/⚳	20°♊32	⯰/☊	12°♊49		
☉/⚷	24°♏26	♀/⚳	24°♒54	♄/⚷	04°♎29	♇/⯰	23°♋33	⯰/⊗	03°♊32		
☉/⚶	01°♎09	♀/⯰	27°♍55	♄/⚶	11°♌13	♇/☊	04°♋11	*☊*	23°♉27		
☉/⚴	16°♑26	♀/☊	08°♓33	♄/⚴	26°♉30	♇/⊗	24°♊54	☊/⊗	14°♉10		
☉/⚵	21°♐00	♀/⊗	29°♒16	♄/⚵	01°♏04	*⚷*	16°♏23	*⊗*	04°♉53		
☉/⚳	14°♒18	*♂*	27°♌47	♄/⚳	24°♊22	⚷/⚶	23°♍06				
☉/⯰	17°♍19	♂/♃	17°♎25	♄/⯰	27°♋23	⚷/⚴	08°♑23				
☉/☊	27°♒58	♂/♄	25°♌11	♄/☊	08°♋01	⚷/⚵	12°♐58				
☉/⊗	18°♒41	♂/♅	26°♋24	♄/⊗	28°♊44	⚷/⚳	06°♒16				

Mercury/Uranus = Sun, direct—sensitive nervous system, tendency to get hyper

Mercury/Neptune = Moon, direct—emotional sensitivity and creative potential

Transits and Progressions

In 1968, when he was hospitalized while at college, secondary progressed Sun was conjoined his Venus. Transiting Pluto was on his MC. Neptune was on his south node. Uranus was inconjunct his Moon, and Saturn was inconjunct Mercury. The solar eclipse of March 28 was opposite his Neptune, while the lunar eclipse of April 13 was opposite his Moon.

In the end of 1986, when he "freaked out" because his marriage was not going well, his secondary progressed Moon was conjoined natal Neptune. Transiting Pluto was semi-square his MC and sesquiquadrate his IC. Uranus was beginning to oppose Uranus. Saturn was transiting between his Sun and Jupiter. The solar eclipse October 3 was conjoined his Neptune, while the lunar eclipse October 17 was conjunct his Moon.

When he had his automobile accident on Easter Sunday in 1991, his secondary progressed Moon was conjoined his ascendant. Pluto was transiting his south node. Neptune was conjoined his progressed Sun. Uranus was inconjunct Pluto, while Saturn was semi-square his fourth house cusp. On January 15, the solar eclipse was exactly square his Moon, while on January 30, the lunar eclipse was conjoined Pluto and square Mercury.

Case History #2

This case is that of a man who had a lot of manic depressive symptoms between the ages of 16 and 21. He started getting depressed in high school; then he would get very "hyper" and remain in a manic state for a while. With a high IQ and a quick mind, he did well in school. During his college years at Kent State, he was hospitalized about 4 times for psychotic incidents and placed on medication. He would usually stay in the hospital for 2 months and then be released; afterwards he would stop his medication. Later, he became a nurse and has been a nurse for some time, but the past few years he has been working in a school with troubled boys who have behavioral problems. Since he turned 21, he has not taken any medication. He has a very high level of energy and does experience becoming very "hyper".

Interpretation of Horoscope

His Sun is conjoined Venus, the south node, Jupiter, and Mercury in Aquarius. This could make him very wired and in need of magnesium and B complex vitamins to help balance his system. Jupiter, Mercury and south node are very close to the MC, showing his need to be involved in some type of communication and humanitarian work. Jupiter conjoined the south node can indicate a very toxic liver, especially as it is square to Neptune. There is a grand square in fixed signs involving the Sun, Venus, south node, Jupiter, and Mercury with Ceres in Taurus, Neptune in Scorpio, and the north node in Leo. This suggests some very fixed aspects of his personality, and also potential problems with circulation. Venus square Neptune can indicate low blood sugar and an attraction to sweets, alcohol, and drugs. His Capricorn Moon is conjoined the asteroid Hygeia, inconjunct Uranus, and sesquiquadrate Pluto, which could make him both "hyper" (Uranus) and depressed (Pluto). This also indicates the need for healing with his mother. His Gemini ascendant is trine Mercury, Jupiter, south node, Venus, and Sun, which gives him a quick mind and a good ability to communicate. The ascendant is also sesquiquadrate Saturn and Mars, the tendency to depression. Mars conjoined Saturn is like driving a car with the brakes on, so he may have suffered some frustrations when he was younger. He was probably bored in school and somewhat rebellious as well. Uranus is also close to an angle in his chart, again giving him a sensitive nervous system and making him restless and wired.

In terms of parallels of declination, the Moon is parallel Mars and Saturn, while being contra parallel Pluto. This could make him very emotional and depressed. The Sun is parallel Venus (blood sugar problems), while Neptune is parallel the south node and contra parallel Ceres. This provides him with a strong sensitivity and nurturing nature.

Midpoints

Mars/Uranus = Sun, Venus, Neptune, and Ceres, direct—hyper-active nervous system, passionate and excitable nature

Mars/Saturn = ascendant, indirect—tendency to depression

Mercury/Neptune = Sun, Venus, Ceres, indirect—unclear in thinking, moody, sensitive to the thoughts of others

Transits and Progressions

In 1978, when both his manic and depressive tendencies began, his progressed Mars was conjoined the Sun and square Neptune. Transiting Pluto was trine his Sun, Venus, and ascendant. Neptune was sitting on his seventh house cusp opposite his ascendant. Uranus was conjoined his Neptune, while square his Sun Venus conjunction. Saturn was conjunct Uranus. On March 24, the lunar eclipse was sesquiquadrate south node, Jupiter, and Mercury.

Bipolar Disorder—Man 2
Natal Chart
Feb 3, 1962, 1:15 PM EST +5:00
Cleveland, Ohio
41N29 58 081W41 44

Geocentric
Tropical
Koch
True Node

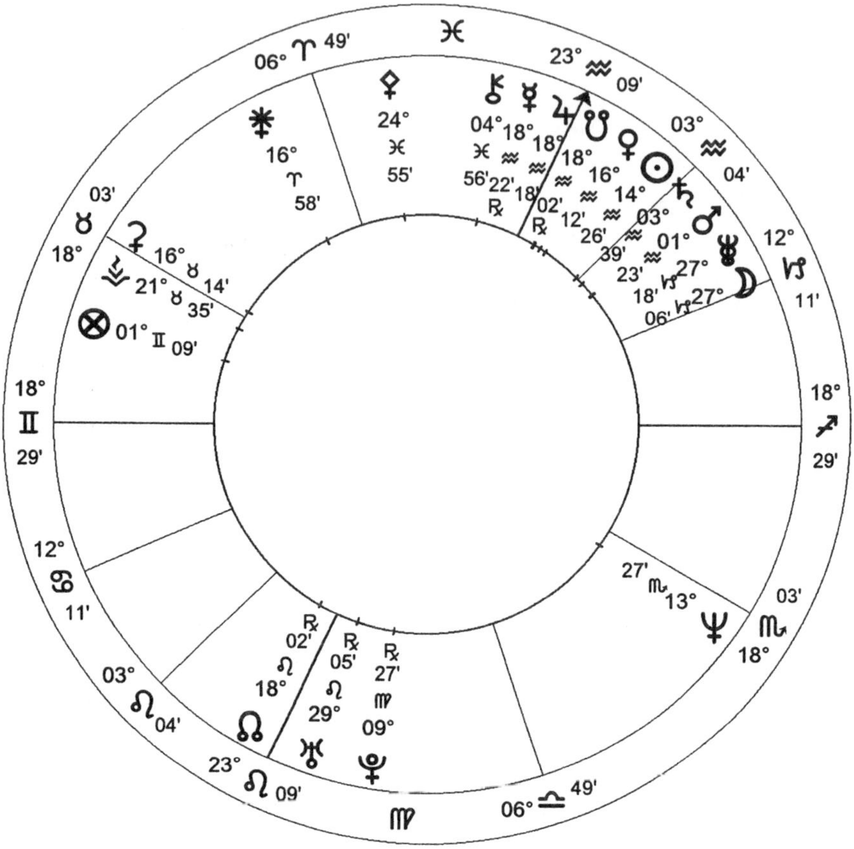

In 1981, he had a psychotic break and was institutionalized for a few months. Progressed Mars was conjunct his Venus, while his progressed Sun was almost conjoined Chiron. Transiting Pluto was beginning to square his Moon, while Neptune was conjoined his Saturn/Neptune midpoint, the health axis. Uranus was square his natal Uranus . Both Saturn and Jupiter at 4 degrees Libra were sesquiquadrate the south node, Jupiter, and Mercury. The solar eclipse of February 4 was conjoined his Sun and Venus, as well as square to Neptune.

Midpoint Listing

Bipolar Disorder• Man 2 • Natal Chart
In Planetery Sequence • Modulus 360°00'

☽	27°♑06	*☿*	18°♒22	♂/♆	22°♐25	*♅*	29°♌05	⚷/Vx	16°♒07
☽/☉	05°♒46	☿/♀	17°♒17	♂/♇	20°♏25	♅/♆	06°♎16	⚷/☊	26°♉29
☽/☿	07°♒44	☿/♂	09°♒53	♂/⚷	18°♒10	♅/♇	04°♍16	⚷/⊗	18°♈02
☽/♀	06°♒39	☿/♃	18°♒20	♂/⚶	26°♓29	♅/⚷	02°♊01	*⚶*	21°♉35
☽/♂	29°♑15	☿/♄	11°♒00	♂/⚴	28°♒09	♅/⚶	10°♋20	⚶/⚴	23°♈15
☽/♃	07°♒42	☿/♅	23°♏44	♂/✱	09°♓11	♅/⚴	12°♊00	⚶/✱	04°♉17
☽/♄	00°♒23	☿/♆	00°♑55	♂/⚳	23°♓49	♅/✱	23°♊02	⚶/⚳	18°♉55
☽/♅	13°♏06	☿/♇	28°♏54	♂/Vx	29°♑20	♅/⚳	07°♋40	⚶/Vx	24°♓26
☽/♆	20°♐17	☿/⚷	26°♒39	♂/☊	09°♏42	♅/Vx	13°♏12	⚶/☊	04°♋48
☽/♇	18°♏16	☿/⚶	04°♈59	♂/⊗	01°♈16	♅/☊	23°♌34	⚶/⊗	26°♉22
☽/⚷	16°♒01	☿/⚴	06°♓38	*♃*	18°♒18	♅/⊗	15°♋07	*⚴*	24°♓55
☽/⚶	24°♓21	☿/✱	17°♓40	♃/♄	10°♒59	*♆*	13°♏27	⚴/✱	05°♈56
☽/⚴	26°♒00	☿/⚳	02°♈18	♃/♅	23°♏42	♆/♇	11°♎27	⚴/⚳	20°♈34
☽/✱	07°♓02	☿/Vx	07°♒50	♃/♆	00°♑53	♆/⚷	09°♑12	⚴/Vx	26°♒06
☽/⚳	21°♓40	☿/☊	18°♉12	♃/♇	28°♏53	♆/⚶	17°♌31	⚴/☊	06°♊28
☽/Vx	27°♑12	☿/⊗	09°♈45	♃/⚷	26°♒37	♆/⚴	19°♑11	⚴/⊗	28°♈02
☽/☊	07°♏34	*♀*	16°♒12	♃/⚶	04°♈57	♆/✱	00°♒13	*✱*	16°♈58
☽/⊗	29°♓07	♀/♂	08°♒48	♃/⚴	06°♓37	♆/⚳	14°♌51	✱/⚳	01°♉36
☉	14°♒26	♀/♃	17°♒15	♃/✱	17°♓38	♆/Vx	20°♐22	✱/Vx	07°♓08
☉/☿	16°♒24	♀/♄	09°♒56	♃/⚳	02°♈16	♆/☊	00°♎44	✱/☊	17°♊30
☉/♀	15°♒19	♀/♅	22°♏39	♃/Vx	07°♒48	♆/⊗	22°♌18	✱/⊗	09°♉03
☉/♂	07°♒55	♀/♆	29°♐50	♃/☊	18°♉10	*♇*	09°♍27	*⚳*	16°♉14
☉/♃	16°♒22	♀/♇	27°♏49	♃/⊗	09°♈44	♇/⚷	07°♐11	⚳/Vx	21°♓46
☉/♄	09°♒03	♀/⚷	25°♒34	*♄*	03°♒39	♇/⚶	15°♋31	⚳/☊	02°♋08
☉/♅	21°♏46	♀/⚶	03°♈54	♄/♅	16°♏22	♇/⚴	17°♊11	⚳/⊗	23°♉41
☉/♆	28°♐57	♀/⚴	05°♓33	♄/♆	23°♐33	♇/✱	28°♊12	*Vx*	27°♑18
☉/♇	26°♏57	♀/✱	16°♓35	♄/♇	21°♏33	♇/⚳	12°♋50	Vx/☊	07°♏40
☉/⚷	24°♒41	♀/⚳	01°♈13	♄/⚷	19°♒17	♇/Vx	18°♏22	Vx/⊗	29°♓13
☉/⚶	03°♈01	♀/Vx	06°♒45	♄/⚶	27°♓37	♇/☊	28°♌44	*☊*	18°♌02
☉/⚴	04°♓41	♀/☊	17°♏07	♄/⚴	29°♒17	♇/⊗	20°♋18	☊/⊗	09°♋35
☉/✱	15°♓42	♀/⊗	08°♈41	♄/✱	10°♓18	*⚷*	04°♓56	*⊗*	01°♊09
☉/⚳	00°♈20	*♂*	01°♒23	♄/⚳	24°♓57	⚷/⚶	13°♈16		
☉/Vx	05°♒52	♂/♃	09°♒51	♄/Vx	00°♒28	⚷/⚴	14°♓55		
☉/☊	16°♏14	♂/♄	02°♒31	♄/☊	10°♏50	⚷/✱	25°♓57		
☉/⊗	07°♈48	♂/♅	15°♏14	♄/⊗	02°♈24	⚷/⚳	10°♈35		

TREATMENTS FOR BIPOLAR DISORDER

1. Obtaining the correct homeopathic constitutional remedy can be very important, as the homeopathic constitutional may replace medications. With the constitutional, natural lithium may not be needed.
2. Cleansing the liver is very important, since the liver detoxifies all chemical substances, as well as anything that may be causing an allergic reaction. In addition, colon cleansing helps the liver and the whole digestive system.

3. Eating a diet that is high in dark leafy green vegetables is important. They have a high nutritional content and also help to cleanse the liver. It is necessary to avoid sugar, dairy products, and wheat, as well as many acidic foods such as fruits, since they contribute to candida, which is very prevalent among those who are bipolar.
4. Utilizing biofeedback and other stress related therapies to access a more meditative state works well.
5. Cranial sacral work can help to balance the nervous system
6. Doing yoga exercises, tai chi, chi gung, and other practices that work with slowing down the breathing and bringing the "chi" to the whole body, can be very helpful.
7. It is a good idea to test for pyroluria, which pulls out both the B-6 and zinc from the body. Most doctors are unaware of this test, but it can be ordered from Norsom Medical Laboratories, 7243-West Wilson Avenue, Harwood Heights, IL. 60656.

SUPPLEMENT RECOMMENDATIONS FOR BIPOLAR DISORDER

L-Taurine is an amino acid that has anti-convulsant properties and is helpful for both epileptics and those suffering from manic depressive tendencies.

GABA may be classified as an amino acid, but it actually serves as a neurotransmitter. (There are more GABA sites in the brain than for any of the other neurotransmitters such as dopamine or serotonin.) It works as an inhibitory transmitter, keeping the brain and body from going into "overdrive". Those with anxiety or manic depression should begin with a low dose, 250 mg. at bedtime or when the anxiety occurs.

B-Complex helps to overcome symptoms of anxiety, depression, irritability, and fatigue.

B-6 should be used in addition to the B complex, especially if one is pyroluric and lacks it.

Zinc—If a diagnosis of pyroluria is made through lab tests, then high doses of zinc should be taken several times a day.

Calcium and Magnesium—Calcium is a difficult mineral to assimilate and needs to be taken with magnesium. Calcium hydroxapatite is one of the best forms. Usually a good supplement has a ratio of twice the amount of calcium to magnesium. However, with manic depressive patients, there is the need for additional magnesium. One way to obtain this is through liquid chlorophyll, which is the magnesium ion, and also through various forms of magnesium in capsule. Calcium supplements should not be taken with meals, but can be taken several times throughout the day.

Manganese is a very important mineral for the nervous system. If it is lacking, fatigue, irritability, and ear noises, such as ringing may be present.

L-Tyrosine is an amino acid that is a precursor to the neurotransmitters norepinephrine and dopamine, which are deficient in many manic depressives during their depressive cycles. L-tyrosine is also recommended when any thyroid conditions are present.

L-Phenylalanine and DL-Phenylalanine—Phenylalanine is a precursor to tyrosine and exhibits many of the same effects. It helps the body to produce a substance called "phenylethylamine" which is deficient in many manic depressives. (Phenylthylamine is present in both chocolate and marijuana, and is created by the body in greater amounts when one is "in love".) The L form seems to work better for manic and depressive states, while the D and DL forms work better for depression.

Methionine is an amino acid that is helpful for some individuals suffering from depression.

L-Tryptophan (and 5-Hydroxy-Tryptophan) is an amino acid that is a precursor to the neurotransmitter serotonin (the one that is affected by drugs such as Prozac and Zoloft). In 1990, L-Tryptophan was pulled from the market in the US, as it was deemed responsible for a number of deaths. Although the deaths were attributed to a contamination of the product made by one particular manufacturer, L-Tryptophan is currently available only by prescription in the US. However, 5-hydroxy-tryptophan is a metabolite of tryptophan , which is available over the counter, and may work better for people who suffer from depression, irritability, and other symptoms.

Glutathione and L-cysteine is an antioxidant which helps to detoxify chemicals into less toxic forms. It is often obtained from L-cysteine or N-acetyl cysteine. Cysteine binds with heavy metals aiding the body's elimination of them.

HERBAL RECOMMENDATIONS

Vervain and Scullcap help to tone the nervous system. They can be used in a formula with wood betony as well.

Hops, Passion flower, Camomile, St. John's wort, and Valerian are herbs that relax the nervous system. Often they are used in combination.

CHAPTER 23

Schizophrenia

SCHIZOPHRENIA IS A CHRONIC DISABLING BRAIN DISEASE. About one percent of the population develops schizophrenia during their life time; more than two million Americans suffer from it each year. People with schizophrenia often suffer psychotic symptoms such as hearing voices, believing that others are controlling their thoughts, or plotting to harm them.

There is no single cause of schizophrenia, although there does seem to be a genetic component. People who have a close relative with schizophrenia are more likely to develop the disorder; an identical twin of a person with schizophrenia has the highest risk. It appears that multiple genes are involved in creating the predisposition to schizophrenia. In addition, factors such as prenatal difficulties like intrauterine starvation, viral infections, and perinatal complications seem to influence the development of it. A recent study implicates genital herpes in the illness. *Herpes simplex 2*, which is transmitted sexually, appears to affect the mothers of schizophrenic patients. Brain chemistry is also being researched, and it is likely that the neurotransmitters dopamine and glutamate are involved.

Developmental neurobiologists have found that schizophrenia may be a developmental disorder, resulting when neurons form inappropriate connections during fetal development. These errors may be dormant until puberty, when changes in the brain that occur normally during this stage, interact adversely with the faulty connections. In other studies, investigators using brain imaging techniques have found evidence of early biochemical changes that may precede the onset of disease symptoms, prompting examination of the neural circuits that are most likely to be involved in producing those symptoms.

Schizophrenia is diagnosed by a variety of symptoms. As with bipolarity, the criteria from the Diagnostic and Statistical Manual of Mental Disorders are generally used. These include impaired overall functioning; thought content that is abnormal such as delusions or illusions; illogical thought forms such as incoherence; distorted perceptions such as visual or auditory hallucinations; impaired sense of self when one has trouble distinguishing the internal reality from the external; altered volition with inadequate drive; impaired social function with withdrawal or aggressiveness; a change in psychomotor functioning such as agitation; and a difficulty in orientation to time and place.

Schizophrenia has been treated through a combination of medications, psychotherapy, group support, and intermittent hospitalization when necessary. Before the 1950's, it was treated through electric shock and insulin coma, both ineffective treatments. Antipsychotic medications have been available since the 1950's and have helped some patients. These medications may reduce the psychotic symptoms and allow individuals to function more effectively. However, they are not a cure, nor do they insure that no further psychotic episodes will occur. Sometimes there are also side effects with the medications. Tardive dyskinesia (TD), like Parkinson's disease, is a disorder characterized by involuntary movements, most often affecting the mouth, lips, and tongue, and sometimes the arms or legs. It usually occurs in about 15-20 per cent of patients receiving antipsychotic medications.

In the late 1940's, two English psychiatrists, Humphrey Osmond, M.D. and John Smythies, M.D., began searching for a biochemical basis of schizophrenia. They knew that drugs like peyote, mescaline, and LSD altered the perceptions and thinking of normal people. These doctors asked whether schizophrenics could be producing mind altering drugs within their own bodies. Dr. Osmond left England in 1951 to become director of a mental hospital in Saskatchewan, Canada, where he met Abram Hoffer, M.D. That meeting led them to develop the first biochemical explanation for schizophrenia. They believed that the cause of schizophrenia was a body produced hallucinogen derived from adrenaline, an important hormone in the body. They called this chemical *adenochrome*. Noradrenaline is usually converted into adrenalin, but in schizophrenics, it is converted into *adenochrome*. To test this theory, Hoffer and Osmond injected themselves with small amounts of *adenochrome*; their perceptions and thinking processes were distorted for periods ranging from hours to days. As he reviewed the chemistry of vitamins, Hoffer realized that *adenochrome* could be countered by interfering with the body's production of adrenalin. Less adrenalin would mean less chance of *adenochrome* formation. Hoffer realized that the B vitamin niacin was known to interfere with adrenalin production. He also knew that a deficiency of niacin resulted in the disease pellagra, symptoms of which included schizophrenic disperceptions.

After a few outstanding recoveries using niacin and niacinamide, Hoffer and Osmond did their first double blind study in 1952. Of those schizophrenic patients given niacin and niacinamide, 75% recovered. Since that time, Hoffer and Osmond have been recognized as the fathers of Orthomolecular Psychiatry. (The word orthomolecular, which means to "straighten molecules," was coined by Dr. Linus Pauling in 1968, when he announced his support of those physicians and psychiatrists using megadoses of vitamins to treat patients.) When powerful tranquillizers were discovered, many psychiatrists felt it was easier to subdue their patients with injections; this suppressed the symptoms, but did not treat the cause. (It also had the support of big drug companies with lots of money advertising in medical journals, unlike Hoffer and Osmond, who had no money behind them.) The work of Hoffer and Osmond has elucidated many unknown aspects of the disease. The types of schizophrenia that respond to niacin, are in part genetically determined. For schizophrenic symptoms to appear, this genetic trait must be combined with either a deficiency of niacin, or an exaggerated need for niacin. If a person capable of producing *adenochrome* takes enough niacin, no schizophrenic symptoms may appear. Someone who does not produce *adenochrome*, but is deficient in niacin, may have symptoms including anxiety and tension, but no schizophrenia.

PSYCHOLOGICAL FACTORS

Schizophrenics have a hard time maintaining relationships and also being part of larger social groups. This causes them to spend many hours alone. If they have strong family support, or a support group, it can be very helpful in enabling them to feel part of society. A support group is also important in allowing them to understand their symptoms, and in finding ways to relate to larger social groups.

ASTROLOGICAL FACTORS

There are many different types of schizophrenia; some are called paranoid schizophrenics and some catatonic; others may be labeled disorganized, undifferentiated, or residual. However, as modern psychiatry changes, and with more bio-chemical research and alternative therapies available, these categories are being dropped. I have looked at schizophrenics as a group without these sub-divisions.

In general, many of these individuals have the sign Libra rising, which often places Capricorn on the fourth house, pointing to some repression in childhood. Aries rising is also found; Aries has more to do with aggressive types and anger. The other rising sign that was found was Sagittarius, which can become too spread out and unfocused; Sagittarius also rules the liver, which may be toxic. A preponderance of mutable signs was evident, especially Pisces. Hard aspects from Mars to Neptune, Mars to Uranus, and Mars to Mercury were common. Hard aspects from Mars to Pluto were prevalent in cases of violence or suicide. There is often a T square in the mutable signs, and frequently the Moon is involved. Quite a few of these cases have a Gemini Moon; Sagittarius and Pisces were also common. Saturn was sometimes in hard aspect to the Sun or Moon, or conjoined another planet such as Venus, Jupiter, or Uranus.

MIDPOINTS

Of the specific health midpoints, Mars/Neptune was found to equal the Moon or the Moon's nodes quite often; this would suggest not seeing things clearly, being "spaced out", or possible hallucinations. It also refers to toxic conditions with a sensitive immune system, low blood sugar, and difficulty assimilating carbohydrates.

Other midpoints that are relevant to check include:

Mercury/Mars—the tendency to exaggerate or magnify, rashness, nervousness, nerve irritation

Mercury/Uranus—disturbances of equilibrium, tendency to scatter one's energies, occasional confusion

Mercury/Neptune—paralysis of the nerves, confused ideas and perceptions, lack of clarity, self-deception

Mercury/Pluto—nervous irritation, hasty speaking and thinking, irritability, impatience

CASE HISTORIES

Case History #1

This is a young woman whose symptoms of adult congenital schizophrenia appeared when she was about thirty-one and half. A year and a half later, she committed suicide. When she was nine years old, her mother began to have symptoms of schizophrenia—hearing voices, walking naked through the house, and not being able to take care of her children. She was hospitalized and later institutionalized. Her father, who was a lawyer, re-married and she was brought up with her two brothers and two step- brothers. Later she went to college, majoring in biology and chemistry, and worked in a medical laboratory. She was also very active in her twenties—hiking, bicycle riding, river rafting. Moving to Santa Fe to attend massage school, she received her license in 1989. She practiced as a massage therapist from the spring of 1989 to the spring of 1991. At that time, she had mood swings, which made it difficult to keep appointments; she became very lethargic, and also started hearing voices, had difficulty sleeping, and lacked motivation. She wrote lots of metaphysical poetry. Finally, she checked herself into a residential treatment center, which worked with a twelve step program. She refused to take medication for her symptoms. Later, she had delusions that she was Jesus and was going to die at the age of 33, as he did. In the summer of 1991, she sustained a head injury from a car battery in her garage, which fell on her head. This may have intensified her symptoms. By Thanksgiving of 1991, a friend of hers drove her back to Tennessee to be with her family. On August 26, 1992, she found her brother's hunting rifle and used it to kill herself.

Interpretation of Horoscope

Her tenth house Sun in Leo is quincunx Saturn in Capricorn near the fourth house cusp, which may indicate her mother's being taken away at an early age. Her Sun is also sesquiquadrate the Moon in Pisces in the sixth house and square Neptune, showing her sensitivity and a tendency to be 'spaced out'. The Pisces Moon is exactly inconjunct Uranus, suggesting an active nervous

Schizophrenia—Woman
Natal Chart
Jul 23, 1959, 10:08 AM CST +6:00
Nashville
36N09 57 086W47 04

Geocentric
Tropical
Koch
True Node

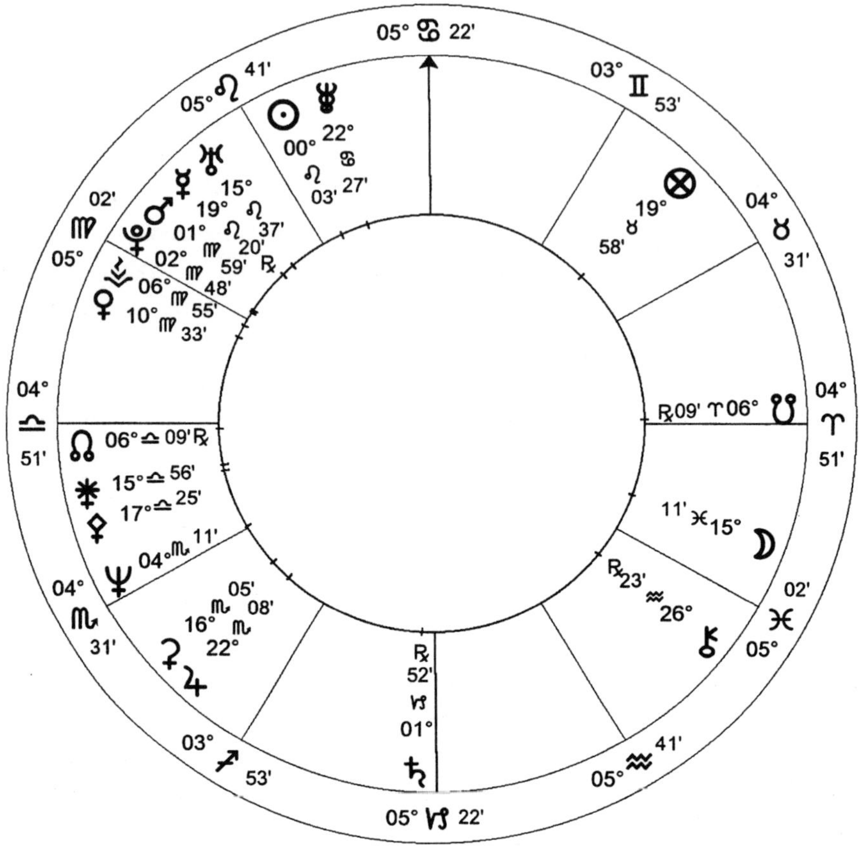

system, and instability in emotional relationships. Her Moon is also opposite Venus, which again refers to her mother and shows a tendency to low blood sugar. The trine from Jupiter in Scorpio to her Moon indicates that she was able to make money from her massage and healing work. She has a Libra ascendant with the north node on the ascendant squaring Saturn in Capricorn; this could tend to make her more tired or lethargic. Mercury is conjoined Uranus, square Jupiter in Scorpio and semi-square her ascendant.

Midpoint Listing

Schizophrenia • Woman • Natal Chart
In Planetery Sequence • Modulus 360°00'

☽	15°♓11	*☿*	19°♌20	♂/♆	03°♎05	*♅*	15°♌37	⚷/⚶	09°♉25
☽/☉	22°♉37	☿/♀	29°♌56	♂/♇	02°♍23	♅/♆	24°♍54	⚷/☊	16°♐16
☽/☿	02°♊15	☿/♂	25°♌40	♂/⚷	29°♏11	♅/♇	24°♌12	⚷/⊗	08°♈11
☽/♀	12°♊52	☿/♃	05°♎44	♂/⚳	04°♍27	♅/⚷	21°♉00	*⚳*	06°♍55
☽/♂	08°♊35	☿/♄	25°♎36	♂/⚴	24°♍42	♅/⚳	26°♌16	⚳/⚴	27°♍10
☽/♃	18°♑39	☿/♅	17°♌28	♂/⚵	23°♍57	♅/⚴	16°♍31	⚳/⚵	26°♍25
☽/♄	08°♒31	☿/♆	26°♍46	♂/⯚	09°♎02	♅/⚵	15°♍46	⚳/⯚	11°♎30
☽/♅	00°♊24	☿/♇	26°♌04	♂/⚶	12°♌13	♅/⯚	00°♎51	⚳/⚶	14°♌41
☽/♆	09°♑41	☿/⚷	22°♉52	♂/☊	19°♍04	♅/⚶	04°♌02	⚳/☊	21°♍32
☽/♇	08°♊59	☿/⚳	28°♌08	♂/⊗	10°♋59	♅/☊	10°♍53	⚳/⊗	13°♋27
☽/⚷	05°♓47	☿/⚴	18°♍23	*♃*	22°♏08	♅/⊗	02°♋47	*⚴*	17°♎25
☽/⚳	11°♊03	☿/⚵	17°♍38	♃/♄	12°♐00	*♆*	04°♏11	⚴/⚵	16°♎40
☽/⚴	01°♑18	☿/⯚	02°♎42	♃/♅	03°♎52	♆/♇	03°♎30	⚴/⯚	01°♏45
☽/⚵	00°♑33	☿/⚶	05°♌54	♃/♆	13°♏10	♆/⚷	00°♑17	⚴/⚶	04°♍56
☽/⯚	15°♑38	☿/☊	12°♍44	♃/♇	12°♎28	♆/⚳	05°♎33	⚴/☊	11°♎47
☽/⚶	18°♉49	☿/⊗	04°♋39	♃/⚷	09°♑16	♆/⚴	25°♎48	⚴/⊗	03°♌42
☽/☊	25°♐40	*♀*	10°♍33	♃/⚳	14°♎32	♆/⚵	25°♎03	*⚵*	15°♎56
☽/⊗	17°♈35	♀/♂	06°♍16	♃/⚴	04°♏47	♆/⯚	10°♏08	⚵/⯚	01°♏00
☉	00°♌03	♀/♃	16°♎20	♃/⚵	04°♏02	♆/⚶	13°♍19	⚵/⚶	04°♍11
☉/☿	09°♌41	♀/♄	06°♏12	♃/⯚	19°♏06	♆/☊	20°♎10	⚵/☊	11°♎02
☉/♀	20°♌18	♀/♅	28°♌05	♃/⚶	22°♍18	♆/⊗	12°♌05	⚵/⊗	02°♌57
☉/♂	16°♌01	♀/♆	07°♎22	♃/☊	29°♎08	*♇*	02°♍48	*⯚*	16°♏05
☉/♃	26°♍05	♀/♇	06°♍40	♃/⊗	21°♒03	♇/⚷	29°♏36	⯚/⚶	19°♍16
☉/♄	15°♎57	♀/⚷	03°♐28	*♄*	01°♑52	♇/⚳	04°♍52	⯚/☊	26°♎07
☉/♅	07°♌50	♀/⚳	08°♍44	♄/♅	23°♎44	♇/⚴	25°♍07	⯚/⊗	18°♌02
☉/♆	17°♍07	♀/⚴	28°♍59	♄/♆	03°♐02	♇/⚵	24°♍22	*⚶*	22°♋27
☉/♇	16°♌25	♀/⚵	28°♍14	♄/♇	02°♏20	♇/⯚	09°♎26	⚶/☊	29°♌18
☉/⚷	13°♉13	♀/⯚	13°♎19	♄/⚷	29°♑08	♇/⚶	12°♌38	⚶/⊗	21°♊13
☉/⚳	18°♌29	♀/⚶	16°♌30	♄/⚳	04°♏23	♇/☊	19°♍28	*☊*	06°♎09
☉/⚴	08°♍44	♀/☊	23°♍21	♄/⚴	24°♏38	♇/⊗	11°♋23	☊/⊗	28°♋04
☉/⚵	07°♍59	♀/⊗	15°♋15	♄/⚵	23°♏54	*⚷*	26°♒23	*⊗*	19°♉58
☉/⯚	23°♍04	*♂*	01°♍59	♄/⯚	08°♐58	⚷/⚳	01°♐39		
☉/⚶	26°♋15	♂/♃	12°♎03	♄/⚶	12°♎10	⚷/⚴	21°♐54		
☉/☊	03°♍06	♂/♄	01°♏55	♄/☊	19°♏00	⚷/⚵	21°♐09		
☉/⊗	25°♊01	♂/♅	23°♌48	♄/⊗	10°♓55	⚷/⯚	06°♑14		

This shows a very wired nervous system and can indicate some allergies. The square to Jupiter shows that the liver could become very toxic from allergens or other substances that she inhales. Mars is exactly conjoined Pluto in Virgo; this indicates potential violence, which she used on herself. It also presents a strong theme of service and healing, especially as Vesta is conjunct the two planets. Mars is trine Saturn, showing that she did have the potential to work hard and follow through with her business.

In terms of parallels of declination, her Moon is contra parallel Venus, again showing low blood sugar. Mercury is parallel Mars and contra parallel Neptune, emphasizing her sensitive nervous system and tendency to become "spaced out."

Midpoints

Sun/Moon = Jupiter, direct—healing ability as well as possible problems with liver

Mars/Saturn = Moon, indirect—lack of nurturing from mother, difficulty expressing emotions

Mars/Neptune = Mercury, indirect—sensitive nervous system and possible respiratory allergies

Saturn/Neptune = Pluto and Mars, direct—possibility of deep depression or serious illness

Transits and Progressions

When she was nine years old, around September of 1968, secondary progressed Mercury was conjoined Uranus, while progressed Moon was conjunct the MC and square the nodes. Transiting Pluto was sextile Jupiter. Neptune was conjoined Jupiter. Uranus was semi-square Uranus. Saturn was inconjunct Jupiter and semi-square Venus. The solar eclipse of September 22 was conjoined the ascendant, while the lunar eclipse of October 6 was opposite Juno.

In 1991, when her symptoms began, the secondary progressed Sun was beginning to conjoin natal Mars. Transiting Pluto was conjunct Jupiter. Neptune was inconjunct Uranus, square the Juno Pallas conjunction, and sextile her Moon. Uranus was on the midpoint of Mercury and Mars (indirect). Saturn was square Neptune and Jupiter was also square Neptune. The solar eclipse of January 15 was sesquiquadrate Venus, while the lunar eclipse of January 30 was conjoined Uranus.

On August 26, 1992, when she committed suicide, the progressed Sun was exactly on natal Mars. Transiting Pluto was on Jupiter. Neptune was inconjunct Uranus, square the Juno Pallas conjunction, and sextile her Moon. Uranus was inconjunct Uranus. Saturn was opposite Uranus. Jupiter was semi-square Neptune. Mars was sesquiquadrate Neptune and inconjunct

Jupiter. Mercury was conjoined Uranus. The solar eclipse of June 30 was conjoined her MC.

Case History #2

This is the case of a young man who has been on anti-psychotic medicine for many years. When he was young, he was very bright and won the science fair at school. At the age of 13, he fell, and after that, he lost muscle control. He started hearing voices telling him to do bad things and was put on medication. He lives at home with his parents, never goes out of the house, and has difficulty communicating with people. The doctors feel his brain is degenerating and he keeps putting on weight; he currently weighs about 200 pounds.

Interpretation of Horoscope

His Sun, Venus, and Mars are all conjunct in Pisces; they are in a T square with the Moon in Gemini and Neptune in Sagittarius. This shows a person who has a sensitive immune system, potential for allergies, and with the Moon opposed Neptune, subject to delusions. Mars being involved could indicate the head injury. Mercury is in Aquarius, forming a grand trine with the Moon and Pluto in Libra in the tenth house. Pluto is exactly inconjunct the Sun and Mars as well; this could indicate the negative voices he heard. Using the asteroids, he has a grand square with Mercury, Vesta, Uranus, and Hygeia. Mercury square Uranus can indicate erratic brain activity, and opposed to Vesta, may indicate compulsivness. Hygeia in the fourth house could show some necessary healing with his family. His Capricorn ascendant is square Pluto, indicating the need for transformation and healing. Saturn, ruler of his chart, is exactly conjoined Jupiter, showing problems with his liver and gall bladder, ruled by Saturn. He would have difficulty assimilating fats and carbohydrates, and tend towards weight gain. The Saturn Jupiter conjunction is trine his south node in Aquarius. The south node is also semi-square Neptune, which can indicate further problems in grounding. His nodes are exactly square the MC as well. Except for Capricorn rising and Chiron, Pallas, and Hygeia in Taurus, he has no earth in his horoscope.

In terms of parallels of declination, Mars is parallel Jupiter and Saturn, but contra parallel the Sun; this again shows problems with the liver and gall bladder. The Moon is parallel Vesta, but contra parallel Neptune, indicating his tendency to lose touch with reality.

Schizophrenia—Man
Natal Chart
Mar 13, 1981, 3:11 AM CST +6:00
St. Louis
38N37 38 090W11 52

Geocentric
Tropical
Koch
True Node

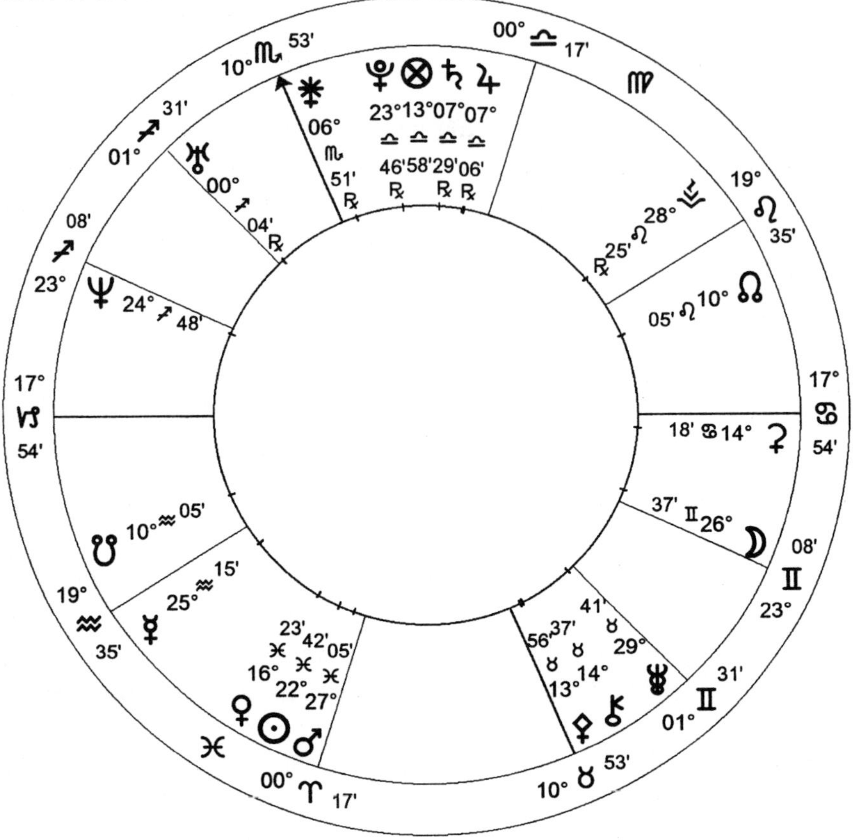

Midpoints

Sun/Moon = Neptune, indirect—sensitive immune system, possible hallucinations, delusions

Mars/Neptune = nodes, direct—possible problems with toxicity and immune system

Mercury/Uranus = Ceres, direct—the need to nurture the nervous system

Midpoint Listing

Schizophrenia • Man • Natal Chart
In Planetery Sequence • Modulus 360°00'

☽	26°♊37	*☿*	25°♒15	♂/♆	10°♒56	*♅*	00°♐04	⚷/⚸	22°♉09
☽/⊙	09°♉40	☿/♀	05°♓49	♂/♇	10°♑26	♅/♆	12°♐26	⚷/☊	27°♊21
☽/☿	25°♈56	☿/♂	11°♓10	♂/⚷	20°♈51	♅/♇	11°♏55	⚷/⊗	29°♋18
☽/♀	06°♉30	☿/♃	16°♐11	♂/⚳	12°♊45	♅/⚷	22°♒21	*⚳*	28°♌25
☽/♂	11°♉51	☿/♄	16°♐22	♂/⚴	20°♈31	♅/⚳	14°♎15	⚳/⚴	06°♋11
☽/♃	16°♌52	☿/♅	12°♑40	♂/⚵	16°♑58	♅/⚴	22°♒00	⚳/⚵	02°♎38
☽/♄	17°♌03	☿/♆	25°♑01	♂/⚶	20°♉41	♅/⚵	18°♏28	⚳/⚶	06°♌22
☽/♅	13°♍21	☿/♇	24°♐31	♂/⚸	28°♈23	♅/⚶	22°♍11	⚳/⚸	14°♋03
☽/♆	25°♍42	☿/⚷	04°♈56	♂/☊	03°♊35	♅/⚸	29°♒52	⚳/☊	19°♌15
☽/♇	25°♌12	☿/⚳	26°♏50	♂/⊗	05°♑32	♅/☊	05°♎05	⚳/⊗	21°♍12
☽/⚷	05°♊37	☿/⚴	04°♈36	*♃*	07°♎06	♅/⊗	07°♏01	*⚴*	13°♉56
☽/⚳	27°♋31	☿/⚵	01°♑03	♃/♄	07°♎18	*♆*	24°♐48	⚴/⚵	10°♌24
☽/⚴	05°♊17	☿/⚶	04°♉46	♃/♅	03°♏35	♆/♇	24°♏17	⚴/⚶	14°♊07
☽/⚵	01°♍44	☿/⚸	12°♈28	♃/♆	15°♏57	♆/⚷	04°♓42	⚴/⚸	21°♉48
☽/⚶	05°♋27	☿/☊	17°♉40	♃/♇	15°♎26	♆/⚳	26°♎37	⚴/☊	27°♊01
☽/⚸	13°♊09	☿/⊗	19°♐37	♃/⚷	25°♋52	♆/⚴	04°♓22	⚴/⊗	28°♋57
☽/☊	18°♋21	*♀*	16°♓23	♃/⚳	17°♍46	♆/⚵	00°♐50	*⚵*	06°♏51
☽/⊗	20°♌18	♀/♂	21°♓44	♃/⚴	25°♋31	♆/⚶	04°♎33	⚵/⚶	10°♍35
⊙	22°♓42	♀/♃	26°♐44	♃/⚵	21°♎59	♆/⚸	12°♓14	⚵/⚸	18°♌16
⊙/☿	08°♓59	♀/♄	26°♐56	♃/⚶	25°♌42	♆/☊	17°♎27	⚵/☊	23°♍28
⊙/♀	19°♓32	♀/♅	23°♑13	♃/⚸	03°♌24	♆/⊗	19°♏23	⚵/⊗	25°♎25
⊙/♂	24°♓54	♀/♆	05°♒35	♃/☊	08°♍36	*♇*	23°♎46	*⚶*	14°♋18
⊙/♃	29°♐54	♀/♇	05°♑04	♃/⊗	10°♎32	♇/⚷	04°♌11	⚶/⚸	21°♊59
⊙/♄	00°♑06	♀/⚷	15°♈30	*♄*	07°♎29	♇/⚳	26°♍06	⚶/☊	27°♋11
⊙/♅	26°♑23	♀/⚳	07°♊24	♄/♅	03°♏47	♇/⚴	03°♌51	⚶/⊗	29°♌08
⊙/♆	08°♒45	♀/⚴	15°♈09	♄/♆	16°♏09	♇/⚵	00°♏19	*⚸*	29°♉41
⊙/♇	08°♑14	♀/⚵	11°♑37	♄/♇	15°♎38	♇/⚶	04°♍02	⚸/☊	04°♋53
⊙/⚷	18°♈40	♀/⚶	15°♉20	♄/⚷	26°♋03	♇/⚸	11°♌43	⚸/⊗	06°♌50
⊙/⚳	10°♊34	♀/⚸	23°♈02	♄/⚳	17°♍57	♇/☊	16°♍56	*☊*	10°♌05
⊙/⚴	18°♈19	♀/☊	28°♉14	♄/⚴	25°♋43	♇/⊗	18°♎52	☊/⊗	12°♍02
⊙/⚵	14°♑47	♀/⊗	00°♑10	♄/⚵	22°♎10	*⚷*	14°♉37	*⊗*	13°♎58
⊙/⚶	18°♉30	*♂*	27°♓05	♄/⚶	25°♌54	⚷/⚳	06°♋31		
⊙/⚸	26°♈11	♂/♃	02°♑06	♄/⚸	03°♌35	⚷/⚴	14°♉17		
⊙/☊	01°♊24	♂/♄	02°♑17	♄/☊	08°♍47	⚷/⚵	10°♌44		
⊙/⊗	03°♑20	♂/♅	28°♑35	♄/⊗	10°♎44	⚷/⚶	14°♊27		

Mercury/Neptune = Pluto, direct—unusual ideas spring from the unconscious

Mercury/Pluto = Moon and Neptune, direct—overly receptive, nervous sensitivity, wanting to pursue strange ideas

Transits and Progressions

In November 1994, when he had his accident, progressed Sun and progressed Mars were conjoined in Aries (the head), while the progressed

Moon was in Sagittarius square natal Venus. Transiting Pluto was square Mercury, conjoined Uranus, square Vesta, and trine Mars. Neptune was conjoined the ascendant, while Uranus was square Pluto exactly. Saturn was inconjunct the Saturn Jupiter conjunction, and semi-square the ascendant. Jupiter was inconjunct the Moon. On November 3, the solar eclipse was conjunct the MC and square the nodes, while the lunar eclipse November 18 was square Mercury and inconjunct Neptune.

TREATMENTS FOR SCHIZOPHRENIA

1. Orthomolecular psychiatry would be the most helpful treatment in determining deficiences of niacin and other important vitamins and minerals.
2. Obtaining the correct homeopathic constitutional can help balance the body biochemically as well.
3. Cleansing the liver is very important, as the liver detoxifies all chemical substances. In addition, colon cleansing helps the liver and the whole digestive system to assimilate nutrients.
4. Ozone treatments bring oxygen into the body, and help to clear the liver. They also oxygenate the brain, which can help interfere with adrenalin production.
5. It is important to eat a balanced diet, high in dark green leafy vegetables that contain essential minerals, and a variety of whole grains such as buckwheat, brown rice, millet, quinoa, amaranth, oats, and barley that contain the B vitamins.
6. Cranial sacral work helps to balance the energy in the brain.
7. Doing yoga exercises, tai chi, chi gung, and other practices help to bring grounding and balance the "chi" energy.

SUPPLEMENT RECOMMENDATIONS FOR SCHIZOPHRENIA

Niacin and niacinamide—Large doses of these can be very helpful in eliminating schizophrenic symptoms. It is important to work with a doctor in determining amounts to be used daily. In extreme cases, intravenous doses of niacin and vitamin C have been given. Most of the time, niacin is given dissolved in a liquid on a full stomach.

B-complex should supplement the niacin and should be taken several times a day as B-100 or B-50.

B-6 is good to use in combination with B-3. B-6 should be taken three times daily after meals.

Vitamin C is not necessary in high doses except if there is a special need. This also should be taken in 3 doses daily, and is best taken in an ascorbate powdered form.

Folic acid and Vitamin B-12 can be taken through injections several times a week. Along with B-3, these are very helpful to schizophrenics. B-12 also improves the blood flow through the frontal lobes of the brain.

GLA oil is found in evening primrose oil and other oils which contain the Omega 6 fatty acids, the precursor to the prostaglandin E 1 series. Prostaglandins are involved in the biochemical pathology of schizophrenia. Several capsules daily should be used.

Zinc in high doses is usually called for by those who have schizophrenic symptoms. This may mean 50 mg. several times daily

Magnesium should also be taken; it is important when taking B-6, especially for children, since B-6 increases their activity level. Magnesium may be obtained through liquid chlorophyll, which is the magnesium ion, as well as through magnesium capsules; about 150 mg. three or four times a day would be helpful.

Manganese is an important mineral for the nervous system. If it is lacking, fatigue, irritability, and ear noises such as ringing may be present. Manganese removes the symptoms of tardive dyskinesia, which is a neuromuscular reaction that is a side effect of using tranquilizers for schizophrenia. Three or four chelated manganese should be used.

Selenium is a good antioxidant with antidepressant qualities. In research, it was found that schizophrenia increased in places where the soil was selenium deficient. A deficiency of selenium increases the difficulty of making prostaglandins in the body.

L-Tryptophan (and 5 Hydroxy-Tryptophan) is a precursor to the neurotransmitter serotonin and may be needed by some schizophrenic patients. The amount needed would be determined by an orthomolecular psychiatrist.

Glutathione and L-cysteine—Glutathione is an antioxidant which helps to detoxify chemicals into less toxic forms. Glutathione also contains selenium. It is obtained from L-cysteine or N-acetyl cysteine to help the body eliminate heavy metals and is used several times daily.

HERBAL RECOMMENDATIONS

Hops, Passion flower, Camomile, St. John's wort, and Valerian—These are herbs that relax the nervous system. Often they are used in combination.

CHAPTER 24

Electional Charts

IN MEDICAL ASTROLOGY, IT IS COMMON TO DO electional charts for surgeries, dental extractions, and other healing procedures where the most harmonious cosmic energies are desired. For emergency surgeries such as appendectomies, of course, there is no question of choosing the time. When I am asked to set up an electional chart for a surgery, I like to consult with the client to see if she or he has tried other alternatives before seeking surgery. So much surgery in this country is totally unnecessary, especially hysterectomies and fibroid surgery for women.

If the client has determined to undergo surgery, she has to provide me with the dates and times that the doctor works, within a period of a few months. Then I study her transits, check any aspects from the progressed Moon, and look at the aspects on the date and time selected.

Some of the old books on horary astrology warn us not to have the Moon or ascendant in the sign ruling the part of the body where the surgery will take place. However, I have seen many clients have surgery where this was the case, and they have had no ill effects. I take this into consideration, but only as a minor factor.

First, I look at the individual's transits. I like to find harmonious transits from Jupiter to the ascendant, Mars, Jupiter, Saturn, or the chart ruler if possible. I also like to avoid hard aspects from Mars to any of the planets, as this could possibly indicate bleeding.

Major transits of Pluto and Uranus often occur during a time when surgery is necessary. Uranus indicates some physiological change. Pluto signifies getting rid of toxins, cells, or organs that are no longer useful to the body. These transits also symbolize the surgery as well as the transformation process the body will go through. There also may be major transits of Saturn in orb during the time period of the surgery. Saturn can indicate a longer recovery period, as well as patience, which is often necessary for complete healing. Most serious dental surgeries take place under Saturn transits since Saturn and Capricorn rule the teeth. Neptune transits may also be prominent during time periods for surgery; these can be tricky as Neptune rules illusion. In fact, the surgery may not be necessary, and if possible, one should wait for a better time.

Once a fairly harmonious time period with the individual's transits is found, I focus on the electional chart itself, the day and time of day. One is not always able to avoid Mercury retrograde, though it would be preferable to have Mercury direct if possible. If not, I have my client double check with the doctor and hospital for the timing and arrangements. I did have one client who appeared for laser surgery on her eye when Mercury was retrograde, and they didn't even have her listed. Of course, she had to make another appointment and return! It may also be impossible to avoid Mars retrograde; however, it would be important to see the aspects Mars is making to the client's natal chart and in the electional chart itself.

There is usually not much of a choice for the ascendant, as doctors operate certain times of day, mostly in the morning. However, there is a choice in terms of aspects of the Moon. I would not schedule surgeries when the Moon is making a hard aspect to Mars, Saturn, Uranus, Neptune, or Pluto. This energy could affect the doctors and nurses as well as the patient. Obviously, full Moons or eclipses should also be avoided. I have not seen any major problems during void of course Moons, and if the rest of the chart looks harmonious, I am less concerned if the Moon is void.

It would be helpful to have Jupiter or Venus in the first house if possible, or near an angle. It would also be good to have the Moon making a favorable aspect to Mars, since Mars rules surgeries and cutting. Another fortunate aspect would be the Moon in harmony with Pluto for the re-generation and healing of the body.

Hysterectomy
Natal Chart
Dec 12, 1942, 3:17 AM EWT +4:00
Great Neck
40N48 02 073W43 44

Geocentric
Tropical
Koch
True Node

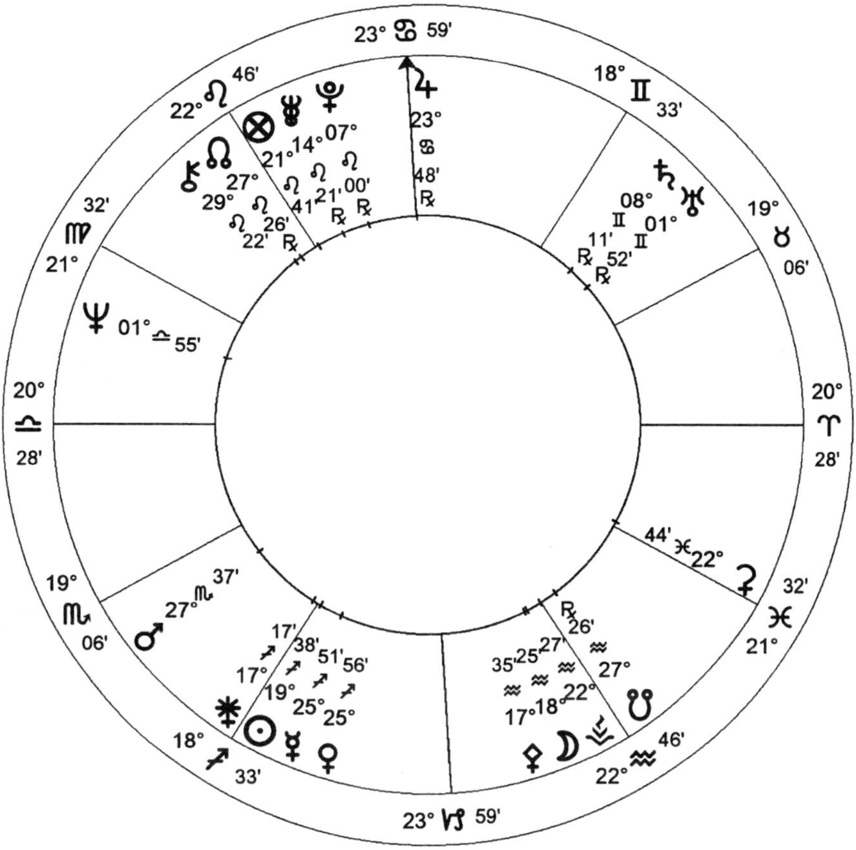

Example #1

This chart is that of a woman who chose to have a hysterectomy to remove fibroids she has had for a long time. She has decided to have a vaginal hysterectomy if possible, which means that she would receive an injection three months before the actual surgery. Since she is 60 years old and has had several children, she feels that this would be appropriate for her body now.

Midpoint Listing

Hysterectomy • Natal Chart
In Planetery Sequence • Modulus 360°00'

☽	18°♒25	*☿*	25°♐51	♂/♆	29°♎46	*♅*	01°♊52	⚷/⛢	21°♌51
☽/☉	19°♑01	☿/♀	25°♐53	♂/♇	02°♎19	♅/♆	01°♌53	⚷/☊	28°♌24
☽/☿	22°♑08	☿/♂	11°♐44	♂/⚷	13°♎29	♅/♇	04°♋26	⚷/⊗	25°♌31
☽/♀	22°♑10	☿/♃	09°♎50	♂/⚶	10°♑02	♅/⚷	15°♋37	*⚶*	22°♒27
☽/♂	08°♑01	☿/♄	17°♓01	♂/⚴	07°♑36	♅/⚶	12°♈09	⚶/⚴	20°♒01
☽/♃	06°♉06	☿/♅	13°♓52	♂/⚵	07°♐27	♅/⚴	09°♈43	⚶/⚵	19°♑52
☽/♄	13°♈18	☿/♆	13°♏53	♂/⚳	25°♑11	♅/⚵	09°♓34	⚶/⚳	07°♓36
☽/♅	10°♈08	☿/♇	16°♎26	♂/⛢	05°♎59	♅/⚳	27°♈18	⚶/⛢	18°♉24
☽/♆	10°♐10	☿/⚷	27°♎36	♂/☊	12°♎31	♅/⛢	08°♋07	⚶/☊	24°♏56
☽/♇	12°♉42	☿/⚶	24°♑09	♂/⊗	09°♎39	♅/☊	14°♋39	⚶/⊗	22°♉04
☽/⚷	23°♏53	☿/⚴	21°♑43	*♃*	23°♋48	♅/⊗	11°♋47	*⚴*	17°♒35
☽/⚶	20°♒26	☿/⚵	21°♐34	♃/♄	00°♋59	*♆*	01°♎55	⚴/⚵	17°♑26
☽/⚴	18°♒00	☿/⚳	09°♒18	♃/♅	27°♊50	♆/♇	04°♍27	⚴/⚳	05°♓09
☽/⚵	17°♑51	☿/⛢	20°♎06	♃/♆	27°♌51	♆/⚷	15°♍38	⚴/⛢	15°♉58
☽/⚳	05°♓34	☿/☊	26°♎38	♃/♇	00°♌24	♆/⚶	12°♐11	⚴/☊	22°♏30
☽/⛢	16°♉23	☿/⊗	23°♎46	♃/⚷	11°♌35	♆/⚴	09°♐45	⚴/⊗	19°♏38
☽/☊	22°♏55	*♀*	25°♐56	♃/⚶	08°♉08	♆/⚵	09°♏36	*⚵*	17°♐17
☽/⊗	20°♏03	♀/♂	11°♐46	♃/⚴	05°♉41	♆/⚳	27°♐19	⚵/⚳	05°♒01
☉	19°♐38	♀/♃	09°♎52	♃/⚵	05°♎32	♆/⛢	08°♍08	⚵/⛢	15°♎49
☉/☿	22°♐45	♀/♄	17°♓03	♃/⚳	23°♉16	♆/☊	14°♍40	⚵/☊	22°♎21
☉/♀	22°♐47	♀/♅	13°♓54	♃/⛢	04°♌05	♆/⊗	11°♍48	⚵/⊗	19°♎29
☉/♂	08°♐37	♀/♆	13°♏55	♃/☊	10°♌37	*♇*	07°♌00	*⚳*	22°♓44
☉/♃	06°♎43	♀/♇	16°♎28	♃/⊗	07°♌45	♇/⚷	18°♌11	⚳/⛢	03°♊33
☉/♄	13°♓54	♀/⚷	27°♎39	*♄*	08°♊11	♇/⚶	14°♉44	⚳/☊	10°♊05
☉/♅	10°♓45	♀/⚶	24°♑11	♄/♅	05°♊01	♇/⚴	12°♉17	⚳/⊗	07°♊13
☉/♆	10°♏46	♀/⚴	21°♑45	♄/♆	05°♌03	♇/⚵	12°♎09	*⛢*	14°♌21
☉/♇	13°♎19	♀/⚵	21°♐36	♄/♇	07°♋35	♇/⚳	29°♉52	⛢/☊	20°♌53
☉/⚷	24°♎30	♀/⚳	09°♒20	♄/⚷	18°♋46	♇/⛢	10°♌41	⛢/⊗	18°♌01
☉/⚶	21°♑02	♀/⛢	20°♎08	♄/⚶	15°♈19	♇/☊	17°♌13	*☊*	27°♌26
☉/⚴	18°♑36	♀/☊	26°♎41	♄/⚴	12°♈53	♇/⊗	14°♌21	☊/⊗	24°♌33
☉/⚵	18°♐27	♀/⊗	23°♎48	♄/⚵	12°♓44	*⚷*	29°♌22	*⊗*	21°♌41
☉/⚳	06°♒11	*♂*	27°♏37	♄/⚳	00°♉27	⚷/⚶	25°♏54		
☉/⛢	16°♎59	♂/♃	25°♍43	♄/⛢	11°♋16	⚷/⚴	23°♏28		
☉/☊	23°♎32	♂/♄	02°♍54	♄/☊	17°♋48	⚷/⚵	23°♎19		
☉/⊗	20°♎40	♂/♅	29°♌45	♄/⊗	14°♋56	⚷/⚳	11°♊03		

Natally, Saturn is in her eighth house and she has just completed her Saturn return. Neptune finished its opposition of her Pluto in January of 2002 when she had the injection. In April of 2002, the time of the surgery, Uranus is conjoined her south node; it will also be square her Mars, but she will have the surgery after the exact square.

The electional chart I set up for April 25, 2002 is for 7:30 AM; the surgery had to be done between 7-9 AM. Taurus is rising with Venus on

Electional Chart #1
Natal Chart
Apr 25, 2002, 7:30 AM EDT +4:00
Charlottesville
38N01 45 078W28 37

Geocentric
Tropical
Koch
True Node

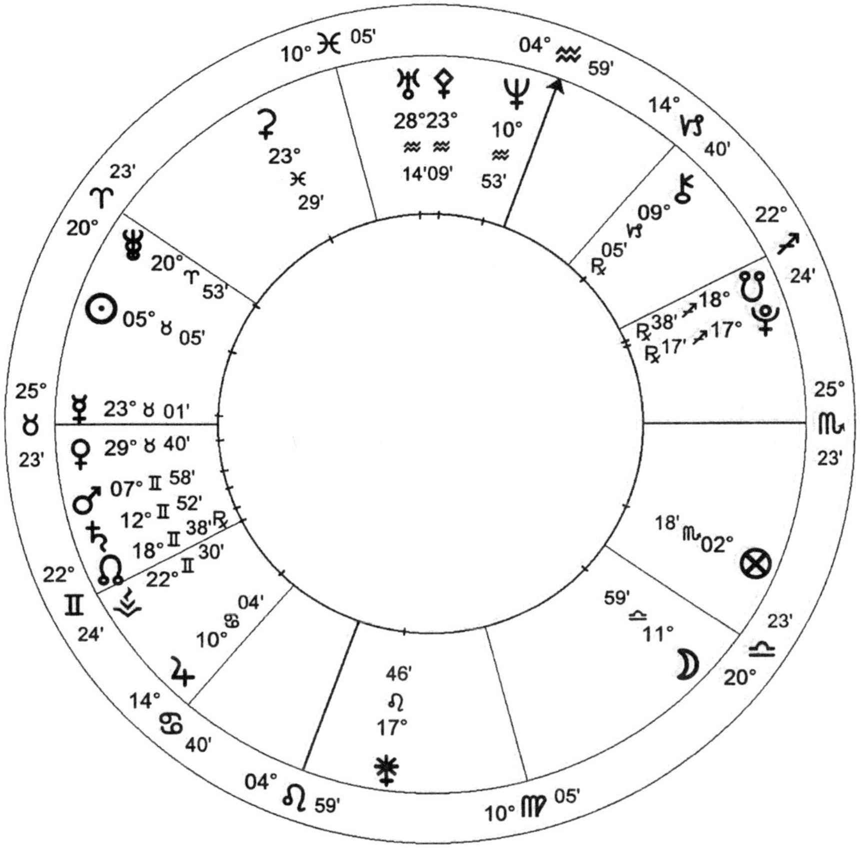

the ascendant, conjoined Mercury in the twelfth house. (She has a Venus Mercury conjunction in her natal horoscope.) Venus is contacting her natal Chiron, in an exact square, showing the healing potential. Mars is conjoined her natal Saturn so this is an opportunity to get rid of old stuff, and Saturn is close to its natal position as well. The north node is exactly trine her natal Moon. Jupiter is in Cancer, the sign of her Jupiter, though it is not conjunct. Uranus is on her south node by 1 degree, and it has just passed the exact square to her natal Mars. Pluto and the south node are approaching a conjunction to her Sun, and Pluto rules the female organs. The asteroid Hygeia is exactly trine her natal Sun, which is another subtle indication for healing.

In the electional chart, the Moon at 12 degrees Libra is forming a grand trine with Mars, Saturn, and the north node in Gemini, as well as Neptune in Aquarius This would be helpful in avoiding excess bleeding and in supporting the immune system. It is sextile Pluto in Sagittarius and square Jupiter in Cancer, which is not a difficult aspect, especially with all the other harmonious aspects. The Sun is in the twelfth house of hospitals, square to her natal Pluto, transformation of her body. Jupiter is opposite Chiron, which can also refer to the healing experience. The Pluto south node conjunction is in the seventh house, which represents the doctor performing the surgery.

Example #2

This is the chart of a woman who needed to have her wisdom teeth extracted. Since she has had problems with chronic fatigue syndrome and anemia, she wanted a harmonious date where her energy would be high.

Natally, her Moon is in the eighth house opposite Chiron, and square both her Sun and Mars. Jupiter is in Sagittarius opposite Uranus in Gemini. Her liver does tend to become toxic and she has done a lot of cleansing. Saturn is conjoined Pluto in Leo square to her nodes, so she has had problems with her teeth and gums. She also has Venus angular, opposite Neptune, indicating a tendency to low blood sugar and a sensitive immune system.

The electional chart that I set up was for April 7, 2000 at 10:00 AM. The surgery had to be done between 8-11 AM on certain weekday mornings. Her time period was the month of April 2000. Since her basic vitality was an issue, it seemed that having the Sun trine her natal Saturn, which also rules the teeth, might be a good idea. I was also able to have the transiting Moon conjoin her Moon within a degree by choosing 10 AM. Transiting Uranus was opposite her natal Saturn and square the nodes, indicating some changes with teeth or bones. It was also trine her natal Uranus. Transiting Pluto was trine her natal Pluto. Transiting Neptune was trine her ascendant and natal Neptune, but sesquiquadrate her Uranus. Transiting Saturn was square her natal Saturn and Pluto, which would be happening all month. This aspect does occur when there is

Dental Surgery
Natal Chart
Feb 17, 1948, 8:22 PM CST +6:00
Evanston
42N02 28 087W41 24

Geocentric
Tropical
Koch
True Node

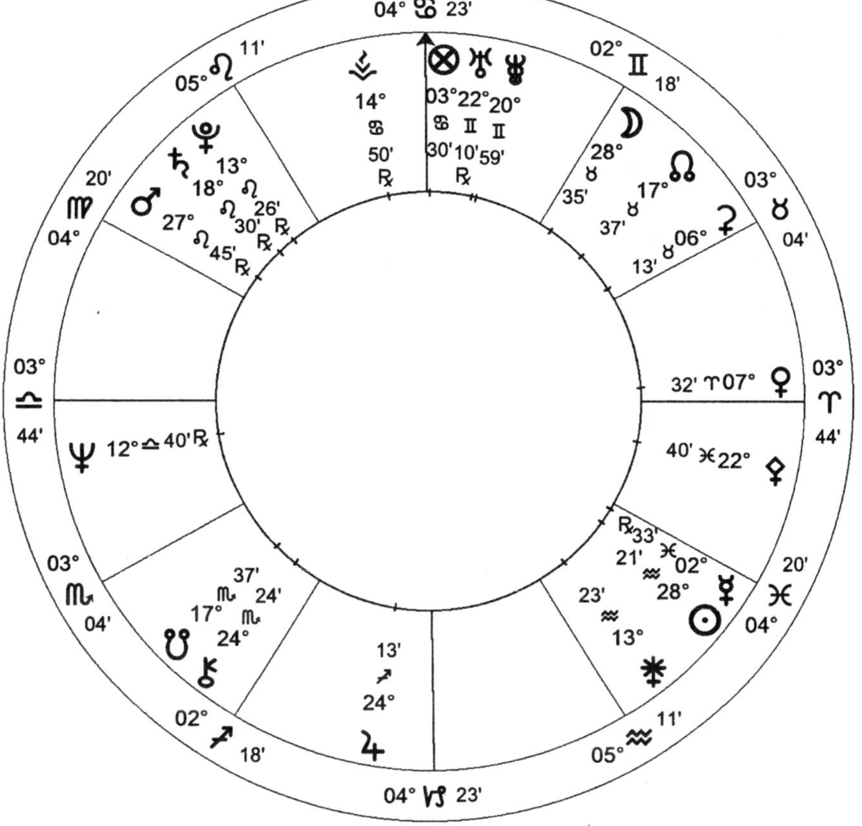

dental surgery. It was also conjoined her north node, indicating this was the time to do it. Transiting Jupiter was also square her natal Pluto as was Mars, indicating some major transformation—losing wisdom teeth. The transiting ascendant was conjoined her natal MC and part of fortune, which was an additional harmonious element, though it was square her natal ascendant. Transiting Mercury was conjoined Pallas Athena in her sixth house, square Uranus and square Jupiter. In fact, Pallas Athena is

Midpoint Listing

Dental Surgery • Natal Chart
In Planetery Sequence • Modulus 360°00'

☽	28°♉35	*☿*	02°♓33	♂/♆	20°♍13	*♅*	22°♊10	⚷/⛢	07°♍41
☽/☉	13°♈28	☿/♀	20°♓03	♂/♇	20°♌35	♅/♆	17°♌25	⚷/☊	21°♒00
☽/☿	15°♈34	☿/♂	00°♊09	♂/⚷	11°♎04	♅/♇	17°♋48	⚷/⊗	13°♍57
☽/♀	03°♉03	☿/♃	28°♑23	♂/⚳	06°♌18	♅/⚷	08°♍17	*⚳*	14°♋50
☽/♂	13°♋10	☿/♄	25°♉32	♂/⚴	10°♊13	♅/⚳	03°♋30	⚳/⚴	18°♉45
☽/♃	11°♓24	☿/♅	27°♈21	♂/⚵	20°♏34	♅/⚴	07°♉25	⚳/⚵	29°♈07
☽/♄	08°♋32	☿/♆	22°♐37	♂/⚶	01°♋59	♅/⚵	17°♈46	⚳/⚶	10°♊32
☽/♅	10°♊22	☿/♇	22°♉59	♂/⛢	24°♋22	♅/⚶	29°♉11	⚳/⛢	02°♋54
☽/♆	05°♌37	☿/⚷	13°♑28	♂/☊	07°♋41	♅/⛢	21°♊34	⚳/☊	16°♊13
☽/♇	06°♋00	☿/⚳	08°♉42	♂/⊗	00°♌38	♅/☊	04°♊53	⚳/⊗	09°♋10
☽/⚷	26°♌29	☿/⚴	12°♓37	*♃*	24°♐13	♅/⊗	27°♊50	*⚴*	22°♓40
☽/⚳	21°♊42	☿/⚵	22°♒58	♃/♄	21°♎22	*♆*	12°♎40	⚴/⚵	03°♓02
☽/⚴	25°♈37	☿/⚶	04°♈23	♃/♅	23°♓11	♆/♇	13°♍03	⚴/⚶	14°♈26
☽/⚵	05°♈59	☿/⛢	26°♈46	♃/♆	18°♏26	♆/⚷	03°♏32	⚴/⛢	06°♉49
☽/⚶	17°♉24	☿/☊	10°♈05	♃/♇	18°♎49	♆/⚳	28°♌45	⚴/☊	20°♈08
☽/⛢	09°♊47	☿/⊗	03°♉02	♃/⚷	09°♐18	♆/⚴	02°♑40	⚴/⊗	13°♉05
☽/☊	23°♉06	*♀*	07°♈32	♃/⚳	04°♎32	♆/⚵	13°♐02	*⚵*	13°♒23
☽/⊗	16°♊03	♀/♂	17°♊39	♃/⚴	08°♒26	♆/⚶	24°♋26	⚵/⚶	24°♓48
☉	28°♒21	♀/♃	15°♒53	♃/⚵	18°♑48	♆/⛢	16°♌49	⚵/⛢	17°♈11
☉/☿	00°♓27	♀/♄	13°♊01	♃/⚶	00°♓13	♆/☊	00°♌08	⚵/☊	00°♈30
☉/♀	17°♓56	♀/♅	14°♉51	♃/⛢	22°♓36	♆/⊗	23°♌05	⚵/⊗	23°♈27
☉/♂	28°♉03	♀/♆	10°♑06	♃/☊	05°♓55	*♇*	13°♌26	*⚶*	06°♉13
☉/♃	26°♑17	♀/♇	10°♊29	♃/⊗	28°♍52	♇/⚷	03°♎55	⚶/⛢	28°♉36
☉/♄	23°♉25	♀/⚷	00°♒58	*♄*	18°♌30	♇/⚳	29°♋08	⚶/☊	11°♉55
☉/♅	25°♈15	♀/⚳	26°♉11	♄/♅	20°♋20	♇/⚴	03°♊03	⚶/⊗	04°♊52
☉/♆	20°♐30	♀/⚴	00°♈06	♄/♆	15°♍35	♇/⚵	13°♏24	*⛢*	20°♊59
☉/♇	20°♉53	♀/⚵	10°♓28	♄/♇	15°♌58	♇/⚶	24°♊49	⛢/☊	04°♊18
☉/⚷	11°♑22	♀/⚶	21°♈53	♄/⚷	06°♎27	♇/⛢	17°♋12	⛢/⊗	27°♊14
☉/⚳	06°♉35	♀/⛢	14°♉15	♄/⚳	01°♌40	♇/☊	00°♋31	*☊*	17°♉37
☉/⚴	10°♓30	♀/☊	27°♈34	♄/⚴	05°♊35	♇/⊗	23°♋28	☊/⊗	10°♊34
☉/⚵	20°♒52	♀/⊗	20°♉31	♄/⚵	15°♏57	*⚷*	24°♏24	*⊗*	03°♋30
☉/⚶	02°♈17	*♂*	27°♌45	♄/⚶	27°♊22	⚷/⚳	19°♍37		
☉/⛢	24°♈40	♂/♃	25°♎59	♄/⛢	19°♋44	⚷/⚴	23°♑32		
☉/☊	07°♈59	♂/♄	23°♌08	♄/☊	03°♋04	⚷/⚵	03°♑53		
☉/⊗	00°♉56	♂/♅	24°♋57	♄/⊗	26°♋00	⚷/⚶	15°♒18		

the goddess of wisdom! Transiting Venus was broadly conjunct her natal Venus.

In the electional chart itself, the Moon trines Ceres in Virgo, which might be good for those assisting her, and sextiles Mercury in Pisces. It has passed the conjunction to Saturn and the square to Uranus. The Sun is trine Chiron in Sagittarius and also trine Pluto, which is helpful for healing. It also sextiles Uranus and squares Vesta in Capricorn. The ascendant is

Electional Chart #2
Natal Chart
Apr 7, 2000, 10:00 AM MST +7:00
Santa Fe
35N41 13 105W56 14

Geocentric
Tropical
Koch
True Node

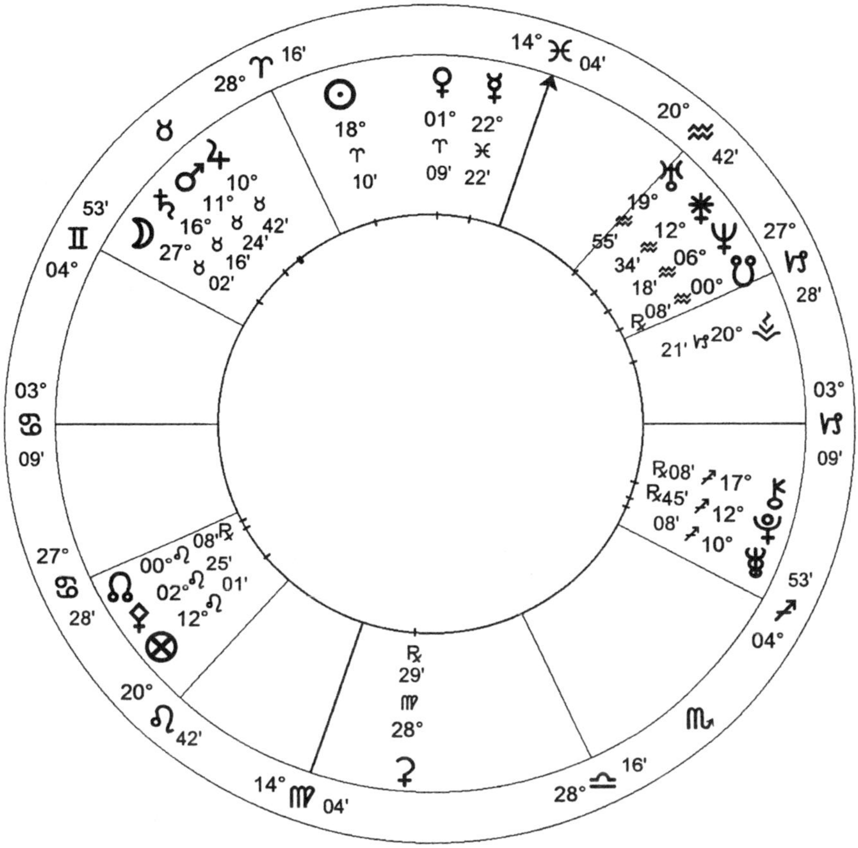

square Venus and sesquiquadrate Uranus. Jupiter and Mars are conjoined in Taurus and inconjunct Pluto in the sixth house, again suggesting physical regeneration. In fact, the extraction of her wisdom teeth went very well, and she recovered quickly.

Appendix A

CALCULATION OF MIDPOINTS

Midpoints should always be calculated by the planets' order in the zodiac. There are several ways of calculating midpoints. Two of the simplest will be illustrated here.

Method I

1. Subtract the difference between the two planets. If the Sun is 4 Gemini and the Moon 17 Scorpio, Gemini to Scorpio would be five signs or 150 degrees. There is an additional 13 degrees to 17 Scorpio.
2. Divide 163° by 2 giving 81.5 degrees.
3. Add 81.5 to 4 Gemini. 60° would be two signs. Adding this, plus 21° more, to 4 Gemini, gives 25.5 degrees Leo. (i.e. 2 signs, plus 21.5).

Method II

The following table can be used:

0 Aries	0 degrees	0 Libra	180 degrees
0 Taurus	30 degrees	0 Scorpio	210 degrees
0 Gemini	60 degrees	0 Sag	240 degrees
0 Cancer	90 degrees	0 Capricorn	270 degrees
0 Leo	120 degrees	0 Aquarius	300 degrees
0 Virgo	150 degrees	0 Pisces	330 degrees

Sun in 4 Gemini is 60 plus 4 = 64 degrees
Moon in 17 Scorpio is 210 plus 17 = 227 degrees

1. 64 plus 227 = 291
2. Divide by 2, which is 145.5
   Translate back into table—25.5 Leo

Appendix B

ANATOMICAL CORRESPONDENCES TO ZODIACAL DEGREES

(translated by Mary L. Vohryzek from "Anatomische Entsprechungen der Tlorkrcisgrade" by Elsbeth and Reinhold Ebertin)

I received these from Mary back in the 70's when I was working with her on Medical Astrology. They are interesting to examine, though I have not found a way to utilize them in my work. When more time and support is available for research in Medical Astrology, we may find these to be significant.

ARIES

1. Cerebrum
2. Mid-brain
3. Cerebellum (abscess)
4. Pineal gland (goiter)
5. Right or left Eye (hair)
6. Orbital cavity (socket of eye)
7. Ear (jaundice)
8. Cheekbone
9. Crystalline lens of eye
10. Eyeballs
11. Optic nerve
12. Tongue (hair)
13. Corpus callosum (band of nerve fibers), rheumatism
14. Frontal lobes (brain)
15. Lateral lobes, stroke, suicide
16. Pons Vareli
17. Spinal cord canal
18. Nerve connections
19. Corpus callosum cerebri
20. Hyoid bone
21. Eye muscle
22. Cheek muscle
23. Masticatory muscle
24. Zygomatic muscle
25. Sternocleidomastoid muscle
26. Skull
27. Fornix (tuberculosis)
28. Fornix (hair)
29. Auditory canal (bronchitis)
30. Paretid gland

TAURUS

1. Palate
2. Opening of throat
3. Uvula
4. Throat or larynx space
5. Larynx
6. Vocal chords
7. Cervical nerves
8. Jugular vein

9. Cervical vein (alcoholism)
10. Neck nerves connecting with the spinal cord (neurasthenia)
11. Neck nerves connecting with the spinal cord (neurasthenia)
12. Neck nerves connecting with the spinal cord (neurasthenia)
13. Neck nerves connecting with the spinal cord (neurasthenia)
14. True vocal chords
15. Epiglottis
16. Abscess carotid artery
17. Thyroid gland tonsils
18. Lymph vessels, (appendix)
19. Maxillary artery
20. Occipital bone (goiter)
21. Sinus artery
22. Hyoid muscle
23. Teeth (rheumatism)
24. Upper jaw
25. Lower jaw, tonsils, glands, (sucide, alcoholism)
26. Nasal bone
27. Cervical vertebrae
28. Deltoid muscles and main neck muscle
29. Deltoid muscles and main neck muscle
30. Trapezius

GEMINI

1. Trachea
2. Esophagus
3. Upper right pulmonary lobe, (appendix)
4. Lower right pulmonary lobe
5. Upper left pulmonary lobe
6. Lower left pulmonary lobe, anxiety, pulmonary inflammation
7. Apex of the lungs, heart
8. Eyesight, bronchial tubes (bronchial system)
9. Pulmonary artery, (rheumatic fever)
10. Hilus (lung root), (typhoid fever)
11. Thymus gland
12. Tracheal mucosa
13. Pulmonary veins
14. Clavicle (collarbone)
15. Scapula (shoulder blade)
16. Pleura
17. Bright's disease, (kidneys), first rib
18. Asthma, second rib
19. Laryngeal muscles
20. Third rib
21. Arm muscles
22. Upper arm, (appendicitis, insanity)
23. Spine
24. Connected with alcoholism, diabetes or low blood sugar
25. Radius (gout, neurasthenia)
26. Wrist, bones, (suicide)
27. Phalanges (fingers)
28. Metacarpal bones, (tuberculosis)
29. Fourth rib
30. Fifth rib

CANCER

1. Sixth rib
2. Seventh rib

3. Eighth rib, visual sense
4. Ninth rib
5. Tenth to twelfth ribs
6. Diaphragm
7. Thoracic canal
8. Hyacus, paralysis
9. Pylorus
10. Gastric fundus
11. Gastric veins, (alcoholism)
12. Large gastric curvature
13. Small gastric curvature
14. Abdominal walls
15. Gastric nerves, (suicide)
16. Pancreas
17. Opening of pancreas into common duct
18. Opening of pancreas into common duct
19. Head of pancreas
20. Upper arterial bend
21. Lower arterial bend
22. Gastric mucosa
23. Gastric blood vessels
24. Blood vessels of digestive organs
25. Blood vessels of digestive organs
26. Mammary glands
27. Nipples
28. Rib, cartilage,(hair)
29. Spleen, (bronchitis)
30. Twelfth dorsal vertebrae

LEO

1. Left coronary artery
2. Aorta
3. Right artery
4. Left carotid artery
5. Right carotid artery
6. Entrance of pulmonary artery, (eyesight)
7. Left coronary vein
8. Vena cave, (anemia, sense of hearing)
9. Upper vena cave, (alcoholism)
10. Jugular vein
11. Clavicular vein
12. Spinal column
13. Right heart chamber
14. Left heart chamber
15. Right atrium
16. Left atrium
17. Right aurical
18. Right cardiac cavity
19. Ventricular septum, spine
20. Mitral valve
21. Left atrium
22. Left auricle, (appendix)
23. Left auricle, (rheumatism)
24. Papillary muscle
25. Pericardium, abscess, (alcoholism)
26. Myocardium
27. Tendons to the goiter
28. Heart valve,
29. Cardiac septum, (neuritis)
30. Back

VIRGO

1. Duodenum
2. Small intestine
3. Cecum (appendix)
4. Ascending colon, asthma
5. Transverse colon
6. Descending colon
7. Rectum

8. Abdominal cavity
9. Right hepatic lobe, (rheumatic fever)
10. Left hepatic lobe, gall, (typhoid fever)
11. Falciform (ligament that attaches liver to diaphragm)
12. Abdominal aorta
13. Hepatic arteries
14. Gallbladder artery
15. Base area of liver
16. Hepatic groove
17. Abdominal muscle
18. Serrate groove
19. Left hepatic groove
20. Bile duct
21. Gall bladder duct, (typhoid fever)
22. Gall bladder
23. Hepatic cartilage, spine
24. Tendons of liver
25. Liver, (cancer, gout, arthritis)
26. Abdominal vein, (suicide)
27. Hip veins, (tuberculosis)
28. Hepatic veins
29. Back lobes of liver
30. Hepatic duct

LIBRA

1. Kidney, pelvis
2. Renal cortex
3. Adrenals, (abscess)
4. Kidney surfaces, (goiter)
5. Renal pyramids
6. Pubis
7. Jaundice, nervous system
8. Nerve supply to kidney and renal pelvis
9. Nerve supply to kidney and renal pelvis
10. Nerve supply to kidney and renal pelvis
11. Nerve supply to kidney and renal pelvis
12. Left renal system
13. Right renal system
14. Left inguinal gland
15. Right inguinal gland, (stroke, suicide)
16. Renal arteries
17. Adrenal arteries, (kidney illness)
18. Fatty capsule of kidneys
19. Great renal calyx
20. Small renal calyx
21. Renal hilus
22. Renal veins
23. Adrenal veins
24. Vascular circulation of the renal cortex
25. Vascular circulation of the renal cortex
26. Vascular system of the skin
27. Vascular system of the skin (tuberculosis)
28. Urinary bladder, (hair)
29. Right ureter, (bronchitis)
30. Left ureter

SCORPIO

1. Urethra (opening)
2. Urethral passage
3. Prostate, uterus
4. Testicles, right side of uterus
5. Testicles, left side of uterus

6. Right epididymis, uterine cavity
7. Left epididymis, right fallopian tube
8. Scrotum, left fallopian tube
9. Spermatic duct, vagina, (alcoholism)
10. Cavernosum of penis
11. Penis, labia majora
12. Seminal vesicles
13. Vulva, labia minora, glans penis
14. Foreskin (prepuce)
15. Cowpers glands
16. Cochlear head, right ovary, (abscess)
17. Testicular lobes, left ovary
18. Efferent ducts, hymen, (appendix, hair)
19. Uterine ligaments
20. Ligaments of penis, Bartholin's gland, (goiter)
21. Sphenoidal cavity
22. Ethmoid (bone) and ligaments
23. Nasal bone, fimbria of fallopian tubes, (rheumatism)
24. Nasal septum
25. Coccyx, ovarian ducts, tonsils, (alcoholism)
26. Perineum
27. Anus
28. Mucous Membranes
29. Vomer
30. Nasal muscles

SAGITTARIUS

1. Pelvic bone
2. Ilium (hip bone)
3. Ischium (tailbone)
4. Femur (thigh)
5. Right large femoral artery, (hair)
6. Left large femoral artery, (anxiety)
7. Right surface femoral artery, heart
8. Left surface femoral artery
9. Right lymphatic vessel, (rheumatic fever, diseases of the eye)
10. Left lymphatic vessels, (typhoid fever)
11. Adductor muscle
12. Large tibial vein
13. Long saphenous vein
14. Surface femoral vein
15. Right hip veins
16. Left hip veins
17. Sciatic nerve
18. Right femoral (kreiser, asthma)
19. Left femoral (kreiser)
20. Right head of femur
21. Left head of femur, (typhoid fever)
22. Right trochanter, (insanity, appendicitis)
23. Left trochanter, spine
24. Hollow of knee, cartilage
25. Condyle of right femur, (neurasthenia, gout)
26. Condyle of left femur, (suicide)
27. Cauteal muscles
28. Right leg muscle
29. Left leg muscle
30. Pear shaped muscle

CAPRICORN

1. Right patella
2. Left patella
3. Cutaneous nerves of upper leg, (eyesight)
4. Cutaneous nerves of tibia
5. Cutaneous nerves of knee
6. Right adductor muscle
7. Left adductor muscle
8. Lymph vessels of knees, (paralysis)
9. Veins of knee
10. Ligaments of right knee
11. Ligaments of left knee
12. Right knee joint
13. Left knee joint
14. Right knee cartilage
15. Left knee cartilage, (suicide)
16. Right knotty protruberance
17. Left knotty protruberance
18. Right ligaments of knee
19. Left ligaments of knee
20. Tendons of right knee
21. Tendons of left knee
22. Muscle endings
23. From upper to lower legs
24. From upper to lower legs
25. Connections between femur and tibia
26. Connections between femur and tibia
27. Deep lying nerves
28. Artery of right knee, (hair)
29. Artery of left knee, (bronchitis)
30. Adductor muscles

AQUARIUS

1. Right shinbone nerve, (fatty degeneration)
2. Left shinbone nerve
3. Right fibula
4. Left fibula
5. Nerve of right fibula
6. Nerve of left fibula, (eyesight)
7. Vein of lower right leg
8. Vein of lower left leg, (anemia)
9. Skin of right lower leg, (alcoholism)
10. Skin of lower left leg
11. Right crural band
12. Left crural band
13. Artery of right lower leg (fibula), (rheumatism)
14. Artery of left lower leg (fibula)
15. Lymph vessel of right lower leg
16. Lymph vessel of left lower leg
17. Bright's disease
18. spinal nervous system
19. spinal nervous system
20. spinal nervous system
21. spinal nervous system
22. Right gastrocnemius, (appendix, cecum)
23. Left gastrocnemius, (rheumatism)
24. Right tibial muscle
25. Left tibial muscle, (alcoholism)
26. Right fibular, (neurasthenia)
27. Left fibular, (goiter)
28. Right tibia
29. Left tibia, (neuritis)
30. Connections in lower leg

PISCES

1. Right heelbone
2. Left heelbone
3. Nerves of right foot, (appendix)
4. Nerves of left foot, (asthma)
5. Right cuboid bone
6. Left cuboid bone
7. Right anklebone
8. Left anklebone
9. Right metatarsus, (rheumatic fever)
10. Left metatarsus, (typhoid fever)
11. Lymph vessels of foot
12. Artery of right foot
13. Artery of left foot
14. Right surface veins
15. Left surface veins
16. Cruciate ligaments of right foot
17. Cruciate ligaments of left foot
18. Right extensor digitorum (toe extensor)
19. Left extensor digitorum
20. Right fibular muscle
21. Left fibular muscle, (typhoid fever)
22. Achilles heel of right foot, (insanity, appendicitis)
23. Achilles heel of left foot, spine
24. Right capsular joint
25. Left capsular joint, (cancer, gout)
26. Nerves of lower foot
27. Phalanges of right foot, (acute nephritis, kidneys)
28. Phalanges of left foot, (tuberculosis)
29. Toe nails of right foot
30. Toe nails of left foot

Appendix C

ASTROLOGICAL BIRTH CONTROL

The concept of Astrological Birth Control has been a very murky issue since the work of Dr. Eugen Jonas was first introduced into this country by Sheila Ostrander and Lynn Schroeder in their book, *Psychic Discoveries Behind the Iron Curtain*. Dr. Jonas, a gynecologist and psychiatrist who was head of the psychiatric department of the state clinic in Nagysurany, Czechoslovakia, had been experimenting with a cosmic fertility cycle based on the angle between the Sun and Moon in a woman's birth chart. Since many good results were achieved through his work, the Czech government allowed him to set up the Astro Research Center for planned parenthood in Nitra, Czechoslovakia. More recently, an organization was started in Vienna, known as Astra International, in order to make Jonas' work available to people all over the world.

However, it is of prime importance to understand that we have never had Dr. Jonas' completed work available in this country. The information that has been popularized is based only on a partial knowledge of his discoveries. I quote from a letter written by Dr. Jonas himself to Jim Shere, an Astrologer and former president of the ICHA (International Committee for a Humanistic Astrology) presently residing in Occidental, Ca. The letter is dated Jan. 23, 1971.

> *"Nobody from the USA has so far been to see me in Czechoslovakia and nobody has asked for any work or publications of mine. Nevertheless I have learned from some extracts of papers that were published in your country that some people had come to see me from the USA and they write such things about my work that I was greatly surprised with what ideas people can have. All the information about myself and my work that I had read and understood is not based on truth"*

The most practical solution to the birth control problem seems to be to incorporate both cycles and to determine carefully the ovulation time through the basal temperature and vaginal mucous method. Both of these methods, along with much fine information on mental birth control and tables for the Sun. Moon angle are given in the *Natural Birth Control Book* by Art Rosenblum. (Aquarian Research Foundation, Philadelphia, Pennsylvania). This book used to be revised every two years to report new developments on the fertility cycles and feedback from women who are using various forms of this method. It is currently out of print but old copies are around. Included in the book are instructions for calculating the lunar angle for those who do not have an astrological chart.

The simplest way to calculate your lunar angle is to subtract the distance between your Sun and Moon. For example, if your Sun is 1 degree of Cancer and your Moon is 3 degrees of Aquarius, you are born a few days after full moon. Your angle is 212 degrees. That means whenever the Sun and Moon are 212 degrees apart, you are at your cosmic fertility peak. However, in order to be safe you need to consider the time period 2½ days before the angle reaches 212 degrees and 1½ days after. If the Moon were 1 degree of Cancer and the Sun 3 degrees of Aquarius, you would start with the Sun in subtracting, and the angle would be 148 degrees. In other words, in the first example you have a disseminating Moon type born after full moon; in the second example you have a gibbous Moon type, born before full moon.

Another older book worth mentioning is *Lunaception* by Louise Lacey (Warner Books, NY, 1971). Louise reports on the twenty. nine women who worked with regulating their ovulation cycle by leaving a light on in the bedroom on the fourteenth, fifteenth and sixteenth nights of their menstrual cycle. In this way ovulation became more regular and only five days of abstention from sexual intercourse was required. The women also charted their basal temperature and vaginal mucous changes to confirm when ovulation was taking place. Among those who followed these instructions, there were no unwanted pregnancies. Louise did not know about the cosmic cycle when she did this study, so consequently it was not observed by these women.

Conscious Conception by Jeannine Parvati Baker, Frederick Baker, and Tamara Slayton (Freestone Publishing and North Atlantic Books, Berkeley, CA) has many good articles on fertility awareness including an article on Astrology and Cosmic Fertility by Yolanda Maarsen Miller and one by Louise Lacey from her book Lunaception.

Appendix D

DECUMBITURE CHARTS

Decumbiture charts are a tool used in classical astrology, deriving from the work of William Lilly and others. A decumbiture chart was erected at the time the patient's urine arrived at the doctor's office. From this chart, a prognosis was made as to whether the patient would recover quickly, whether the illness would lead to her death, whether the doctor would be a contributing cause of death, what means of curing might be helpful, and other information of a predictive nature. Decumbiture charts are related to horary charts in the way they are interpreted and used.

An example of the type of information an astrologer would obtain from the decumbiture chart by looking at the Moon is by determining if the Moon is approaching a benefic or malefic— if a benefic, this would indicate the "disease" is neither serious nor long lasting; if a malefic, the condition would get worse. If the Moon is in difficult aspects already, then the patient has no resources to draw upon. Other types of information involve the ruler of the sixth house in the eighth house in which case the individual dies from the disease, or the ruler of the seventh in the eighth, in which case the doctor may be a contributing cause of death.

My own work with Medical Astrology and astrology in general is as a tool for healing and transformation. Utilizing this approach, I attempt to connect the physiological symptoms to psychological problems as well as spiritual imbalances in one's life. I work both with balancing the physical body through natural supplements, herbs, and other alternative therapies, as well as finding outlets through creative projects and supportive groups that utilize self-awareness techniques and spiritual practices. I do not find decumbiture charts useful as a healing tool, though they may be interesting to those curious about astrological techniques.

Studying the natal chart with secondary progressions and transits provides a lot of information about an individual. The roots of our physical symptoms often begin years before they manifest in the body, and this can be seen through the tools of basic natal astrology. The types of healing that an individual would respond to can also be seen through the natal horoscope.

For those interested in pursuing the study of decumbiture charts, I recommend the publications on classical astrology from Arhat Media Inc., P.O. Box 2008, Reston, VA 20195 and also the Traditional Astrologer magazine from England, which tends to publish articles on Decumbitures. Their address is 3 Avondale Bungalows, Sherwood Hall Road, Mansfield. Notts, NG18 2NJ, United Kingdom.

Appendix E

SUPPLEMENT RECOMMENDATIONS

There are many types of supplements that are important for balancing our bodies. Each person is different and will require various combinations of these nutritional supplements and different amounts. It is important to work with a health practitioner such as a Naturopathic physician or nutritional consultant when setting up an individual program.

Bioflavonoids or Vitamin P help in absorption of Vitamin C and in protecting the Vitamin C molecule from oxidation. Bioflavonoids increase the strength of the capillaries which link the arteries to the veins; this is especially important in bleeding gums, bruising, and bleeding ulcers as well as in hemorrhoids, varicose veins, nosebleeds, and excess menstrual bleeding. One of the bioflavonoids, Quercetin, is especially important for asthma, allergies, multiple chemical sensitivities, bursitis, arthritis, colds, flus, and protection from radiation. It stabilizes certain cells and inhibits release of histamine and other inflammatory chemicals. Quercetin is found with hesperidin, rutin, and catechin in Bioflavonoid supplements. One needs a total of 1200 or 1600mg. daily; it is recommended to take 400 mg. three or four times a day.

Vitamin C produces an immunological response which helps to fight viruses and bacteria. It supports the adrenal function and aids in producing the adrenal hormones so that the body can handle infections and stress. Vitamin C helps in maintaining healthy collagen so that it brings healing to injured and aging tissues. Vitamin C also activates white blood cells and increases production of lymphocytes, the white cells important in antibody response. It can decrease the production of histamine and thus can reduce allergic reactions. It also increases interferon production and so can activate the immune response to viruses. Through its antioxidant effect, it reduces the effect of pollution and helps to protect from smog, carbon monoxide, lead, and heavy metals. Vitamin C should only be used in an ascorbate form such as magnesium ascorbate. Basic dose should be from 500 mg. to 1,000 mg. daily; more may be required in serious conditions, up to bowel tolerance, (too much Vitamin C can cause diarrhea) which varies with each individual.

Vitamin E is an antioxidant which helps to prevent the breakdown of nutrients by oxygen; this is enhanced by other antioxidants as Vitamin C, beta carotene, glutathione and L-cysteine, as well as the mineral selenium. Oxidation in our bodies of substances as the fat molecules causes free radicals, unstable molecules that may lead to cellular and tissue damage and eventually chronic inflammation. Vitamin E helps heart and muscle cell respiration by improving their function with less oxygen and therefore increases stamina and endurance. It also has some anti-clotting properties and can be used before and after surgery. It is not advisable for people with high blood pressure to use Vitamin E. Recommended dosage is 400-600 i.u's daily, preferably in its water dispersible form as Vitamin E succinate.

Vitamin A is an antioxidant that is crucial not only for the eyes and the skin, but it moisturizes the mucous linings helping to fight off infectious agents and environmental toxins. Deficiencies reduce cellular immunity and antibody production. Preformed Vitamin A (retinol) comes from animal products with its highest concentration in liver and fish liver oil. Beta carotene or provitamin A is found in yellow and orange colored vegetables and fruits as well as leafy green vegetables. Many people, however, especially those who are ill, cannot convert beta carotene to A, so they need to take Vitamin A and not just beta carotene. 25,000 i.u's a day is recommended; sometimes more is used for a shorter time period.

B-Complex vitamins work with enzymes to convert carbohydrates to glucose; they are also important in fat and protein metabolism. B complex vitamins aid the nervous system in its functioning, relaxing individuals who are stressed or fatigued. Healthy skin, hair, eyes, nails and liver are made possible with sufficient amounts of B complex. They enhance the muscle tone of the gastrointestinal system, allowing the bowels to function properly. Some of the B vitamins can also be made in the body by microorganisms in the large intestine. Deficiencies of the B vitamins include fatigue, depression, irritability, insomnia, nervousness, cracks at the corner of the mouth, and sore mouth and tongue. The germ or bran of cereal grains are important sources of B complex as are some beans and nuts. Organic liver is an excellent source of B complex. Antibiotics, which kill intestinal bacteria flora, lower the potential to produce B vitamins; replacing intestinal bacteria is important in maintaining the health of the colon. A good B complex should be taken three times a day since the body does not store B complex, and commonly used substances such as sugar, alcohol, and coffee deplete B vitamins. B complex tends to be sold as B-50 (50 mg. of some of the B vitamins, 50 mcg. of a few, and 400 or 800 mcg. of folic acid); 3 of these a day is usually recommended.

Pantothenic Acid or Vitamin B-5 is also known as coenzyme A or the ant-stress vitamin since it supports the adrenal glands in the production of cortisone and other adrenal hormones to help counteract stress. Through supporting the adrenals, it helps to reduce toxic effects of antibiotics and radiation. It is also used in nerve disorders such as neuritis, epilepsy, multiple sclerosis, and other mental disorders. 500 mg. taken 2 or 3 times daily is a good therapeutic dose. It should be taken at a separate time from B-complex.

Vitamin B-6 or Pyridoxine is an especially important vitamin for women as it is connected to hormonal balance and water regulation. It is necessary in amino acid metabolism and supporting the central nervous system. B-6 helps to maintain the potassium-sodium balance in the body, thereby aiding in the fluid regulation as well as in the electrical functioning of the nerves, heart, and musculoskeletal system. Pyridoxine aids protein metabolism and many amino acid reactions. There is a high requirement of B-6 during pregnancy and it is also used for premenstrual symptoms, especially water retention, along with magnesium. Whenever estrogen levels are higher in using birth control pills or estrogen therapy, as well as in pregnancy, more B-6 is needed. B-6 and magnesium are used for hyperactivity in children as well as in neuritis, multiple sclerosis, and Parkinson's disease. It is also important for the immune system and may help to protect against radiation. Therapeutic doses of pyridoxine range from 200-500 mg. per day. This vitamin should not be taken without B complex, but preferably at a different time.

Vitamin B-12 or Cobalamin is often lacking in those who are vegetarian since it is only found in usable amounts in animal proteins. It is necessary for the formation of red blood cells and is often indicated in cases of extreme tiredness. Cobalamin is absorbed from the small intestine; if digestion and absorption problems are present, there may be a deficiency. Methyl cobalamin is the more usable form of B-12; some people take it sublingually, but if there is any real deficiency, it is given intramuscularly in doses of 500-1,000 mcg. several times a week for a given time period.

Folic Acid or its coenzyme tetrahydrofolic (THFA) has functions similar to vitamin B-12. It aids in red blood cell production by carrying the carbon molecule to the larger molecule, which is the iron containing part of hemoglobin. Folic acid also helps in the breakdown of protein and amino acid conversions, along with B-12. It is especially needed during pregnancy since it is important for cell multiplication and division. It is also called for in alcoholics, in women who are taking birth control pills, in psychiatric patients, epileptics, those who have taken large doses of antibiotics and depleted the intestinal bacteria in the colon, and those who are eating diets of processed foods. Folic acid (foliage) is highest in the green leafy vegetables which lose their folate quickly as they are transported or sit on shelves in supermarkets. A daily dose may be 800 mcg. and it may be taken sublingually. Higher amounts are available by prescription and are usually injected along with B-12.

PABA or Para-aminobenzoic acid is part of the folic acid molecule; it nourishes the hair and skin as well as being useful as a sunscreen. As part of the coenzyme tetrahydrofolic acid, it aids in the metabolism of amino acids and is also supportive of red blood cells. PABA is useful for skin problems such as Vitiligo, a skin de-pigmenting condition; it is also used for burns and to reduce wrinkles and skin aging. Found in liver, whole grains such as rice and egg yolks, a normal dose would be 50-100 mg. three times a day but 1,000 mg. is used as a therapeutic dose. This should also be taken at a different time from B complex.

Niacin or Vitamin B-3 refers to two compounds, nicotinic acid and niacinamide, which can be manufactured from the amino acid L-Tryptophan. Niacin stimulates circulation, reduces cholesterol levels in the blood, and is crucial to normal brain function and a healthy nervous system. The coenzymes of niacin help break down proteins, fats, and carbohydrates in the diet; thus, niacin is used to increase energy through improving food utilization. It is helpful in treating digestive disorders such as diarrhea and constipation, helps with hypoglycemia, anxiety, and depression. With migraine type headaches and arthritis, it helps stimulate blood flow in the capillaries. Niacin is also good for reducing blood pressure and lowering serum cholesterol. It is used to treat a wide variety of psychological problems such as senility, alcoholism, drug problems, depression, and schizophrenia. Taken as nicotinic acid, it can produce redness, warmth, and itching over areas of the skin. (This is a result of the release of histamine by the cells which causes vaso-dilation.) For those who do not like this flush, it can be used in the form of niacinamide. Supplements may provide as much as 50-100 mg. a day, but 2-3 grams may be necessary therapeutically to treat certain conditions mentioned.

Vitamin D is known as the "sunshine" vitamin because it is manufactured in the human skin when it is in contact with ultraviolet light from the sun's rays. From this interaction, D-3 or cholecalciferol is produced; this form of vitamin D is found in fish liver oils. Many people are deficient in Vitamin D because of fear of the Sun and also avoidance of animal products. D-2 or activated ergocalciferol is the major synthetic form of provitamin D; it is found in fortified milk and in many vitamin pills and should be avoided. Vitamin D helps to regulate calcium metabolism and normal calcification of the bones as well as helping us to utilize phosphorus. It helps increase the absorption of calcium from the gut as well as decrease excretion from the kidneys. Because of its regulation of calcium and phosphorus metabolism, vitamin D is important for children's growth, especially for healthy bones and teeth. It is also important in maintaining the nervous system, heart functions, and for blood clotting. Without proper amounts of Vitamin D, blood levels of calcium and phosphorus decrease, and the body has to get these minerals from the bones. Osteomalacia may occur, which is a loss of bone mineral. Osteoporosis is a loss of bone mass. More vitamin D is required during the winter, and for those who are not exposed to the Sun. Vitamin D is best utilized with vitamin A so many supplements contain both.

Calcium is the most important mineral in our bodies; it works with magnesium to regulate heart and muscle contraction as well as nerve conduction. Vitamin D is needed for calcium and phosphorus to be absorbed from the digestive tract. Parathyroid hormone and calcitonin, secreted by the thyroid, help maintain normal blood calcium levels along with vitamin D. Calcium is necessary in maintaining our bones and teeth. It is helpful for nerve transmission and pre-menstrual problems such as cramps and irritability. Calcium absorption becomes less efficient as we age. Foods that are high in oxalic acid such as spinach, rhubarb, chard, beet greens, and chocolate interfere with calcium absorption; so also does phytic acid found in whole grains, beans, or foods rich in fiber. Taking calcium and magnesium at bedtime or between meals, when the stomach is more acidic, is helpful for better absorption. Certain leafy green vegetables such as collard greens, turnip greens, kale, and mustard greens are excellent sources of calcium. The form in which calcium is absorbed is crucial as it is difficult to assimilate this mineral from supplements. The most assimilable form of calcium is microcrystalline calcium hydroxyapatite, which is an animal product. Calcium aspartate is also a good form. . Most adults need 1,000 mg. a day but pregnant women and nursing mothers need more. Post menopausal women need at least 1,500 mg.

Magnesium is the iron of the plant world; chlorophyll provides magnesium in the same way that hemoglobin provides iron. Magnesium is necessary to calcium absorption; deficiencies of magnesium are related to cramps and spasms, high blood pressure, heart attacks due to coronary artery spasm, kidney stones, and pre-menstrual symptoms. As a natural tranquilizer, magnesium is considered the "anti-stress" mineral. It helps relax skeletal muscles as well as muscles of the gastrointestinal tract. Magnesium is a key mineral in working with hyperactivity and autism in children. Magnesium needs calcium for its assimilation in the ratio of 1:1; the old formula was 2 parts calcium, but now it is being realized that even more magnesium is needed. Often magnesium is required in addition to its use in supplements with calcium; liquid chlorophyll is one way of providing additional magnesium. Magnesium, like calcium, can be destroyed by foods containing oxalic acid as well as by phytic acid. Using sugar, alcohol, and coffee also destroy magnesium. Dark green leafy vegetables, which are high in chlorophyll, contain lots of magnesium. If 1,500 mg. of calcium is being used daily, then 1,500 mg. of magnesium should be used.

Potassium may be the mineral most needed therapeutically. It is one of the electrolyte minerals (the others are sodium and chloride) so it carries a tiny electrical charge. Potassium is the positive ion within the cells; the potassium sodium balance is crucial to cardiovascular health and physical stamina, among other things. However, with a diet so rich in sodium (fast foods, chips, packaged foods with added sodium), potassium is often lacking. Diuretics prescribed by doctors also lower potassium as does alcohol, caffeine drinks, and sugar. The kidneys regulate our body's potassium sodium balance; the adrenal hormone aldosterone stimulates elimination of potassium by the kidneys. Potassium deficiency often occurs during bouts of diarrhea and other gastrointestinal problems. Low potassium may impair glucose metabolism and lead to elevated blood sugar. Hypertension, cardiac arrythmias, depression, and fatigue are other symptoms. Potassium rich foods include parsley, especially made as a tea, and dark green leafy vegetables. The potassium. sodium ratio should be 2 to 1. If additional potassium is required, a prescription would be about 640-1280 mg. a day (10-20 mcg).

Chromium is part of the GTF (glucose tolerance factor), and is therefore necessary in regulating carbohydrate metabolism since it prepares insulin function for proper use of glucose in the body. Chromium is used to treat diabetes and is also being used, along with niacin, for hypoglycemia and high blood cholesterol. Countries with low chromium in the soil seem to have a high incidence of both diabetes and cardiovascular disease. This is also true of countries where processed foods and refined grains are a large part of the diet. Chromium is found in nutritional yeast, which is difficult to digest for many people, but it is also found in liver, beef, rye, wheat germ, and whole wheat. Supplementation for chromium is about 200-300 mcg daily.

Iodine is a trace mineral whose deficiency creates goiter and hypothyroidism, which manifests as weight gain, sluggishness, and low energy. Iodine is necessary for the production of thyroid hormones that regulate the metabolic rate of the body. The thyroid hormones are needed for normal growth, protein synthesis, and energy metabolism. The formation of our bones and nerves, reproduction, and our speech and mental state are all influenced by our thyroid. Fish, shellfish, and sea vegetables from the ocean contain plenty of iodine. Kelp, in particular, is an excellent source, and is a good salt substitute. Iodized salt contains other unneeded chemicals that are not so good. A 6 ounce portion of ocean fish contains 500 mcg of iodine, which is more than the RDA of 150 mcg.

Iron, when it is lacking, produces less hemoglobin and therefore less oxygen to our tissues. Iron deficient anemia is common; poor absorption from the intestines is usually the cause. However, with vegetarians, the "nonheme" form of iron from vegetable sources is not as well absorbed as the "heme" form, which is found predominantly in liver and beef. Oxalic acid found in certain vegetables (see calcium) and phytic acid found in whole grains also tend to bind the iron. Vitamin C helps iron absorption as does copper, manganese, and cobalt. The primary function of iron in the body is to form hemoglobin, which is the oxygen carrying component of the red blood cell. Those who need iron the most are menstruating women, pregnant women, nursing mothers, people taking high amounts of pharmaceutical drugs that interfere with absorption, and vegetarians. The best assimilated form of iron is chelated iron; this should be taken between meals, about 50 mg. twice a day with 250 mg. of vitamin C. It is also best not to take iron at the same time as vitamin E, which may bind it. Many men and post menopausal women have toxic levels of iron; they should use supplements that are iron free.

Manganese is a trace mineral which is essential to many enzyme systems for energy production, bone formation, protein metabolism, and other functions. Manganese is part of the enzyme SOD (*superoxide dismutase)* which can bind oxygen free radicals, protecting cell membranes and tissues from degeneration. Manganese seems to have a role in the production of thyroxine, in glucose metabolism, and in reproduction. Along with B vitamins, it has been used to treat Parkinson's disease, multiple sclerosis, epilepsy, and myasthenia gravis; it may alleviate fatigue and weakness by enhancing nerve impulses. Manganese is found in dark leafy green vegetables, nuts, and whole grains. Taking supplemental manganese may decrease iron utilization. For therapeutic purposes, manganese may be taken in its chelated form or as manganese sulfate or gluconate, 10-15 mg. per day in between meals so it doesn't interact with other minerals.

Molybdenum is rich in certain soils and deficient in others; this affects our grains and vegetables and the amount of molybdenum they contain. Molybdenum has a key role in three important enzyme systems; therefore it is vital in uric acid formation, iron utilization, carbohydrate metabolism, and sulfite detoxification. Molybdenum reduces the production of nitrosamines, cancer causing chemicals in the colon. Liver, organ meats, and brewer's yeast are fairly high in molybdenum. As a supplement, 150-500 mcg. a day is used.

Zinc is the most important mineral for the immune system. It improves antibody response and helps regulate the function of the white blood cells. A high amount of zinc in the diet can increase the production of T lymphocytes. Because zinc is important in many enzyme reactions, it is used for chemical detoxification. Zinc deficiency may be noted in people who have MCS because it helps detoxify environmental chemicals. Zinc is also involved in metabolism; it is a part of *alcohol dehydrogenase*, which helps the liver detoxify alcohol, including drinking alcohol. It also helps heal wounds and may be used before and after surgery. It is useful as well in copper toxicity which is common in peri menopausal and post menopausal women. 30-60 mg daily but more for zinc deficiency

Selenium is an antioxidant and a component of the enzyme, glutathione peroxidase. It is low in most soils and therefore required as a supplement. It helps prevent cell degeneration from free radicals and protects from the toxic effects of heavy metals and other substances. Selenium is also found to have a anti-carcinogenic effect. It works well with Vitamin E. in carrying out antioxidant functions. A usual dose is between 100-200 mcg.

GLA oil (Gamma linolenic acid) is found in evening primrose oil, borage oil, and black currant seed oil; GLA is the active critical form of Omega 6 fatty acids which provides the prostaglandin E1 series. This series is probably the most important of the hormonelike prostaglandins; it protects the liver from alcohol, other irritating drugs and toxins, and helps the immune system. In addition, it is very important for allergies and asthma, skin disorders such as eczema and dermatitis, MCS, multiple sclerosis, rheumatoid arthritis, premenstrual syndrome, and cardiovascular disease. GLA helps to reduce arterial spasm and clotting, which contribute to cardiac problems. A usual dose would be between 500-1000 mg. a few times a day.

EPA and DHA (Eicosapentaenoic acid and Decosahexaenoic acid) are the active critical form of Omega 3 long chain fatty acids that are found in fish oils. They affect prostaglandin series 3 as well as PGE1. These oils, often referred to as marine oils, help lower blood fat and cholesterol levels as well as being helpful in rheumatoid arthritis, asthma, migraine, and MCS. They can be obtained by eating coldwater fish such as salmon, herring, mackerel, trout, butterfish, bluefish, and sardines that feed on plankton. For those who do not eat these fish a few times a week, a capsule of 500 mg. is recommended twice daily. Cold pressed flaxseed oil is a good source of the Omega 3 fatty acids but many people cannot convert the Omega 3's into EPA and DHA and therefore need supplementation if they are not eating fish.

Lipoic Acid is a strong antioxidant that contains sulfur and is manufactured in trace amounts in the body. It has the ability to increase levels of the most important antioxidant compound in the body, glutathione. Glutathione protects the body from free radicals produced by alcohol consumption, cigarette smoking, exposure to toxic chemicals, and radiation. Lipoic acid is recommended for blood sugar disorders like diabetes and hypoglycemia, and liver ailments.

Probiotics include various strands of intestinal bacteria especially *lactobacillus acidophilus and lactobacillus bifidus*. They are used to re-implant friendly bacteria into the colon and assist in producing folic acid, biotin, B-12, and vitamin K, as well as breaking down foods. Important for stomach and digestive upset, they also help inflammatory problems of the gastrointestinal tract. They produce immunity in the body, help with food allergies, and in herpes infections. Obtained in powder, capsule or liquid form, probiotics should be used a couple of times a day. They are especially important if one is taking antibiotics or traveling to a country where there could be microorganisms in the food.

Digestive Enzymes are sometimes called for when there are digestive problems. Usually it is pancreatic enzymes that are most helpful which include lipases, amylases, and proteases; these help with carbohydrate digesetion. Some people also need a formula that contains ox bile to help digest fats.

Glandulars or protomorphogens are extracts of tissues from glands which can be taken orally to help support those tissues in humans. **Adrenal glandular** is helpful for fatigue, stress, allergies, environmental sensitivities, and low blood sugar. 300mg. twice daily may be taken along with other stress reducing supplements such as vitamins B, C, A, and zinc. **Pancreas glandular** is used to aid digestion by providing extra digestive enzymes, as well as helping those with hypoglycemia (low blood sugar) and diabetes. One pancreas glandular is often taken before each meal. **Thyroid glandular** is helpful in supporting the gland to work better. It has been used for fatigue and to support immune function. Usually it is taken three times a day after meals. **Thymus glandular** contains the active hormone thymosin, which stimulates T cell production. It is taken two or three times a day when recurrent infections, fatigue, or immune deficiency persist. Organic glandulars are available from range grazed cattle and sheep in New Zealand.

L-carnitine is necessary to transform fatty acids into energy for muscular activity. Carnitine transports fatty acids into the cell as well as increases the rate at which the liver oxidizes cells. It is being used for those who have MCS and experience tiredness with difficulty exercising. Those who are vegetarians and those who avoid red meat often have deficiencies of L-carnitine which manifest as fatigue, muscle weakness, and confusion. 1,000-2,000 mg. daily is a recommended dosage.

Glutathione and L-cysteine—Glutathione is an antioxidant that helps to protect against environmental toxins, heavy metals, cigarette smoke, and radiation exposure by detoxifying these chemicals into less toxic forms. It is especially good for skin conditions. Glutathione must be obtained from or N-acetyl cysteine which raises glutathione levels in the body. Cysteine is a sulfur containing amino acid that is synthesized in the liver. Cysteine binds with heavy metals such as lead, cadmium, and mercury aiding the body's elimination of them. 500 mg. twice daily is a recommended dose.

L-Glutamine is important to brain function and proper digestion; it is the only amino acid metabolized in the brain. L glutamine is needed to heal the intestines. Taken as a dose of 500 mg. 4 times a day, it reduces the craving for alcohol and also for sugar. L-glutamine can be converted into the excitotoxin glutamic acid and also into **GABA (gamma-aminobutyric acid)**, a brain tranquillizer working in the central nervous system. It is an inhibitory transmitter, keeping the body and brain from going into "overdrive". To heal the intestines or curb sugar cravings, a recommended dose is 5 grams per day. Those with anxiety or manic depression should begin with a low dose, 250 mg. either at bedtime or when the anxiety occurs.

Lysine helps in the absorption of calcium from the intestinal tract and in the formation of collagen, the body protein that is the matrix for the connective tissues, skin, cartilage, and bones. Adequate lysine may help prevent osteoporosis through better absorption of calcium. Lysine has also been used in the treatment of herpes simplex infections; particularly for cold sores (herpes type 1). A therapeutic dose for lysine would be 500 mg. three times a day. Sometimes using 3,000 mg. all at once will stop the cold sore when it is coming on.

Methionine is one of the sulfur containing amino acids which helps prevent problems of the skin and nails. It is also useful as a lipotropic agent to prevent excess fat build up in the liver. Among its other functions are relieving fatigue and use as an antidepressant. A therapeutic dose would be from 500-2000 mg. daily.

Phenylalanine helps form norepinephrine in the brain which is a neurotransmitter important for learning, memory, and alertness. Phenylalanine has been used in the treatment of depression marked by lethargy or apathy in its L form. The D and DL forms are helpful pain relievers in certain musculoskeletal conditions. For pain, D or DL phenylalanine can be taken in doses of 500-750 mg. two or three times a day on an empty stomach.

Tryptophan's dietary intake is lower than most amino acids; tryptophan is an essential vitamin as it is a precursor of niacin and its deficiency can cause symptoms of pellagra. It is the precursor for serotonin which influences moods and sleep patterns. Tryptophan is used for insomnia; it is also effective in manic depression and depression associated with menopause. As a therapeutic dose, 1 gm. of tryptophan may be taken before bedtime; this may be increased by 500 mg. or up to 3,000 mg. Calcium and magnesium may also be taken to help. Other uses are for Parkinson's disease, epilepsy, and schizophrenia. However, currently, tryptophan cannot be obtained without a prescription from a doctor.

L-Tyrosine is a precursor of both adrenaline and thyroid hormones, which stimulate the metabolism and nervous system. It is also used as an antidepressant as well as for Parkinson's disease, macular degeneration, and in drug programs. As a supplement to boost the thyroid or as an antidepressant, 500-1,000 mg. of tyrosine can be taken 2 or 3 times daily on an empty stomach.

Taurine functions in electrically active tissues such as the brain and heart to help stabilize cell membranes. Because it is an inhibitory neurotransmitter, one of its uses is to help treat epilepsy and other brain states where it is used as a mild sedative. Taurine is also used for cardiovascular problems, especially arrhythmias and hypertension. Dosage used ranges from 500 mg. to 5-6 grams per day with the higher amounts used for the cardiovascular problems (2 grams three times daily.).

Coenzyme Q-10 or Ubiquinone is an antioxidant and immune stimulant. It can be obtained in the diet through oily fish, organ meats and whole grains. It works along with certain enzymes to stimulate the metabolism and also carries electrons to the cells. Co Q 10 helps heart functioning, both with cardiac muscle function and electrical functioning; it also helps to lower blood pressure. 10-20 mg. should be taken twice a day along with 60-800 i.u's of Vitamin E.

Chondroitin Sulfate and Glucosamine Sulfate—Chondroitin sulfates are contained in mussels and oysters; chondroitin sulfates, which are high in sulfur, help alleviate joint problems and rebuild degenerating cartilage. They may also help in maintaining elasticity of the artery walls and in reducing potential inflammation and blood clotting time. Chondroitin sulfates and Glucosamine sulfates have been used for arthritis, bursitis, ulcers, angina, and allergies.

MSM or Methylsulfonyl Methane is a sulfur compound that may have some anti-inflammatory and antioxidant properties. It is currently being used in treating inhalant allergies, arthritis, and to heal the intestines.

Organo-Germanium is a trace mineral; in its form as Ge-132, it has been found to have an effect on the immune system in restoring the function of T cells and stimulating interferon production. It is being used in the treatment of viral disorders such as Epstein Barr, cancer, gastrointestinal diseases, circulatory problems, and other conditions where improved oxygenation is needed. I have used it for climbing in high altitudes such as in Peru. Some germanium is found in the soil; it is also found in certain herbs such as garlic, ginseng, aloe vera, and shitake mushrooms. Germanium is being marketed in capsules and powder form; suggested dosages range from 50-300 mg. daily. Organo-germanium should only be used in its form as

GE-132; other types are less expensive but may be dangerous and have been known to cause kidney damage.

Octacosanol is the active ingredient in wheat germ responsible for its ability to increase endurance and energy. (Wheat germ itself often becomes rancid when exposed to the air.) Octacosanol helps bring more oxygen to the lungs as well as decreases blood cholesterol. It is used as a brain fuel, to prevent muscle pain and for neuromuscular disorders such as muscular dystrophy. I have found it to work well for respiratory allergies and colds. A therapeutic dose would be 40 to 80 mg. daily.

Appendix F

HERBAL RECOMMENDATIONS

There are many herbs that are important in supporting the immune system and also in detoxifying the liver. These herbs can be purchased dried in herb stores and natural food stores. It is preferable to use them as teas or food supplements in order for them to be effective. Using herbs as tinctures may be convenient but alcohol is used in the tinctures so the effect is not helpful to the liver or pancreas. By using herbs in capsules, little value of the herb is obtained since the herbs are older and dried. To have any effect, one would need to take many capsules. Making herbs into teas is relatively simple—for dried leaves, put 1 or 2 teaspoons per cup of water and simmer for 5-10 minutes. For roots or stems, put a small amount in water and simmer for 20 minutes.

Alfalfa is a very important herb which is high in chlorophyll, contains the eight essential amino acids along with vitamins A, D, E ,B-6, and small amounts of calcium and phosphorus. It is helpful for those with allergies and those with MCS as it is such a strong source of nutrients. It makes a good morning tea in combination with nettle leaves which are high in iron, and horsetail leaves that contain large amounts of silica.

Aloe vera juice and gel are very healing for the whole body. Aloe is mucilaginous and is particularly helpful for constipation and other conditions involving the digestive tract. Drinking one quarter of a cup of aloe before bedtime works well; also eating one aloe leaf a day if you have a fresh plant.

Astragalus is a Chinese herb which is both a stimulant and a tonic for the spleen, kidney, lungs and blood. Astragalus is used to build up the immune system; it is often used in combination with Chinese licorice and other herbs.

Chaparral is an excellent blood purifier and will help to rebuild the immune system. It is also a natural antibiotic and helpful in treating bacterial and viral infections. A combination of chaparral and red clover is excellent. Spearmint or peppermint may be added to help with the bitter taste. Simmer 3 teaspoons of chaparral and 3 teaspoons of red clover in four cups of water for 10-15 minutes. Drink three cups daily or on alternate days.

Echinacea root is a powerful herb to purify the blood and the lymph. It is excellent for treating skin problems such as acne, boils, poison ivy and oak. It is also good for colds and flus. Recently, it has been found that echinacea can increase the white blood cell count and stimulate the production of T cells. As a tea, often red clover is added, which is also a strong blood purifier

Garlic is a natural antibiotic with some immune stimulating properties. It treats bacterial and fungal conditions, including candida/yeast problems, helps with colds and flus, and may reduce blood pressure. Eating fresh garlic with foods is the best way to obtain its benefits.

Goldenseal root—Goldenseal powder from the root has many uses including antibacterial and antiparasitic; it is good for yeast, worms, and other types of germs. It is also a bitter herb and so works well for certain liver and gastrointestinal problems. Golden seal can be taken in a large capsule 3 times a day. It is best to use it for a short period of time, usually no more than a week, or there may be possible liver irritation.

Goldenseal leaf is excellent to detoxify and tone the liver. Two teaspoons of the leaf may be used in 3 or 4 cups of water and simmered. It is also possible to add spearmint or peppermint to the goldenseal leaf, which cuts the bitter taste and is helpful to the digestion.

Horsetail is a diuretic used for all urinary disorders and is also rich in minerals, especially silica and selenium. In combination with alfalfa and nettles, it is a nutritive tonic.

Kelp is an important supplement. It is high in iodine, which improves thyroid function. It is also high in other minerals and vitamins as calcium, magnesium, potassium, niacin, riboflavin, and choline. Algin, which is found in kelp, is also helpful in pulling out intestinal toxins. Using kelp as a salt substitute is helpful as well as taking several capsules a day. If the body does not need much iodine, do not overuse kelp.

Nettles are an expectorant for the lungs, a good remedy for bleeding and anemia, and an important source of iron, potassium, and silica. Fresh nettle leaves are often steamed as a vegetable.

Parsley is very beneficial for the kidneys in detoxifying them. It is also helps to make the body more alkaline. Simmering some fresh organic parsley in water and drinking a couple of cups first thing in the morning is very helpful.

Wheatgrass juice is cleansing to the liver and is also an additional source of iron. It can be mixed with other vegetable juices or taken alone in water. One or two ounces are usually taken a few times a week.

Bibliography: General Astrology

Arroyo, Stephen, *Astrology, Psychology, and the Four Elements*, CRCS Publications, Davis, CA, 1975.

Bach, Eleanor and Climas, George, *Ephemerides of the Asteroids*, Ceres, Pallas, Juno, Vesta, 1900-2000, Celestial Communications, NY, 1973.

Brady, Bernadette, *Predictive Astrology—the Eagle and the Lark*, Samuel Weiser, York Beach, ME, 1992.

Brady, Bernadette, *Brady's Book of Fixed Stars*, Samuel Weiser, York Beach, ME, 1998.

Bogart, Gregg, *Therapeutic Astrology*, Dawn Mountain Press, Berkeley, CA, 1996.

Carter, Charles, *Encyclopedia of Psychological Astrology*, Theosophical Publishing House, London, England, 1924.

Cunningham, Donna, *Healing Pluto Problems*, Samuel Weiser, York Beach, ME, 1988.

Cunningham, Donna, *Furthur Dimensions of Healing Addictions*, Cassandra Press, San Rafael, CA, 1990.

Dean, Geoffrey, *Recent Advances in Natal Astrology*, The Astrological Association, Kent, England, 1977.

Dobyns, Zipporah, *Finding the Person in the Horoscope*, TIA Publications, Los Angeles, CA, 1973.

Dobyns, Zipporah, (Introduction by) *The Asteroid Ephemeris*, TIA Publications, Los Angeles, CA, 1977.

Donath, Emma Belle, *Asteroids in the Birth Chart*, Gemini World, Dayton, OH, 1976.

Ebertin, Reinhold, *Combination of Stellar Influences*, Ebertin. Verlag, Aalen, Germany, 1960.

Ebertin, Reinhold and Hoffman, Enid, *Fixed Stars and Their Interpretation*, Ebertin. Verlag, Aalen, Germany, 1971.

Forrest, Steven, *The Inner Sky*, ACS Publications, San Diego, CA, 1988.

Forrest, Steven, *The Night Speaks*, ACS Publications, San Diego, CA, 1993.

George, Demetra, *Asteroid Goddesses*, ACS Publications, San Diego, CA, 1986.

Greene, Liz, *Saturn—a New Look at an Old Devil*, Samuel Weiser, NY, 1974.

Greene, Liz, *The Astrology of Fate*, Samuel Weiser, York Beach, ME, 1984.

Greene, Liz, *The Astrological Neptune and the Quest for Redemption*, Samuel Weiser, York Beach, ME, 1996.

Hand, Robert, *Horoscope Symbols*, Para. Research, Rockport, MA, 1981.

Jansky, Robert, *Interpreting the Eclipses*, ACS Publications, San Diego, CA., 1979.

Jones, Marc Edmund, *The Guide to Horoscope Interpretation*, Sabian Publishing Society, Stanwood, WA, 1969.

Merriman, Raymond, *Evolutionary Astrology*, Seek. It Publications, W. Bloomfield, MI, 1991.

Meyer, Michael, *A Handbook for the Humanistic Astrologer*, Doubleday, Garden City, NY, 1974.

Moore, Marcia and Douglas, Mark, *Astrology, the Divine Science*, Arcane Publications, York Harbor, ME, 1971.

Oken, Alan, *Alan Oken's Complete Astrology*, Bantam, Toronto, NY, and London, England, 1988.

Reinhart, Melanie, *Chiron and the Healing Journey*, Arkana Books, London, England, 1989.

Robson, Vivian E., *The Fixed Stars and Constellations in Astrology*, Samuel Weiser, NY, 1969.

Rudhyar, Dane, *The Astrology of Personality*, Servire/ Wassenaar, the Netherlands, 1963.

Sullivan, Erin, *Saturn in Transit*, Arkana Books, London, England, 1991.

Sullivan, Erin, *Retrograde Planets*, Arkana Books, London, England, 1992.

Bibliography: Medical Astrology

Baker, Douglas Dr., *Esoteric Healing, Part III*, Flower Remedies and Medical Astrology, Samuel Weiser, NY, 1978.

Cornell, H. L., *Encyclopedia of Medical Astrology*, Llewellyn Publications, St. Paul, MN, 1972.

Cunningham, Donna, *Astrology and Vibrational Healing*, Cassandra Press, San Rafael, CA, 1988.

Clogstoun. Willmott, Jonathan, *Western Astrology & Chinese Medicine*, Destiny Books, NY, 1985.

Davidson, Wm., M.D., *Lectures on Medical Astrology*, Astrological Bureau, Monroe, NY, 1973.

Garrison, Omar V., *Medical Astrology*, University Books, NY, 1971.

Gibson, Mitchell E., M.D., *Signs of Mental Illness*, Llewellyn, St.Paul, MN, 1998.

Jansky, Robert, *Modern Medical Astrology*, AstroAnalytics, Venice, CA, 1974.

Jansky, Robert, *Astrology, Nutrition and Health*, ParaResearch, Rockport, MA., 1977.

Millard, Margaret, M.D., *Casenotes of a Medical Astrologer*, Samuel Weiser, NY, 1980.

Nauman, Eileen, *The American Book of Nutrition & Medical Astrology*, ACS Publications, San Diego, CA, 1982.

Naiman, Ingrid, *The Astrology of Healing*, Monograph series, Santa Fe, NM, 1984.

Perry, Inez and Carey, George, *The Zodiac and the Salts of Salvation*, Samuel Weiser, NY.

Sawtell, Vanda, *Astrology and Biochemistry*, Health Science Press, Devon, England, 1975.

Starck, Marcia, *Astrology: Key to Holistic Health*, Seek-It Books, W. Bloomfield, MI, 1982.

Starck, Marcia, *Healing with Astrology*, Crossing Press, Freedom, CA, 1997.

Tobyn, Graeme, *Culpeper's Medicine*, Element Books, Rockport, MA, 1997

Bibliography: Health and Healing

Airola, Paavo, N. D. *How to Get Well*, Health Plus Publishers, Phoenix, AZ, 1974.

Airola, Paavo, N. D., *Hypoglycemia: A Better Approach*, Health Plus Publishers, Phoenix, AZ, 1977.

Asimov, Isaac, *The Human Body: Its Structure and Operation*, Signet, New American Library, NY, 1963.

Baker, Jeannine Parvati, *Hygieia; A Woman's Herbal*, Freestone Collective, Monroe, UT, 1978.

Baker, Jeannine Parvati, with Baker, Frederick, and Slayton, Tamara, *Conscious Conception*, Freestone Publishing, Monroe, UT, 1986.

Ballentine, Rudolph, M.D., *Diet and Nutrition: A Holistic Approach*, Himalayan International Institute, Honesdale, PA, 1978.

A Barefoot Doctor's Manual, Running Press, Philadelphia, PA, 1977.

Clark, Hulda, N.D., *The Cure for All Diseases*, New Century Press, San Diego, CA, 1995.

Friedman, Meyer M.D. and Rosenman, Ray M.D., *Type A Behavior and Your Heart*, Alfred A. Knopf, NY, 1974.

Gerson, Max, M.D., *A Cancer Therapy: Results of 50 Cases*, Totality Books, Del Mar, CA, 1958.

Graedon, Joe, *The People's Pharmacy*, St. Martin's Press, NY, 1976.

Green, James, *The Male Herbal*, Crossing Press, Freedom, CA, 1991.

Haas, Elson, M.D., *Staying Healthy with the Seasons*, Celestial Arts, Millbrae, CA, 1981.

Haas, Elson, M.D., *Staying Healthy with Nutrition*, Celestial Arts, Berkeley, CA, 1992.

Hill, Ann (ed. by), *A Visual Encyclopedia of Unconventional Medicine*, Crown Publishers, NY, 1979.

Hoffman, David, *The Holistic Herbal*, Element Books, Shaftesbury, Dorset, England, 1983.

Hoffer, Abram, M.D., *Orthomolecular Treatment for Schizophrenia*, Keats Publishing, Los Angeles, CA, 1999.

Jackson, Mildred, N. D. & Teague, Terri, *The Handbook of Alternatives to Chemical Medicine*, Terri Teague and Mildred Jackson, Oakland, CA, 1975.

Jackson, Mildred, N. D. and Teague, Terri, *Mental Birth Control,* Lawton. Teague Publications, Oakland, C., 1978.

Kaptchuk, Ted, O.M.D., *The Web That Has No Weaver,* Congdon & Weed, NY, 1983.

Ladd, Vasant, *Ayurveda—the Science of Self-healing*, Sunstone, Santa Fe, NM, 1984

Luce, Gay Gaer, *Body Time*, Pantheon Books, Random House, NY, 1971.

McNaught, Ann and Callander, Robin, *Illustrated Physiology*, Churchill Livingstone, NY, 1979

Miller, Benjamin and Keane, Claire, *Encyclopedia and Dictionary of Medicine and Nursing*, W. B. Saunders Co., Philadelphia, PA, 1972

Murphy, Robin, N.D. *Fundamentals of Materia Medica*, transcribed lectures, 1988.

Pelletier, Kenneth, *Mind as Healer, Mind as Slayer,* Delta, NY, 1977.

Pfeiffer, Carl, M.D., *Nutrition and Mental Illness*, Healing Arts Press, Rochester, VT, 1987.

Rosenblum, Art, *The Natural Birth Control Book*, Aquarian Research Foundation, Philadelphia, PA, 1976.

Seaman, Barbara and Seaman, Gideon, M.D., *Women and the Crisis in Sex Hormones*, Rawson Associates Publishing Inc. NY, 1977.

Selye, Hans, *The Stress of Life*, McGraw Hill, NY, 1976.

Sheehy, Gail, Passages: *Predictable Crises of Adult Life*, E. P. Dutton and Co., NY, 1974.

Simonton, O. Carl M.D., Simonton, Stephanie M. and Creighton, James, *Getting Well Again*, J. P. Torcher Inc., Los Angeles, CA, 1978.

Starck, Marcia, *Handbook of Natural Therapies*, Crossing Press, Freedom, CA, 1998.

Svoboda, Robert, *Prakruti—Your Ayurvedic Constitution*, Geocom, Albuquerque, NM, 1988.

Tierra, Michael, *The Way of Herbs*, Unity Press, Santa Cruz, CA, 1980.

Walker, Norman, *Colon Health*, O'Sullivan, Woodside & Co., Phoenix, AZ, 1979.

Weed, Susun, *Menopausal Years—The Wise Woman Way*, Ash Tree Publishing, Woodstock, NY, 1992.

Weed, Susun, *Breast Health—The Wise Woman Way*, Ash Tree Publishing, Woodstock, NY, 1996.

Williams, Roger, *Biochemical Individuality*, University of Texas Press, Austin, TX, 1956.

Williams, Roger, *Alcoholism: The Nutritional Approach*, Univ. of Texas Press, Austin, TX, 1978

Wittenberg, Janice, with Baker, Randy, *The Rebellious Body: Reclaim Your Life from Environmental Illness or Chronic Fatigue Syndrome*, Perseus Books, NY, 1996